Edexcel GCSE Mathematics *foundation* book 2

Keith Pledger

Gareth Cole

Peter Jolly

Graham Newman

Joe Petran

Sue Bright

www.heinemann.co.uk
✓ Free online support
✓ Useful weblinks
✓ 24 hour online ordering

01865 888058

Heinemann Educational Publishers
Halley Court, Jordan Hill, Oxford OX2 8EJ
Part of Harcourt Education Limited

Heinemann is the registered trademark of
Harcourt Education Limited

© Harcourt Education Ltd, 2006

First published 2006

10 09 08 07 06
10 9 8 7 6 5 4 3 2 1

British Library Cataloguing in Publication Data is available from the British Library on request.

10-digit ISBN: 0 435 53619 2
13-digit ISBN: 978 0 435536 19 0

Copyright notice
All rights reserved. No part of this publication may be reproduced in any form or by any means (including photocopying or storing it in any medium by electronic means and whether or not transiently or incidentally to some other use of this publication) without the written permission of the copyright owner, except in accordance with the provisions of the Copyright, Designs and Patents Act 1988 or under the terms of a licence issued by the Copyright Licensing Agency, 90 Tottenham Court Road, London W1T 4LP. Applications for the copyright owner's written permission should be addressed to the publisher.

Typeset by Tech-Set Ltd, Gateshead, Tyne and Wear
Original illustrations © Harcourt Education Limited, 2006
Illustrated by Adrian Barclay and Mark Ruffle
Cover design by mccdesign
Printed by CPI Bath Press
Cover photo: Photolibrary.com ©

Acknowledgements
Harcourt Education Ltd would like to thank those schools who helped in the development and trialling of this course.

This high quality material is endorsed by Edexcel and has been through a rigorous quality assurance programme to ensure that it is a suitable companion to the specification for both learners and teachers. This does not mean that its contents will be used verbatim when setting examinations nor is it to be read as being the official specification – a copy of which is available at www.edexcel.org.uk

The publisher's and authors' thanks are due to Edexcel Limited for permission to reproduce questions from past examination papers. These are marked with an [E]. The answers have been provided by the authors and are not the responsibility of Edexcel Limited.

The authors and publisher would like to thank the following individuals and organisations for permission to reproduce photographs: Getty Images/PhotoDisc p**431**; Corbis pp**332, 347, 389, 410, 494**; Empics pp**384, 426**; iStockPhoto.com/Gloria-Leigh Logan p**285**; iStockPhoto.com/James Goldsworthy p**304**; Brand X Photos p**399**; Digital Vision p**419**; Alamy Images/David Tipping p**450**; iStockPhoto.com/Stephen Gibson p**454**; Empics/AP Photo p**462**

Every effort has been made to contact copyright holders of material reproduced in this book. Any omissions will be rectified in subsequent printings if notice is given to the publishers.

Publishing team
Editorial	James Orr, Lindsey Besley, Evan Curnow, Nick Sample, Jim Newall, Alex Sharpe, Laurice Suess, Katherine Pate, Elizabeth Bowden, Ian Crane
Design	Phil Leafe
Production	Siobhan Snowden
Picture research	Chrissie Martin

Websites
There are links to relevant websites in this book. In order to ensure that the links are up-to-date, that the links work, and that the sites aren't inadvertently linked to sites that could be considered offensive, we have made the links available on the Heinemann website at www.heinemann.co.uk/hotlinks. When you access the site, the express code is **4084P**.

Tel: 01865 888058   www.heinemann.co.uk

Quick reference to chapters

15 Percentages   277

16 Coordinates and graphs   299

17 Ratio and proportion   322

18 Symmetry   338

19 Simple perimeter, area and volume   347

20 Presenting and analysing data 1   369

21 Formulae and inequalities   391

22 Transformations   411

23 Probability   425

24 Presenting and analysing data 2   447

25 Pythagoras' theorem   466

26 Advanced perimeter, area and volume   475

27 Describing transformations   504

28 Expressions, formulae, equations and graphs   523

Examination practice papers   548
Formulae sheet   557
Answers   A1
Index to Books 1 and 2   I1

Introduction

Introduction

These revised and updated editions have been carefully matched to the new two-tier specification for GCSE Maths. Books 1 and 2 cover everything you need to know to achieve success in your exam, up to and including Grade C. The author team is made up of Senior Examiners, a Chair of Examiners and Senior Moderators, all experienced teachers with an excellent understanding of the requirements of the Edexcel specification.

Key features

- **Chapters** are divided into **sections**, each with a simple explanation followed by clear examples or a worked exam question. These show you how to tackle questions. Each section also contains practice exercises to develop your understanding and help you consolidate your learning.

- **Key points** are highlighted throughout, like this:

  To find the **square** of any number, multiply the number by itself.

  Each chapter ends with a summary of key points you need to remember.

- **Hint boxes** are used to make explanations clearer. They may also remind you of previously learned facts or tell you where in the book to find more information.

  > a means $1a$
  > so $1a + 1a = 2a$

- **Mixed exercises** are designed to test your understanding across each chapter. They include past exam questions which are marked with an [E]. You will find a mixed exercise at the end of every chapter.

- **Examination practice papers** are included to help you prepare for the exam at the end of your course.

- **Answers** are provided at the back of the book to use as your teacher directs.

Quick reference and detailed Contents pages

- Use the thumb spots on the edge of the **Quick reference** page to help you turn to the right chapter quickly. Note that Book 1 contains Chapters 1–14 and Book 2 contains Chapters 15–28.

- Use the detailed **Contents** to help you find a section on a particular topic. The summary and reference codes on the right show your teacher the part(s) of the specification covered by each section in the book. (For example, NA3h refers to Number and Algebra, section 3 Calculations, subsection h.)

Use of a calculator or a computer

These symbols show you where you must, or must not, use a calculator. Sometimes you will need to use a spreadsheet package on a computer. There are also links to websites and suggested activities that require an internet search.

Coursework

A Coursework Guide is available online at www.zebramaths.co.uk

Contents

15 Percentages

15.1	Understanding percentages	277–278	Introducing percentages	NA2e
15.2	Percentages, fractions and decimals	278–281	Writing percentages as decimals and fractions in their lowest terms	NA2c/e/3c
15.3	Working out a percentage of an amount	282–283	Calculating percentages of different amounts	NA3c/m
15.4	Increasing a number by a percentage	283–285	Adding a percentage of an amount	NA3m
15.5	Decreasing a number by a percentage	285–286	Reducing an amount by a percentage	NA3m
15.6	VAT	286–287	Adding VAT on to an amount	NA3m
15.7	Index numbers	288–289	Using an index to look at increases and decreases over time	NA2e/HD5k
15.8	Writing one quantity as a percentage of another quantity	290–292	Writing one number as a percentage of another	NA3e
15.9	Comparing different proportions using percentages	292–293	Using percentages to compare different fractions and decimals	NA2e
15.10	Interest and depreciation	293–295	Solving numerical problems involving compound interest	NA3m
	Summary of key points	297–298		

16 Coordinates and graphs

16.1	Coordinates in the first quadrant	299–301	Using coordinates in the first quadrant to draw shapes and find the mid-point of a line segment	NA6b/SSM3e
16.2	Linear graphs	301–304	Drawing linear graphs from tabulated data	NA6c
16.3	Conversion graphs	304–306	Using conversion graphs to convert from one measurement to another	NA6c
16.4	Distance–time graphs	306–309	Reading distance–time graphs and calculating speed	NA6c
16.5	Curved graphs	309–311	Drawing curved graphs for real-life situations	NA6e
16.6	Coordinates in four quadrants	312	Plotting coordinates that include negative numbers	NA6b/SSM3e
16.7	Using algebra to describe lines	313–316	Drawing the graphs of straight line equations	NA6b
16.8	1-D, 2-D or 3-D?	316–318	Using coordinates in 1-D, 2-D and 3-D	SSM3e
	Summary of key points	321		

17 Ratio and proportion

17.1	What is a ratio?	322–324	Examples of ratios used in everyday life	NA2f
17.2	Simplifying ratios	324–326	Writing ratios in their lowest terms by cancelling	NA2f
17.3	Equivalent ratios	326–327	Finding and using equivalent ratios	NA2f/3n
17.4	Writing ratios in unitary form	327–328	Ratios as $1:n$ or $n:1$	NA2f
17.5	Dividing quantities in a given ratio	328–330	Sharing in a given ratio	NA3f
17.6	Solving ratio and proportion problems by the unitary method	330–332	Examples of direct proportion	NA3n
17.7	Direct proportion	332–334	Examples in which increasing one quantity causes another quantity to increase in the same ratio	NA3n
17.8	Scales in maps and diagrams	334–335	Using a scale to convert between map distances and ground distances	NA2f
	Summary of key points	337		

18 Symmetry

18.1	Reflective symmetry in 2-D shapes	338–340	Finding lines of symmetry and completing shapes given their lines of symmetry	SSM3a/3b
18.2	Reflective symmetry in pictures and patterns	340–342	Line symmetry in more complicated shapes	SSM3a/3b
18.3	Rotational symmetry	342–343	Finding the order of rotational symmetry of various shapes	SSM3a/3b
18.4	The symmetry of regular polygons	344	Line symmetry and rotational symmetry of regular polygons	SSM3a/3b
	Summary of key points	346		

19 Simple perimeter, area and volume

19.1	Perimeter	347–349	Perimeters of shapes made up of straight lines and circumferences of circles	SSM4f
19.2	Area	349–351	Finding areas by counting squares	SSM4f
19.3	Volume	351–352	Finding volumes by counting cubes	SSM4g
19.4	Finding areas using formulae	352–355	Using formulae to find areas of rectangles, triangles and composite shapes	SSM2e/4f
19.5	Finding volumes of cuboids using formulae	355–356	Using the formulae for the volume of a cuboid	SSM4g
19.6	Surface area	357–358	Finding the surface area of cuboids and prisms	SSM4f
19.7	Fitting boxes into larger boxes	358–359	Division of volumes	SSM4g

19.8	Area and volume problems	360–361	Solving problems involving area and volume	SSM4f/g
19.9	Converting units of area and volume	361–363	Changing from one unit to another	SSM4a/4i
19.10	Compound measures: speed	363–364	Relationship between speed, time and distance and assorted questions	SSM4c
19.11	Problem solving with a spreadsheet	365	Maximising areas using a spreadsheet	SSM4f/NA5f
Summary of key points		368		

20 Presenting and analysing data 1

20.1	The mode	369–370	Finding the most common item in a set of data	HD4b
20.2	The median	371–372	Finding the middle value in a set of data	HD4b
20.3	The mean	373–374	Finding the mean (ordinary average) of a set of data	HD4b/j
20.4	The range	374–375	Using the range of a set of data to compare it with other sets of similar data	HD4b/5ad
20.5	Using appropriate averages	376–378	The advantages/disadvantages of each kind of average	HD4b/5a
20.6	Stem and leaf diagrams	378–381	Drawing and using stem and leaf diagrams	HD4a/5b
20.7	Pie charts	381–387	Drawing and using pie charts	HD4a/5b
Summary of key points		390		

21 Formulae and inequalities

21.1	Using word formulae	391–393	Using words to state the relationship between different quantities	NA5f
21.2	Writing algebraic formulae	394	Using letters to state the relationship between different quantities	NA5f
21.3	Using algebraic formulae	394–397	Substituting into algebraic formulae	NA5f
21.4	Using negative numbers	397–399	Addition, subtraction and multiplication using negative numbers	NA3a
21.5	Substituting into more complicated formulae	399–402	Substituting into formulae which include powers of a variable	NA5f
21.6	Using algebraic equations	402–405	Finding the solution to a problem by writing an equation and solving it	NA5e
21.7	Inequalities	405–408	Solving linear inequalities	NA5d
Summary of key points		410		

22 Transformations

| 22.1 | Translation | 411–414 | Understanding translation is a sliding movement with two components | SSM3b |

22.2	Rotation	414–416	Understanding that rotation is a turning motion about an angle and with a centre	SSM3b
22.3	Reflection	417–419	Reflecting various shapes in mirror lines in different positions	SSM3b
22.4	Enlargement	419–421	Making various shapes larger using different centres of enlargement and scale factors	SSM3c
	Summary of key points	424		

23 Probability

23.1	The probability scale	425–426	Comparing probabilities. How likely is it?	HD4c/5g
23.2	Using numbers to represent probabilities	426–428	Finding a number to represent a probability	HD4d
23.3	Certain and impossible events	429–430	Simple probability	HD4c
23.4	The probability that something will *not* happen	430–432	Working out the probability that something will not happen if you know the probability that it will happen	HD4f
23.5	Finding an estimated probability by experimenting	432–434	Estimating a probability from the results of an experiment	HD4d/5i/j
23.6	Using a sample space diagram to find theoretical probabilities	435–437	Using a diagram to record all the possibilities	HD4e
23.7	Using two-way tables to find probabilities	438–440	Using the information contained in a two-way table to find an estimate for a probability	HD3c/4d
23.8	Relative frequency	441–442	Estimating probability by relative frequency	HD4d/5g/h/i/j
	Summary of key points	446		

24 Presenting and analysing data 2

24.1	Scatter diagrams	447–452	Drawing and using scatter diagrams and lines of best fit; correlation	HD4a/h/5b/f
24.2	Finding averages	452–454	Finding the mean, median and mode of a set of data; using appropriate averages	HD4b
24.3	Averages from frequency distributions	454–457	Finding the mean, mode and median from frequency tables	HD4g/j
24.4	Spread from frequency distributions	457–458	Finding the range and interquartile range from a frequency table	HD4b
24.5	Averages from grouped data	459–461	Finding the mean, mode, median from grouped frequency tables	HD4g
	Summary of key points	465		

25 Pythagoras' theorem

25.1	Using Pythagoras' theorem to find the hypotenuse	466–470	Using Pythagoras' theorem to calculate the length of the hypotenuse	SSM2h/NA4d
25.2	Using Pythagoras' theorem to find one of the shorter sides of a triangle	470–472	Using Pythagoras' theorem to find one of the shorter sides of a right-angled triangle	SSM2h/NA4d
Summary of key points		474		

26 Advanced perimeter, area and volume

26.1	Perimeters and areas of 2-D shapes	475–477	Perimeter and area of triangles and quadrilaterals	SSM4f
26.2	Circumference of a circle	477–481	Introducing π and the formula for the circumference of a circle	SSM2i/4h
26.3	Area of a circle	481–485	Developing the formula for the area of a circle	SSM4h
26.4	Parts of circles	486–487	Compound shapes made from circle parts e.g. semicircles, quadrants	SSM2i/4h
26.5	Volumes and surface areas of 3-D shapes	488–492	Surface areas and volumes of prisms	SSM4f/g
26.6	Accuracy of measurement	492–493	Degrees of accuracy of given measurements	SSM4a
26.7	Choosing an appropriate degree of accuracy	493–495	Using sensible units for various measurements	SSM4a
26.8	Compound measures: density	495–497	Using speed and density formulae	SSM4c
26.9	Changing units	497–498	Converting between units of speed	SSM4a
26.10	Comparing measurements	499–500	Changing units as necessary	SSM4a
Summary of key points		503		

27 Describing transformations

27.1	Translations	504–506	Describing translations using column vectors	SSM3a/b/f
27.2	Reflections	506–508	Describing a reflection by giving the equation of a mirror line	SSM3a/b
27.3	Rotations	508–512	Describing a rotation by giving the angle, the direction and the centre of rotation	SSM3a/b
27.4	Enlargements	512–518	Describing an enlargement by giving the scale factor and centre	SSM3c/3d
Summary of key points		521–522		

28 Expressions, formulae, equations and graphs

28.1	Simplifying algebraic expressions	523–528	Multiplying out brackets	NA5b

28.2	Drawing graphs of simple quadratic functions	528–530	Graphs of functions $y = ax^2 + c$ where a and c can be positive or negative	NA6e
28.3	Drawing graphs of more complex quadratic functions	530–531	Graphs of functions $y = ax^2 + bx + c$	NA6e
28.4	Solving quadratic equations	532–534	Using graphs to solve equations such as $ax^2 + bx + c = d$	NA6e
28.5	Graphs that describe real-life situations	535–539	Assorted situations treated graphically	NA6d
28.6	Rearranging formulae	539–541	Changing the subject of a formula	NA5f
28.7	Solving simple quadratic and reciprocal equations	541–542	Solving equations of the form $ax^2 + b = c$ or $\dfrac{a}{x} = b$	NA5e
28.8	Solving equations by trial and improvement	542–543	Solving cubic equations using trial and improvement	NA5m
28.9	Trial and improvement on a spreadsheet	543–545	Using a spreadsheet to solve cubic equations by trial and improvement	NA5m

Summary of key points   547

Examination practice paper Non calculator   548–551

Examination practice paper Calculator   552–556

Formulae sheet   557

Answers   A1–A28

Index to Books 1 and 2   I1–I10

15 Percentages

15.1 Understanding percentages

Percentage
%
pc
} means 'number of parts per hundred'.

Look at the large square below. It has been divided into 100 equal small squares.

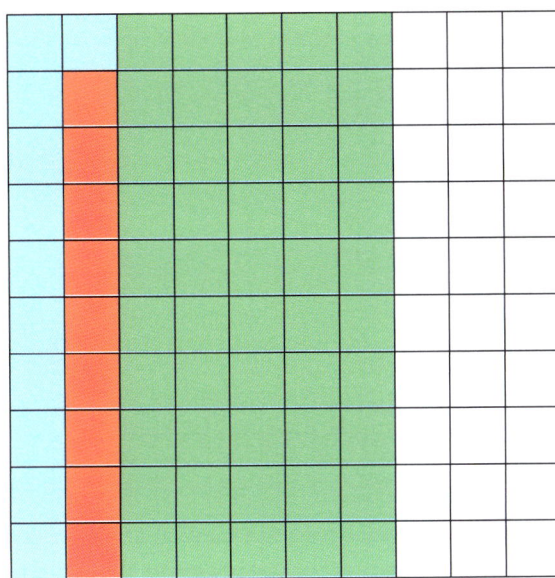

11 of the 100 small squares are shaded blue.
So 11% of the large square is shaded blue.

9 of the 100 small squares are shaded red.
So 9% of the large square is shaded red.

50 of the 100 small squares are shaded green.
So 50% of the large square is shaded green.

30 of the 100 small squares are unshaded.
So 30% of the large square is unshaded.

Exercise 15A

1 This large square is divided into 100 equal small squares.
   (a) What percentage of the large square is shaded
       (i) blue
       (ii) red
       (iii) green?
   (b) What percentage of the large square is unshaded?
   (c) What fraction of the large square is unshaded?

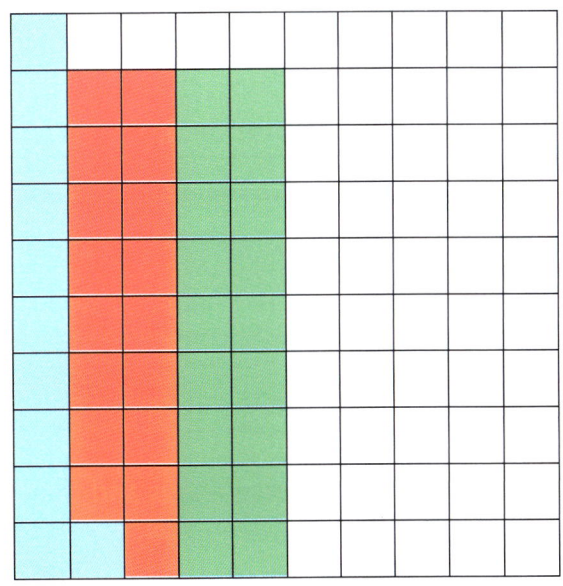

2 This large rectangle is divided into 100 equal small rectangles.
  (a) What percentage of the large rectangle is shaded
      (i) yellow   (ii) blue
      (iii) red   (iv) green?
  (b) What percentage of the large rectangle is unshaded?
  (c) What fraction of the large rectangle is unshaded?

3 Draw a 10 by 10 square on squared paper. Shade in the following percentages:
  (a) 25% in grey   (b) 40% in red   (c) 28% in green
  (d) What percentage of the large square is not shaded?

4 Draw a large rectangle divided into 100 small rectangles as in question 2. Shade in the following percentages:
  (a) 30% in grey   (b) 22% in blue   (c) 36% in yellow
  (d) What percentage of the large rectangle is not shaded?

15.2 Percentages, fractions and decimals

In this large rectangle, 50% is shaded blue and 50% is unshaded.

50% means 50 in a hundred, which can be written as $\frac{50}{100}$

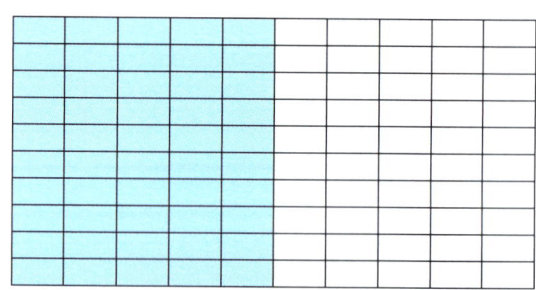

$\frac{50}{100}$ simplifies to $\frac{1}{2}$

So 50% is the same as $\frac{1}{2}$. You can write 50% = $\frac{1}{2}$ = 0.5

In this large square, 25% is shaded red and 75% is unshaded.

25% means 25 in a hundred, which can be written as $\frac{25}{100}$

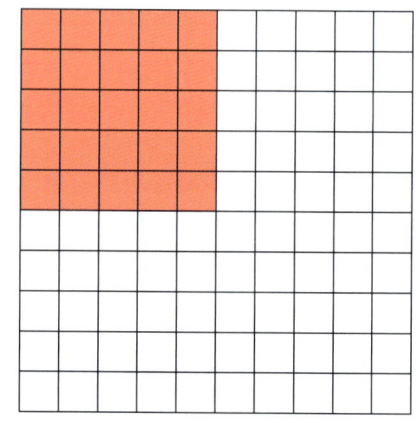

$\frac{25}{100}$ simplifies to $\frac{1}{4}$

So 25% is the same as $\frac{1}{4}$. You can write 25% = $\frac{1}{4}$ = 0.25

Similarly, 75% = $\frac{75}{100}$ = $\frac{3}{4}$ = 0.75

> Remember these percentages and their equivalent fractions:
>   50% = $\frac{1}{2}$ 25% = $\frac{1}{4}$ 75% = $\frac{3}{4}$ $33\frac{1}{3}$% = $\frac{1}{3}$ $66\frac{2}{3}$% = $\frac{2}{3}$

15.2 Percentages, fractions and decimals

Converting percentages to fractions and decimals

A percentage can be written as a fraction, with denominator (bottom) 100.

Example 1

Write 19% as a fraction.

$$19\% = \frac{19}{100}$$

Notice that 5 is the highest common factor of 85 and 100

Example 2

Write 85% as a fraction.

$$85\% = \frac{85}{100}$$

Simplify $\frac{85}{100}$ →(85 ÷ 5)→ $\frac{17}{20}$ (100 ÷ 5)

So $85\% = \frac{17}{20}$

Example 3

Write $3\frac{1}{2}\%$ as a fraction.

$$3\frac{1}{2}\% = \frac{3\frac{1}{2}}{100}$$

Simplify $\frac{3\frac{1}{2}}{100}$ →($3\frac{1}{2} \times 2$)→ $\frac{7}{200}$ (100 × 2)

So $3\frac{1}{2}\% = \frac{7}{200}$

To write a percentage as a decimal:
- write the percentage as a fraction
- convert the fraction to a decimal.

Remember:
Fractions can be changed into decimals by dividing the numerator by the denominator.

Example 4

Write 63% as a decimal.

$$63\% = \frac{63}{100} = 63 \div 100 = 0.63$$

Example 5

Write 15% as a decimal.

$$15\% = \frac{15}{100} = 15 \div 100 = 0.15$$

Exercise 15B

1 For this large rectangle, state
   (a) (i) what percentage is shaded blue
       (ii) what fraction is shaded blue
   (b) (i) what percentage is shaded red
       (ii) what fraction is shaded red
   (c) (i) what percentage is shaded green
       (ii) what fraction is shaded green
   (d) (i) what percentage is unshaded
       (ii) what fraction is unshaded.

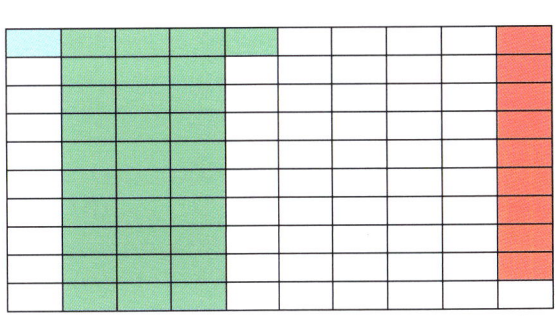

2 For this large rectangle, state
   (a) (i) what percentage is shaded red
       (ii) what fraction is shaded red
   (b) (i) what percentage is shaded green
       (ii) what fraction is shaded green
   (c) (i) what percentage is shaded blue
       (ii) what fraction is shaded blue
   (d) (i) what percentage is unshaded
       (ii) what fraction is unshaded.

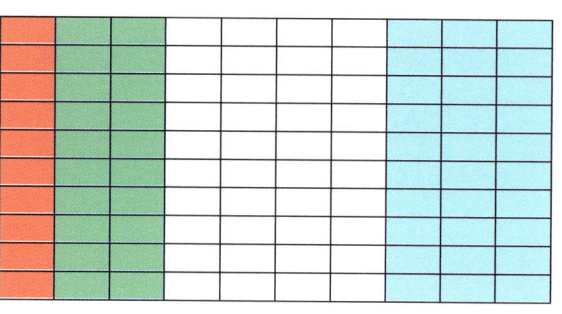

3 Write these percentages as fractions in their simplest form.
   (a) 17%   (b) 99%   (c) 41%   (d) 3%
   (e) 60%   (f) 80%   (g) 90%   (h) 30%
   (i) 10%   (j) 70%   (k) 22%   (l) 6%
   (m) 64%   (n) 96%   (o) 15%   (p) 65%

4 Write these percentages as decimals.
   (a) 37%   (b) 49%   (c) 87%   (d) 7%   (e) 40%
   (f) 15%   (g) 8%   (h) 28%   (i) 36% (j) 95%
   (k) 45%   (l) 3%   (m) $3\frac{1}{2}$%   (n) $6\frac{1}{2}$%   (o) $12\frac{1}{2}$%

5 Jack goes to the cinema with his little brother Joey. As they're both under 16, they're offered the special deal of the week. Jack decides to take the 12% discount off the price of a ticket, while Joey decides to take the $\frac{1}{12}$ off the price of a ticket. Who saves more money?

6 At the same cinema, 56% of people going at the weekend decide to see the latest blockbuster release.
   (a) Express this as a fraction in its simplest form.
   (b) Express this as a decimal.
   (c) Express the percentage that saw another film as a fraction in its simplest form.

Converting decimals and fractions to percentages

To convert a decimal to a percentage, multiply the decimal by 100.

Example 6

Change to a percentage:
(a) 0.47   (b) 0.075

(a) 0.47 × 100 = 47%   (b) 0.075 × 100 = 7.5%

15.2 Percentages, fractions and decimals

To write a fraction as a percentage:
- change the fraction to a decimal
- multiply the decimal by 100.

Example 7

Change to a percentage:
(a) $\frac{7}{10}$ (b) $\frac{17}{40}$

(a) $\frac{7}{10} = 7 \div 10 = 0.7$
$0.7 \times 100 = 70$
So $\frac{7}{10} = 70\%$

(b) $\frac{17}{40} = 17 \div 40 = 0.425$
$0.425 \times 100 = 42.5$
So $\frac{17}{40} = 42.5\%$

Exercise 15C

1 Change these decimals to percentages.
(a) 0.37   (b) 0.59   (c) 0.11   (d) 0.1   (e) 0.36
(f) 0.7   (g) 0.03   (h) 0.771   (i) 0.09   (j) 0.055
(k) 0.83   (l) 0.56   (m) 0.075   (n) 0.125   (o) 0.675

2 Write these fractions as percentages.
(a) $\frac{1}{2}$ (b) $\frac{3}{4}$ (c) $\frac{2}{5}$ (d) $\frac{4}{5}$ (e) $\frac{9}{10}$
(f) $\frac{7}{20}$ (g) $\frac{8}{25}$ (h) $\frac{19}{25}$ (i) $\frac{3}{20}$ (j) $\frac{3}{8}$
(k) $\frac{5}{8}$ (l) $\frac{3}{16}$ (m) $\frac{7}{50}$ (n) $\frac{9}{100}$ (o) $\frac{13}{1000}$

3 Copy and complete this table:

Percentage	Decimal	Fraction
	0.61	
		$\frac{7}{10}$
35%		
$8\frac{1}{2}\%$		
	0.15	
		$\frac{3}{25}$
	0.07	
$1\frac{1}{4}\%$		
		$\frac{2}{3}$

4 Out of 720 visitors to the Big Splash Water Sports complex, 90 decided to go windsurfing. Express this as a percentage, a decimal and a fraction in its simplest form.

15.3 Working out a percentage of an amount

There are a number of different methods of working out a percentage of an amount.

Example 8

Work out 15% of 40 kg.

Method 1

Change the percentage to a fraction:

$15\% = \frac{15}{100}$

Multiply the amount by the fraction:

$\frac{15}{100} \times 40\,\text{kg} = \frac{15 \times 40\,\text{kg}}{100} = \frac{600\,\text{kg}}{100} = 6\,\text{kg}$

So 15% of 40 kg = 6 kg.

Your calculator may have a short way of doing this with the % key.

Method 2

Change the percentage to a decimal:

$15\% = \frac{15}{100} = 15 \div 100 = 0.15$

Multiply the amount by the decimal:

$0.15 \times 40\,\text{kg} = 6\,\text{kg}$

So 15% of 40 kg = 6 kg.

Method 3

Work from 10%.

To find 10% of 40 kg means find one tenth of 40:

10% of 40 is 4

5% of 40 is 2 ——— half of 10%

15% of 40 is 6 kg.

Example 9

Work out 7.5% of £35.

Method 1

1% of £1 is 1p so 1% of £35 is 35p

7.5% is therefore 35 × 7.5 = 262.5p

To the nearest penny this is £2.63

Method 2

$7.5\% = \frac{7.5}{100} = 0.075$

$0.075 \times £35 = £2.625$

Method 3

Working from 10%:

10% of £35 is £3.50

5% of £35 is £1.75 ——— half of 10%

2.5% of £35 is 87.5p ——— half of 5%

7.5% is 10% − 2.5% = £3.50 − 87.5p = £2.625 or £2.63

Exercise 15D

Work out these percentages.

1. 60% of 165
2. 45% of 920 kg
3. 17% of £7000
4. 90% of 80
5. 6% of £420
6. 10% of £16.80
7. 17.5% of £164
8. 30% of £264
9. 5% of £31 240
10. 0.3% of 250 tonnes
11. 7.2% of £600
12. 96% of 32 000 m
13. 25% of 36 km
14. 25% of 15.2 km
15. 6.8% of £9840
16. 4.8% of 3.6 litres

15.4 Increasing a number by a percentage

Prices and salaries often increase by a percentage. In this section you will be finding a percentage of an amount, and then adding it to the original amount.

When you invest money you get paid for lending other people your money.

The money you are paid is called **interest**. The interest is usually paid each year (often called per annum).

Example 10

Find the interest on £250 invested at 5% for one year.

Find 10% first ⟶ 10% of £250 = £25
5% is half of 10% → so 5% of £250 = £12.50

The interest is £12.50 for one year.

Example 11

Satinder earns £160 per week working at the supermarket. She is awarded a 5% pay rise.

(a) Work out the amount of the rise.
(b) Work out her new weekly wage.

(a) **Method 1** $5\% = \dfrac{5}{100}$

$\dfrac{5}{100} \times £160 = \dfrac{5 \times £160}{100} = \dfrac{£800}{100} = £8$

Rise = £8

Chapter 15 Percentages

> **Method 2** $5\% = 0.05$
> $0.05 \times £160 = £8$
> Rise $= £8$
>
> **Method 3**   Find 10% first:
> 10% of £160 = £16
> 5% of £160 = £8 ——— half of 10%
>
> **(b)** Either   £160 + £8 = £168
> or   New wage is 100% + 5% = 105% of old wage
> So new wage = 105% of £160
>
> $$= \frac{105}{100} \times £160$$
>
> $$= \frac{105 \times £160}{100}$$
>
> $$= \frac{£16\,800}{100}$$
>
> $$= £168$$
>
> or $105\% = 1.05$
> $1.05 \times £160 = £168$

To increase a number by a percentage, you find the percentage of that number and then add this to the starting number.

Exercise 15E

1 Increase
  (a) £50 by 10%
  (b) 60 l by 5%
  (c) 400 m by 20%
  (d) £150 by 15%
  (e) 35 g by 20%
  (f) £450 by 12%
  (g) £85 by 8%
  (h) 300 by 15%
  (i) 2 tonnes by 35%

2 Find the interest on £350 invested for one year at
  (a) 10%   (b) 11%   (c) 9%   (d) 15%
  (e) 1%   (f) 5%   (g) 8%   (h) 4%

3 Ray buys a bike for £200. He sells it for 15% more than he paid for it. How much does he sell the bike for?

4 Sandra buys an antique painting for £2000. Six months later she sells it, making a profit of 5%. How much does she sell the painting for?

5 Tommy invests £150 at an interest rate of $7\frac{1}{2}\%$. How much interest will Tommy get after one year?

6 A market trader buys knitted jumpers for £8.60 each and sports shirts for £4.80 each. She sells them for 65% more than she bought them for.
Work out the selling price of each item.

7 Janice left £450 in her building society account for one year. The building society paid interest of $6\frac{1}{2}\%$ per annum.
How much interest did Janice's money earn in the year?

8 Last year, a skiing holiday in Italy cost £276. The price was made up of fares £80, hotel £120, skiing instruction £30 and hire of equipment £46.

This year, the cost of fares had risen by 12%, hotel costs had risen by 8%, the cost of instruction had increased by 50% and hire of equipment by 10%.

Work out the total cost of the holiday this year.

15.5 Decreasing a number by a percentage

Reductions in numbers or prices are often described using percentages. There are several ways you can work out the actual numbers involved.

A 12% discount means that the price is reduced by 12%.

Example 12

At the beginning of a year the number of unemployed people in a city was 5500. This number fell by 1% during the year.

(a) Work out the fall in the number of unemployed people.
(b) Work out the number of people remaining.

(a) Fall in the number of unemployed people:

Either $\quad 1\% = \dfrac{1}{100}$ $\qquad$ **or** $\quad 1\% = 0.01$

$\dfrac{1}{100} \times 5500 = \dfrac{1 \times 5500}{100} = \dfrac{5500}{100} = 55$ $\qquad 0.01 \times 5500 = 55$

(b) Number of people remaining:

Either $\quad 5500 - 55 = 5445$
or $\qquad$ New number is $100\% - 1\% = 99\%$ of old number

So the number remaining = 99% of 5500

$= \dfrac{99}{100} \times 5500 \qquad$ **or** $\quad 99\% = 0.99$

$= \dfrac{99 \times 5500}{100} \qquad\qquad 0.99 \times 5500 = 5445$

$= \dfrac{544\,500}{100} = 5445$

To decrease a number by a percentage, you find the percentage of that number and then take it away from the starting number.

Exercise 15F

1 Work out the sale price of a TV that normally costs £120 if the discount is
  (a) 10%
  (b) 20%
  (c) 5%
  (d) 15%

2 Gareth is offered a discount of 10% for paying cash for a car that has an original price of £3000.
How much does Gareth pay for the car?

3 Rob gets a discount of 5% off his ticket to Paris.
The original price was £150.
How much does Rob have to pay for his ticket?

4 In their spring sale, Sonic Sound reduced the price of all CDs and DVDs by 30%.
Calculate
  (a) the reduction in price
  (b) the new price of a CD usually costing £12.

5 A furniture store reduced all normal prices by 15% for the spring sale.
Work out
  (i) the reduction in price   (ii) the spring sale price of
  (a) a table normally priced at £80
  (b) a settee normally priced at £740
  (c) a TV table normally priced at £40.60

6 Fun In The Sun Holidays advertises a discount of 18% off all holiday prices.
How much would it cost for
  (a) a fly drive holiday originally priced at £360
  (b) an activity holiday originally priced at £168?

15.6 VAT

VAT or value added tax is a tax imposed by the government on sales of some goods and services.

In 2005, VAT was set at $17\frac{1}{2}$%.

> To apply VAT you add $17\frac{1}{2}$% extra onto the original cost.

Example 13

$17\frac{1}{2}$% VAT is added to Harry's bill of £24.
What is the total bill?

To work this out you have to find $17\frac{1}{2}$% of £24 and then add it on to the £24.

There is an easy non-calculator method for working out VAT at $17\frac{1}{2}$%.

First find 10% of £24	£2.40	10%
Then halve it to find 5%	£1.20	5%
Then halve this to find $2\frac{1}{2}$%	£0.60	$2\frac{1}{2}$%
	£4.20	$17\frac{1}{2}$%

£24 + £4.20 = £28.20

VAT can be worked out by finding   10%
                          then   5%
                          then $2\frac{1}{2}$% +
                                  ─────
                                  $17\frac{1}{2}$%

Exercise 15G

1 Find $17\frac{1}{2}$% of these amounts:
   (a) £10   (b) £30   (c) £32   (d) £40
   (e) £16   (f) £120   (g) £250   (h) £360

2 Work out the total bill in each of these cases when VAT is added at $17\frac{1}{2}$%.
   (a) £100   (b) £300   (c) £320   (d) £40
   (e) £160   (f) £120   (g) £2500 (h) £3600

3 Value added tax (VAT) is charged at the rate of $17\frac{1}{2}$%. How much VAT is there to pay on
   (a) a telephone bill of £52.40 before VAT
   (b) a restaurant bill of £28 before VAT
   (c) a wedding reception costing £1980 before VAT
   (d) a builder's bill for repairs of £158.80 before VAT?

15.7 Index numbers

An **index number** shows how a quantity changes over time.

A **price index** shows how the price of something changes over time.

Index numbers are often used to mark changes in retail prices. The amount an average family spends on food, fuel etc. is worked out for a particular year, known as the **base year**. Any changes in prices are collected and the overall rise or fall in the amount of money spent by an average family is given as a percentage of the base year price.

The index always starts at 100.

If the price (or quantity) rises over time, the index rises above 100.

If the price (or quantity) falls over time, the index falls below 100.

This table shows an index of retail prices for January to April last year.

January	February	March	April
100	104.5	103.0	106.8

This means that prices rose by 4.5% from January to February. Although in March they fell by 1.5 percentage points compared with February, prices were still 3% above the January figure. April shows a rise of 6.8% on the January figure.

Example 14

The table shows the index numbers for the sales of ice cream each month.

Month	August	September	October	November
Index	100	95	87	76

(a) What was the percentage change from August to November?
(b) In which period was there the greatest fall in sales?
(c) What is the overall trend in sales figures?

(a) From August to November: 100 − 76 = 24; a fall of 24%.
(b) August to September: 5
    September to October: 8
    October to November: 11
    The greatest fall was in the period October to November.
(c) The sales fell each month:

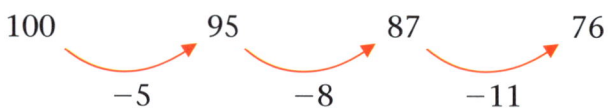

15.7 Index numbers

Exercise 15H

1. The table shows an index for the number of winter coats sold by a shop.

Month	Jan	Feb	Mar	Apr
Index	100	110	102	98

   (a) What happened to the sale of winter coats between March and April?
   (b) In which period was there the greatest decrease in sales?
   (c) What is the difference in sales between January and April?

2. The table shows an index for the service costs of a car, over a period of time.

Year	2001	2002	2003	2004
Index	100	120	135	130

   (a) Write down the base year for the index table.
   (b) In which period was there the greatest increase in costs?
   (c) What was the percentage change from 2001 to 2004?

3. The table shows an index for the value of a computer over time.

Year	2000	2001	2002	2003	2004
Index	100	80	62	44	28

   (a) In which period was there the greatest change in value?
   (b) There was an 80% reduction from 2000 to 2005. What is the index for 2005?

4. The table shows an index for the number of newspapers sold by a shop in a week.

Day	Mon	Tue	Wed	Thu	Fri
Index	100	105	92	96	110

   (a) Write down the base day for the table.
   (b) What was the percentage change from Monday to Wednesday?
   (c) Between which two days was there the greatest change in newspaper sales?

15.8 Writing one quantity as a percentage of another quantity

Example 15

The top mark in a test is 34 out of 40.
What is this as a percentage?

To find one quantity as a percentage of another follow these steps:

Step 1 Write the two amounts as a fraction: $\frac{34}{40}$

Step 2 Convert the fraction to a decimal:
$$\frac{34}{40} = 34 \div 40 = 0.85$$

Step 3 Multiply the decimal by 100:
$$0.85 \times 100 = 85$$

The top mark is 85%.

Example 16

A jacket is reduced in price from £80 to £62.
What is the percentage reduction?

The actual reduction is £80 − £62 = £18

Step 1 Write this as a fraction of the original price: $\frac{18}{80}$

Step 2 Convert to a decimal:
$$18 \div 80 = 0.225$$

Step 3 Multiply by 100:
$$0.225 \times 100 = 22.5\%$$

The percentage reduction is 22.5%.

To write one amount as a percentage of another:
- write the amounts as a fraction
- convert the fraction to a decimal
- multiply the decimal by 100.

$$\text{Percentage change} = \frac{\text{actual change}}{\text{original amount}} \times 100$$

Exercise 15I

1 (a) What percentage of £100 is £5?
   (b) What percentage of 5 kg is 600 g?
   (c) What percentage of £160 is £24?
   (d) What percentage of 2 l is 150 ml?
   (e) What percentage of 3 hours is 1 hour 15 mins?
   (f) What percentage of £4.20 is 35p?
   (g) What percentage of £16 000 is £480?
   (h) What percentage of 20 tonnes is 200 kg?
   (i) What percentage of 3.6 m is 180 cm?

2 (a) Write £15 as a percentage of £200.
   (b) Write £600 as a percentage of £3000.
   (c) Write 15 minutes as a percentage of 1 hour 15 mins.
   (d) Write 6.3 m as a percentage of 157.5 m.
   (e) Write £5.60 as a percentage of £140.
   (f) Write 36 kg as a percentage of 900 kg.
   (g) Write 20 tonnes as a percentage of 320 tonnes.
   (h) Write 4.5 mm as a percentage of 90 cm.
   (i) Write £850 as a percentage of £4000.
   (j) Write £1575 as a percentage of £63 000.

3 Shoes in a sale are reduced in price from £60 to £42.
What is the percentage reduction?

4 A factory employing 300 people made 18 people redundant.
What percentage of the employees were made redundant?

5 Peter bought a new motor bike for £840 and sold it two years later for £378.
By what percentage had its value fallen compared with the two years?

6 A games console, normally sold for £215, is offered for sale at £180.60.
Calculate the percentage reduction.

7 A shopworker received a wage increase from £160 per week to £165 per week.
What was the percentage increase?

8 Shona deposited £450 in a bank savings account.
Interest paid after a year increased the amount in her account to £478.80.
What percentage rate of interest did the bank pay?

9 Ali paid a deposit of £108 on a secondhand car costing £1350.
What percentage of the price was the deposit?

10 Last year the number of students in a school grew from 1050 to 1500.
What was the percentage increase in the number of students?

15.9 Comparing different proportions using percentages

Example 17

Write in order of size, smallest first:

65%, $\frac{3}{5}$, 0.66, $\frac{5}{8}$

First, change them to percentages:

$\frac{3}{5} = 3 \div 5 = 0.6 = 60\%$

$0.66 = 66\%$

$\frac{5}{8} = 5 \div 8 = 0.625 = 62.5\%$

Then write in order: $\frac{3}{5}$, $\frac{5}{8}$, 65%, 0.66

60%	62.5%	65%	66%
$\frac{3}{5}$	$\frac{5}{8}$	65%	0.66

Example 18

In three class tests, Robin scored 8 out of 10 in English, 17 out of 20 in science and 42 out of 50 in history. Which was his best result?

First, change the marks to percentages:

English: 8 out of 10 = $\frac{8}{10}$ = 8 ÷ 10 = 0.8 = 80%

Science: 17 out of 20 = $\frac{17}{20}$ = 17 ÷ 20 = 0.85 = 85%

History: 42 out of 50 = $\frac{42}{50}$ = 42 ÷ 50 = 0.84 = 84%

So Robin's best result was for science.

To compare percentages, fractions and decimals, you can first change them all to percentages.

Exercise 15J

1. Rearrange in order of size, smallest first:
   (a) 52%, 0.53, $\frac{9}{15}$
   (b) 72%, $\frac{7}{10}$, 0.71
   (c) 0.07, $\frac{1}{10}$, 8%
   (d) $\frac{3}{8}$, 30%, 0.36

2. In end of term tests, Sheila's results were:
   English: 16 out of 24   Geography: 58 out of 100
   Maths: 27 out of 40   Science: 11 out of 20
   History: 31 out of 50   Technology: 33 out of 60
   (a) Which was her best result?   (b) Which was her worst result?

3. Top Cooks Catering offered two different courses to its students. 45 out of 50 recommended Cake Baking, whilst 37 out of 40 recommended Pizza Making. Which scored the higher percentage of recommendations from students?

15.10 Interest and depreciation

When you invest money in a bank or building society, you receive interest on the amount you invest.

> Example 10 in Section 15.4 showed you how to calculate simple interest.

Simple interest is when the same interest is added each year. You find the interest for one year and multiply it by the number of years.

Example 19

Find the simple interest on £1000 invested for two years at 5% per annum.
Year 1:   10% of £1000 is £100   so   5% of £1000 is £50
Year 2:   5% of £1000 is £50
Total interest is £50 + £50 = £100

However, you can choose to add the interest for one year to the amount already in your account. In that case, interest for the next year is based on the combined amounts.

Example 20

Tanvi invests £1000 at 5% per annum. She adds the interest for Year 1 to the money already in her account. Find the total interest at the end of Year 2.
Year 1:   10% of £1000 is £100   so   5% of £1000 is £50
The interest is added on, so there is £1050 in the account at the end of Year 1.
Year 2:   10% of £1050 is £105   so   5% of £1050 is £52.50
The interest is added on, so there is £1102.50 in the account at the end of Year 2.
Total interest is £50 + £52.50 = £102.50

When you buy a car the value of the car gets smaller and smaller as time goes by. This is called **depreciation**.

Example 21

Find the value of a car that was bought for £10 000 after depreciation at 10% per annum for two years.

Year 1:   10% of £10 000 is £1000

The car has a value of £10 000 − £1000 = £9000 at the end of Year 1.

Year 2:   10% of £9000 is £900

The car has a value of £9000 − £900 = £8100 at the end of Year 2.

Exercise 15K

1. Find the simple interest when
   (a) £100 is invested for two years at 10% per annum.
   (b) £500 is invested for three years at 10% per annum
   (c) £200 is invested for two years at 5% per annum
   (d) £1000 is invested for two years at 4% per annum
   (e) £50 is invested for four years at 5% per annum.

2. Find the total interest after two years when the interest for the first year is added to the amount already in the account.
   (a) £100 invested at 10% per annum
   (b) £500 invested at 10% per annum
   (c) £200 invested at 5% per annum
   (d) £1000 invested at 4% per annum
   (e) £50 invested at 5% per annum.

3. Jasmine invested £1000 for two years at 8%. She left the interest for the first year in her account.
   How much money was in Jasmine's account at the end of the two years?

4. James invested £100 for two years at 4%. He left the interest for the first year in his account.
   How much money was in James's account at the end of the two years?

5. Ben bought a car for £12 000. The value of the car depreciated at 10% a year. What was the value of Ben's car after two years?

6. Jane bought a car for £8000. The value of the car depreciated at 20% a year. What was the value of Jane's car after two years?

7 Susan bought a flute for £200. The value of the flute depreciated at 10% a year.
   What was the value of the flute after two years?

8 Joe buys a new truck for £100 000. The value of the truck depreciates at 20% a year.
   What is the value of Joe's truck after two years?

Mixed exercise 15

1 Copy and complete this table of equivalent fractions, decimals and percentages.

Fraction	Decimal	Percentage
$\frac{1}{2}$		
	0.6	
		20%
	0.35	
$\frac{1}{20}$		

2 James bought a new boat for £10 000.
   It had lost 60% of its value after three years.
   (a) Work out the loss in value.
   (b) What is the value of the boat after three years?

3 The same sort of bike is for sale in two shops.
   Work out the price you would have to pay in each shop.

WHEELIE'S
Mountain bikes $\frac{1}{4}$ OFF
Price was £198
Price now

CHEAPER BIKES
Mountain bikes
30% OFF
BIGGEST REDUCTION
Last week's price was £239
This week's price is

4 Find the percentage reduction on the Mega Games System in the sale.

Mega Games System
Normal Price   £300
Sale Price   £225

5 Janet invests £50 in a building society for one year.
   The interest rate is 4% per year.
   (a) How much interest, in pounds, does Janet get?

Nisha invests £20 in a different building society. She gets £3 interest after one year.

(b) Work out the percentage interest rate that Nisha gets.

6 Nigel works in a service station and earns £12 500 per year. He is given a pay rise of 15%.
Ryan is a football player earning £17 500 per year. He is given a pay rise of 1.5%.
Who has the bigger rise in pay?

7 Work out the cost of each item after VAT at 17.5% is added.
(a) Kevin's TV, cost £80 plus VAT.
(b) Julie's microwave, cost £64 plus VAT.
(c) Sophie's saxophone, cost £240 plus VAT.
(d) Roger's boat, cost £720 plus VAT.
(e) Terri's motorbike, cost £360 plus VAT.

8 Rearrange the following in order of size, starting with the smallest:
(a) 36%, $\frac{7}{19}$, 0.37
(b) 0.09, 19%, $\frac{1}{6}$
(c) $\frac{17}{27}$, 60%, $\frac{5}{8}$, 0.62

9 The table shows an index for the price of vintage comics.

Year	2001	2002	2003	2004
Index	100	104	109	117

(a) What was the percentage price rise from 2001 to 2002?
(b) What was the percentage price rise from 2001 to 2004?
(c) Jim paid £50 for a comic in 2001. What would the price be in 2004?

10 A shopkeeper increases the prices of goods in the shop in line with the rate of inflation.
The rate of inflation is 2.1%.
Calculate
(a) the increase in the price of a table marked at £160
(b) the new price of a chair marked at £85
(c) the increase in the price of a bed marked at £249
(d) the new price of a settee marked at £1350.

11 In an election, 6600 people were eligible to vote. 45% voted for Edwards, 28% voted for Philips and 6% voted for Fortescue. The remainder did not vote.

(a) What percentage of voters did not vote?

(b) How many votes did each candidate receive?

12 House prices in a town increased on average by 8% during the year 2000. Calculate

(a) the price increase of a house previously valued at £84 000

(b) the new price of a house previously valued at £102 250.

13 An insurance agent is paid 2% commission on the value of any policies she sells. How much commission is she paid when she sells a policy worth

(a) £4500   (b) £6550?

14 A new chainsaw costs £240. With depreciation its value is expected to fall each year by 15% of its value at the beginning of the year.

What will be the value of the chainsaw in 2 years' time?

15 £900 is invested for two years at $4\frac{1}{2}$%. The interest at the end of the first year is left in the account.

What is the total interest earned?
Give your answer to the nearest penny.

Summary of key points

1 Percentage

%
pc
} means 'number of parts per hundred'.

2 Remember these percentages and their equivalent fractions:

$50\% = \frac{1}{2}$ $25\% = \frac{1}{4}$ $75\% = \frac{3}{4}$ $33\frac{1}{3}\% = \frac{1}{3}$ $66\frac{2}{3}\% = \frac{2}{3}$

3 A percentage can be written as a fraction with denominator (bottom) 100.

4 To write a percentage as a decimal:
- write the percentage as a fraction
- convert the fraction to a decimal

5 To convert a decimal to a percentage, multiply the decimal by 100.

6 To write a fraction as a percentage:
   - change the fraction to a decimal
   - multiply the decimal by 100.

7 To increase a number by a percentage, find the percentage of that number and then add this to the starting number.

8 To decrease a number by a percentage, you find the percentage of that number and then take it away from the starting number.

9 VAT can be worked out by finding   10%
   then   5%
   then $2\tfrac{1}{2}\%$ +
   _____
   $17\tfrac{1}{2}\%$

10 An **index number** shows how a quantity changes over time.

   A **price index** shows how the price of something changes over time.

   The index always starts at 100.

   If the price (or quantity) rises over time, the index rises above 100.

   If the price (or quantity) falls over time, the index falls below 100.

11 To write one amount as a percentage of another:
   - write the amounts as a fraction
   - convert the fraction to a decimal
   - multiply the decimal by 100.

12 Percentage change = $\dfrac{\text{actual change}}{\text{original amount}} \times 100$

13 To compare percentages, fractions and decimals, you can first change them all to percentages.

14 **Simple interest** is when the same interest is added each year. You find the interest for one year and multiply it by the number of years.

16 Coordinates and graphs

16.1 Coordinates in the first quadrant

You can describe the position of a place on a grid by using two numbers.

You write the number of units across first and the number of units up second.

On this map 6 across, 3 up gives the position of the Water Hole. You can write this as the point (6, 3). The numbers 6 and 3 are the **coordinates**.

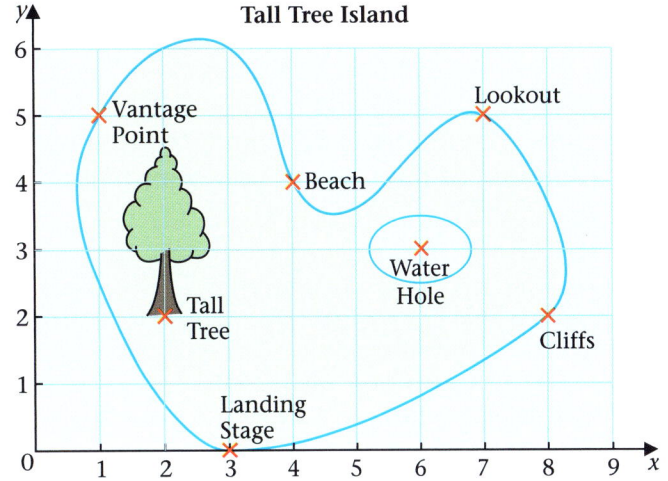

Exercise 16A

1. Write down the names of the places on the map above with these coordinates:

   (a) (8, 2)   (b) (7, 5)   (c) (1, 5)

2. Write down the coordinates of these places on the map of Tall Tree Island above:

   (a) Tall Tree   (b) Landing Stage   (c) Beach

3. On squared paper draw a coordinate grid and number it from 0 to 12 across the page and 0 to 6 up the page. Join these points in the order given:

   (2, 3) (3, 1) (10, 1) (11, 3) (7, 3) (9, 5) (6, 5) (4, 3) (2, 3)

4. Write down the coordinates of all the points marked red in the diagram below.

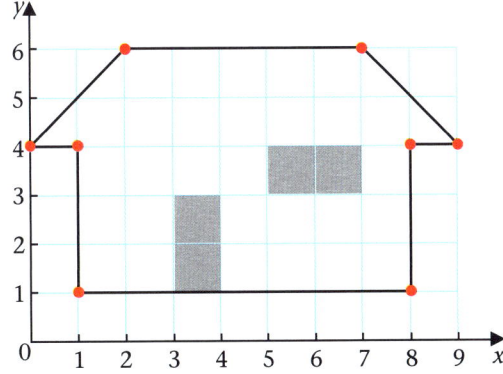

5 Write down the coordinates of all the corner points that make up this ship.

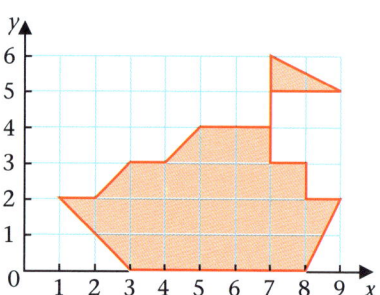

6 Draw a coordinate grid from 0 to 10 in both directions. On your grid plot each of these sets of points and join them in the order given.
(a) (1, 1) (4, 1) (4, 4) (1, 4) (1, 1)
(b) (6, 1) (9, 1) (9, 6) (6, 6) (6, 1)
(c) (0, 6) (5, 6) (0, 10) (0, 6)
(d) (5, 7) (5, 10) (8, 10) (5, 7)

7 Draw a coordinate grid from 0 to 10 in both directions. On your grid draw a shape of your own and label the coordinates of each point.

8 Invent an island of your own and mark positions on it using a coordinate grid. List all the places with their coordinates.

Coordinates of the mid-point of a line segment

Here is a straight line through points *A* and *B*.
The section of line between *A* and *B* is called a **line segment** *AB*.
A has coordinates (1, 1)   *B* has coordinates (3, 6)
Halfway along line segment *AB* is *M*.
M is called the **mid-point of the line segment** *AB*.
You can find the coordinates of the mid-point.

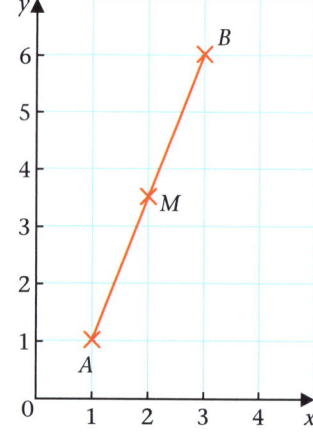

1 Add the *x*-coordinates and divide by 2:
$$\frac{1+3}{2} = \frac{4}{2} = 2$$
2 Add the *y*-coordinates and divide by 2:
$$\frac{1+6}{2} = \frac{7}{2} = 3\frac{1}{2}$$
So the coordinates of the mid-point are $(2, 3\frac{1}{2})$.

Example 1

Work out the coordinates of the mid-point of the line segment *AB* where *A* is (2, 3) and *B* is (7, 11).

Mid-point *x*-coordinate is $\frac{2+7}{2} = \frac{9}{2} = 4\frac{1}{2}$

Mid-point *y*-coordinate is $\frac{3+11}{2} = \frac{14}{2} = 7$ So the mid-point is $(4\frac{1}{2}, 7)$.

Exercise 16B

1 Work out the coordinates of the mid-point of each of these line segments on the grid below.
   (a) AB   (b) CD   (c) EF   (d) GH

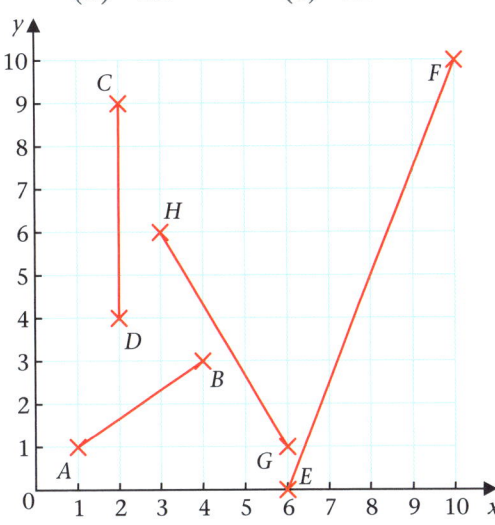

2 Work out the coordinates of the mid-point of each of these line segments:
   (a) AB where A(0, 0) and B is (4, 5)
   (b) CD where C(3, 1) and D is (4, 9)
   (c) EF where E(5, 7) and F is (1, 6)
   (d) GH where G(1, 0) and H is (5, 8)
   (e) IJ where I(9, 10) and J is (3, 7)

16.2 Linear graphs

You can use graphs to show relationships. For example, if you buy several packets of crisps the price you pay is related to the number of packets you buy.

> **Example 2**
>
> Stan sells packets of crisps at 30p each. He wants a quick way of remembering how much different numbers of packets cost.
>
> He makes a table:
>
> | Number of packets | 1 | 2 | 3 | 4 | 5 | 6 |
> |---|---|---|---|---|---|---|
> | Cost in pence | 30 | 60 | 90 | 120 | 150 | 180 |
>
> Notice that the cost goes up by 30p for each extra packet.
>
> A pattern like the one in the table is known as a **linear relationship**. Linear relationships can be spotted very easily by drawing a graph.

Plot the points (1, 30), (2, 60), (3, 90), (4, 120), (5, 150) and (6, 180) to draw a graph of Stan's table.

When the points are they plotted make a straight line.

If the line of Stan's graph is made longer, the cost of 7 and 8 packets can be read off. Check the broken lines to see that the costs of 7 and 8 packets are 210p and 240p.

0 packets cost 0p, so extend the graph back to (0, 0).

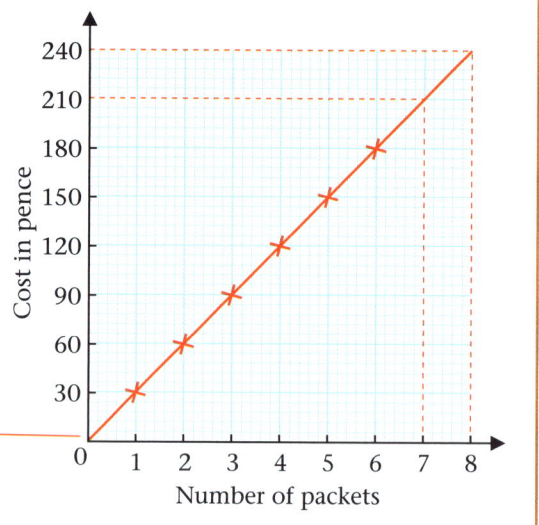

A graph representing a **linear relationship** always has a straight line.

Example 3

Sharon charges £2 for the use of her taxi and £1.50 per mile after that.

(a) Use this information to draw up a table
(b) Plot the points on a graph.

Work out the cost for these journeys

(c) 7 miles   (d) 1 mile.

(a) The table gives the charges for some journeys up to 6 miles long.

Distance in miles	0	2	4	6
Cost in £	2	5	8	11

(b) Plot the points (0, 2), (2, 5), (4, 8), (6, 11). The graph gives a straight line.

(c) The cost of a 7 mile journey is £12.50

(d) The cost of a 1 mile journey is £3.50

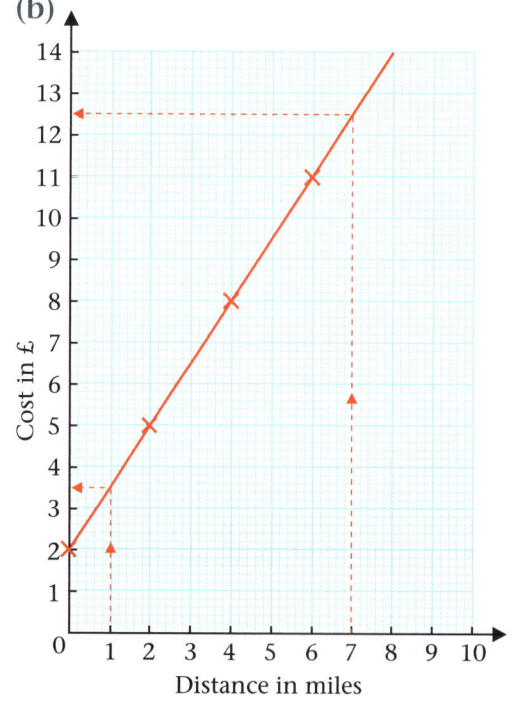

Because the relationship is linear, you can use the graph to find the cost of a journey of more than 6 miles and for journeys between the values that you have worked out.

Exercise 16C

1. The table shows the cost of potatoes per kg.

Weight in kg	1	2	3	4	5
Cost in pence	30	60	90	120	150

   (a) Draw a graph for this table.
   (b) Work out how much 2.5 kg of potatoes would cost.
   (c) Extend the graph to work out the cost of 6 kg of potatoes.

2. The table shows the cost of ice lollies.

Number of ice lollies	1	2	3	4	5
Cost in pence	25	50	75	100	125

   (a) Draw a graph for the cost of ice lollies from the table.
   (b) Extend the graph and then use it to work out the cost of
      (i) 8 ice lollies   (ii) 6 ice lollies.

3. The table shows the number of litres of petrol left in a car's petrol tank on a journey.

Travelling time in hours	1	2	3	4	5	6	7	8
Number of litres left	55	50	45	40	35	30	25	20

   (a) Draw a graph from the information given in the table.
   (b) How many litres were in the tank at the start of the journey (after 0 hours)?
   (c) How many litres were in the tank after $5\frac{1}{2}$ hours?

4. A car uses 2 litres of petrol for every 5 km it travels.
   (a) Copy and complete the table showing how much petrol the car uses.

Distance travelled in km	0	5	10	15	20	25
Petrol used in litres	0	2	4			

   (b) Draw a graph from the information in your table.
   (c) Work out how much petrol is used to travel 4 km.
   (d) Work out how many kilometres had been travelled by the time 15 litres of petrol had been used.

5. The water in a reservoir is 144 m deep. During a dry period the water level falls by 4 m each week.

   (a) Copy and complete this table showing the expected depth of water in the reservoir.

Weeks	0	1	2	3	4	5	6	7	8
Expected depth of water in m	144	140							

   (b) Draw a graph from the information in your table.
   (c) How deep would you expect the reservoir to be after 10 weeks?

   If the water level falls to 96 m the water company will divert water from another reservoir.

   (d) After how long will the water company divert water?

16.3 Conversion graphs

A **conversion graph** is used to convert a measurement into different units.

This conversion graph relates temperatures in degrees Fahrenheit (°F) to temperatures in degrees Celsius (°C).

To draw a conversion graph you need to know two pairs of values linking the two sets of units.

In this case use the facts that

   0 °C = 32 °F   (the freezing point of water)
and 100 °C = 212 °F (the boiling point of water).

To make the conversion graph you draw a horizontal axis from 0 to 100 for °C and a vertical axis from 0 to 212 for °F. Then plot the two points and join them with a straight line.

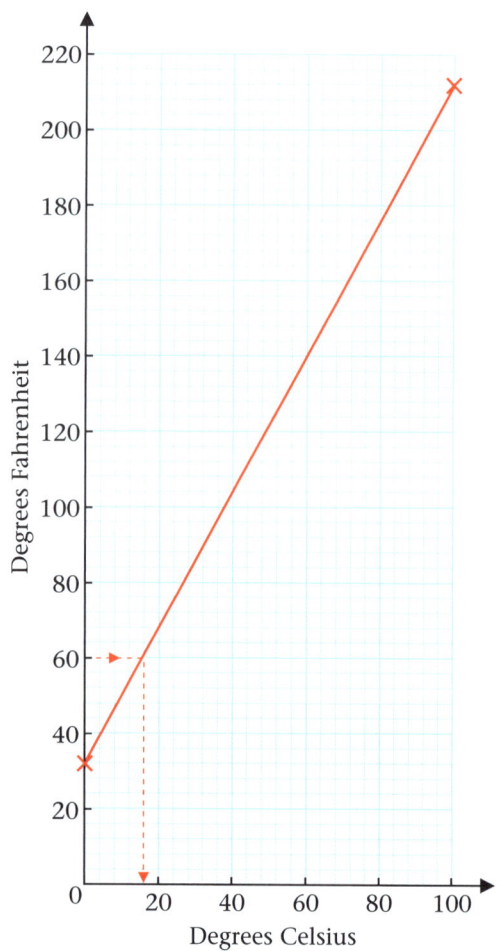

16.3 Conversion graphs

Example 4

Change 60° Fahrenheit to degrees Celsius.
- Draw a horizontal line from 60 °F across to the straight line on the graph.
- From the line draw a vertical line down to the °C axis.
- Read off the scale.

The answer is 16 °C.

Exercise 16D

1 Copy the table and use the temperature conversion graph on page 304 to complete it.

°C	5	20		28			35	80		40
°F			80		50	100			200	

2 (a) Draw a conversion graph from pounds to kilograms. Use the fact that 0 pounds is 0 kilograms and 50 kilograms is approximately 110 pounds.
On your graph draw axes for kilograms and pounds using scales of 1 cm = 10 pounds and 1 cm = 10 kg. Plot the points (0, 0) and (50, 110) and join them with a straight line.

(b) Copy and complete this table using your conversion chart to help you.

Kilograms	0			45	30	15			35	50
Pounds	0	10	20				50	14		110

3 Copy this table and then use the information in the table to draw a conversion graph from inches into centimetres. Use your graph to help you fill in the missing values.

Inches	0	1	2				9	8		12
Centimetres	0			10	15	20			25	30

4 Copy this table and then use the information in the table to draw a conversion graph from miles into kilometres. Use your graph to help you fill in the missing values.

Miles	0	5		40		30			24	50
Kilometres	0		16		36		72	20		80

5 Copy this table and then use the information in the table to draw a conversion graph from acres into hectares. Use your graph to help you fill in the missing values.

Hectares	0			12	15	17			3	20
Acres	0	20	30				24	45		50

16.4 Distance–time graphs

Distance–time graphs give information about journeys. You always use the horizontal axis for time and the vertical axis for distance.

Example 5

Mary travels to work by bus.

She walks the first 750 metres in 10 minutes, waits at the bus stop for 5 minutes, then travels the remaining 3000 metres by bus. She arrives at the work bus stop 21 minutes after she set off from home.

> Use squared paper.
> Distance is the vertical axis.
> Time is the horizontal axis.

(a) Draw a distance–time graph of her journey.

(b) Work out the average speed of the bus in kilometres per hour.

(a)
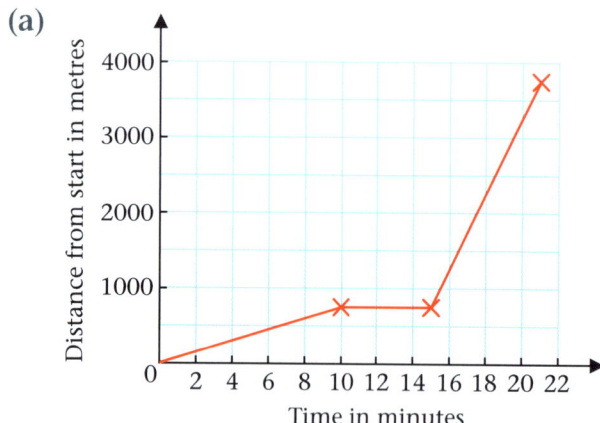

(b) From the graph, the bus travels
   3000 m (3 km) in 6 minutes.
So in 1 hour (= 6 minutes × 10)
it travels 3 km × 10 = 30 km
The speed is 30 km per hour.

16.4 Distance–time graphs

Example 6

This is a graph showing the journey made by an ambulance.

On the graph from O to A the ambulance travels 10 km in 10 minutes. From A to B the ambulance travels 20 km in 10 minutes. From B to C the ambulance does not go anywhere for 5 minutes. The 30 km journey back to base takes 15 minutes.

Work out the speed of the ambulance for each part of the journey.

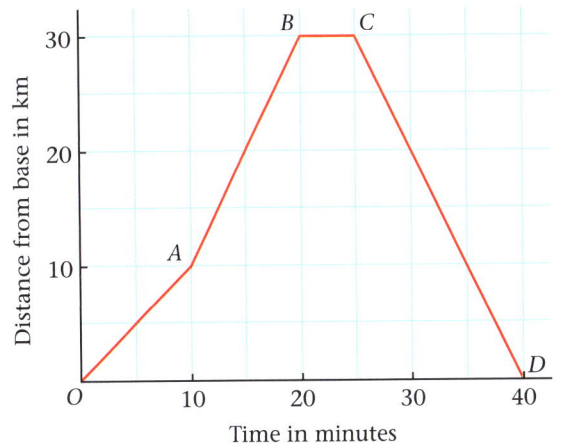

Between O and A:
  speed = 10 km in 10 minutes
       = 1 km per minute
       = 60 km per hour

There are 60 minutes in 1 hour, so speed = 1 × 60 km per hour (km/h).

Between A and B:
  speed = 20 km in 10 minutes
       = 2 km per minute
       = 120 km per hour

Between B and C: speed = 0 km per hour

Between C and D:
  speed = 30 km in 15 minutes
       = 2 km per minute
       = 120 km per hour

Distance–time graphs are used to relate the distance travelled to the time taken, and to calculate speeds.

Exercise 16E

1 Jane walks to the shops, does some shopping then walks home again.
   (a) How many minutes did it take Jane to walk to the shops?
   (b) How far away were the shops?
   (c) How many minutes did Jane spend shopping?
   (d) How many minutes did it take Jane to walk home?
   (e) Work out the speed at which Jane walked to the shops. First give your answer in metres per minute, then change it to km per hour.
   (f) Work out the speed at which Jane walked back from the shops. First give your answer in metres per minute, then change it to km per hour.

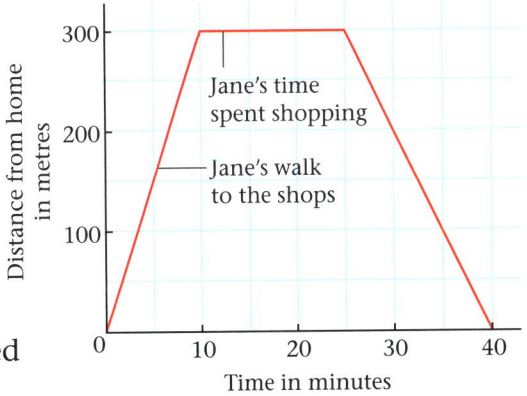

Remember:
1000 m = 1 km

2 Here is a graph of David's car journey to see his aunt.

(a) Write a story of the journey explaining what happened during each part of it.

(b) Work out David's speed during each part of the journey. Give your answers in km per hour.

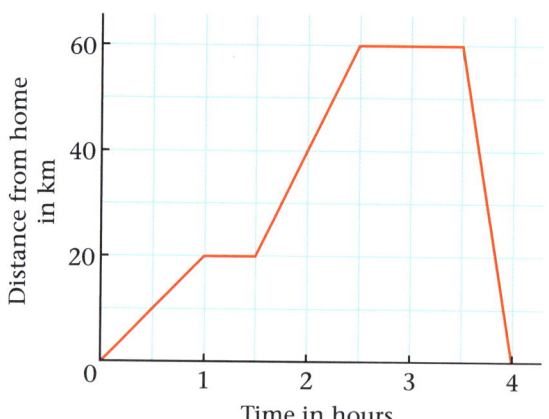

3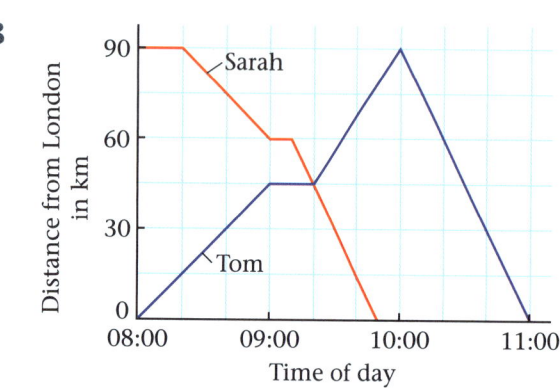

This graph shows Tom's and Sarah's journeys. Tom sets off from London at 08:00 and travels to a town 90 km away to meet his girlfriend Sarah. He stops for a rest on the way. Once he gets to Sarah's he turns around and drives straight home because he discovers that she set off for London some time ago to see him.

(a) Describe Tom's journey in detail explaining after what distance he stopped on the way and for how long.

(b) Describe Sarah's journey in detail explaining after what distance she stopped on the way and for how long.

(c) At what time did Sarah and Tom pass each other and what distance were they from London when it happened?

4 Imran has a bath. The graph shows the depth of the bath water.

He starts at O by turning the hot and cold water taps on.

Between O and point A on the graph the depth of water goes up to 20 cm in 5 minutes.

Explain what happens between points A and B, B and C, C and D, D and E, and E and F on the graph and how long each part of the process takes.

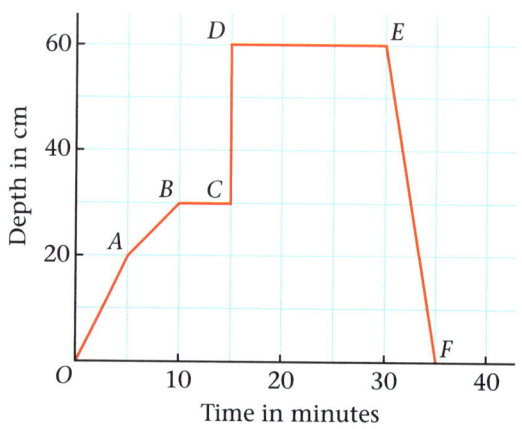

5 Gerald walked to the post box near his house to post a letter. It took him 4 minutes to walk to the post box, which was 400 m away. Gerald chatted to a friend for 2 minutes and he walked home in 3 minutes. Use graph paper to draw a distance–time graph for this journey.

6 Kirsti took a trip in a hot-air balloon. The balloon rose 400 metres in the air in one hour and stayed at this height for two and a half hours. The balloon then came back to the ground in half an hour. Use graph paper to draw a distance–time graph for this balloon flight.

7 Annabel travels to school. She walks the 250 metres to the bus stop in 4 minutes, waits at the bus stop for 5 minutes and then travels the remaining 1000 metres by bus. She arrives at the bus stop outside the school 15 minutes after she sets off from home.
   (a) Draw a distance–time graph of the journey.
   (b) Work out the speed of the bus, first in metres per minute, then in km per hour.

8 Mae went shopping by car. She drove the 10 miles to the shops in 30 minutes. She stayed at the shops for 30 minutes and then started to drive home. The car then broke down after 5 minutes when she had travelled 4 miles from the shops. It took 10 minutes to repair the car and another 5 minutes to get home. Draw a distance–time graph for Mae's journey.

16.5 Curved graphs

Sometimes you will come across a distance–time graph where the line is curved.

Example 7

The distance fallen by a stone when it is dropped from a cliff is shown on this graph.
(a) What distance did the stone fall in 2 seconds?
(b) How long did the stone take to fall 32 metres?

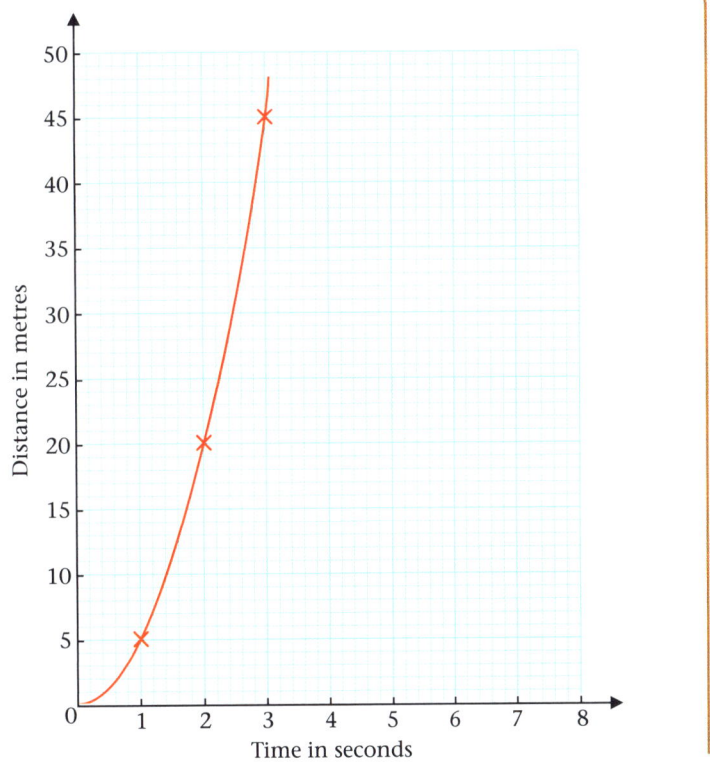

(a) Draw a line up from 2 seconds to meet the curve. Then draw across to the distance axis. It cuts it at 20 metres. The stone fell 20 metres in 2 seconds.

(b) Draw a line across from 32 metres to the curve. Then draw down to the time axis. It cuts it at about 2.6 seconds. The stone took 2.6 seconds to fall 32 metres.

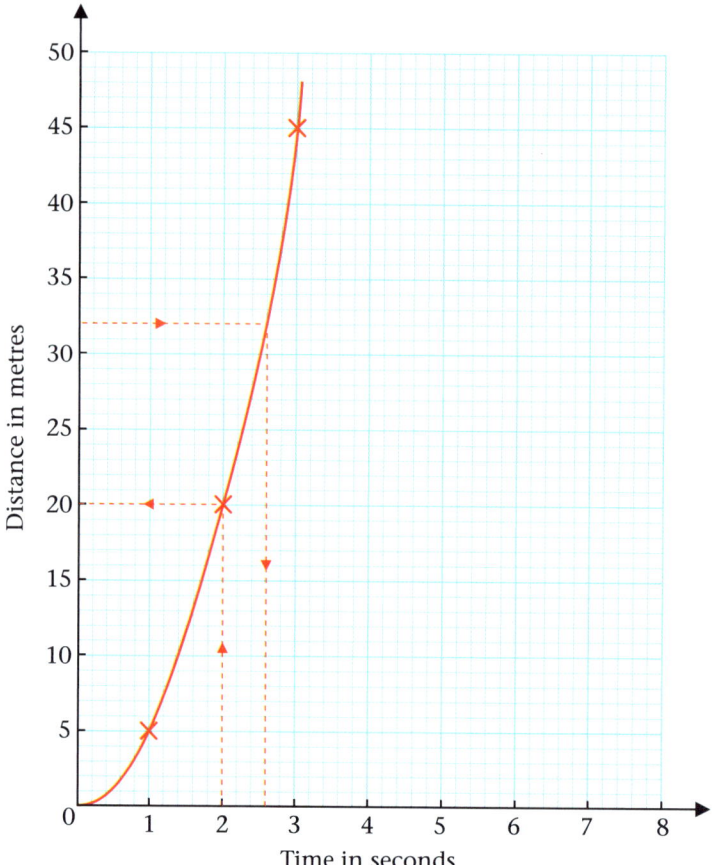

Exercise 16F

1 Use the graph in Example 7 to find
   (a) the distance fallen by the stone in
       (i) 1.5 seconds
       (ii) 3 seconds
   (b) the time taken for the stone to fall
       (i) 40 metres
       (ii) 25 metres.

2 Karen skis down a mountain. This graph shows her run.

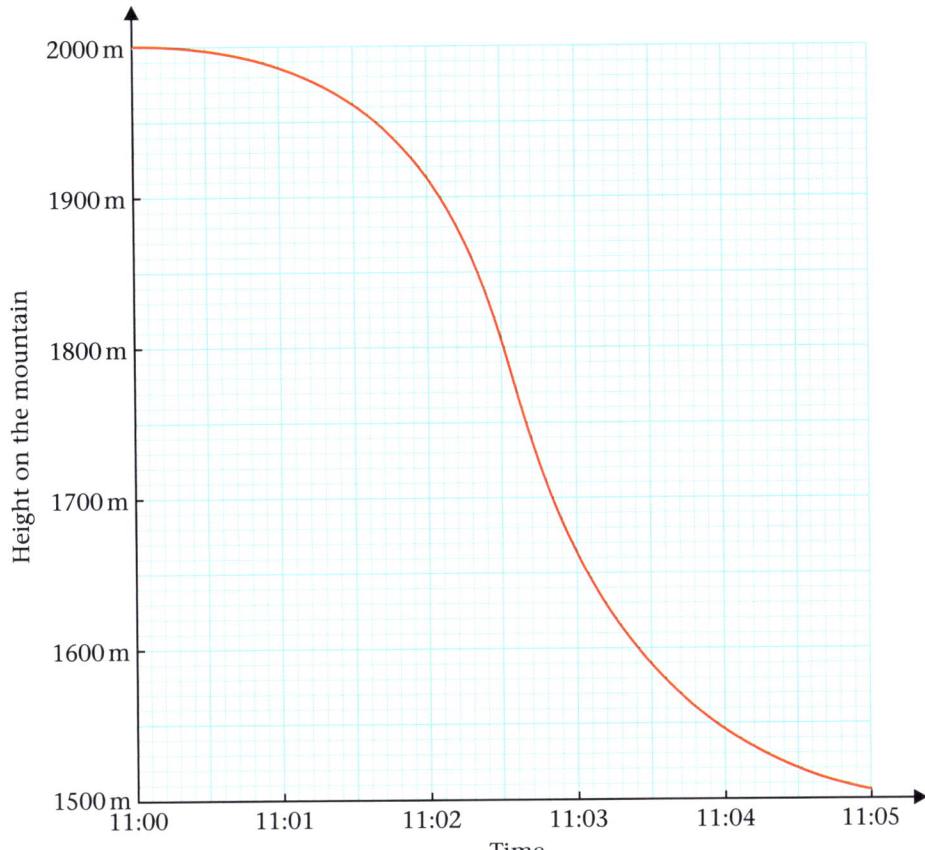

(a) From the graph write down the height Karen was at after
   (i) 1 minute
   (ii) 2 minutes 30 seconds
   (iii) 4 minutes 15 seconds.
(b) Use the graph to write down the time at which Karen was at the following heights:
   (i) 1900 m   (ii) 1750 m   (iii) 1625 m

3 The speed of a ball when it is dropped is shown in the following table of values.

Distance in metres	0	5	10	15	20	25
Speed in metres per second	0	10	14	17	20	22

(a) Draw a graph using the information given in the table.
(b) Use the graph to work out the speed when the distance fallen is 12 metres.
(c) Use the graph to work out the distance fallen when the speed is 18 metres per second.

Join up your points with a **smooth** curve.

16.6 Coordinates in four quadrants

In Section 16.1 you learned how to plot points on a grid with positive coordinates only. You also need to be able to plot coordinates that include negative numbers.

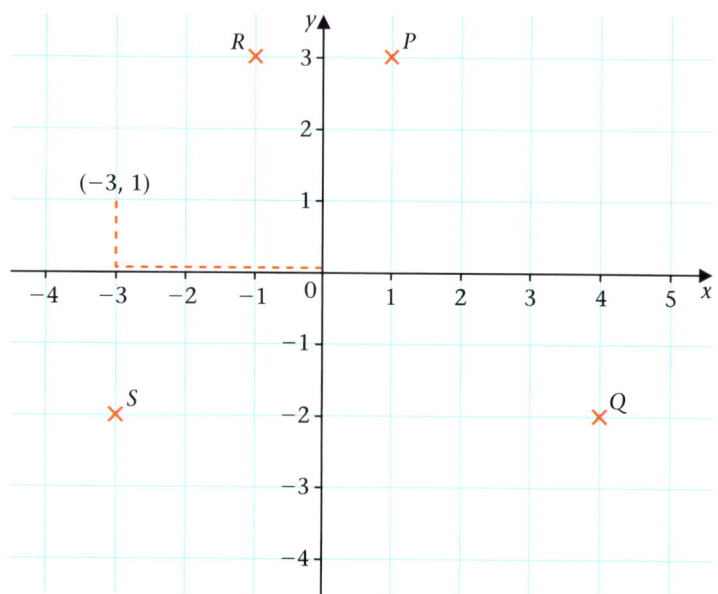

The horizontal axis is called the **x-axis**.
The vertical axis is called the **y-axis**.
The point (0, 0) is called the **origin** and is labelled 0.
Point P is (1, 3).
Point R is at −1 along the x-axis and 3 up the y-axis, so R is (−1, 3).
Point Q is (4, −2) and point S is (−3, −2).
To plot the point (−3, 1), move to −3 on the x-axis, then up 1.

Exercise 16G

1 Write down the coordinates of all the points A to L marked on the coordinate grid.

2 Draw a coordinate grid with the horizontal axis (the x-axis) marked from −4 to +4 and the vertical axis (the y-axis) marked from −10 to +10.
Plot the following points and join them in the order given:
(−1, 6) (−2, 6) (−4, 5) (−4, 6) (−2, 7) (0, 8)
(1, 7) (1, −2) (2, −6) (1, −8) (0, −9) (−1, −9)
(−2, −8) (−3, −6) (−2, −5) (−1, −5) (0, −6) (−2, −6)
(−1, −8) (0, −8) (1, −6) (−1, −2) (−3, 0) (−3, 2) (−1, 6)

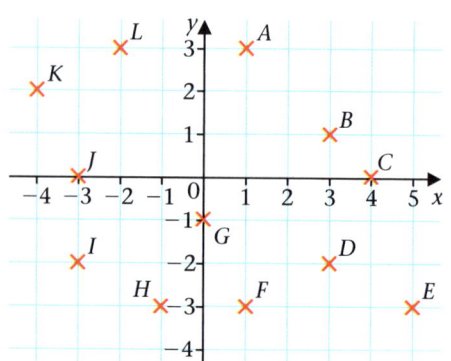

16.7 Using algebra to describe lines

This graph shows a linear (straight line) relationship between the numbers on the horizontal and vertical axes. You can use algebra to describe the relationship and the line.

> **Remember:**
> The horizontal axis is called the *x*-axis and the vertical axis is called the *y*-axis.

In a pair of numbers the *x*-coordinate is given first; the *y*-coordinate is given second:

(x, y)

For example, in the point (3, 2) the *x*-coordinate is 3 and the *y*-coordinate is 2.

Look for a number pattern connecting the coordinates to give the line a name. On the grid above all the *x*-coordinates are 2 so the line is called $x = 2$

The **equation** of the line is $x = 2$

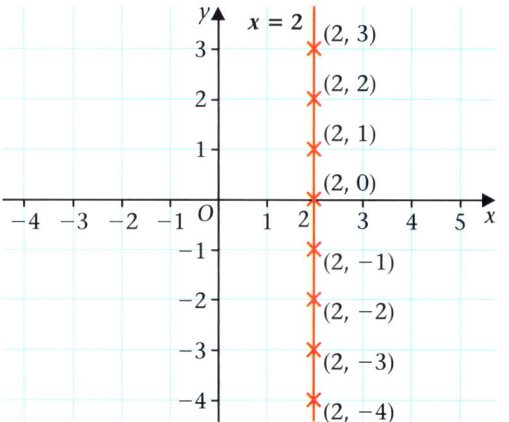

In the graph on the right, all the *y*-coordinates are -2 so the line is called $y = -2$

The **equation** of the line is $y = -2$

> The **equation of a line** uses algebra to show a relationship between the *x*- and *y*-coordinates of points on the line.

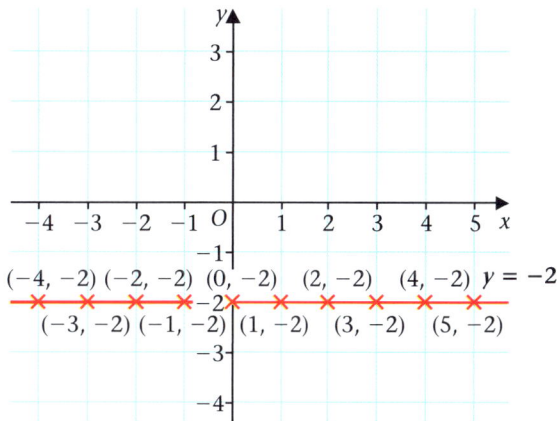

Exercise 16H

1. Write down the equations of the lines marked **(a)** to **(d)** in this diagram.

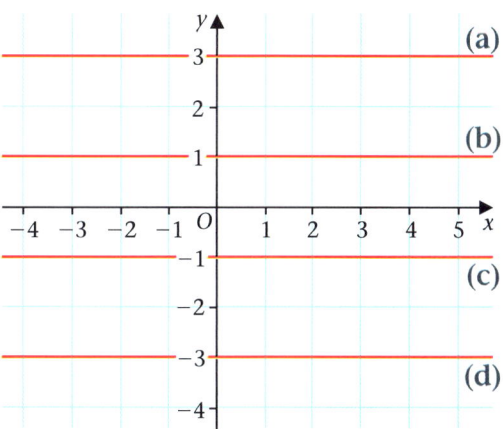

Chapter 16 Coordinates and graphs

2 Write down the equations of the lines labelled (a) to (d) in this diagram.

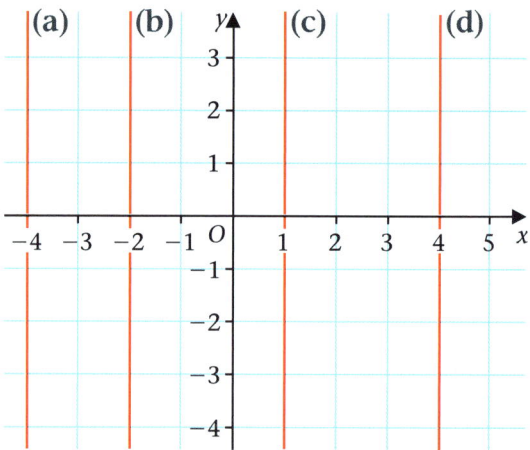

3 Draw a coordinate grid with x- and y-axes labelled from −5 to 5. On the grid draw and label the graphs of
(a) $x = 4$ (b) $x = -2$ (c) $x = -4$ (d) $x = 1$

4 Draw a coordinate grid with axes labelled from −5 to 5. On the grid draw and label the graphs of
(a) $y = 4$ (b) $y = -2$ (c) $y = -4$ (d) $y = 1$

5 Draw a coordinate grid with axes labelled from −5 to 5. On the grid draw and label the graphs of
(a) $y = 3$ (b) $x = -1$
(c) Write down the coordinates of the point where the two lines cross.

Example 8

Draw the graph of $y = x - 1$

Step 1 Choose some values for x, for example let $x = -2$, 0 and +2

Step 2 Put these values of x into the equation $y = x - 1$:
When $x = -2$: $y = -2 - 1 = -3$
When $x = 0$: $y = 0 - 1 = -1$
When $x = 2$: $y = 2 - 1 = 1$

Step 3 Write these pairs of values in a table.

x	−2	0	2
y	−3	−1	1

Step 4 Plot the points $(-2, -3)$, $(0, -1)$ and $(2, 1)$ and join them. Extend the line to the edges of the grid.

Step 5 Label the line.

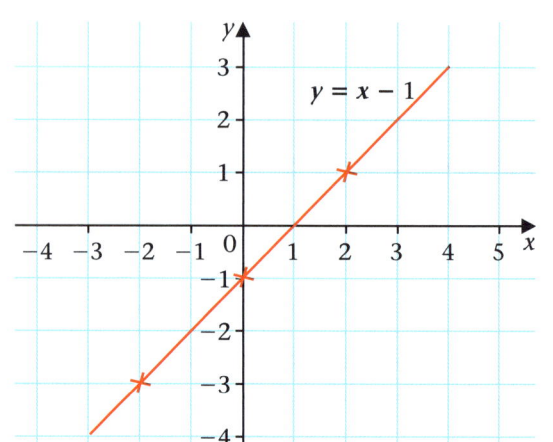

16.7 Using algebra to describe lines 315

Worked examination question

Draw and complete a table of values for the graphs of $y = 2x - 1$ and $y = -x + 1$.

Draw the graphs and write down the coordinates of the point where they cross.

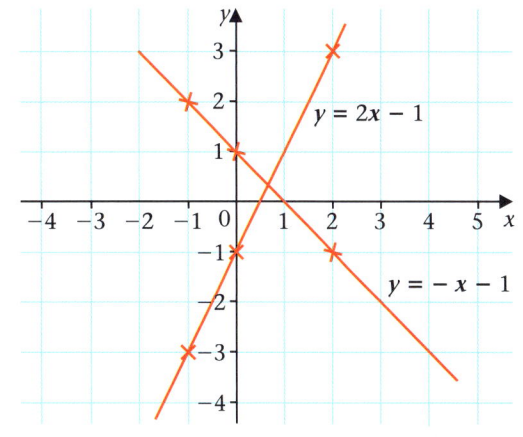

Step 1
Choose three values for x.
For example $x = -1, 0, 2$

Step 2
Put these values of x into each equation:

$y = 2x - 1$ $x = -1$ $y = -2 - 1 = -3$
 $x = 0$ $y = 0 - 1 = -1$
 $x = 2$ $y = 4 - 1 = 3$

$y = -x + 1$ $x = -1$ $y = 1 + 1 = 2$
 $x = 0$ $y = 0 + 1 = 1$
 $x = 2$ $y = -2 + 1 = -1$

These pairs of values make $y = 2x - 1$ true:

x	−1	0	2
y	−3	−1	3

These pairs of values make $y = -x + 1$ true:

x	−1	0	2
y	2	1	−1

Step 3
Plot the points $(-1, -3)$, $(0, -1)$ and $(2, 3)$ and join them with a straight line.

Plot the points $(-1, 2)$, $(0, 1)$ and $(2, -1)$. and join them with a straight line.

Make sure you read the coordinates accurately from your graph.

The lines cross at about $(\frac{2}{3}, \frac{1}{3})$.

$y = mx + c$ is the general equation of a straight line.
m is the gradient and c is where the line crosses the y-axis.

Exercise 16I

1 On a coordinate grid with axes labelled from −5 to 5 draw the following graphs:

   (a) $y = x + 2$ (b) $y = x + 4$ (c) $y = x + 1$
   (d) $y = x - 2$ (e) $y = x - 4$ (f) $y = x - 1$

   Choose three values from −5 to 5

2 On a coordinate grid with the x-axis labelled from −4 to 4 and the y-axis labelled from −10 to 10 draw the following graphs and write the values of m and c.

   (a) $y = x + 2$ (b) $y = 2x + 3$ (c) $y = 3x - 2$ (d) $y = \frac{1}{2}x + 3$

   Hint for (a):
   Compare with $y = mx + c$.
   ($m = 1$ and $c = 2$)

3 On a coordinate grid with the x-axis labelled from −3 to 6 and the y-axis labelled from −2 to 6 draw the graph of $x + y = 4$.

> Hint: The coordinates of the points on the line $x + y = 4$ always add up to 4.

4 On a coordinate grid with the x-axis labelled from −4 to 4 and the y-axis labelled from −6 to 6 draw the following graphs.
  (a) $y = -2x - 1$
  (b) $y = x + 2$
  (c) Write down the coordinates of the point where they cross.

5 (a) Copy and complete this table of values for $y = 3x + 1$.

x	−2	−1	0	1	2	3
y	−5		4			10

  (b) On a coordinate grid with the x-axis labelled from −2 to 3 and the y-axis labelled from −5 to 10 draw the graph of $y = 3x + 1$.

  (c) Use your graph to find the value of x when $y = 6$. [E]

16.8 1-D, 2-D or 3-D?

The number line goes in one direction (either horizontally or vertically).

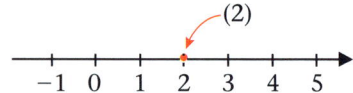

> The number line is **1-dimensional** or **1-D**. You can describe position on the number line using one number or coordinate, for example (2).

Coordinate grids and flat shapes go in two directions.

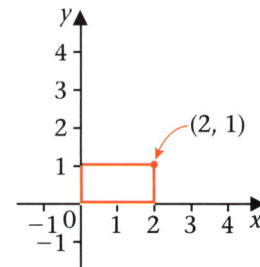

> Flat shapes are **2-dimensional** or **2-D**. You can describe position on a flat shape using two numbers or coordinates, for example (2, 1).

Solid shapes go in three directions.

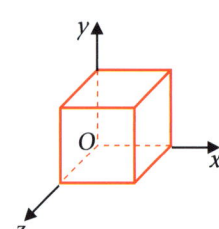

> Solid shapes are **3-dimensional** or **3-D**. You can describe position in a solid shape using three numbers or coordinates, for example (4, 1, 2).

16.8 1-D, 2-D or 3-D?

This diagram shows a 3-D grid. The *x*-, *y*- and *z*-axes are all at right angles to each other. The lengths of the edges of the cuboid are 2, 2 and 1 units.

To get to point *P* from *O*, you go 4 units along the *x*-axis, then 1 unit parallel to the *y*-axis, then 2 units parallel to the *z*-axis.

The coordinates of point *P* are (4, 1, 2).

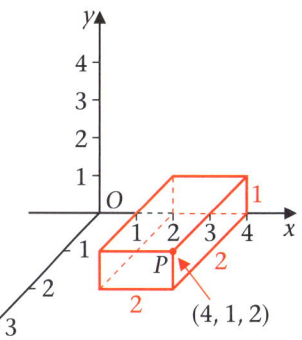

Example 9

Say whether each shape is 1-D, 2-D or 3-D.

(a)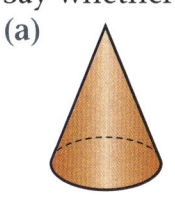
Cone

(b)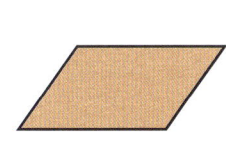
Parallelogram

(c)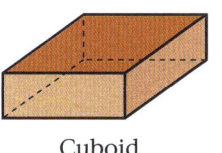
Cuboid

(a) 3-D   (b) 2-D   (c) 3-D

Example 10

The diagram represents a cuboid on a 3-D grid.
OR = 2 units, *OP* = 5 units and *OS* = 4 units.
Find the coordinates of
(a) *S* (b) *P* (c) *R* (d) *V* (e) *U* (f) *O*

(a) To get to *S* from *O* you go 0 along the *x*-axis,
4 units up the *y*-axis and 0 units parallel to the *z*-axis.
So *S* = (0, 4, 0)
(b) Similarly *P* = (0, 0, 5)
(c) *R* = (−2, 0, 0)
(d) *V* = (−2, 4, 0)
(e) To get to *U* from *O* you go −2 units along the *x*-axis,
4 units parallel to the *y*-axis and 5 units parallel to the *z*-axis.
So *U* = (−2, 4, 5)
(f) *O* = (0, 0, 0)

Exercise 16J

1 Say whether each shape is 1-D, 2-D or 3-D.

(a)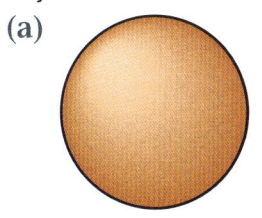
Sphere

(b)
Square

(c)
Line

(d)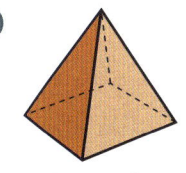
Pyramid

318 Chapter 16 Coordinates and graphs

2 Say whether each shape is 1-D, 2-D or 3-D.
   (a) Hexagon   (b) Cylinder
   (c) Circle   (d) Cube

3 Write down all the 3-dimensional coordinates from this list:
   (6)   (3, 1, 1)   (4, 2)   (6, 6, 9)   (3)
   (12, 8) (4, 1, 16) (9, 3)   (28, 1, 8) (126)

4 Write down the coordinates of each vertex of this cuboid:

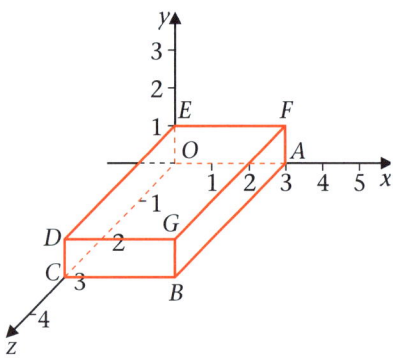

5 Write down the coordinates of each vertex of this cuboid:

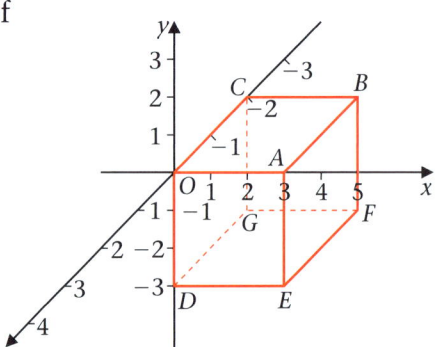

Mixed exercise 16

1 (a) Write down the coordinates of the point
       (i) P
       (ii) Q
   (b) Draw a pair of coordinate axes.
       (i) Plot the point (4, −3). Label the point A.
       (ii) Plot the point (0, 3). Label the point B.
   (c) Work out the mid-point of the line PQ.

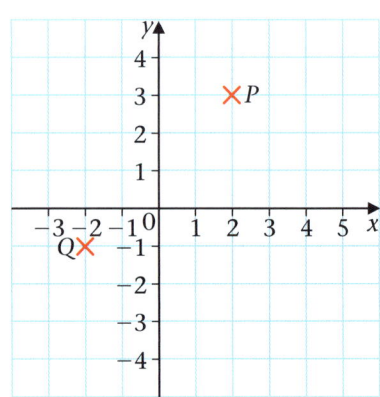

2 This table gives information about the cost of ice creams.

Number of ice creams	1	2	3	4	5
Cost of ice creams in pence	60	120	180	240	300

(a) Draw a graph for the cost of ice creams.
(b) Extend the graph to find the cost of
  (i) 9 ice creams (ii) 6 ice creams.
(c) How many ice creams can be bought for £4.20?
(d) How much would you have to pay for 25 ice creams?

3 This table gives some approximate conversion between inches and centimetres.

Centimetres	2.5	5	10	30	50
Inches	1	2	4	12	20

(a) Draw a conversion graph from inches to centimetres.
(b) Use your graph to find the number of centimetres in
  (i) 6 inches (ii) 10 inches
(c) Use your graph to find out the number of inches in
  (i) 25 cm (ii) 40 cm

4 Here is part of a travel graph of Siân's journey from her house to the shops and back.

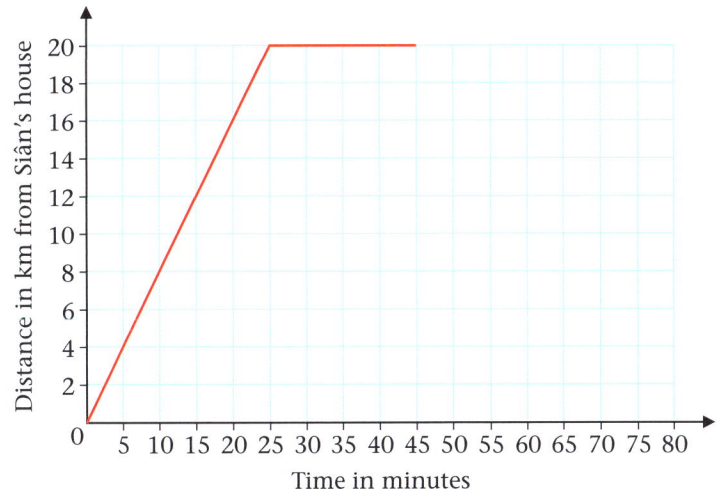

(a) Work out Siân's speed for the first 20 minutes of her journey. Give your answer in km/h.

Siân spends 20 minutes at the shops. She then travels back to her house at 60 km/h.

(b) Copy and complete the travel graph. [E]

5 Draw a coordinate grid with x values from −4 to +4 and y values from −6 to +6. On the grid draw the graphs of the following straight lines:

(a) $x = 3$ (b) $y = -2$
(c) $x = -1$ (d) $y = 4$
(e) $y = x$ (f) $y = -x$
(g) $y = 2x - 1$ (h) $y = -2x + 1$

6 This cuboid has sides of 3, 3 and 2 units. Write down the coordinates of each vertex.

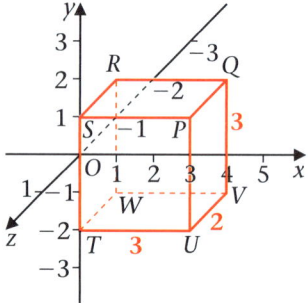

7 On a coordinate grid with the x-axis labelled from −4 to 4 and the y-axis labelled from −10 to 10 draw the following graphs:

(a) $y = x + 1$ (b) $y = 2x - 2$ (c) $y = 2x - 3$

(d) Write down the coordinates of the points where they cross as accurately as you can.

8 (a) Copy and complete the table of values for the following graphs:

(i) $y = 3x - 2$ (ii) $y = 5 - x$

x	−1	0	1	2
y				

x	−1	0	1	2
y				

(b) Draw the graphs on graph paper and write down the coordinates of the point where they cross.

9 List the coordinates of all the vertices of the cuboid.

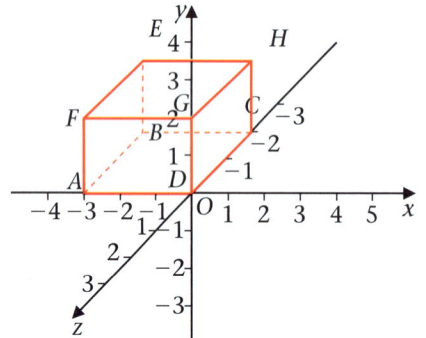

10 Jon went to Spain.
He changed £300 into euros (€).
The exchange rate was £1 = €1.50
(a) How many euros did he get?

When he came home he changed €14.70 back into pounds.
The exchange rate was now £1 = €1.40
(b) How many pounds did he get?

11 Prendeep bought a necklace in the United States of America.
Prendeep paid $108.

Arthur bought an identical necklace in Germany.
Arthur paid €117.

The exchange rates are

| £1 = $1.44 |
| £1 = €1.6 |

Calculate, in pounds, the difference between the prices paid for the two necklaces.
Explain how you worked out your answer. [E]

Summary of key points

1 A graph representing a **linear relationship** always has a straight line.

2 A **conversion graph** is used to convert a measurement into different units.

3 **Distance–time graphs** are used to relate the distance travelled to the time taken, and to calculate speeds.

4 The **equation of a line** uses algebra to show a relationship between the x- and y-coordinates of points on the line.

5 The number line is **1-dimensional** or **1-D**. You can describe position on the number line using one number or coordinate, for example (2).

6 Flat shapes are **2-dimensional** or **2-D**. You can describe position on a flat shape using two numbers or coordinates, for example (2, 1).

7 Solid shapes are **3-dimensional** or **3-D**. You can describe position in a solid shape using three numbers or coordinates, for example (4, 1, 2).

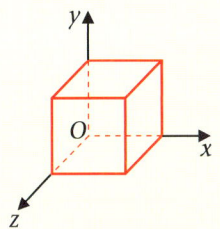

17 Ratio and proportion

17.1 What is a ratio?

A **ratio** is a way of comparing two numbers or quantities.

Ratios can be used to compare costs, weights and sizes …

On the deck there are 2 women and 1 man.
So $\frac{2}{3}$ of the people on deck are women and $\frac{1}{3}$ of the people are men.
You can also say that:

the ratio of men to women is 1 to 2. This is written as 1 : 2
the ratio of women to men is 2 to 1, written 2 : 1

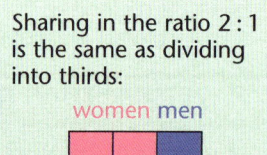

Sharing in the ratio 2 : 1 is the same as dividing into thirds:

women men

On the deck there are also 5 cars and 2 bicycles. So you can say that:

the ratio of cars to bicycles is 5 to 2, or 5 : 2
the ratio of bicycles to cars is 2 to 5, or 2 : 5

Ratios are used to work out the exact quantities needed in mixtures. Pharmacists making up medicines, manufacturers making biscuits, cooks baking cakes and builders mixing concrete all need to be able to make exact mixtures.

Example 1

Frank is making fruit smoothies for 5 of his friends. How much of each ingredient does he need?

oranges $4 \times 5 = 20$ oranges
apples $2 \times 5 = 10$ apples

I use 4 oranges and 2 apples to make a smoothie for one person.

In Example 1 the ratio of oranges to apples is 4 : 2.

17.1 What is a ratio?

Example 2

To make a mixer full of concrete you need 15 shovels of sand, 9 shovels of gravel and 6 shovels of cement. Vijay needs 4 mixers full of concrete.

(a) How much sand, gravel and cement will he need?
(b) Write the ratio of sand to gravel to cement.

15 shovels of sand
9 shovels of gravel and
6 shovels of cement

(a) sand $15 \times 4 = 60$ shovels
    gravel $9 \times 4 = 36$ shovels
    cement $6 \times 4 = 24$ shovels

(b) The ratio of sand to gravel to cement is $15 : 9 : 6$

Example 3

For the tile pattern below find
(a) the fraction of the pattern that is blue
(a) the ratio of white tiles to blue tiles.

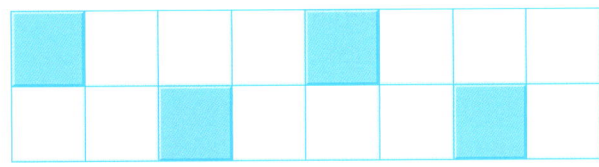

(a) $\frac{4}{16}$ or $\frac{1}{4}$ is blue

(b) white : blue
    $12 : 4$ which can be simplified to
    $3 : 1$

Divide both sides of the ratio by 3.

Exercise 17A

1 Here are some tile patterns. For each one write down
(i) the fraction of the pattern that is red
(ii) the ratio of red tiles to blue tiles in the pattern.

(a)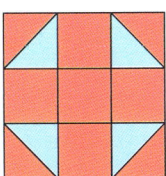

(b)

(c)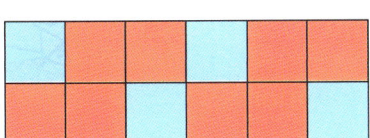

(d)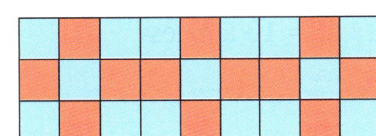

2 A recipe for 6 rock cakes needs 40 g of margarine and 100 g of flour. How much margarine and flour are needed to make
  (a) 12 rock cakes (b) 18 rock cakes (c) 30 rock cakes
  (d) 3 rock cakes (e) 15 rock cakes?

3 A recipe for a rice cake weighing 1200 g is:
  200 g of butter   400 g of ground rice
  400 g of sugar   4 eggs (eggs weigh 50 g each)
How much of each ingredient would you use to make a rice cake weighing
  (a) 2400 g (b) 600 g (c) 1800 g (d) 3000 g?

4 42 strawberries, 6 bananas and 12 apples are used to make 6 glasses of fruit smoothie. How much of each ingredient is needed to make
  (a) 3 glasses (b) 4 glasses (c) 1 glass?

5 A builder prepares 120 kg of mortar by mixing 20 kg of cement with 10 kg of lime and 90 kg of sand. How much cement, lime and sand does he use to prepare
  (a) 60 kg of mortar   (b) 180 kg of mortar
  (c) 12 kg of mortar?

6 To make 25 kg of bronze you mix 6 kg of tin with 19 kg of copper.
How much tin and copper do you need to make
  (a) 50 kg of bronze (b) 250 kg of bronze
  (c) 100 kg of bronze?

7 Brass is an alloy (mixture) of zinc and copper in the ratio 3 : 17
How much copper would you expect to be in a brass cross which contains 120 g of zinc?

17.2 Simplifying ratios

You need to be able to solve problems using ratios. It is often easier if you simplify the ratios first.

These ratios below are **equivalent** – the relationship between each pair of numbers is the same:

  10 : 20
  3 : 6
  2 : 4
  1 : 2   This ratio is the **simplest form** of the ratio 10 : 20

> To **simplify** a ratio you divide both its numbers by a common factor.

17.2 Simplifying ratios

Example 4

Simplify the ratio 30 : 100

10 is a common factor of 30 and 100. Dividing both numbers by 10 gives:

$$30 : 100$$
$$\div 10 \qquad \div 10$$
$$3 : 10$$

When a ratio cannot be simplified it is said to be in its **lowest terms**. Ratios are usually written in their lowest terms.

Example 5

Write 40p to £1 as a ratio.

First, you make the units the same so you are comparing pennies with pennies: 40p to 100p

The ratio is:

40 : 100

4 : 10 ——— Divide by 10.

2 : 5 ——— Divide by 2.

The ratio of 40p to £1 is 2 : 5 in its lowest terms.

Always write the ratio in its lowest terms.

Exercise 17B

1 Write these ratios in their lowest terms.
   (a) 2 : 4   (b) 3 : 9   (c) 3 : 18   (d) 6 : 24
   (e) 8 : 24   (f) 16 : 24   (g) 10 : 2   (h) 28 : 4
   (i) 32 : 48   (j) 15 : 9

2 Write these ratios in their lowest terms.
   (a) 20 cm : 100 cm   (b) 20 cm : 1 m
   (c) 25p : £2   (d) £3 : 60p

Remember that the units must be the same before you write a ratio without units.

3 Write these ratios in their simplest form.
   (a) 2 cm : 1 m   (b) 350 mg : 1 g
   (c) 10 ml : 2 l   (d) 64 g : 4 kg
   (e) £3 : 40p : £1.20   (f) 150 mm : 40 cm
   (g) 340 m : 1.2 km   (h) 40 min : 2 h : $\frac{1}{2}$ h
   (i) 45 g : 1 kg   (j) 42p : £1.05
   (k) 45 cm : 0.1 m   (l) 2.4 tonnes : 132 kg

4 Write the ratios of these comparisons in their lowest terms.
 (a) A small loaf cost 49p and a large loaf cost 63p.
 (b) Jeanette weighs 40 kg and Pauline weighs 44 kg.
 (c) Spey School has 660 boys and Tree School has 750 boys.
 (d) Mr Johnson takes 1 hour to get to work by train but 2 hours by car.
 (e) A salesman made 27 successful calls and 21 unsuccessful calls.
 (f) A factory employs 66 craft workers, 18 clerical staff and 12 sales staff.

5 Abi buys a bracelet for £120, whilst Hayley buys some beads for 72p.
Write these prices as a ratio in its lowest terms.

17.3 Equivalent ratios

In Section 17.2 you learned how to simplify a ratio. Sometimes it is useful to find other equivalent ratios.

For example, if the ratio of teachers to students is 1 : 30 (or one per class of 30) then three classes will need a ratio of 3 : 90 since 1 : 30 and 3 : 90 are **equivalent ratios**.

> Two ratios are **equivalent** when one simplifies to the other.

Example 6

A hotel used to employ 2 cooks and 7 waiters.

The hotel then expanded and the number of cooks was increased to 10.

If the number of waiters is kept in proportion to the number of cooks, how many waiters should there be?

	cooks : waiters
ratio before increase:	2 : 7
ratio after increase:	10 : ?

You need to find the number that makes these ratios **equivalent**.

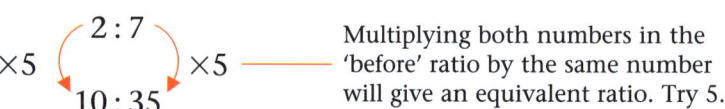

Multiplying both numbers in the 'before' ratio by the same number will give an equivalent ratio. Try 5.

2 : 7 and 10 : 35 are equivalent ratios.

The number of waiters after the increase is 35.

Exercise 17C

1. Calculate the missing numbers in these ratios:
   (a) $3:5 = 12:?$
   (b) $4:7 = 16:?$
   (c) $6:5 = 3:?$
   (d) $4:5 = ?:35$
   (e) $8:3 = ?:15$
   (f) $7:? = 49:63$

2. The numbers of mugs made in a pottery in the morning and in the afternoon are in the ratio $4:9$. They are always completed in this ratio.
   (a) How many mugs are made in the afternoon when 60 are made in the morning?
   (b) How many are made in the morning when 189 are made in the afternoon?

3. The ratio of students going home for lunch to students staying at school for lunch is $3:5$. When 273 students go home for lunch how many stay at school?

4. The ratio of the length of a room to its width is $5:4$. The length of the room is 6 metres. What is the width?

5. An alloy contains iron and tungsten in the ratio $5:1$. If there is 15 kg of iron in a quantity of the alloy, how much tungsten is there?

6. A mortar mix is made by adding sand and cement in the ratio $4:1$. Five buckets of cement are used. How much sand is needed?

7. The ratio of males to female in the crowd at a rock concert is $5:4$. There are 120 males in the crowd. How many females are there?

8. The ratio of the lengths of two rectangles is $5:6$. The length of the first rectangle is 12.5 cm. What is the length of the second rectangle?

17.4 Writing ratios in unitary form

Ratios can be written in the form $1:n$ or $n:1$.
The number n is written as a decimal (unless it is a whole number). When one of the numbers in a ratio is 1, the ratio is in **unitary form**.

Chapter 17 Ratio and proportion

Example 7

(a) Write these ratios in the form $1:n$.
   (i) $8:10$ (ii) $5\,\text{cm}:1\,\text{km}$ (iii) $20:1$

(b) Write these ratios in the form $n:1$.
   (i) $21:5$ (ii) $1\,\text{kg}:4\,\text{g}$

(a) (i) $8:10$
        $1:\frac{10}{8}$ —— Divide both numbers by 8.
        $1:1.25$

    (ii) $5\,\text{cm}:1\,\text{km}$
        $5:100\,000$ —— Write both numbers in cm.
        $1:20\,000$ —— Divide by 5.

    (iii) $20:1$
        $1:\frac{1}{20}$ —— Divide by 20.
        $1:0.05$

(b) (i) $21:5$
        $4.2:1$ —— Divide by 5.

    (ii) $1\,\text{kg}:4\,\text{g}$
        $1000\,\text{g}:4\,\text{g}$ —— Write both quantities in g.
        $250:1$ —— Divide by 4.

$10 \div 8 = \frac{10}{8}$

Exercise 17D

1 Write these ratios in the form $1:n$.
  (a) $2:5$ (b) $32\,\text{g}:8\,\text{g}$
  (c) $10\,\text{cm}:10\,\text{m}$ (d) $4:10$
  (e) $32\text{p}:£2$ (f) $2:15$
  (g) $5:11$ (h) $25\,\text{g}:1\,\text{kg}$

2 Write these ratios in the form $n:1$.
  (a) $6:8$ (b) $1\,\text{km}:2\,\text{cm}$
  (c) $3\,\text{h}:\frac{1}{2}\text{h}$ (d) $£3:40\text{p}$
  (e) $5\,l:10\,\text{ml}$ (f) $2\,\text{m}:2\,\text{mm}$
  (g) $1000:30$ (h) $5\text{p}:25\text{p}$

17.5 Dividing quantities in a given ratio

Ratios can be used to share or divide quantities.

Example 8

Patrick and Colleen share £35 in the ratio $3:4$
How much does each person get?

The total number of shares is $3+4=7$

17.5 Dividing quantities in a given ratio

Each share is worth $\frac{£35}{7} = £5$

$3 : 4$

Patrick gets $3 \times £5 = £15$

Colleen gets $4 \times £5 = £20$

£15   £20

You could also write that Patrick gets $\frac{3}{7}$ of the total amount of money: $\frac{3}{7} \times £35 = £15$

Exercise 17E

1. £360 is divided between Sally and Nadir in the ratio 5 : 4. How much should each person receive?

2. Nick, Mark and Gavin share £480 in the ratio 4 : 5 : 3. How much should each person receive?

3. Share 40 sweets in the ratio 2 : 5 : 1.

4. Henry, Sue and Rebecca agree to look after the cake stall in the ratio 2 : 4 : 3. Rebecca looked after it for 1 hour. How long did
   (a) Henry   (b) Sue
   spend looking after the stall?

5. Copy and complete this table. The first one is done for you.

Quantity	Divided in the ratio		
	4 :	3 :	2
£27	£12	£9	£6
9 lb			
36 km			
63 miles			
81 tonnes			
£144			

In questions 6, 7 and 8 divide the quantities in the ratios given.

6. (a) £14.91 in the ratio 2 : 5   (b) £45 in the ratio 4 : 5
   (c) £51.92 in the ratio 2 : 9   (d) £170.52 in the ratio 1 : 4 : 7

7. (a) 600 g in the ratio 3 : 2   (b) 32 cm in the ratio 3 : 5
   (c) 23.4 l in the ratio 1 : 5   (d) 34.65 m in the ratio 2 : 4 : 5

8 (a) 30.78 m in the ratio 4 : 5
(b) 75 cm in the ratio 3 : 2
(c) 48 kg in the ratio 3 : 5
(d) £357 in the ratio 1 : 2 : 4

9 The ratio of girls to boys in a class is 4 : 3.
There are 28 students in the class.
How many are (a) girls (b) boys?

10 The angles of a triangle are in the ratio 6 : 5 : 7.

Find the sizes of the three angles.

Remember:
the angles of a triangle add up to 180°.

11 Shortcrust pastry is made from flour and fat in the ratio 2 : 1.
How much flour do you need to make 600 g of pastry?

12 A business makes a profit of £660. The directors divide it in the ratio 3 : 4 : 8.
How much do they each receive?

13 An alloy is made from iron, copper, nickel and phosphorus in the ratio 6 : 4 : 3 : 1.
Find the weight of (a) copper (b) nickel in 714 g of the alloy.

14

Mortar is made by mixing 5 parts by weight of sand with 1 part by weight of cement. How much sand is needed to make 8400 kg of mortar? [E]

17.6 Solving ratio and proportion problems by the unitary method

A useful way of solving ratio problems is to first find the value of one unit of the quantity. This is called the **unitary method**.

Example 9

If 6 similar CDs cost £30, how much will 8 CDs cost?

6 CDs cost £30 — **Find the cost of one CD.** It costs less.

1 CD costs $\dfrac{£30}{6}$

8 CDs cost $\dfrac{£30}{6} \times 8 = £40$ — Eight CDs cost 8 × the cost of one CD.

17.6 Solving ratio and proportion problems by the unitary method

Example 10

If 6 men can build a shed in 3 days, how long will it take 4 men working at the same rate?

6 men take 3 days

1 man takes 3×6 days — **Find how long it would take one man.** It takes longer.

4 men take $\dfrac{3 \times 6}{4} = 4\tfrac{1}{2}$ — Four men take $\tfrac{1}{4}$ the time taken by one man.

$\dfrac{3 \times 6}{4}$ is the same as $3 \times 6 \times \tfrac{1}{4}$

Example 11

Zoe paid £3.20 for 8 mince pies. How much would 12 mince pies cost?

8 mince pies cost 320 pence

1 mince pie costs $\dfrac{320}{8}$ — **Find how much one mince pie costs.**

12 mince pies cost $\dfrac{320}{8} \times 12$ — 12 pies cost $12 \times$ the cost of one mince pie.

12 mince pies cost 480 pence or £4.80

Exercise 17F

1 Ten leisure centre tickets cost £48.
   What would 25 tickets cost?

2 Twenty daffodil bulbs cost £2.50.
   What would 36 bulbs cost?

3 Paul paid £7.20 for 24 Christmas cards.
   How much would he have to pay for 36 similar cards?

4 Camilla paid £40 for 15 CDs.
   How much would she have to pay for 24 similar CDs?

5 Vijay buys 18 postcards for £2.16.
   How much would he pay if he buys 27?

6 Bronwen bought 15 roses for £9.
   How many roses could she have bought for £12.60?

7 A train travels at 80 miles per hour.
   How long will it take to travel
   (a) 140 miles   (b) 440 miles   (c) 640 miles?

8 A cyclist travels at an average speed of 16 km per hour. At the same rate
   (a) how far would she travel in 4 hours
   (b) how long would it take her to cycle 100 km?

9 A wall took 6 hours for 4 men to build. At the same rate
   (a) how long would it have taken 10 men
   (b) how many men would have been needed to build it in 12 hours?

10 Eight men can build a chalet in 18 days. Working at the same rate how long would it take
   (a) 12 men   (b) 5 men?
   (c) How many men would be needed to build it in 3 days?

17.7 Direct proportion

Two quantities are in **direct proportion** if their ratio stays the same as the quantities increase or decrease.

Example 12

A car uses 8 litres of petrol to travel 124 km. If the amount of petrol used is in direct proportion to the distance travelled, how far can the car travel on 1 litre?

8 litres is used for 124 km, a ratio of 8 : 124.

Dividing both numbers by 8 gives

$$1 : \frac{124}{8}$$

So on 1 litre the car can travel $\frac{124}{8} = 15.5$ km.

Example 13

Method 1
Seven pencils cost 63p. The cost is directly proportional to the number of pencils. How much will 12 pencils cost?

First find out what one pencil costs:

   7 pencils cost 63p

So   1 pencil costs $\frac{63p}{7} = 9p$

12 pencils cost 9p × 12 = £1.08

> You used this method to solve problems in Section 17.6

Method 2

The ratio of the number of pencils to the cost is 7 : 63.

If the cost of 12 pencils is x, the ratio of the number of pencils to the cost is 12 : x.

To get from 7 to 12 you multiply 7 by $\frac{12}{7}$:

To get from the cost of 7 pencils to the cost x of 12 pencils you multiply 63p by $\frac{12}{7}$.

$$\frac{12}{7} \curvearrowright \begin{matrix} 7 & : & 63 \\ 12 & : & x \end{matrix} \curvearrowleft \frac{12}{7}$$

So the cost of 12 pencils $x = 63 \times \frac{12}{7}$ pence
$ = 108$ pence $= £1.08$

> You saw this method in Section 17.3

Worked examination question

Here is a list of ingredients for making some Greek food. These amounts make enough for six people:

    2 cloves of garlic
    4 ounces of chick peas
    4 tablespoons of olive oil
    5 fluid ounces of Tahina paste

Change the amounts so that there will be enough for nine people. [E]

Nine people is one and a half times as much as six (six has been multiplied by 1.5 to give nine).

    The 2 cloves of garlic become 3.
    The 4 ounces of chick peas become 6.
    The 4 tablespoons of olive oil become 6.
    The 5 fluid ounces of Tahina paste become $7\frac{1}{2}$.

> Using the unitary method
>   9 : 6
>   1.5 : 1

> 2 : 4 : 4 : 5
> is equivalent to
> 3 : 6 : 6 : $7\frac{1}{2}$

Exercise 17G

1 Dress material costs £23.40 for 4 metres.
How much does 1 metre cost?

2 14 cm^3 of copper weighs 126 g.
What is the weight of 1 cm^3?

3 Betty is paid £38.50 for seven hours' work at a nursing home.
How much should she receive for five hours' work?

4 Six stamps cost £2.52.
How much will ten stamps cost?

5 A machine makes 490 engine parts in 35 minutes.
How many engine parts will the machine make in one hour?

6 Four packets of tea cost £1.28.
How much will three packets cost?

7 Six tickets to the theatre cost £19.80.
How much would eight tickets cost?

8 Seven tubes of toothpaste have a total weight of 854 g.
Work out the weight of eight tubes of toothpaste.

9 Anisha buys 12 bananas for £1.80.
How much would 15 bananas cost?

10 Five bottles of detergent have a capacity of 1560 cm^3.
Work out the total capacity of nine similar bottles.

11 The recipe for eight small cakes includes the following:

   480 g flour, 720 g fat, 2 eggs.

   Change the amounts so there will be enough to make 12 small cakes.

12 A telegraph pole 60 feet high casts a shadow 12 feet long.
At the same time of day, how long is a shadow cast by
   (a) a 90 foot pole   (b) a 40 foot pole   (c) a 25 foot pole?

13 A machine can produce 1120 plastic mugs in 8 hours.
At that rate
   (a) how many plastic mugs will it produce in 10 hours
   (b) how long will it take to produce 840 plastic mugs?

14 A car travels 126 miles on 18 litres of petrol.
   (a) How far will it travel on 40 litres?
   (b) How many litres will be needed to travel 540 miles?

15 Mario is paid £31.50 for working 6 hours in the supermarket. At that rate
   (a) how much will he be paid for working 8 hours
   (b) how long would it take him to earn £63?

17.8 Scales in maps and diagrams

> Ratios called **scales** are used to show the relationship between distances on a map and distances on the ground.

A common scale is 1 : 50 000; this means that 1 cm on the map represents 50 000 cm on the ground.

   50 000 cm = 500 m = 0.5 km

So 1 cm on the map represents 0.5 km on the ground.

Remember:
10 mm = 1 cm
100 cm = 1 m
1000 m = 1 km

17.8 Scales in maps and diagrams

Example 14

Two towns are 5.2 cm apart on a map whose scale is 1 : 50 000. How far apart are the towns in real life?

    1 cm   represents   0.5 km
    5.2 cm represents   0.5 km × 5.2 = 2.6 km

The towns are 2.6 kilometres apart.

> To convert from cm to m, divide by 100:
> 260 000 cm ÷ 100 = 2600 m
>
> To convert from m to km, divide by 1000:
> 2600 m ÷ 1000 = 2.6 km

Exercise 17H

1 A map has a scale of 1 : 50 000. What is the distance on the ground if the distance on the map is
  (a) 2.5 cm   (b) 3.6 cm
  (c) 5.2 cm   (d) 6.2 cm?

2 What is the distance on the map from question **1** if the distance on the ground is
  (a) 6 km   (b) 5.2 km
  (c) 8.4 km   (d) 25.6 km?

3 A town map has a scale of 1 : 6000.
  (a) The town hall is 1500 metres from the station. How far is this on the map?
  (b) On the map the hotel is 4.6 cm from the harbour. How far is this on the ground?
  (c) Adrian plans a walk round the town. He measures it on the map to be 36.5 cm. How far is he planning to walk?

4 A model radio-controlled aircraft is built to scale, using 1 cm to represent 1.4 metres.
  (a) Write this scale as a ratio.
  (b) What is the length of the model if the length of the real aircraft is 42 metres?

5 A model of a van is made to a scale of 1 : 20. The height of the model is 10 cm. Work out the height, in metres, of the full-size van.

6 A map is drawn on a scale of 3 cm to 1 km.
  (a) Work out the real length of a lake which is 4.2 cm long on the map.
  (b) The distance between the church in Canwick and the town hall in Barnton is 5.8 km. Work out the distance between them on the map.

> 'A scale of 3 cm to 1 km' This means that a real length of 1 km is represented on the map by a length of 3 cm.

Chapter 17 Ratio and proportion

Mixed exercise 17

1 Robert used these ingredients to make 24 buns:

    100 g of sugar   90 g of flour
    80 g of butter   30 ml of milk
    2 eggs

Robert wants to make 36 similar buns.

Write down how much of each ingredient he needs for 36 buns. [E]

2 Jack shares £180 between his two children Ruth and Ben. The ratio of Ruth's share to Ben's share is 5 : 4.
Work out how much each child is given. [E]

3 7200 people took part in a survey, with a ratio of 5 : 4 people preferring the taste of Ice Cool's new lemonade drink to the old drink. How many people liked each drink?

4 Anna, Beth and Cheryl share the total cost of a holiday in the ratio 6 : 5 : 4. Anna pays £294.
  (a) Work out the total cost of the holiday.
  (b) Work out how much Cheryl pays. [E]

5 Kelly bought 4 identical computer disks for £3.60.
Work out the cost of 9 of these computer disks.

6 A city map has a scale of 1 : 14 000.
  (a) Cornhill Street is 18 mm long on the map.
     Work out the real distance in metres.
  (b) Commercial Street is 840 metres long.
     What is the length of the street on the map, in millimetres?

7 In Year 11 at Tree Valley High School there were 108 boys and 132 girls. Write this as a ratio in its simplest form.

8 The ratio of hurdlers to long jumpers at the local athletics club is 3 : 5. If there are 15 hurdlers, how many long jumpers are there?

9 Seven tickets to the cricket match cost £86.10. If the cost of tickets is directly proportional to the number of tickets, how much will three tickets cost?

10 A map is drawn on a scale of 2 cm to 1 km.
  (a) Work out the real length of a bridge which is 1.5 cm long on the map.
  (b) The distance between Clifton and Hitchin is 6.5 km.
     Work out the distance between them on the map.

11 Bill gave his three daughters a total of £32.40.
The money was shared in the ratio 4 : 3 : 2.
Jane had the largest share.
Work out how much money Bill gave to Jane. [E]

Summary of key points

1. A **ratio** is a way of comparing two numbers or quantities. For example 3 : 2.

2. To **simplify** a ratio you divide both its numbers by a common factor.
   For example:

   $\div 2 \begin{pmatrix} 2 : 6 \\ 1 : 3 \end{pmatrix} \div 2$ Divide by the common factor 2.

   2 : 6 simplifies to 1 : 3

3. When a ratio cannot be simplified it is said to be in its **lowest terms**. Ratios are usually written in their lowest terms.

4. Two ratios are **equivalent** when one simplifies to the other.

5. Ratios can be written in the form $1 : n$ or $n : 1$. The number n is written as a decimal (unless it is a whole number).
   When one of the numbers in a ratio is 1, the ratio is in **unitary form**. For example, 2 : 3 can be written as 1 : 1.5 in unitary form.

6. Ratios can be used to share or divide quantities.

7. A useful way of solving ratio and proportion problems is to first find the value of one unit of the quantity. This is called the **unitary method**. For example, to find the cost of 12 pies when you know the cost of 8 pies:

8 pies cost	320 pence
1 pie costs	$\frac{320}{8}$ — Find the cost of one pie.
So 12 pies cost	$\frac{320}{8} \times 12$ — 12 × the cost of one pie

8. Two quantities are in **direct proportion** if their ratio stays the same as the quantities increase or decrease.

9. Ratios called **scales** are used to show the relationship between distances on a map and distances on the ground.
   On a 1 : 50 000 scale map, 1 cm represents 50 000 cm (or 0.5 km) on the ground.

18 Symmetry

18.1 Reflective symmetry in 2-D shapes

The two-dimensional (2-D) picture of a butterfly on the right is **symmetrical**. If you could fold it in half along the dotted line each half would fit exactly on top of the other.

The dotted line is called a **line of symmetry**. One half of the shape is a mirror image of the other half.

Some shapes have more than one line of symmetry. The flags below have more than one line of symmetry.

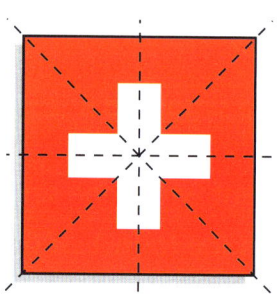

A good way to find the lines of symmetry of a shape is to draw it on tracing paper. Then you can actually fold the shape and check that each half fits exactly on top of the other. Another method is to use a mirror.

> A 2-D shape has a **line of symmetry** if the line divides the shape into two halves and one half is the mirror image of the other half.

> A line of symmetry is sometimes called a **mirror line**.

Example 1

Half of a symmetrical shape is shown here. The dotted line is a line of symmetry. Copy and complete the shape.

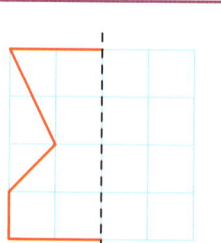

Method 1

Mark the mirror images of the points (or vertices) in first...

... then join the dots.

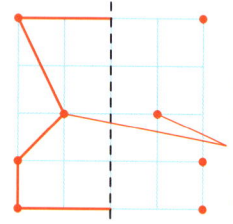
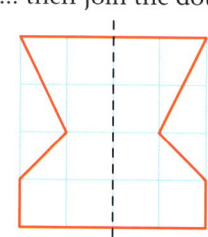

Each point has a mirror image the same distance away from the line of symmetry, but on the other side.

18.1 Reflective symmetry in 2-D shapes   339

Method 2

You could copy the shape onto tracing paper, flip it over and use the reflected image to draw the reflected shape.

Copy...   ... then draw

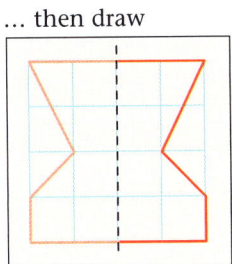

Exercise 18A

1   This question is about the following tiles.

   A    B 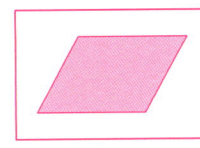   C 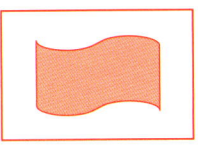   D

   E    F 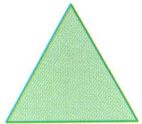   G    H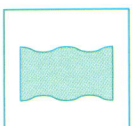

   Which shape(s) have
   (a) only one line of symmetry
   (b) no lines of symmetry
   (c) exactly three lines of symmetry
   (d) exactly four lines of symmetry
   (e) exactly two lines of symmetry?

2   Copy these shapes and draw all the lines of symmetry on each.

   (a) 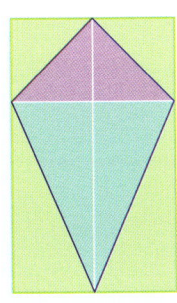   (b) 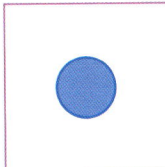   (c)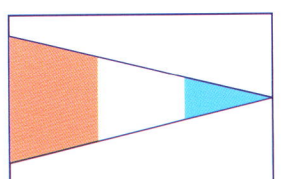

3 In each of these shapes the dotted line is a line of symmetry. Copy and complete each shape.

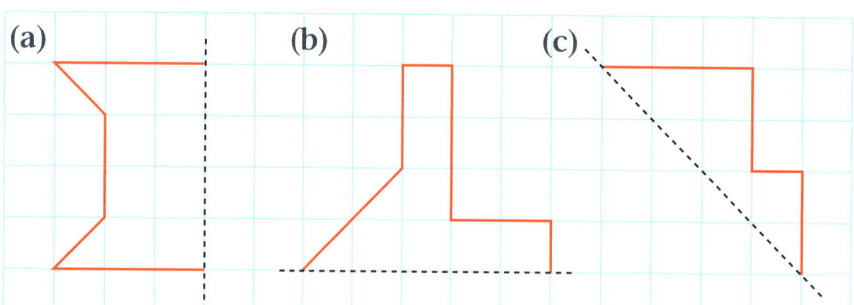

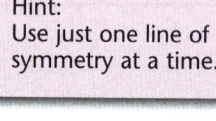

In questions 3 and 4 you need a larger grid than is shown.

4 Use the two lines of symmetry to copy and complete each of these shapes.

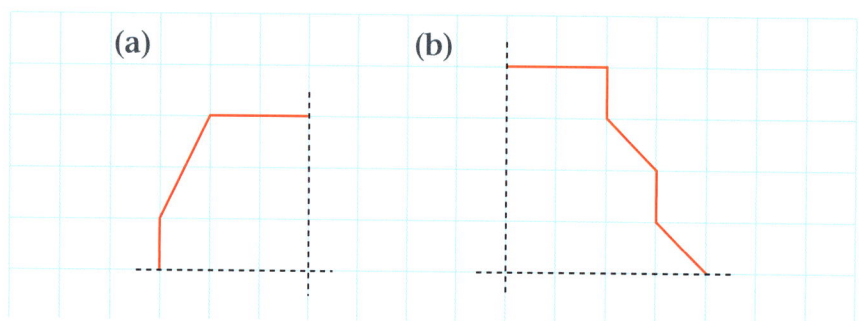

Hint:
Use just one line of symmetry at a time.

5 Write out the capital letters of the alphabet which have
   (a) one line of symmetry
   (b) more than one line of symmetry
   (c) no lines of symmetry.

18.2 Reflective symmetry in pictures and patterns

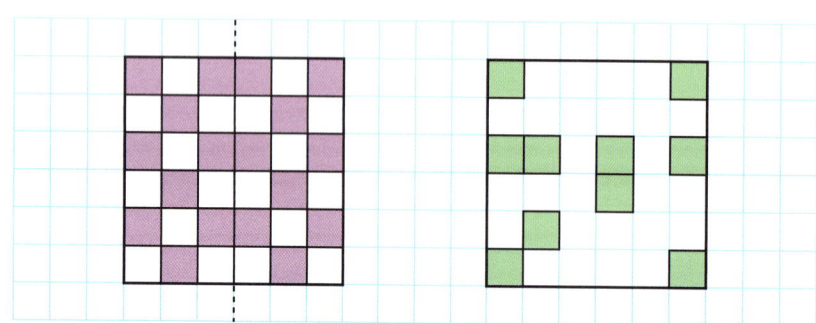

This pattern is **symmetrical**. It can be divided into two halves that are mirror images of each other.

This pattern is **asymmetrical** (not symmetrical). One half is **not** a mirror image of the other.

18.2 Reflective symmetry in pictures and patterns   341

Exercise 18B

You may want to use a mirror or tracing paper in this exercise.

1   Look at these patterns.

    A 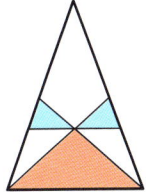   B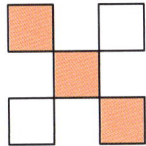

    C 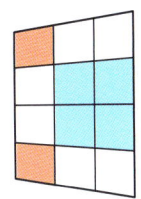   D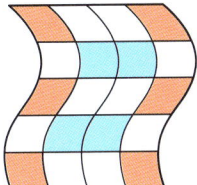

    E 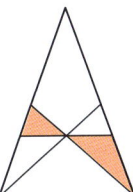   F

   (a) Which patterns have only one line of symmetry?
   (b) Which of these patterns are asymmetrical?
   (c) Which of these patterns have two lines of symmetry?

   Remember:
   Asymmetrical shapes have no lines of symmetry.

2   Copy these patterns. Draw in all the lines of symmetry on each one.

   (a) 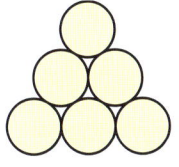   (b)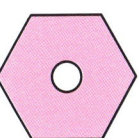

   (c)    (d)

   (e)    (f)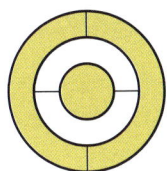

3 In how many different ways can you arrange six squares (which must touch) to form a symmetrical pattern?

Draw your patterns. Two are done for you.

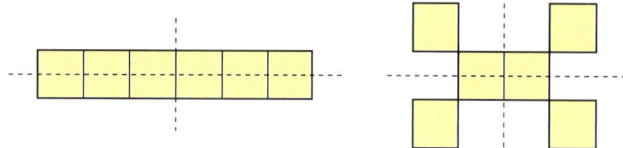

18.3 Rotational symmetry

When a square is rotated or turned through 360° it looks exactly as it did at the start on four different occasions during the rotation.

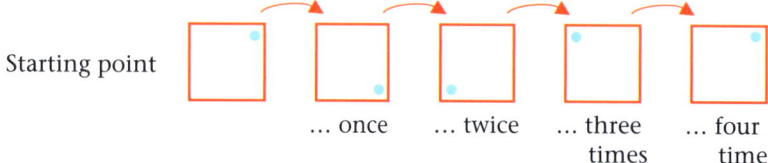

A 2-D shape with **rotational symmetry** repeats the appearance of its starting position two or more times during a full turn.

The **order** of rotational symmetry is the number of times the original appearance is repeated in a full turn.

A square has order of rotational symmetry 4 as it looks the same four times during one complete turn.

Looking for rotational symmetry

Sometimes rotational symmetry can be hard to spot, so you may want to try one of the following ideas.

Either actually turn the book or paper the shape is drawn on, **or** trace the shape onto tracing paper and turn it on top of the shape in the book. Then you will be able to see when the shapes match.

This image of a zebra does not have rotational symmetry.

Example 2

Does a kite have rotational symmetry?

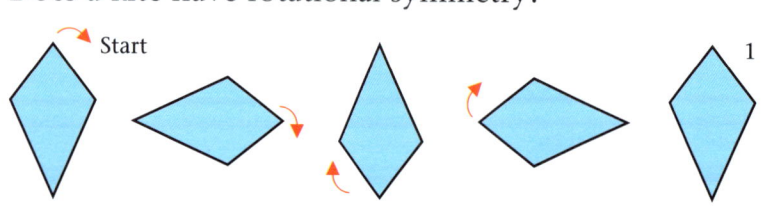

A kite only looks the same once during a complete turn, so it does not have rotational symmetry.

18.3 Rotational symmetry

Example 3

Write down the order of rotational symmetry of this flag:

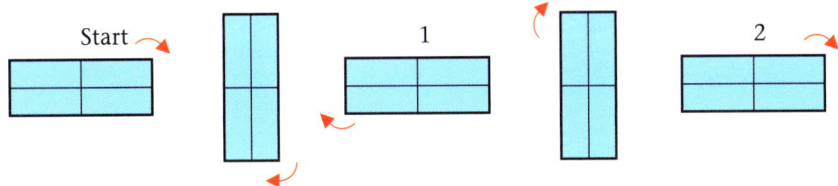

As the flag is turned through 360° it looks the same twice.
The order of rotational symmetry is 2.

Exercise 18C

You may want to use tracing paper in this exercise.

1 Write down whether or not each of these shapes has rotational symmetry.

(a) 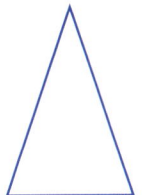   (b) 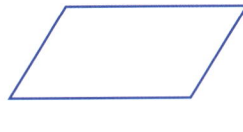   (c)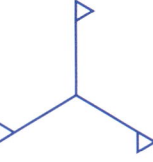

(d) 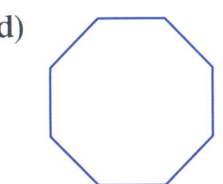   (e)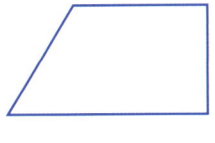

2 State the order of rotational symmetry of each of these shapes.

(a) 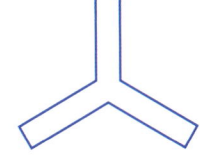   (b)    (c)

(d) 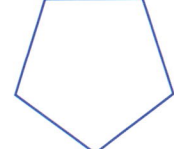   (e)

18.4 The symmetry of regular polygons

A regular hexagon has
  6 sides
  6 lines of symmetry
  order of rotational symmetry 6.

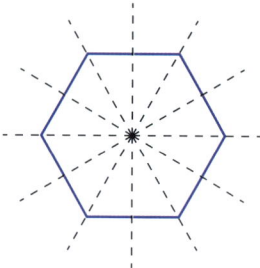

Regular polygons have the same number of lines of symmetry as they have sides.

The order of rotational symmetry of a regular polygon is the same as the number of sides.

Exercise 18D

For each of these regular polygons, find:
(a) the number of lines of symmetry
(b) the order of rotational symmetry.

1 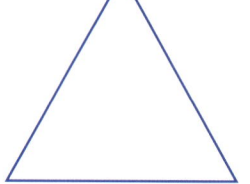 2 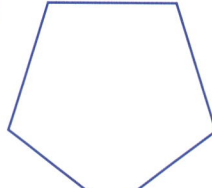 3 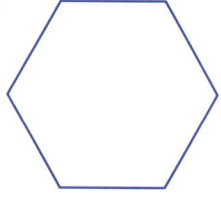 4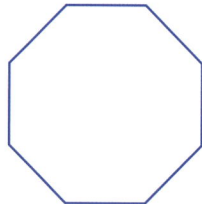

Mixed exercise 18

1 How many lines of symmetry does a kite have?
2 Draw a rectangle showing all the lines of symmetry.
3 Which regular polygon has five lines of symmetry?
4 Sketch a regular octagon showing its lines of symmetry.
5 What is the order of rotational symmetry of a regular octagon?
6 Which special triangle has rotational symmetry of order 3?

Mixed exercise 18

7 Copy or trace the shapes below. Draw all the lines of symmetry and write down the order of rotational symmetry for each shape.

(a)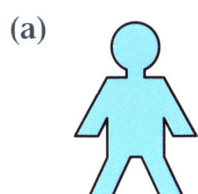
(b)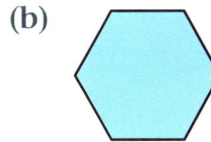
(c)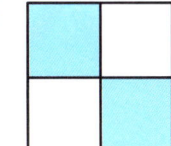
(d)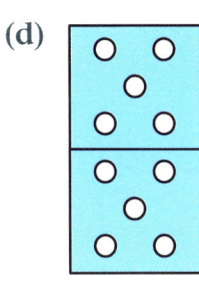
(e)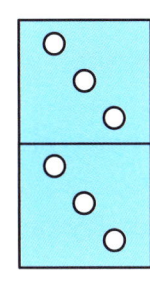

8 Copy and complete the shapes below using the lines of symmetry given.

In questions 8 and 9 you need a larger grid than is shown.

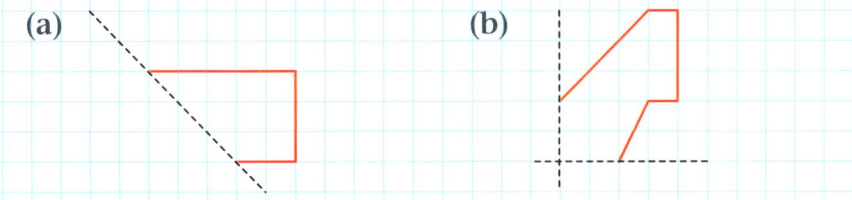

9 Using the lines of symmetry shown, copy and complete the missing parts of the patterns.

10 On a copy of each of these shapes, draw all of its lines of symmetry, if it has any.

(a)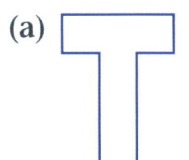
(b)
(c)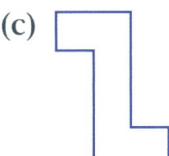

[E]

11 These shapes each have at least one line of symmetry.

(a) Copy these shapes and show all the lines of symmetry.
(b) Explain how you could check whether or not a line of symmetry was correct.

12 *ABCDE* is a regular pentagon. *O* is the centre of the pentagon.

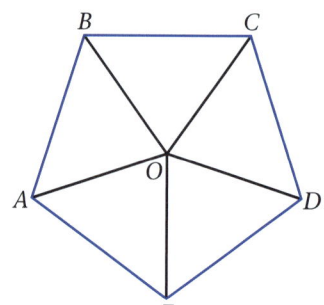

(a) Write down the order of rotational symmetry of the regular pentagon.
(b) Write down the number of lines of symmetry of triangle *OCD*.

13 Which of the designs below have line symmetry?

A	B	C	D	E
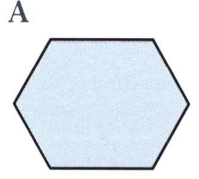		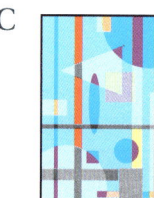		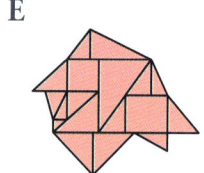
Floor tile	Asian carpet design	Contemporary art	Wallpaper pattern	Tile design

Summary of key points

1 A 2-D shape has a **line of symmetry** if the line divides the shape into two halves and one half is the mirror image of the other half.

2 A line of symmetry is sometimes called a **mirror line**.

3 A 2-D shape with **rotational symmetry** repeats the appearance of its starting position two or more times in a full turn.

4 The **order** of rotational symmetry is the number of times the original appearance is repeated in a full turn.

5 Regular polygons have the same number of lines of symmetry as they have sides.

6 The order of rotational symmetry of a regular polygon is the same as the number of sides.

19 Simple perimeter, area and volume

19.1 Perimeter

The **perimeter** of a 2-D shape is the distance around the edge of the shape.

Example 1

Find the perimeter of this rectangle.

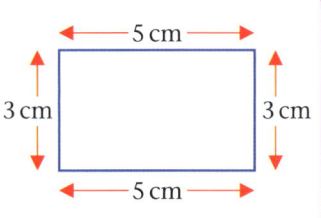

The rectangle has two sides of length 5 cm and two sides of length 3 cm. The perimeter is

5 + 3 + 5 + 3 = 16 cm

Exercise 19A

1 Work out the perimeters of these shapes:

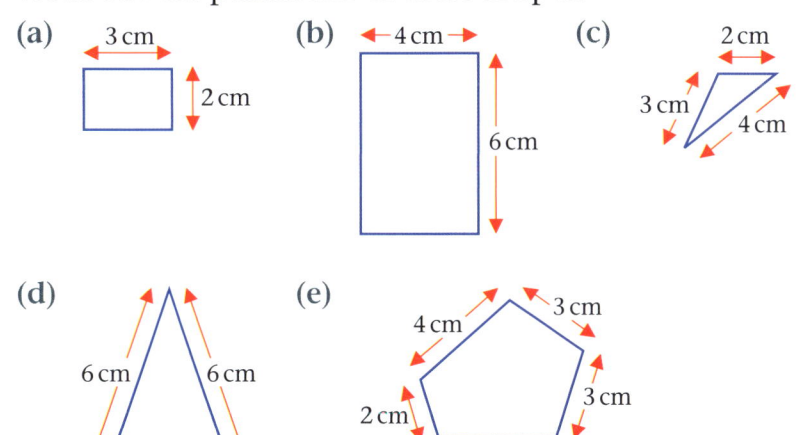

The perimeter of the outer walls of the Pentagon Building is just over 1.4 km.

2 Work out the perimeters of these shapes:
   (a) a square with side 5 cm
   (b) a rectangle with sides 4 cm and 2 cm
   (c) an equilateral triangle with all sides 6 cm
   (d) an isosceles triangle with two sides of 5 cm and one of 6 cm.

Perimeter of composite shapes

Example 2

Find the perimeter of this shape.

The shape is made up from a rectangle and a triangle. The rectangle is 9 cm by 6 cm and the triangle has sides 8 cm, 6 cm and 10 cm.

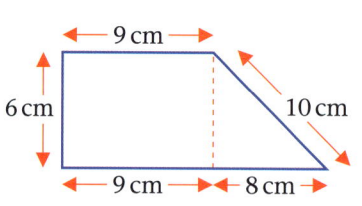

Remember that the perimeter is the distance around the outside edge of the shape. It does not include any lines inside the shape.

The perimeter is

$6 + 9 + 10 + 8 + 9 = 42$ cm

Exercise 19B

Find the perimeters of these shapes.

1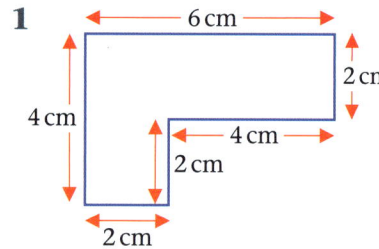

2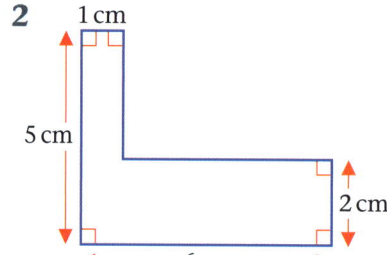

3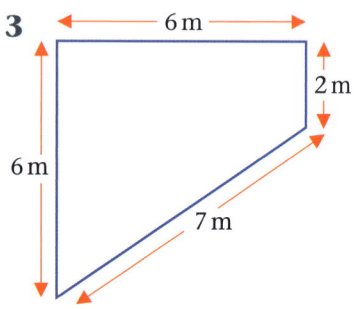

4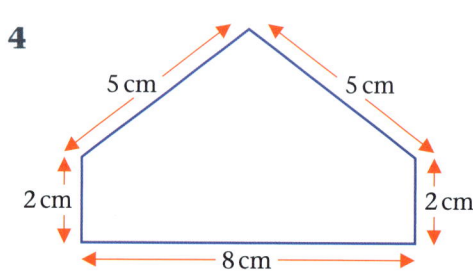

5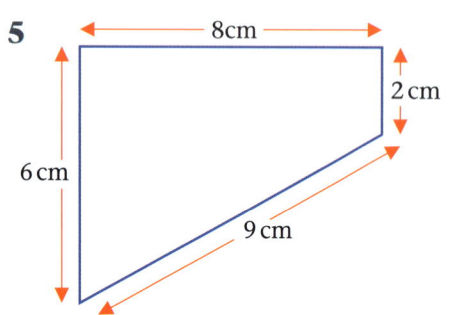

6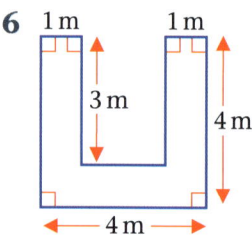

Measure these shapes and then find their perimeters.

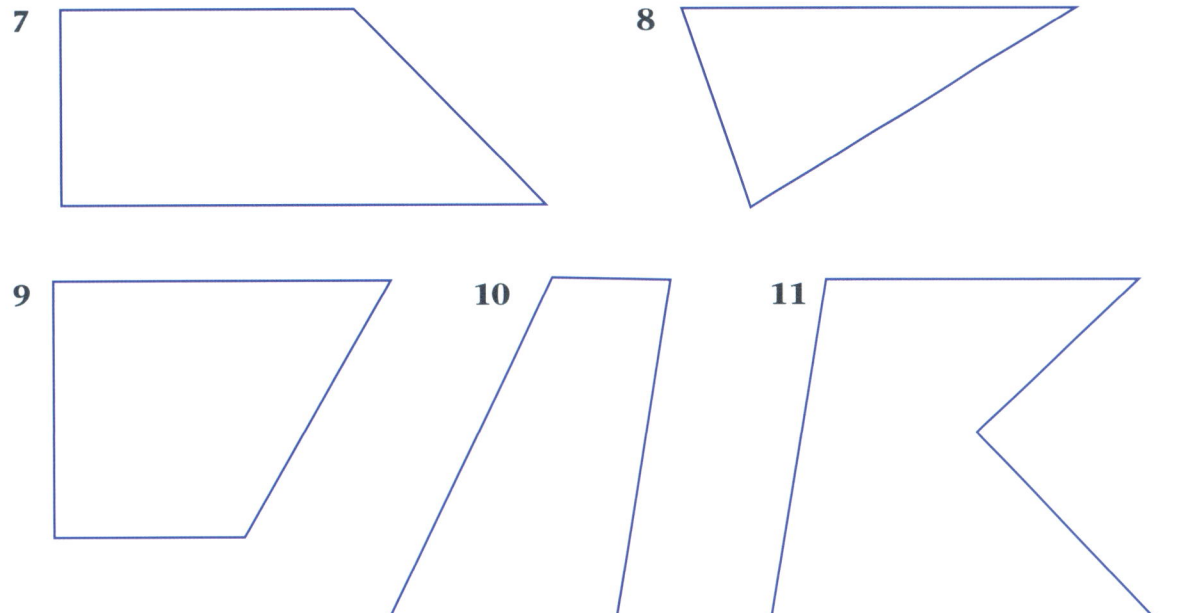

19.2 Area

The **area** of a 2-D shape is a measure of the amount of space it covers. Typical units of area are square centimetres (cm²), square metres (m²) and square kilometres (km²).

You can use a cm² grid to work out the area of a shape.

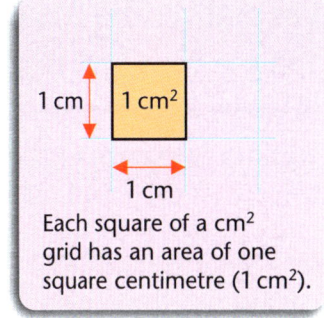

Each square of a cm² grid has an area of one square centimetre (1 cm²).

Example 3

Find the area of this rectangle.

This rectangle covers up 6 squares.

Each square is 1 cm by 1 cm and has an area of 1 square centimetre or 1 cm².

The rectangle has an area of 6 cm².

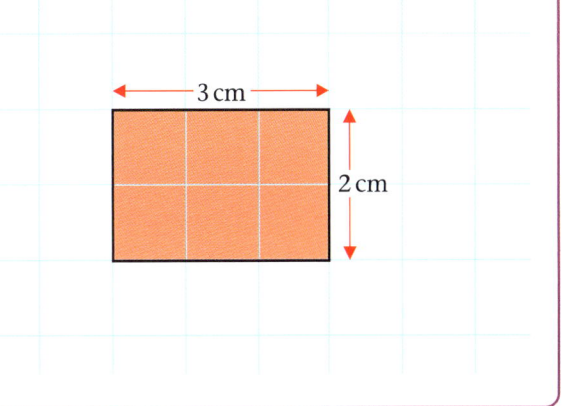

Chapter 19 Simple perimeter, area and volume

Exercise 19C

Find the areas of these shapes in cm² by counting squares.

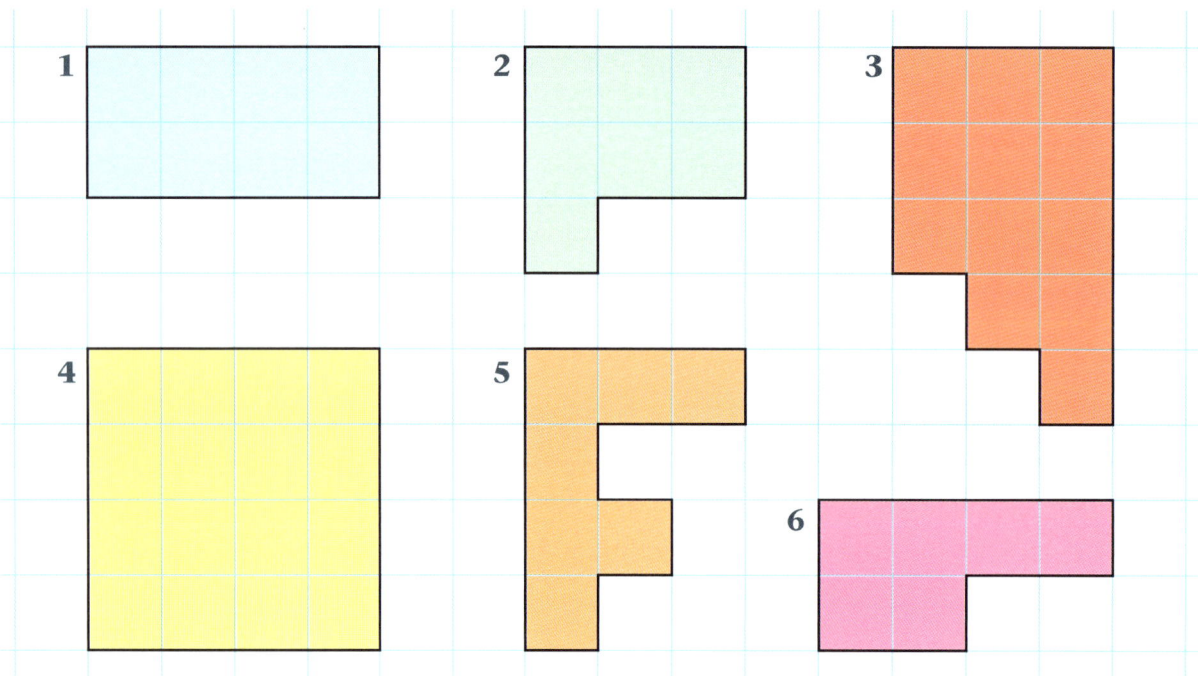

Estimating the areas of irregular shapes

You can use a cm² grid to help you estimate the area of an irregular shape.

Sometimes shapes do not fit exactly into whole squares. In these cases try and match up part squares to make whole ones.

Example 4

Estimate the area of this shape in cm² by counting squares.

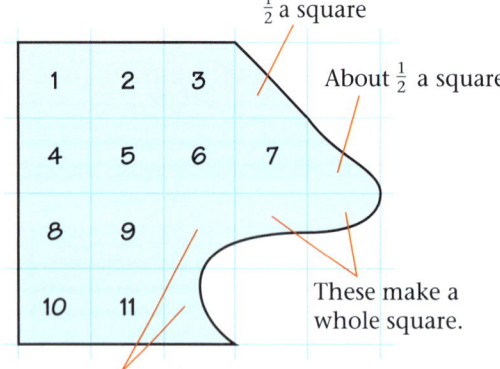

It is a good idea to number the squares as you count to make sure that you don't miss a square or part of a square.

This shape has a total area of about
$11 + 1\frac{1}{2} + 1 + \frac{1}{2} + \frac{1}{2} = 14\frac{1}{2}$ cm².

Exercise 19D

Estimate the areas of these shapes in cm² by counting squares.

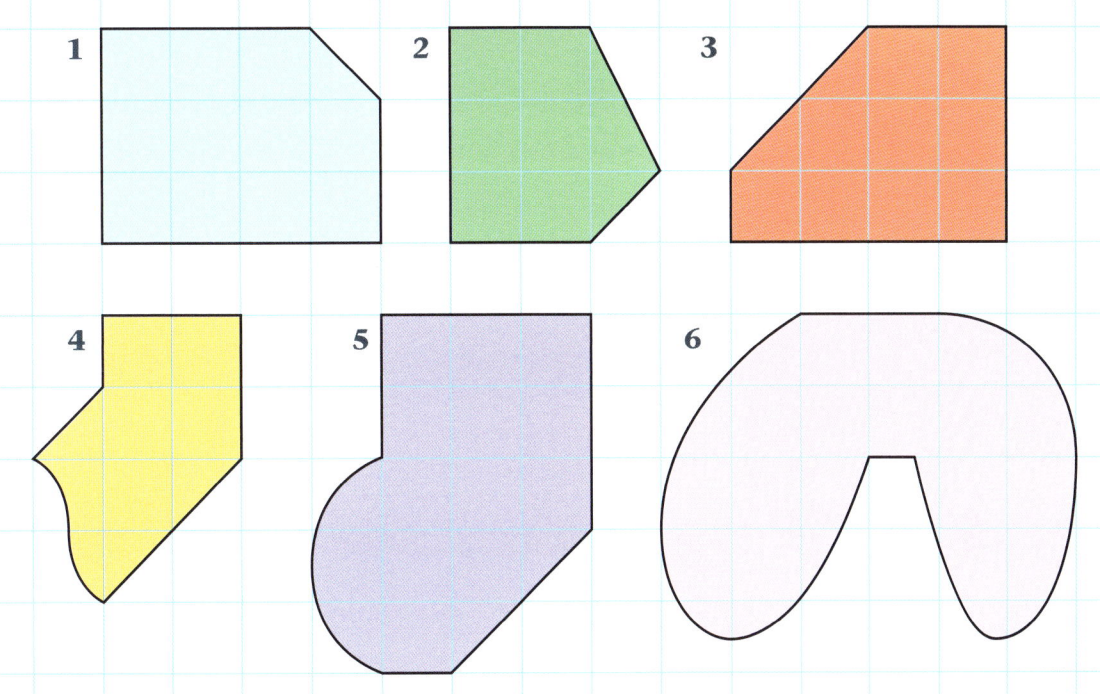

19.3 Volume

The **volume** of a 3-D shape is a measure of the amount of space it occupies. Typical units of volume are cubic centimetres (cm³) and cubic metres (m³).

In Section 19.2 you estimated an area using a grid of squares with area 1 cm². To estimate a volume you can use cubes of volume 1 cm³.

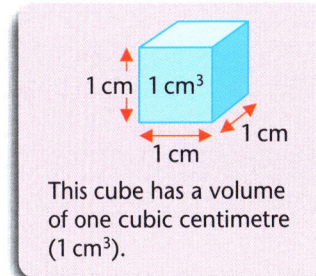

This cube has a volume of one cubic centimetre (1 cm³).

Example 5

This cuboid is made from cubes with sides all 1 cm long. Find the volume of the cuboid.

There are 8 (= 4 × 2) cubes in the top layer. There are 3 layers of cubes so the total number of cubes is 8 × 3 = 24.

This can be worked out from 4 × 2 × 3 which is length × width × height for the cuboid.

The volume of the cuboid is 24 cm³.

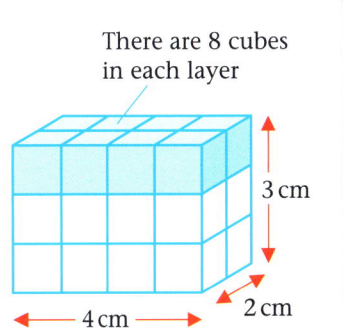

There are 8 cubes in each layer

Exercise 19E

Find the volumes of these shapes in cm³ by counting cubes.

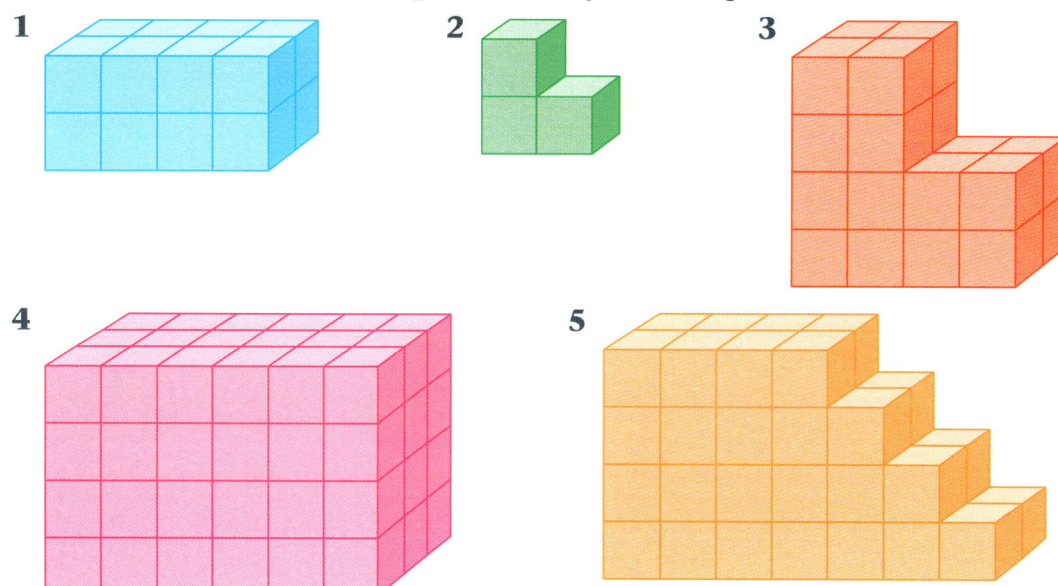

19.4 Finding areas using formulae

You can find the areas of some shapes using formulae:

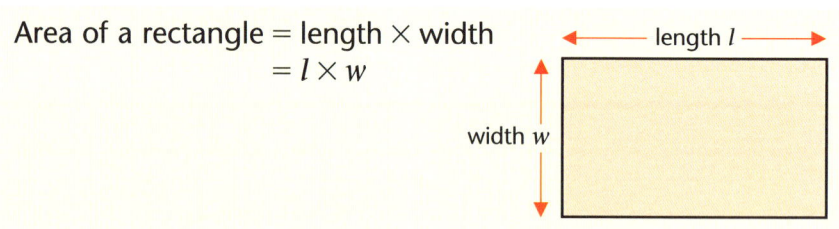

Area of a rectangle = length × width
= $l \times w$

A **formula** is a relationship between quantities, written using either letters or words. There is more about formulae in Chapter 21.

Since a square is a special type of rectangle then:

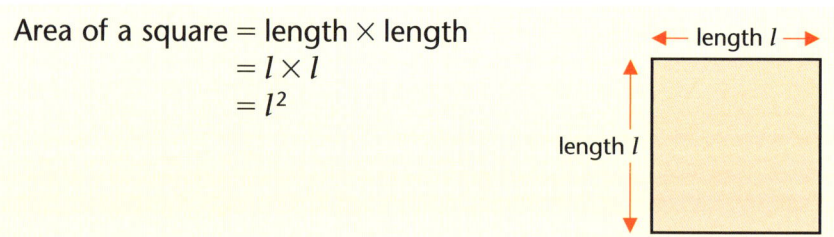

Area of a square = length × length
= $l \times l$
= l^2

The area of a triangle is half the area of a rectangle that encloses it so:

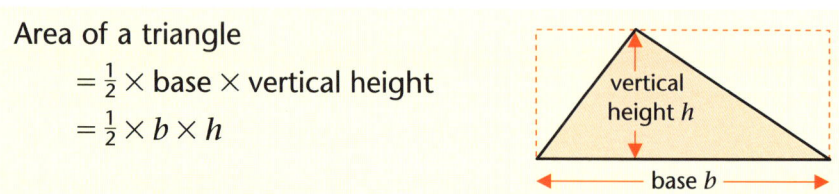

Area of a triangle
= $\frac{1}{2}$ × base × vertical height
= $\frac{1}{2} \times b \times h$

19.4 Finding areas from formulae

You can cut a corner off a rectangle and replace it on the other side to make a parallelogram so:

Area of a parallelogram = base × vertical height
= $b \times h$

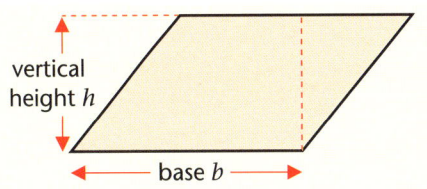

You will need to learn these formulae for your exam.

Example 6

Find the areas of these shapes.

(a) 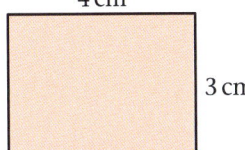 (b) 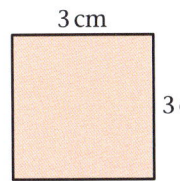 (c)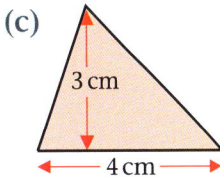

(a) Area of rectangle = $l \times w$
$= 4 \times 3 = 12 \, cm^2$

(b) Area of square = $l \times l$
$= 3 \times 3 = 9 \, cm^2$

(c) Area of triangle = $\frac{1}{2} \times b \times h$
$= \frac{1}{2} \times 4 \times 3$
$= \frac{1}{2} \times 12 = 6 \, cm^2$

Exercise 19F

Find the areas of these shapes.

1 (a) 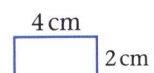 (b) 5 cm / 3 cm (c) 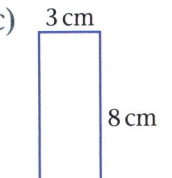 (d)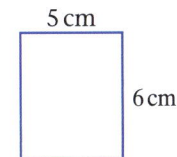

2 (a) 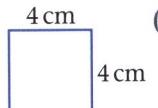 (b) 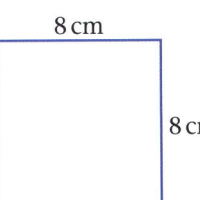 (c) 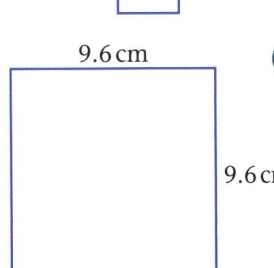 (d)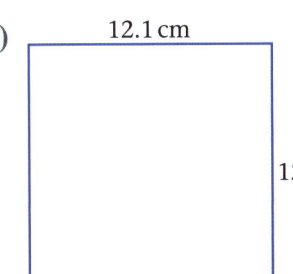

354 Chapter 19 Simple perimeter, area and volume

3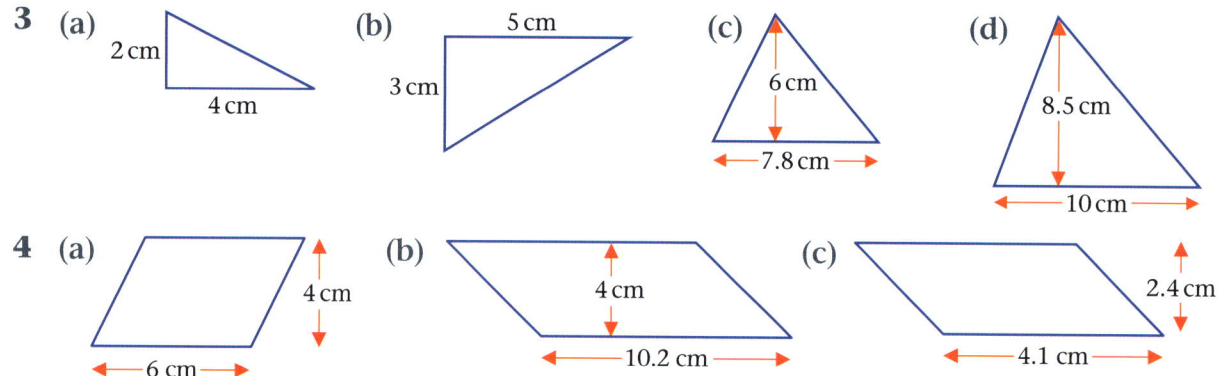

4

5 Copy this table and complete the columns.

	Shape	Length	Width	Area
(a)	Rectangle	5 cm	6 cm	
(b)	Rectangle	4 cm		20 cm²
(c)	Rectangle	2 cm		20 cm²
(d)	Rectangle		5 cm	40 cm²
(e)	Rectangle		12 cm	60 cm²

6 Copy this table and complete the columns.

	Shape	Base	Vertical height	Area
(a)	Triangle	10 cm	5 cm	
(b)	Triangle		12 cm	60 cm²
(c)	Triangle		5 cm	40 cm²
(d)	Triangle	4 cm		32 cm²
(e)	Triangle	16 cm		64 cm²

Area of a composite shape

You can find the area of a more complicated shape by splitting it up into simple shapes.

Example 7

Find the area of this shape.

Area of rectangle $= l \times w$
$= 8 \times 6$
$= 48 \text{ cm}^2$

Area of triangle $= \frac{1}{2} \times b \times h$
$= \frac{1}{2} \times 5 \times 8$
$= 20 \text{ cm}^2$

Total area $= 48 + 20 = 68 \text{ cm}^2$

You can split this shape into a rectangle and a triangle.

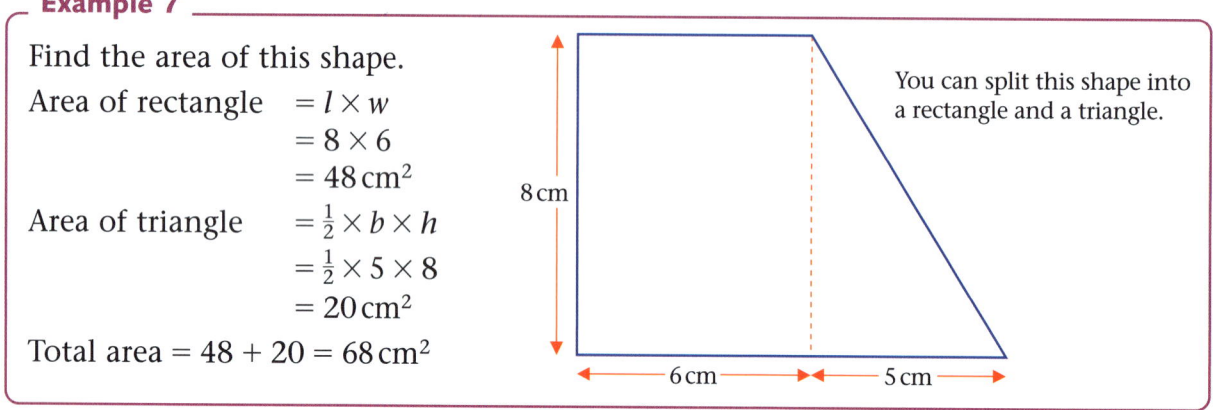

Exercise 19G

Find the areas of these shapes.

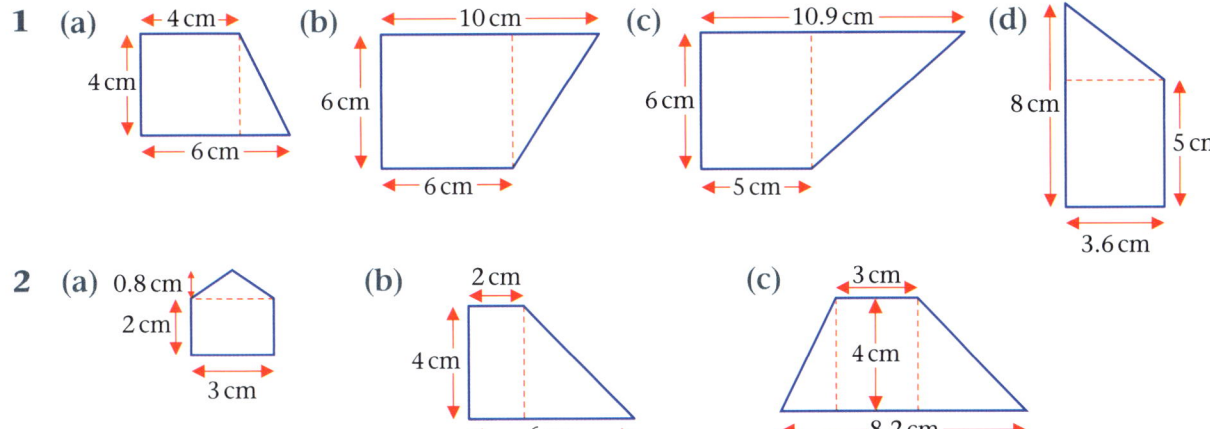

19.5 Finding volumes of cuboids using formulae

In Section 19.3 you found the volumes of cuboids by counting cubes. There is also a formula for finding the volume of such shapes:

Volume of a cuboid = length × width × height
= $l \times w \times h$

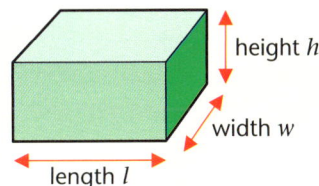

In a cube the length, width and height are all the same size so the formula is:

Volume of a cube = length × length × length
= $l \times l \times l$
= l^3

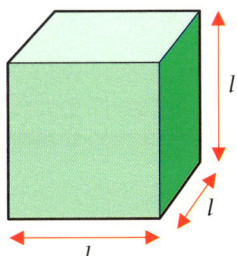

Example 8

Find the volume of a cuboid with length 8 cm, width 6 cm and height 4 cm.

Volume = $l \times w \times h$
= $8 \times 6 \times 4 = 192$ cm³

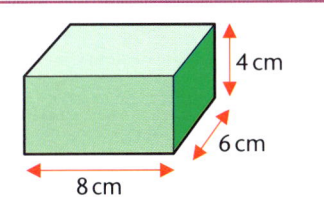

Chapter 19 Simple perimeter, area and volume

Example 9

This solid shape is made from 2 cm cubes.
Find its volume.

For each cube:

volume = $l \times l \times l$
= $2 \times 2 \times 2 = 8 \text{ cm}^3$

There are 7 cubes in the shape so the total volume is

$7 \times 8 = 56 \text{ cm}^3$

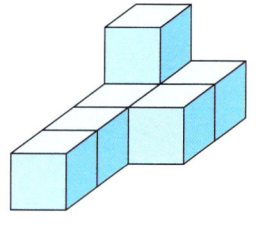

You cannot see one of the base cubes.

Exercise 19H

Find the volumes of these shapes.

1

2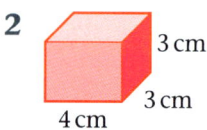

3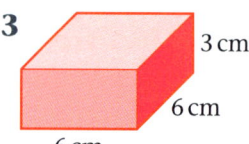

4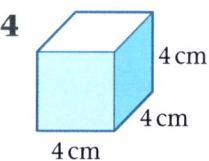

5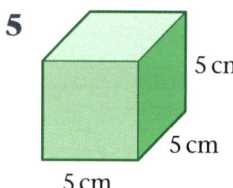

6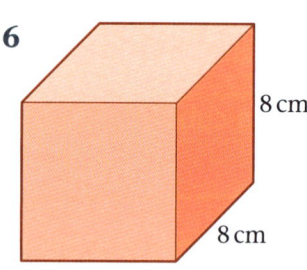

7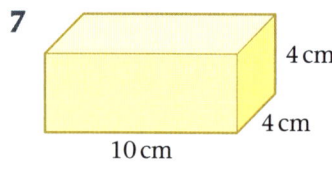

8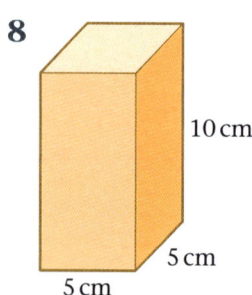

9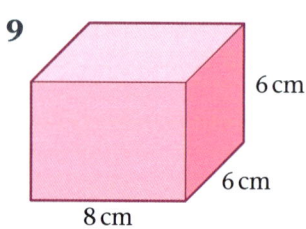

10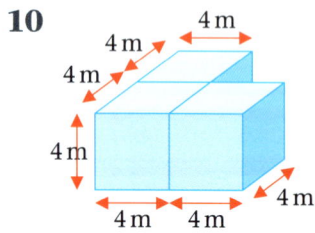

11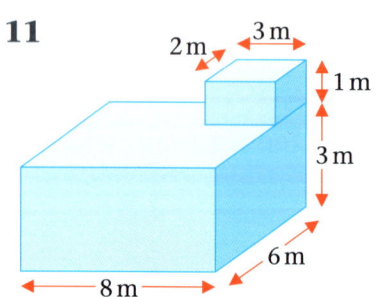

19.6 Surface area

You also need to be able to work out the surface area of simple solid shapes.

The **surface area** is the total area of all the faces of a solid shape.

Example 10

Work out the surface area of this cuboid.

The top and bottom faces are 5 m × 8 m rectangles.
They each have area 40 m².
The sides are 2 m × 5 m rectangles. They each have area 10 m².

The front and back faces are 2 m × 8 m rectangles.
They each have area 16 m².

The total surface area of the cuboid is

top + bottom + right side + left side + front + back = 40 + 40 + 10 + 10 + 16 + 16
= 132 m²

Example 11

Work out the surface area of this prism.

Area of sloping face = 5 × 9   = 45 cm²
Area of back face   = 3 × 9   = 27 cm²
Area of base   = 4 × 9   = 36 cm²
Area of side   = ½ × 4 × 3 = 6 cm²
Area of side   = ½ × 4 × 3 = 6 cm²

Total = 120 cm²

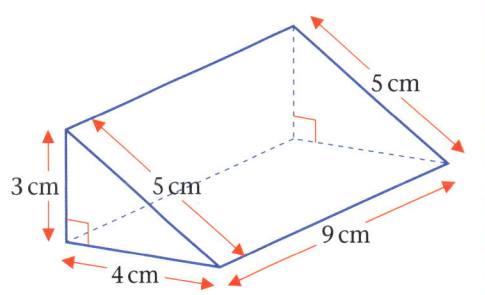

Remember: A prism is a shape with uniform cross-section.

Exercise 19I

Work out the surface areas of these shapes.

1.

2.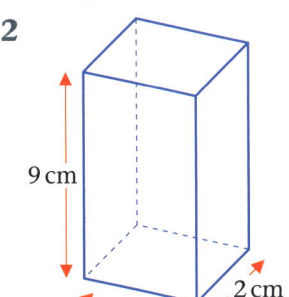

3.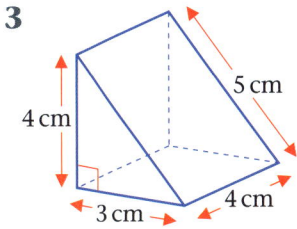

358 Chapter 19 Simple perimeter, area and volume

4, 5, 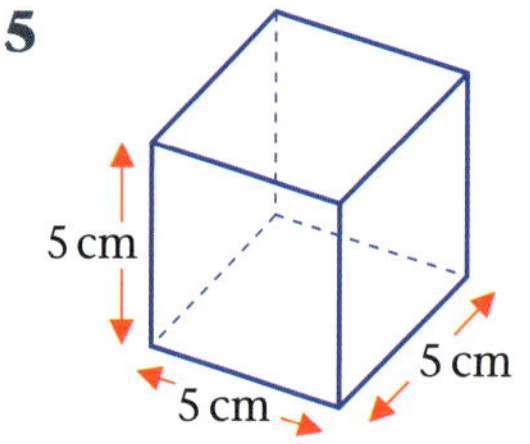 6, 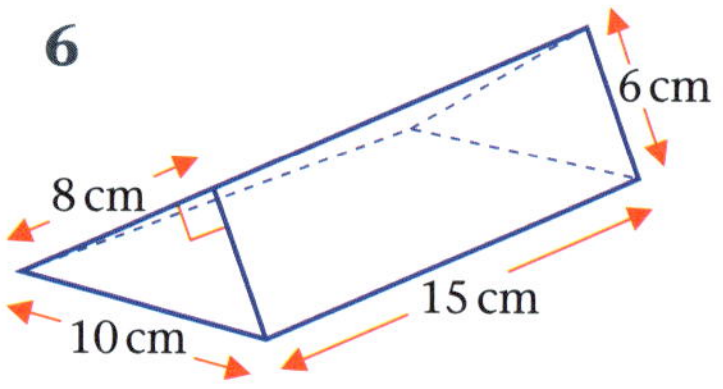 7, 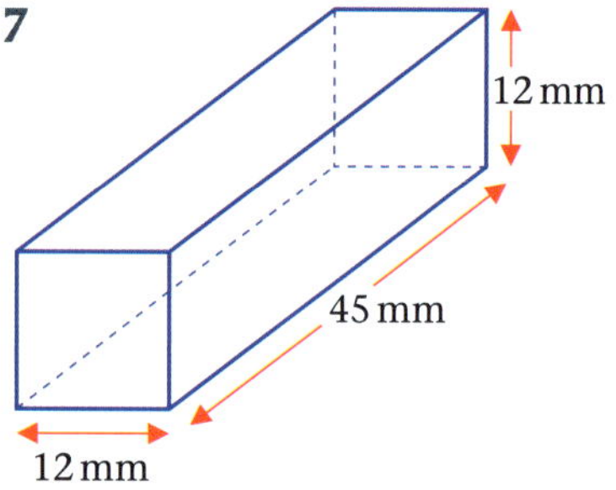 8, 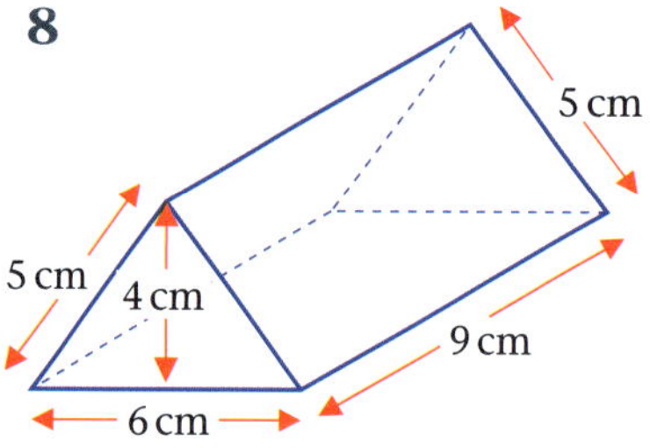 9, 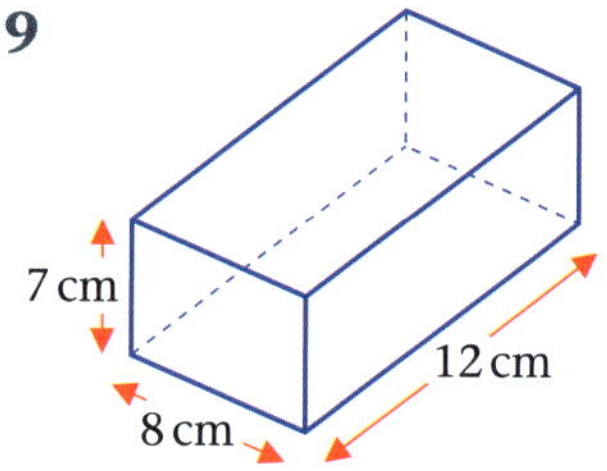 10, 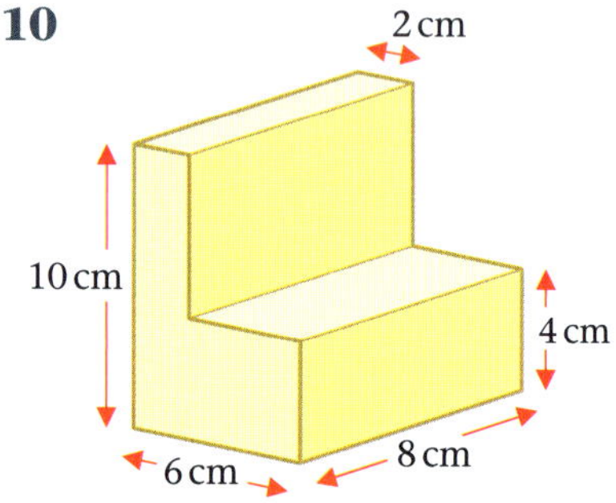 11, 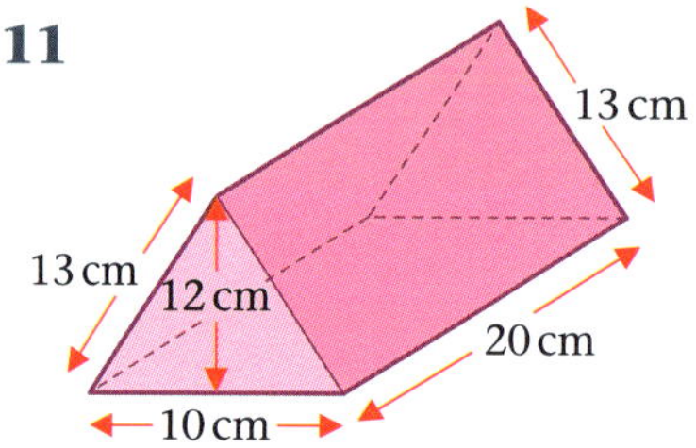 12

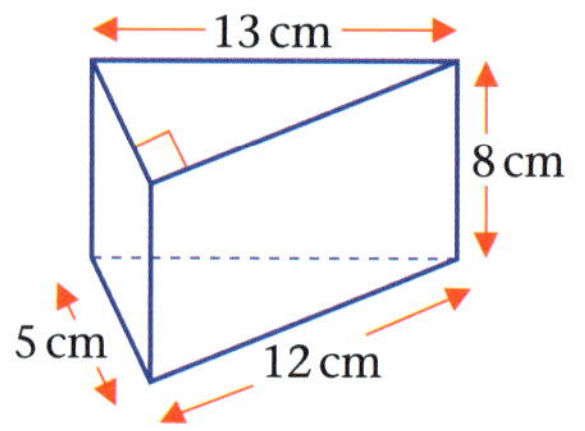

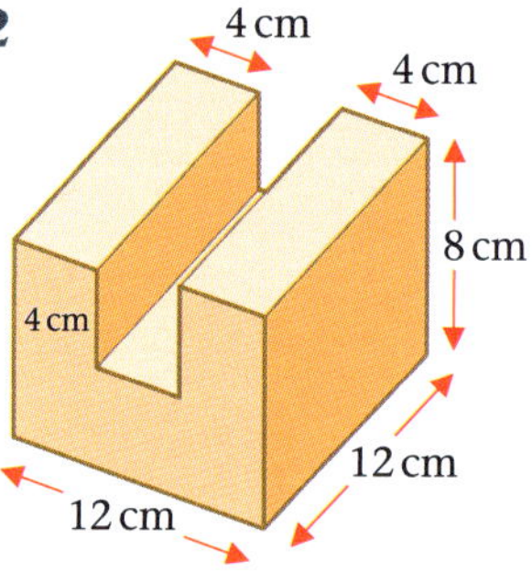

19.7 Fitting boxes into larger boxes

Sometimes we have to calculate how many times small boxes will fit into a larger box.

Example 12

The diagram shows a packet for a sharpener 4 cm × 2 cm × 2 cm, and a box for packets of sharpeners 40 cm × 20 cm × 20 cm.

How many packets will completely fill the box?

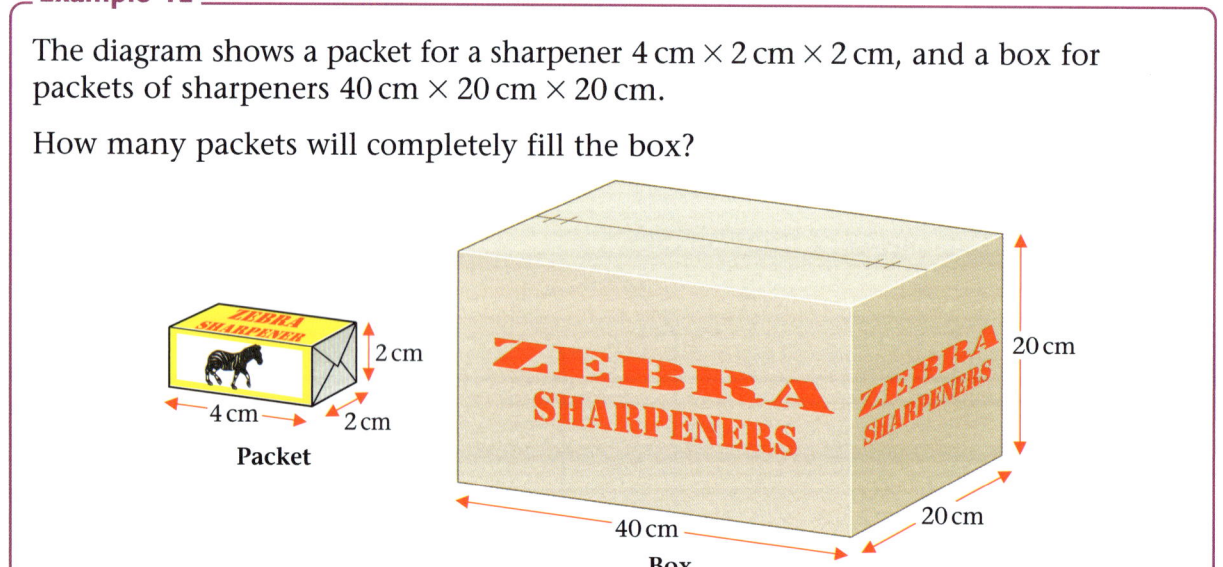

19.7 Fitting boxes into larger boxes

Compare each of the corresponding sides of the packet and the box.

The length of the packet (4 cm) will fit into the length of the box (40 cm) 10 times. That is, 10 packets can fit along the length of the box.

The width of the packet (2 cm) will fit into the width of the box (20 cm) 10 times. That is, 10 packets can fit across the width of the box.

The height of the packet (2 cm) will fit into the height of the box (20 cm) 10 times. That is, 10 packets can fit up the height of the box.

The total number of packets that will fit in the box is
$$10 \times 10 \times 10 = 1000$$

Exercise 19J

In each question the diagrams show a packet and a box. Find out how many packets will completely fill the box.

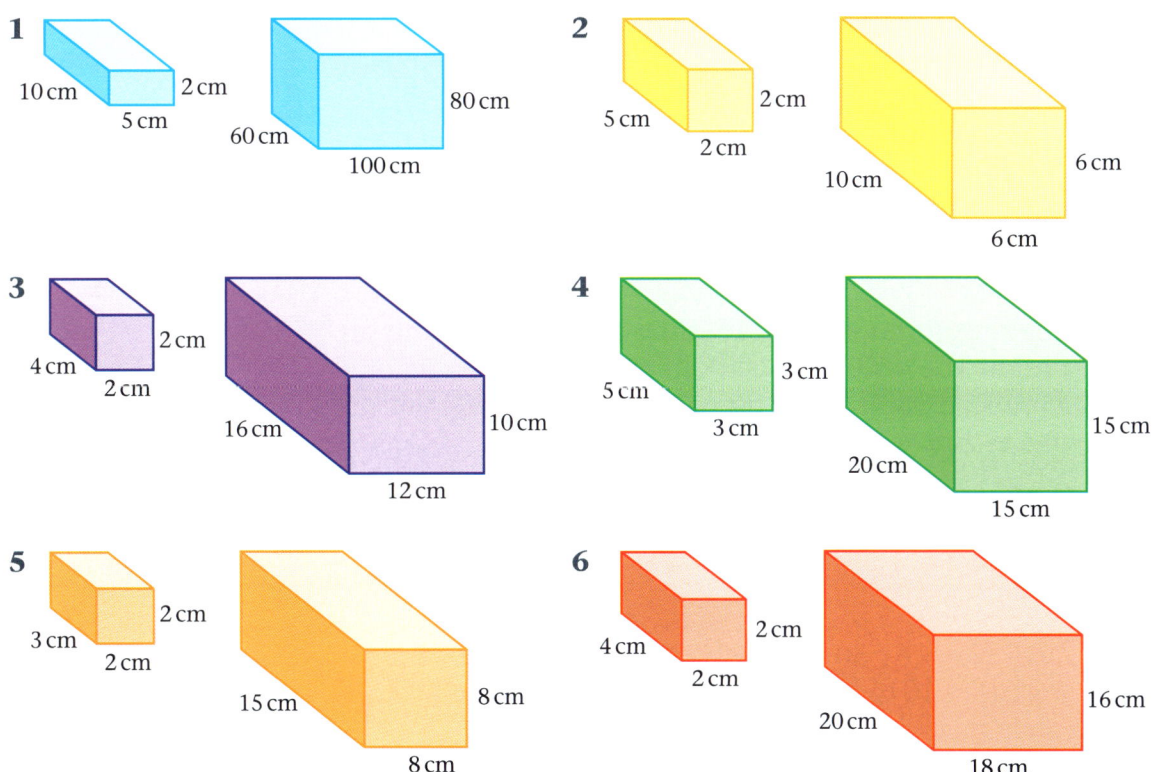

Chapter 19 Simple perimeter, area and volume

19.8 Area and volume problems

In real-life problems you sometimes need to round answers.

Example 13

A wall is 10 m long and 4 m high.
A tin of paint covers 12 m².
How many tins of paint are needed to paint the wall?

Area of wall = 10 × 4 = 40 m²

40 ÷ 12 = 3.33...

4 tins of paint are needed.

You cannot buy 0.33... tins of paint. Round the answer up.

Exercise 19K

Keith and Mary have bought an old house and are having some work done on it.

1. The lounge is a rectangle 4 m by 3 m and the carpet they buy covers it completely. The carpet costs £7.95 per square metre. How much does the carpet cost them?

2. The kitchen is rectangular and measures 3.4 m by 2.7 m. They have to buy a whole number of square metres of vinyl to cover the floor. The vinyl costs £12.50 per square metre. How much will it cost to cover the floor?

3. The bathroom walls need to be tiled to a height of 1.5 m. The tiles are all 15 cm square. The bathroom measures 3 m by 3 m. The tiles cost 65p each.
   (a) How many tiles are needed for the height?
   (b) How many tiles are needed for the length of one wall?
   (c) How many tiles are needed for all 4 walls? You can ignore the space taken up by the door.
   (d) Work out the cost of all the tiles.

4. The small bedroom measures 3 m by 2 m and the walls are 2.5 m high. The walls of this room are going to be painted with emulsion paint. Each tin of paint will cover 15 m². How many tins will they need?

5. The central heating system runs on oil. The oil tank is a cuboid with length 2.5 m, width 1 m and height 1.5 m. How many litres of oil will the tank contain?

Remember that 1 l = 1000 ml or 1000 cm³.

6. All the tiles on the roof need to be replaced. Each tile measures 30 cm by 30 cm. Each of the two sides of the roof measures 10 m by 8 m. There needs to be an allowance of an extra 50% for overlaps.
   How many tiles are needed for the roof?

7 The lawn needs replacing and they decide to replace the worn-out grass with strips of turf that measure 2 m by 0.3 m. The new lawn is to measure 20 m by 12 m.
Work out how many strips they need to buy.

8 Keith wants to replace the surface of the drive, which measures 12 m by 8 m. He needs to dig out the old surface to a depth of 30 cm.
(a) Work out the volume of rubble that Keith needs to dig out.
(b) How many 4 m³ skips will be needed to carry away the rubble?

19.9 Converting units of area and volume

You may be asked in the examination to convert square centimetres (cm²) to square metres (m²) or m² to cm².

Here are two pictures of the same square. The only difference is that one is measured in metres and the other in centimetres.

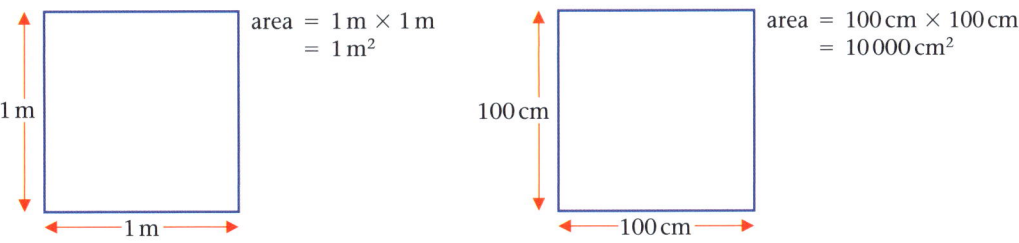

1 m² = 100 × 100 cm² = 10 000 cm²

Similarly you may be asked to convert cubic centimetres (cm³) to cubic metres (m³).

Here are two pictures of the same cube. The only difference is that one is measured in metres and the other in centimetres.

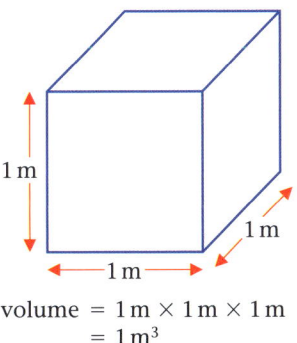
volume = 1 m × 1 m × 1 m
= 1 m³

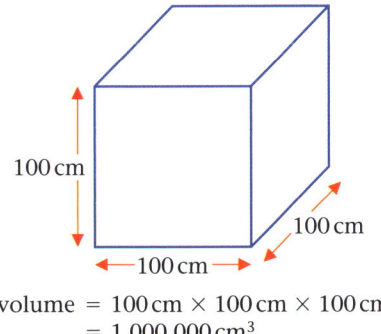
volume = 100 cm × 100 cm × 100 cm
= 1 000 000 cm³

1 m³ = 100 × 100 × 100 cm³ = 1 000 000 cm³

Chapter 19 Simple perimeter, area and volume

Example 14

A square has an area of 1.2 m².
What is its area in cm².

$$1 \text{ m}^2 = 10\,000 \text{ cm}^2$$
So $1.2 \text{ m}^2 = 1.2 \times 10\,000 \text{ cm}^2$
$= 12\,000 \text{ cm}^2$

Example 15

The volume of an oil drum is 2 340 000 cm³.
Write down the volume of the oil drum in m³.

$$1 \text{ m}^3 = 1\,000\,000 \text{ cm}^3$$
So $2\,340\,000 \text{ cm}^3 = \dfrac{2\,340\,000}{1\,000\,000} \text{ m}^3$
$= 2.34 \text{ m}^3$

Exercise 19L

1 Work out the number of
  (a) cm² in 2 m²
  (b) cm² in 13 m²
  (c) cm² in 2.4 m²
  (d) cm² in 15.2 m²
  (e) m² in 120 000 cm²
  (f) m² in 23 000 cm²
  (g) m² in 164 300 cm²
  (h) cm² in 0.42 m²
  (i) cm² in 0.03 m²
  (j) m² in 3000 cm²
  (k) m² in 100 cm²

2 Work out the number of
  (a) cm³ in 7 m³
  (b) cm³ in 15 m³
  (c) cm³ in 3.5 m³
  (d) cm³ in 4.78 m³
  (e) m³ in 4 000 000 cm³
  (f) m³ in 3 780 000 cm³
  (g) m³ in 14 789 000 cm³
  (h) cm³ in 0.8 m³
  (i) cm³ in 0.002 m³
  (j) cm³ in 0.000 024 m³
  (k) m³ in 37 800 cm³
  (l) m³ in 142 000 cm³
  (m) m³ in 3000 cm³

3 The area of a pane of glass is 12 000 cm².
Write down the area of the pane of glass in m².

4 The diagram shows a door.
  (a) Work out the area of the surface of the door in m².
  (b) Write down your answer to part (a) in cm².

5 The volume of a large packing case is 2.3 m³.
Write down the volume of the packing case in cm³.

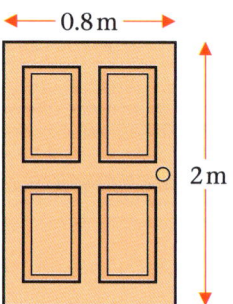

6 The dimensions of a washing machine are shown in the diagram.

(a) Work out the volume of the washing machine in cm³.

(b) Write down your answer to part (a) in m³.

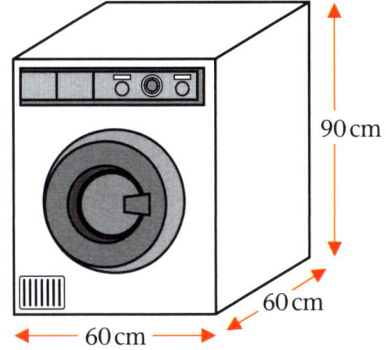

19.10 Compound measures: speed

Sometimes you need to work with two units at the same time. For example, the speed of a car can be measured in miles per hour – a measurement involving a unit of length and a unit of time.

For an object moving at a constant speed:

$$\text{speed} = \frac{\text{distance}}{\text{time}} \qquad \text{time} = \frac{\text{distance}}{\text{speed}}$$

$$\text{distance} = \text{speed} \times \text{time}$$

Typical units are miles per hour, and metres per second.

Usually the speed of a car is not constant for the whole journey so you use the average speed:

$$\text{average speed} = \frac{\text{total distance travelled}}{\text{total time taken}}$$

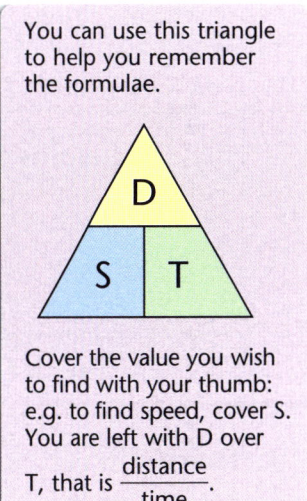

You can use this triangle to help you remember the formulae.

Cover the value you wish to find with your thumb: e.g. to find speed, cover S. You are left with D over T, that is $\frac{\text{distance}}{\text{time}}$.

Example 16

What speed does my car average if I travel 90 miles in 3 hours?

$$\text{average speed} = \frac{\text{total distance travelled}}{\text{total time taken}}$$

$$= 90 \div 3 = 30 \text{ miles per hour}$$

Example 17

How long does it take to travel 400 miles at a constant speed of 50 miles per hour?

$$\text{time} = \frac{\text{distance}}{\text{speed}}$$

$$= 400 \div 50 = 8 \text{ hours}$$

Example 18

How far can you go if you travel for 3 hours at 10 miles per hour?

distance = speed × time
= 10 × 3
= 30 miles

Exercise 19M

1 Elizabeth walked for 3 hours at 4 miles per hour.
   How far did she walk?

2 Andrew drove 100 miles in 4 hours.
   At what average speed did he travel?

3 Karen drove 300 miles at an average speed of 60 miles per hour.
   How long did her journey take her?

4 David was travelling by canal boat and went 30 miles in 8 hours.
   At what average speed was he travelling?

5 Amanda rode her bike for 3 hours and travelled 21 miles.
   At what average speed was she travelling?

6 Gerry ran for 2 hours and covered 16 miles.
   At what average speed was he running?

7 Brigit swam for 3 hours and travelled 4 miles.
   At what average speed was she swimming?

8 Alfred set off from home at 8 am. He travelled 200 miles by car and arrived at 11 am.
   At what average speed was he travelling?

9 Jason set off for work at 07:55. He arrived at work at 08:10.
   If he lives 5 miles from work, at what average speed did he travel?

10 Frances was using a keep fit treadmill. She ran for 40 minutes and 'travelled' 10 kilometres.
   At what average speed was she running?

19.11 Problem solving with a spreadsheet

Look at this problem:

A farmer has 200 metres of fencing. He wants to use all the fencing to enclose a rectangular area of his field for his animals to graze. Find the length and width of the rectangle which gives his animals the maximum grazing area.

You can solve problems like this on a computer by using a spreadsheet.

Exercise 19N

1. Think of all the rectangles you can draw whose perimeters are 200 metres. For example, some could be long and thin; others short and wide.

   Use a spreadsheet to record the length L and width W of each rectangle.

   Then multiply the values of L and W to get the area of each rectangle.

   Formula
   A3 = A2 + 10

   (W = 100 − L)
   Formula
   B2 = 100 − A2

   (A = L × W)
   Formula
   C2 = A2 × B2

	A	B	C	D
1	L	W	LW	
2	0	100	0	
3	10			
4	20			
5				
6				

   > The perimeter of each rectangle is 200 metres, so
   > $$2L + 2W = 200$$
   > You can divide by 2 to make this equation simpler:
   > $$L + W = 100$$
   > Use your spreadsheet to try lots of values for L from $L = 0$ to $L = 100$ metres.
   > Increase L by 10 metres each time. For each value of L calculate a value for W using
   > $$W = 100 - L$$

   > Make sure your spreadsheet has at least 12 rows and 3 columns. Use column A for the length, column B for the width and column C for the area of each rectangle.

   What is the maximum value for the area?

2. Draw a graph of the data in your spreadsheet.

   > Drawing a graph of the data can give you a better understanding of how the area changes as the lengths and widths of the rectangles change.

Mixed exercise 19

1 (a) Work out the perimeter of this shape:

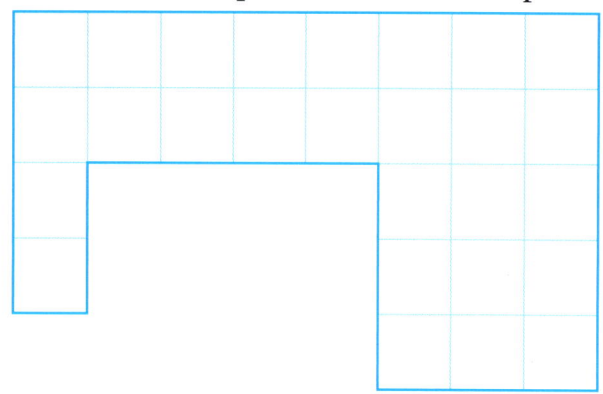

  (b) Work out the area of the shape.

2 Measure and write down the perimeter of this shape.

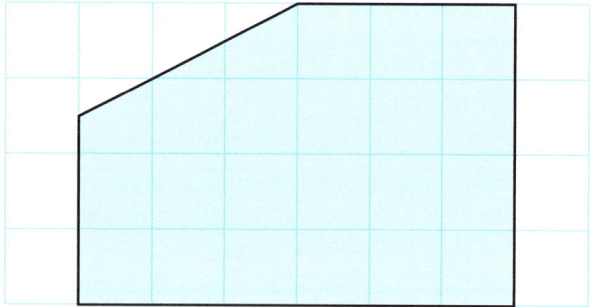

3 Work out the perimeter of the shape on the right.

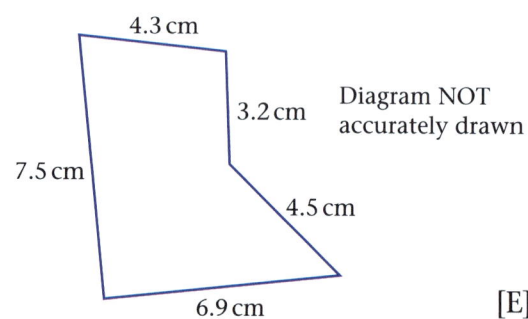

[E]

4 The diagram represents an L-shaped room whose corners are all right angles.

  (a) (i) Work out the value of x.
  (ii) Work out the value of y.
  (b) Work out the perimeter of the shape.
  (c) Work out the area of the shape.

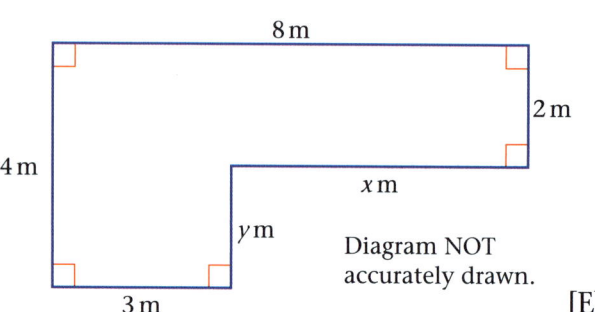

[E]

5 The diagram represents the babies' pool, with paving around, at a leisure centre. The pool is rectangular, 8 m long by 5 m wide, and has a depth of 0.6 m throughout.

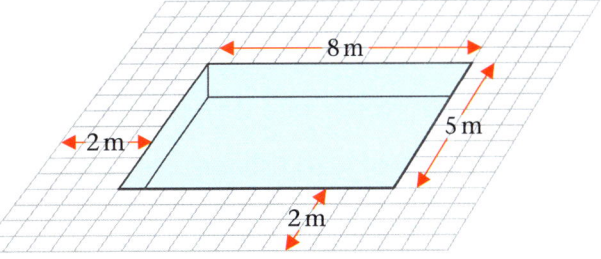

(a) Work out the volume of the pool in m³.

The paving around the pool is 2 m wide.

(b) Work out the area of the paving.

6 The diagram shows a paved surface.
All the corners are right angles.
Work out the area of the paved surface. [E]

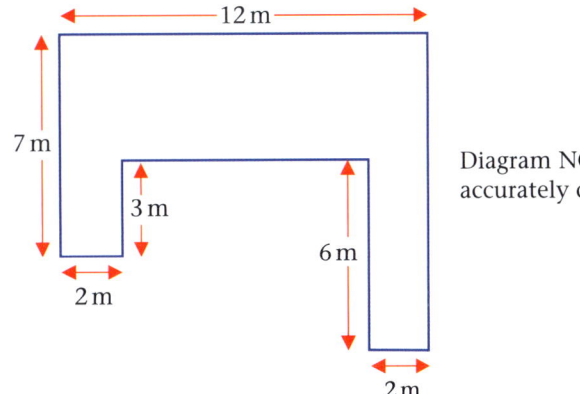

Diagram NOT accurately drawn

7 The diagram represents a large tank in the shape of a cuboid.
The tank has a base. It does not have a top.
The width of the tank is 2.8 metres.
The length of the tank is 3.2 metres.
The height of the tank is 4.5 metres.

Diagram NOT accurately drawn

The outside of the tank is going to be painted.
1 litre of paint will cover 2.5 m² of the tank.
The cost of the paint is £2.99 for each litre tin.

Calculate the cost of the paint needed to paint the outside of the tank.

8 Daniel leaves his house at 07:00.
He drives 87 miles to work.
He drives at an average speed of 36 miles per hour.
At what time does Daniel arrive at work? [E]

9 Change 8 m³ to cm³. [E]

10 Ben fills a container with boxes. Each box is a cube of side 0.5 m. The container is a cuboid of length 9 m, width 4 m and height 3 m.
Work out how many boxes will fit exactly into the container. [E]

Summary of key points

1. The **perimeter** of a 2-D shape is the distance around the edge of the shape.

2. The **area** of a 2-D shape is a measure of the amount of space it covers. Typical units of area are square centimetres (cm^2), square metres (m^2) and square kilometres (km^2).

3. **Area formulae** for 2-D shapes:

   Area of a rectangle $=$ length $\times$ width
   $= l \times w$

   Area of a square $=$ length $\times$ length
   $= l \times l = l^2$

   Area of a triangle $= \frac{1}{2} \times$ base $\times$ vertical height
   $= \frac{1}{2} \times b \times h$

   Area of a parallelogram $=$ base $\times$ vertical height
   $= b \times h$

4. The **volume** of a 3-D shape is a measure of the amount of space it occupies. Typical units of volume are cubic centimetres (cm^3) and cubic metres (m^3).

5. **Volume formulae** for cuboids (3-D):

   Volume of a cuboid $=$ length $\times$ width $\times$ height
   $= l \times w \times h$

   Volume of a cube $=$ length $\times$ length $\times$ length $= l \times l \times l = l^3$

6. The **surface area** is the total area of all the faces of a solid shape.

7. $1\, m^2 = 100 \times 100\, cm^2 = 10\,000\, cm^2$
   $1\, m^3 = 100 \times 100 \times 100\, cm^3 = 1\,000\,000\, cm^3$

8. For an object moving at a constant speed:

   $$\text{speed} = \frac{\text{distance}}{\text{time}} \quad \text{time} = \frac{\text{distance}}{\text{speed}} \quad \text{distance} = \text{speed} \times \text{time}$$

   Typical units are miles per hour, and metres per second.

   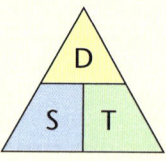

9. When an object's speed varies as it travels:

   $$\text{average speed} = \frac{\text{total distance travelled}}{\text{time taken}}$$

20 Presenting and analysing data 1

The word average is often used. Think about these statements:

'Jenny is of average height.'
'A centre forward averages one goal a game.'
'Teenagers in Britain spend an average of £5 a week on hair care products.'

Here the word average means that something is typical, or describes something that typically happens.

In mathematics an **average** is usually a single value which is used to represent a set of data. It is in some way typical of the data and gives an idea of what the data is like.

Three different averages are commonly used:

- the **mode**   • the **median**   • the **mean**.

This chapter shows you how each one is found and why it is useful.

On average this family size box contains 500 g of cereal. The weight of cereal in the box is only allowed to vary within a very small range.

20.1 The mode

The **mode** of a set of data is the value which occurs most often.

Example 1

The numbers of goals scored by a team in ten matches were:

   1, 5, 2, 0, 4, 2, 1, 2, 2, 3

Find the mode of this data.

The score that occurred most often was 2 goals, so the mode is 2.

Example 2

Find the mode of this team's scores:

   3, 1, 0, 1, 4, 3, 6, 2, 1, 3

There are two modes: 1 and 3.

Example 3

Find the mode of this team's scores:

   2, 5, 3, 4, 0, 1, 6

There is no mode since each score occurred only once.

Chapter 20 Presenting and analysing data 1

Exercise 20A

1   Four students recorded the number of text messages they got on each day in a week. Here are their results:

John: 8, 8, 7, 6, 8, 5, 8
Kit: 6, 7, 5, 4, 6, 5, 8
Mary: 6, 5, 4, 8, 7, 3, 9
Tina: 3, 4, 4, 7, 3, 6, 6

   (a) For each student, write down the mode(s) of the numbers of text messages.
   (b) What is the overall mode for all the numbers of text messages?

2   Here are the CPU speeds, in GHz, of 18 computers in an office:

   1.6   1.8   2.2   1.8   2.2   1.8
   1.6   1.5   1.8   1.6   2.0   2.0
   1.4   2.0   2.1   2.3   1.6   1.7

   (a) Write down (i) the fastest speed, (ii) the slowest speed.
   (b) Write down the modal speed.

3   Here are some sets of numbers. Add a number, or numbers, to each set so that the new set has the mode shown on the right.

   (a) 8, 5, 9, 6, 3, 7, 4   : mode 6
   (b) 3, 7, 5, 8, 4, 3, 6, 9   : mode 5
   (c) 2, 6, 7, 8, 5, 3, 2   : mode 4
   (d) 11, 7, 15, 12, 15, 8, 9   : modes 11 and 15
   (e) 6, 3, 8, 9, 4, 6, 5   : mode 7
   (f) 8, 3, 6, 2, 7, 9, 7, 5   : modes 5 and 6

4   The table shows the numbers of goals scored by the teams in a hockey competition.

Number of goals	0	1	2	3	4	5
Number of teams	3	3	6	4	3	1

   (a) Make a list of all the numbers of goals scored by all the teams.
   (b) Write down the modal number of goals.
   (c) How many teams were in the competition?

20.2 The median

The **median** is the middle value when the data is arranged in order of size.

Example 4

Find the median of Brian's homework marks for
(a) English: 5, 7, 9, 4, 1, 3, 7, 4, 6
(b) history: 6, 8, 3, 7, 5, 3, 7, 2

(a) Arrange the English marks in order of size:

   1, 3, 4, 4, 5, 6, 7, 7, 9

The middle mark is 5. Brian has four marks higher and four marks lower than this.

The median is 5.

(b) Arrange the history marks in order of size:

   2, 3, 3, 5, 6, 7, 7, 8

The 'middle mark' lies between the 5 and 6 so the median is $5\frac{1}{2}$.

> Notice that the median history mark is not a mark Brian has actually scored.
> Because there is an even number of marks there is no 'middle mark' in the data.
> Instead the value of a middle mark has been calculated.

Example 5

The table shows the shoe sizes of a group of students. Find the median shoe size.

Shoe size	7	$7\frac{1}{2}$	8	$8\frac{1}{2}$	9	$9\frac{1}{2}$
Number of students	2	2	5	4	3	3

To find the median you could list all the shoe sizes:

7, 7, $7\frac{1}{2}$, $7\frac{1}{2}$, 8, 8, 8, 8, 8, $8\frac{1}{2}$, $8\frac{1}{2}$, $8\frac{1}{2}$, $8\frac{1}{2}$, 9, 9, 9, $9\frac{1}{2}$, $9\frac{1}{2}$, $9\frac{1}{2}$

You can see that the middle value or median is $8\frac{1}{2}$.

An easier way of finding the middle value is to add up the numbers of students. There are 19 students altogether so the middle student is the 10th.

Starting at the left of the data table, the 10th student is in the '$8\frac{1}{2}$' column, so the median shoe size is $8\frac{1}{2}$.

Exercise 20B

1. Rearrange the following marks in order and write down the median in each case.
   (a) 5, 8, 3, 2, 7, 9, 6
   (b) 15, 18, 9, 11, 17, 8, 12, 10, 9
   (c) 9, 4, 7, 3, 1, 6, 3, 8
   (d) 8, 12, 18, 9, 14, 7, 10, 6

2. Give examples of
   (a) seven different numbers with a median of 12
   (b) nine different numbers with a median of 8
   (c) eight different numbers with a median of 10
   (d) six different numbers with a median of 4.5

3. Here are some sets of numbers. Add a number to each set to obtain the median given on the right.
   (a) 1, 8, 5, 2   : median 5
   (b) 8, 4, 5, 3, 8, 4, 2, 9   : median 4
   (c) 7, 5, 3, 6, 8, 2, 7   : median $6\frac{1}{2}$
   (d) 7, 4, 3, 6, 2, 6, 8, 4   : median 5

   Hint: you need to make 5 the middle number.

4. The table shows some students' results from a quiz.

Marks	0	1	2	3	4	5	6	7	8	9	10
Number of students	0	0	2	3	1	1	2	5	4	6	4

   (a) Write down the median mark.
   (b) Write two statements making use of the median.

5. The chart below shows the numbers of parking tickets issued by a traffic officer on seven days of a week.

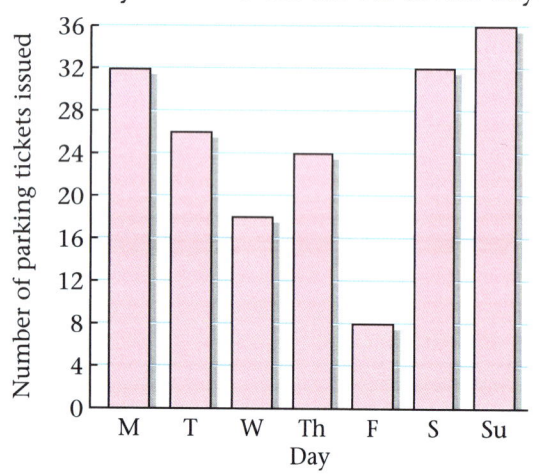

   (a) Work out the median number of tickets issued per day.
   (b) Write down the modal number.

20.3 The mean

The **mean** of a set of data is the sum of the values divided by the number of values:

$$\text{mean} = \frac{\text{sum of the values}}{\text{number of values}}$$

Example 6

Find the mean of 3, 8, 4, 7, 7, 6, 4, 1

The sum of the values is:

$3 + 8 + 4 + 7 + 7 + 6 + 4 + 1 = 40$

There are 8 values, so divide 40 by 8:

$40 \div 8 = 5$

The mean is 5.

Example 7

The mean of three numbers is 5, and the mean of four other numbers is 8. What is the mean of all seven numbers?

The sum of the three numbers is 15 — $\frac{15}{3} = 5$

The sum of the four numbers is 32 — $\frac{32}{4} = 8$

Mean of all seven numbers $= \dfrac{\text{Total sum}}{7} = \dfrac{15 + 32}{7} = \dfrac{47}{7} = 6.7$

Example 8

The mean of four numbers is 6. Three of the numbers are 4, 8 and 3. Find the value of the other number.

The sum of the four numbers is 24 — $\frac{24}{4} = 6$

If x is the missing number, $4 + 8 + 3 + x = 24$

$15 + x = 24$

$x = 9$

The other number is 9.

Exercise 20C

1 Calculate the mean for each set of data.
   (a) 12, 18, 9, 14, 8, 17
   (b) 23, 15, 37, 26, 16, 21, 33, 23
   (c) 15, 25, 22, 34, 19, 20
   (d) 25, 12, 31, 26, 31, 19, 30, 16

2 The heights of a group of students, in centimetres, are:
   158, 162, 172, 157, 161
   (a) Calculate the mean height.
   (b) Another student joins the group. His height is 159 cm.
       Calculate the new mean height.

> You can use your calculator to work out the mean. Either add the numbers then divide, or use the data entry key then press the MEAN key.

3 The weights of four parcels, in grams, are:
   515, 620, 542, 563
   (a) Calculate the mean weight.
   (b) A fifth parcel is added. The new mean is 710 g.
       Calculate the weight of the parcel.

4 The mean of four numbers is 94, and the mean of another nine different numbers is 17. What is the mean of all thirteen numbers?

5 Here are some sets of numbers. Find one more number for each set to obtain the mean given on the right.
   (a) 8, 3, 6, 7, 8, 4   : mean 7
   (b) 17, 14, 8, 11, 15, 17   : mean 14
   (c) 6, 3, 9, 7, 2, 6, 5   : mean 5.5
   (d) 23, 31, 20, 27, 32, 24   : mean 26

20.4 The range

The mean of a set of data is an average value. It does not tell you how spread out the data is.

One way of measuring the spread of a set of data is to find its **range**:

> The **range** of a set of data is the difference between the highest value and the lowest value:
>   the range = highest value − lowest value

Two sets of data may have the same mean but different ranges. Compare these two batsmen's scores after four innings:

   Peter: 0, 96, 100, 0   Mean 49   Range 100 − 0 = 100
   Hanif: 49, 51, 46, 50   Mean 49   Range 51 − 46 = 5

Both have the same mean or average score but Hanif has a much smaller range. His scores are less spread out which shows he is a more consistent player.

Exercise 20D

1 Here are the distances thrown by two athletes in a javelin competition:

Fiona Yass: 18, 17, 14, 18, 16, 22, 17, 16
Ulga Perez: 17, 15, 15, 18, 18, 15, 18, 20

(a) Work out the range for each athlete.
(b) Which athlete was (i) better (ii) more consistent? Give reasons for your answers.

2 Here are the scores of three students on a computer game:

Tim: 47, 51, 36, 78, 43, 20, 39, 27
Franz: 35, 38, 42, 55, 28, 43, 61, 54
Pani: 45, 51, 57, 44, 50, 48, 43, 49

(a) Which student was least consistent? Give a reason for your answer.
(b) One of the students scored 75 in his next game. His range is now 32. Who was it?

3 Copy and complete the table below. The first one is done for you.

Make	Basic model	Top model	Price range
Audi 2.0	£21 025	£26 265	£5240
Citroën C4 2.0	£16 695	£20 495	
Ford Focus 2.0		£16 680	£2180
Mazda 2.0	£15 200		£4000
Nissan Almera 2.0		£15 650	£3000
Peugeot 407 2.0	£16 950		£4000
Renault Mégane 2.0	£13 900	£18 600	
Toyota Corolla 2.0		£15 895	£1700
Volkswagen Golf 2.0	£12 990	£18 250	

4 The table shows the maximum and minimum temperatures one day last year in degrees Fahrenheit.

(a) Calculate the range in each city.
(b) List the cities in order, highest range first.
(c) Give a reason why someone might want to know these ranges.

City	Maximum	Minimum
London	64	42
Paris	69	47
Moscow	38	9
New York	72	59
Luxor	101	88

20.5 Using appropriate averages

The different types of averages are useful in different situations.

The **mode** is useful when you need to know, for example:
- which shoe size is most common
- which brand of cat food is most popular.

The **mean** is useful for finding a 'typical' value when most of the data is closely grouped, for example the height of a typical student in your class.

The mean may not give a very typical value if the data is very spread out, or if it includes a few values that are very different from the rest. For example:

> A company chairwoman earns £200 000 a year and her nine employees each earn £15 000.
> Their mean pay is £33 500.

The mean height of the students in your class will be 'typical' unless some people are very much taller or shorter than the rest.

In situations like this, the **median** or middle value may be more typical. Median earnings in this company are £15 000.

Example 9

Shah records the number of hits on his web page every day. Here are his results:

   1, 3, 17, 18, 19, 20, 21, 21, 24

Find the mode, median and mean of these numbers.

The mode is 21.   Two days had 21 hits.

The mean is $\frac{144}{9} = 16$.   Notice that only two days had fewer hits than this.

The median is 19.   There were four days with more hits and four days with fewer hits.

You can see that the two days with low numbers of hits lowered the result for the mean. If the days with 1 and 3 hits had 15 and 16 hits, the mean would have been 19, but the mode and median would have remained the same.

Example 10

Here are the numbers of rooks in each of 10 rookeries in Yorkshire:

   38, 35, 35, 35, 30, 29, 28, 28, 11, 5

Find the mode, median and mean of the numbers of rooks and the range. Comment on your results.

The mode is 35, the median is 29.5, the mean is 27.4 and the range is 33.

Here the median gives the best idea of a 'typical' number of rooks – half the rookeries have more and half have fewer.

The mean has been distorted by the two very low numbers of rooks, and only two rookeries have fewer rooks.

The mode is not representative as only one rookery has more rooks.

The range just tells you that there is a wide spread of the numbers of rooks.

Advantages and disadvantages of the three averages

	Advantages	Disadvantages
Mode	Easy to see or pick out Not influenced by extreme values	There can be more than one mode Cannot be used for further calculations
Median	Not influenced by extreme values	Actual value may not exist (see Example 4)
Mean	Can easily be calculated Uses all the data Can be used for further calculations	Extreme values can distort the result

Activity – Bicycles

How many bicycles are there in your home?
- Collect data for the whole class.
- Work out the mode, median and mean of your data.
- Comment on your findings.

Exercise 20E

1 Find the mode, median and mean in each of the following and make a comment about each.
   (a) The numbers of cars left in the station car-park overnight during one week were:
       12, 6, 14, 9, 13, 6, 10
   (b) The numbers of passengers boarding the train between 9 am and 12 noon were:
       24, 17, 32, 24, 35, 32, 28
   (c) The costs of the first five tickets sold were:
       £1.15, £12.40, £3.60, £3.60, £2.95

2 The weekly wages for the station staff were:

1 station manager	£400
2 ticket office clerks	£280 each
2 train dispatch officials	£240 each
3 cleaners	£200 each
2 trainees	£185 each

(a) Calculate the total weekly wages bill.

(b) What is
  (i)   the modal wage
  (ii) the median wage
  (iii) the mean wage
  (iv) the range?

(c) Comment on your answers to part **(b)**.

3 Find six numbers which have a mean of 5, a mode of 2 and a median of $4\frac{1}{2}$.

20.6 Stem and leaf diagrams

A stem and leaf diagram is another way of presenting data. It has the advantage that the shape of the way the data is distributed can be seen without losing the detail of the original data.

0	5, 8
1	2, 5, (7) — This leaf represents 17
2	4, 4, 5, 8
3	0, 3, 9
4	1, 5, 6

Key
4│1 means 41

Remember:
You must always add a key to the diagram to show how the stem and leaf combine.

The data represented is

5, 8, 12, 15, 17, 24, 24, 25, 28, 30, 33, 39, 41, 45, 46

Example 11

Here are the total numbers of medals won by Great Britain in the Olympic Games since 1896.

7, 30, 2, 145, 41, 44, 34, 20, 16, 14, 23, 11
24, 20, 18, 13, 18, 13, 21, 37, 24, 20, 15, 28, 30

(a) Show this data in a frequency chart.
(b) Represent the data in a stem and leaf diagram.
(c) Find the median.

(a)

Class interval	Tally	Frequency
0–9	||	2
10–19	⌁⌁⌁ |||	8
20–29	⌁⌁⌁ |||	8
30–39	||||	4
40–49	||	2
140–149	|	1

(b) Write the data as stem and leaves.

0	2, 7
1	5, 3, 8, 3, 8, 1, 4, ⑥ — This leaf represents 16
2	8, 0, 4, 1, 0, 4, 3, 0
3	0, 7, 4, 0
4	4, 1
14	5

Key
2 | 8 means 28

Now write the leaves in order:

0	2, 7
1	1, 3, 3, 4, 5, 6, 8, 8
2	0, 0, 0, 1, 3, 4, 4, 8
3	0, 0, 4, 7
4	1, 4
14	5

Key
2 | 8 means 28

(c) There are 25 data values, so the median (the middle number) is the 13th data value.

If you had only drawn a frequency chart you would not have been able to find the median value. You can count across your ordered stem and leaf diagram to find the 13th data value. The median is 20.

Chapter 20 Presenting and analysing data 1

A **stem and leaf** diagram shows the shape of the distribution and keeps the original data values.

Always include a **key** with a stem and leaf diagram to show how the stem and leaf are combined.

Activity – World temperatures

(a) From a newspaper, collect one day's temperatures for cities around the world.
(b) Represent the data in a stem and leaf diagram.
(c) Find the mode, median, mean and range of your data.
(d) Comment on your findings.

Exercise 20F

1 Forty people were asked 'What are the last two digits of your telephone number?' The results were:

45	15	55	26	43	27	22	36	98	81
17	36	24	36	55	30	43	08	24	26
25	08	23	45	72	29	57	17	67	69
44	53	68	14	90	26	36	49	52	37

(a) Copy and complete this stem and leaf diagram. The 10–19 class interval is done for you.

0	
1	4, 5, 7, 7
2	
3	
4	
5	
6	
7	
8	
9	

Key
1│4 means 14

(b) What is the median?

2 Forty-one pupils recorded the time taken in seconds to solve a puzzle at the school fête. The times were:

    25 38 50   9 35 48   9 12 47 34
    52 11 32 41 36 29   7 44 18 23
    39 22 17   4 49 38 57 15 33 58
    14   8 35 27 17 43 20 37   6 26 24

(a) Represent this data using a stem and leaf diagram, including a key.
(b) What is the median time?

3 Marks (out of 60) in a mock examination were:

    25 42 54 37 18 35 29 53 47 53
    44 56 35 26 34 43 37 15 55 34
    52 35   9 43 58 27 52 45 50 20
    24 43 55 46 35 14 38 27 44 32
    35 19 36 28 46 34 45 34 40 59

(a) Using class intervals 0–9, 10–19, etc. draw a frequency chart to represent this data.
(b) Draw a stem and leaf diagram to represent this data, including a key.
(c) In which class interval is (i) the mode (ii) the median?
(d) Calculate the mean of the marks in the class interval 30–39. Give your answer to 1 decimal place.
(e) If the pass mark was 2 above the median, what percentage passed?

20.7 Pie charts

A **pie chart** is a good way of displaying data when you want to show how something is shared or divided.

How Wayne spent the last 24 hours

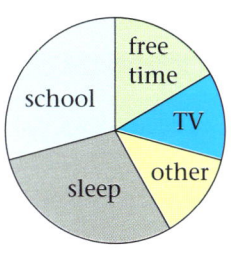

Land use in the UK

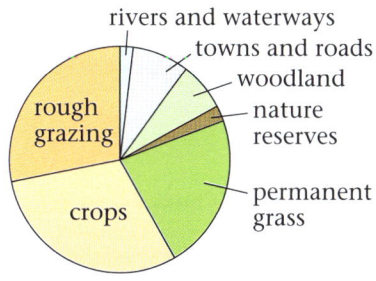

The market share for different cat food brands

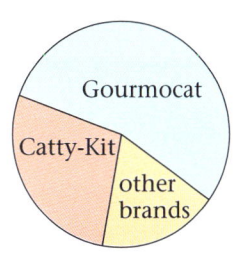

Chapter 20 Presenting and analysing data 1

Drawing a pie chart

Each slice of a pie chart is called a **sector**.

When you know the angle of each sector at the centre of a pie chart, here is how to draw it.

Example 12

Draw a pie chart whose angles at the centre are: 108°, 90°, 72°, 60° and 30°.

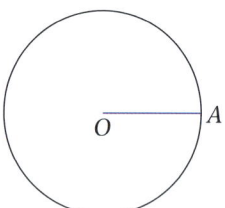

Draw a circle. Draw a line OA from its centre to its circumference.

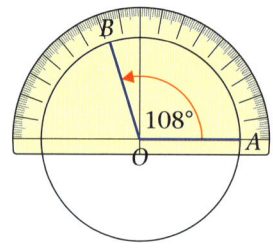

Use your protractor to measure the angle 108°. Mark it and draw the line OB.

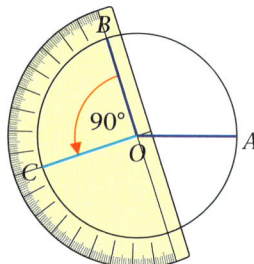

Place your protractor along OB. Measure the angle 90°, mark it and draw the line OC.

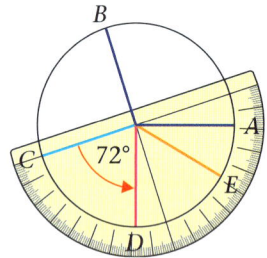

Place your protractor along OC. Measure the angle 72°, mark it and draw OD.

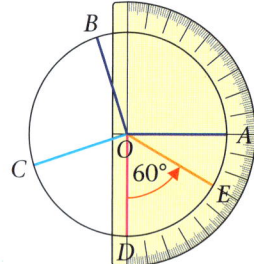

Place your protractor along OD. Measure the angle 60°, mark it and draw OE.

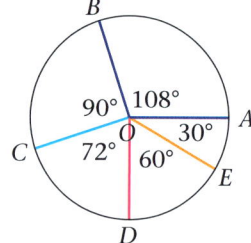

Check that the angle remaining is 30° and mark it.

The angles at the centre of a pie chart add up to 360°.

Exercise 20G

1. Clive wants to draw a pie chart to show the result of his traffic survey. He calculates these angles:

Speed (mph)	Under 70	70–80	More than 80
Angle	210°	90°	60°

Draw a pie chart for Clive's traffic survey.

2. Tarina wants to draw a pie chart to show the votes in the General Election in 2005. Here are some of the angles she calculates:

   (a) Copy and complete the table.
   (b) Draw the pie chart.

	Angle
Labour	127°
Conservative	116°
Liberal Democrat	
Other	38°

> **Activity – The General Election**
> (a) From the internet, find the number of Parliamentary seats won by
>   (i) the Labour party
>   (ii) the Conservative party
>   (iii) the Liberal Democrat party
>   (iv) all the other parties,
>   in the General Election in 2005.
> (b) Draw a pie chart to display your findings.
> (c) Compare your pie chart to the one you drew in question 2.

Calculating the angles

Twenty students were asked on which day they would help paint the scenery for the school play. The replies were: Monday 5, Tuesday 4, Wednesday 8 and Thursday 3. Here is the data shown on a pie chart.

The circle represents all 20 students and each section represents one of the days.

Separating the sections shows that to fit together again the shaded angles must add up to 360°: the total sum of the angles at the centre of the circle.

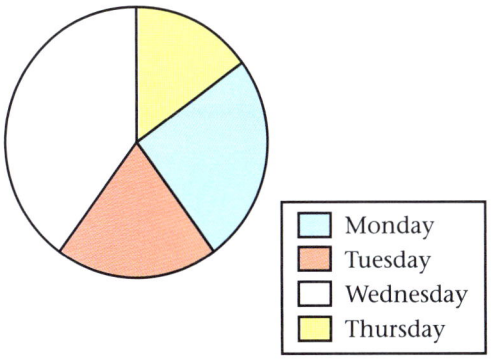

- Monday
- Tuesday
- Wednesday
- Thursday

The angles at the centre of a pie chart add up to 360°.

Here is how to calculate the angles of each sector:

20 students are represented by 360°

1 student is represented by $\frac{360}{20} = 18°$

Monday: 5 students so the angle is $5 \times 18° = 90°$
Tuesday: 4 students so the angle is $4 \times 18° = 72°$
Wednesday: 8 students so the angle is $8 \times 18° = 144°$
Thursday: 3 students so the angle is $3 \times 18° = 54°$

Check: 20 students so the angle is $20 \times 18° = 360°$

Another way of calculating the angles is to find what fraction of 360° the students represent:

Monday: $\frac{5}{20} \times 360° = 90°$

Tuesday: $\frac{4}{20} \times 360° = 72°$

Wednesday: $\frac{8}{20} \times 360° = 144°$

Thursday: $\frac{3}{20} \times 360° = 54°$

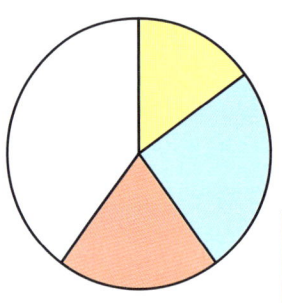

Interpreting pie charts

Example 13

This pie chart shows the proportions of gold, silver and bronze medals won by Great Britain in the Olympic Games in Athens in 2004.

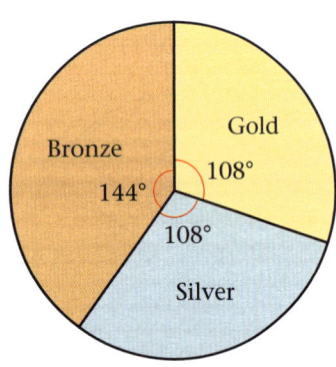

The total number of medals won by the UK was 30.
Find the numbers of gold, silver and bronze medals.

Method 1
30 medals are represented by 360°

1 medal is represented by $\frac{360°}{30} = 12°$

Gold: The angle is 108° so the number of medals is $\frac{108°}{12°} = 9$ medals

Silver: The angle is 108° so the number of medals is $\frac{108°}{12°} = 9$ medals

Bronze: The angle is 144° so the number of medals is $\frac{144°}{12°} = 12$ medals

Method 2
Find what fraction of the 30 medals each angle represents.

Gold:
$\frac{108°}{360°} \times 30 = 9$ medals

Silver:
$\frac{108°}{360°} \times 30 = 9$ medals

Bronze:
$\frac{144°}{360°} \times 30 = 12$ medals

Worked examination question

720 students were asked how they travelled to school.

The pie chart shows the results of this survey.

Work out

(a) how many of the students travelled to school by bus

(b) how many students walked to school.

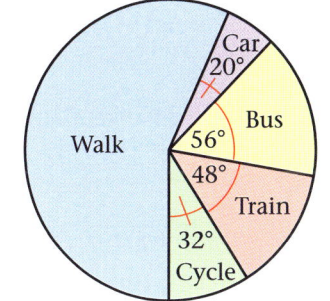

(a) **Method 1**

360° represents 720 students

1° represents $\frac{720}{360} = 2$ students

The angle of the bus sector of the pie chart is 56°, so the number of students is:

$56 \times 2 = 112$

Method 2

The bus sector is 56° and the whole pie chart is 360°,

so the fraction travelling by bus is $\frac{56}{360}$

There are 720 students so the number of students travelling by bus is

$\frac{56}{360} \times 720 = 112$

(b) First, find the angle of the 'walk' sector:
360 − (20 + 56 + 48 + 32) = 360 − 156
= 204°

Either each 1° represents 2 students   **or** $\frac{204}{360} \times 720 = 408$ students

204 × 2 = 408 students

Exercise 20H

1 In a survey 300 people were asked 'Do you believe in God?' The results are summarised in the pie chart.

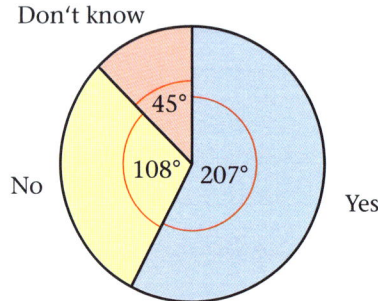

Use the information in the pie chart to work out the number of people who said 'No'.

2 The pie chart gives information about the medals won by Great Britain in the Olympic Games at Seoul in 1988.

Copy and complete the table.

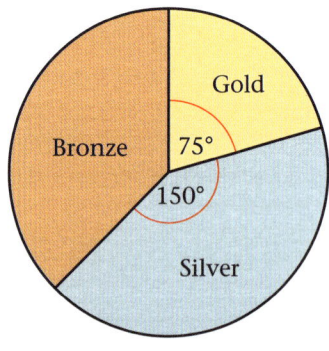

	Degrees	Number of medals
Gold	75°	
Silver	150°	
Bronze		9
Total	360°	24

3 Thirty students were asked to name their favourite ice cream. The results are shown in this pie chart.

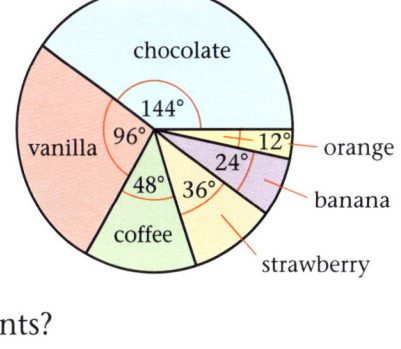

(a) What does the whole circle represent?
(b) Which ice cream does the largest sector represent?
(c) What does the smallest sector represent?
(d) Use the given angles to calculate the number of students who liked strawberry ice cream.
(e) How could you select a randon sample of 30 students?

4 (a) Kasha takes home £240 per week. He allocates his money like this:

Rent £60   Travel £18   Clothes £28
Food £80   Savings £40   Spare £14

Draw a pie chart to show how he allocates his money.

(b) Kasha has a £60 rise. He now allocates his money as shown in the pie chart.
  (i) Calculate how much he now spends on rent, travel, clothes, food, savings and how much he has spare.
  (ii) Which items have not changed?

5 The numbers of pens and pencils in five students pencil cases are shown in the table.

Name	Number	Angle needed
Gwyneth	3	45°
Peter	8	
Wes	4	
Mario	2	
Nesta	7	

(a) Copy and complete the table by calculating the angles needed to draw a pie chart.
(b) Draw the pie chart.

6 The table shows the numbers and types of tickets sold at a cinema box office.

Type of ticket	Standard	Student	Senior
Number sold	38	24	10

Draw a pie chart to illustrate this data.

Mixed exercise 20

1. A rugby team played 10 games.
   Here are the numbers of points the team scored.

   12 22 14 11 7 18 22 14 36 14

   (a) Write down the mode.
   (b) Work out the range.
   (c) Work out the mean.
   (d) Work out the median.

2. Here are the times, in minutes, to do the washing up:

   6 11 16 13 8 9 21 36 25 16
   21 34 16 26 10 9 10 20 17 11

   (a) Draw a stem and leaf diagram to show these times.
   (b) Work out the median.
   (c) Calculate the mean.

3. Jan measures the heights, in millimetres, of 20 plants in her greenhouse. Here are her results:

   178 189 147 147 166
   167 153 171 164 158
   189 166 165 155 152
   147 158 148 151 172

   (a) Copy and complete the stem and leaf diagram to show this information.

   (b) Work out the median. [E]

4 A fire service put out 90 fires last year.
The table shows information about the months when the fires were put out.
Sam is going to draw a pie chart to show this information.

(a) Complete the table to show the sizes of the angles Sam needs to draw the pie chart.

Months	Number of fires put out	Angle
January to March	15	
April to June	26	
July to September	35	
October to December	14	

(b) Draw an accurate pie chart to show this information.

5 40 passengers at Gatwick Airport were asked which country they were flying to. Here is a frequency table which shows that information:

Country	Number of passengers
USA	14
France	10
Spain	11
Greece	5

Draw an accurate pie chart to show this information. [E]

6 The table shows the maximum and minimum temperatures, in degrees Celsius, for one day last year.

City	Maximum	Minimum
Vienna	12	1
Rome	13	4
Madrid	19	3
Cape Town	35	16
Melbourne	26	14

(a) Calculate the range in each city.
(b) List the cities in order, highest range first.
(c) Which city has the smallest range?

Chapter 20 Presenting and analysing data 1

7 Sita spent £90 as in the table.

(a) Calculate the angle of each sector.

(b) Draw a pie chart to show her spending.

Items	Amount spent	Angle of sector
Bus fares	£12	
Going out	£25	
Clothes	£30	
Records	£15	
Other	£8	
Total spending	£90	**Total angles 360°**

[E]

Summary of key points

1 The **mode** of a set of data is the value which occurs most often.

2 The **median** is the middle value when the data is arranged in order of size.

3 The **mean** of a set of data is the sum of the values divided by the number of values:

$$\text{mean} = \frac{\text{sum of values}}{\text{number of values}}$$

4 The **range** of a set of data is the difference between the highest value and the lowest value:

range = highest value − lowest value

5 A **stem and leaf diagram** shows the shape of the distribution and keeps all the data values.

Always include a **key** with a stem and leaf diagram to show how the stem and leaf are combined.

6 A **pie chart** is a good way of displaying data when you want to show how something is shared or divided.

7 The angles at the centre of a pie chart add up to 360°.

21 Formulae and inequalities

You learned about equations in Chapter 11 (in Book 1). This chapter shows you how to use word and algebraic formulae and equations to help solve problems.

21.1 Using word formulae

Example 1

David works in a factory. He is paid by the hour and is given an extra bonus at the end of the week. His pay can be calculated using this **word formula**:

pay = rate of pay × hours worked + bonus

Work out his pay when he works for 40 hours at a rate of pay of £7 an hour and earns a bonus of £20.

pay = £7 × 40 + £20
    = £280 + £20 = £300

He earns £300.

Exercise 21A

1. To work out his pay Keith uses the word formula:

   pay = rate of pay × hours worked + bonus

   (a) Work out his pay when he works for 30 hours at a rate of pay of £6 an hour and earns a bonus of £30.
   (b) Work out his pay when he works for 35 hours at a rate of pay of £5.50 an hour and earns a bonus of £15.

2. To work out the distance around her bicycle wheel Davina uses the formula:

   distance = 3 × diameter

   (a) Work out the distance around the wheel if the diameter is 60 cm.
   (b) Work out the distance around the wheel if the diameter is 50 cm.

Chapter 21 Formulae and inequalities

3 Use the formula

cost of pens = cost of one pen × number of pens

to work out the cost of 17 pens if one pen costs 25p.

Writing word formulae

Sometimes you will need to write a word formula from information you are given.

Example 2

Jill worked for 30 hours at a rate of pay of £8 an hour. How much should she get paid?

You can write a word formula to find her pay for any number of hours she works:

pay = hours worked × rate of pay
    = 30 × £8
    = £240

Example 3

Rashmi buys 24 pens at 65 pence each.
Work out the total cost of the pens.

Here is a suitable word formula:

cost = number of pens × cost of one pen
     = 24 × 65p
     = 1560p = £15.60

A **word formula** uses words to represent a relationship between quantities.

Exercise 21B

For each of the following questions, first write down a word formula, then use it to help you find the answers.

1 Daniel works for 30 hours at a rate of pay of £9 an hour. How much should he get paid?

2 Helen works for 20 hours at a rate of pay of £7.50 an hour. How much should she get paid?

21.1 Using word formulae

3 Abdul works for 30 hours at a rate of pay of £5.75 an hour. How much should he get paid?

4 Susan buys 12 pens at £1.20 each. Work out the total cost of the pens.

5 Roger buys 24 pens at 50p each. Work out the total cost of the pens.

6 Rachel buys 12 books at 28p each. Work out the total cost of the books.

7 Keith buys 15 stamps at 30p each. Work out the total cost of the stamps.

8 Andy buys 20 stamps at 42p each. Work out the total cost of the stamps.

9 Karen sells 50 cakes at 40p each. How much money does she collect?

10 Louise sells 45 loaves of bread at 92p each. How much money does she collect?

11 Mark adds together his age and the age of his sister Pauline. He gets a total of 28. If Mark is 16 how old is Pauline?

12 James loses some £1 coins from his money bag. He had £12 to start with and now only has £7. How many coins has he lost?

13 A chocolate bar machine holds 48 bars of chocolate. After 23 are sold how many are left?

14 At Anne's birthday party there were 48 cans of drink. Everybody at the party had 4 cans. How many people were at the party?

15 Naomi shared a bag of sweets equally between herself and her 6 friends. There were 56 sweets in the bag. How many sweets did the 7 people have each?

16 Evan and his 9 friends were playing football and smashed a window. The cost of repairing the window was £126. The 10 friends decided to split the cost equally between them. How much did they each have to pay?

21.2 Writing algebraic formulae

It is usual in algebra to write a word formula using letters.

For example:
Area of a rectangle = $l \times w$
$A = lw$

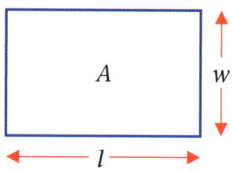

> **Remember:**
> $2a$ means 'double a' or '$2 \times a$' or '2 multiplied by a'
> $ab = a \times b$ means 'a multiplied by b'
> $a + b$ means 'a added to b'

Example 4

Write the word formula used in Example 2 as an algebraic formula.

   pay = hours worked × rate of pay

Use the letters P for pay, H for hours worked, and R for rate of pay. The algebraic formula is:

   $P = H \times R$ or $P = HR$

Example 5

Write the word formula used in Example 3 as an algebraic formula.

   cost = number of pens × cost of one pen

Use the letters C for cost, N for number of pens, and P for cost of one pen. The algebraic formula is:

   $C = N \times P$ or $C = NP$

An **algebraic formula** uses letters to repressent a relationship between quantities.

Exercise 21C

Write an algebraic formula for questions **10–16** in Exercise 21B. Remember to explain what each letter stands for.

21.3 Using algebraic formulae

Section 21.2 showed you how to write **algebraic formulae**. You also need to know how to use algebraic formulae, by substituting number values for the letters.

> In algebra, 'substitute' means 'replace a letter with a number value'.

The next two exercises provide practice in substituting numbers into algebraic expressions.

21.3 Using algebraic formulae

Example 6

Let $a = 3$, $b = 2$ and $c = 5$

Work out the value of (a) $a + b$ (b) ab (c) $3c - 2a$

(a) $a + b = 3 + 2 = 5$
(b) $ab = a \times b = 3 \times 2 = 6$
(c) $3c - 2a = 3 \times c - 2 \times a$
$= 3 \times 5 - 2 \times 3$
$= 15 - 6 = 9$

Exercise 21D

In this exercise $a = 3$, $b = 2$, $c = 5$ and $d = 0$
Work out the value of these expressions.

1. $a + c$
2. $b + c$
3. $a + b + c$
4. $2a$
5. $3c$
6. $5d$
7. ac
8. ad
9. $5b + 2a$
10. $4c - 2b$
11. $5a + 2b$
12. $2a + 3b + 4c$
13. $c - a$
14. $c - 2d$
15. $ab - c$
16. $4b + 2d$
17. $3c - 2b$
18. $5a - 3c$
19. $ac - ab$
20. abc
21. $2c - ad$

Exercise 21E

In this exercise $p = 2$, $q = 4$, $r = 3$ and $s = 0$
Work out the value of these expressions.

1. $3p$
2. $4q$
3. $5r$
4. $10s$
5. $p + q$
6. $q + r$
7. $r + s$
8. $p + q + r$
9. $2p + 4q$
10. $3s + 3p$
11. $5r - 2q$
12. $4r - 3q$
13. pq
14. qr
15. rs
16. pqr
17. $5q - 8p$
18. $3p - 2r + 3pq$
19. $4p - 2s$
20. $3q - pr$
21. $2pq + 3qr - 2pqr$

Using numbers in algebraic formulae

Example 7

Write
(a) a word formula
(b) an algebraic formula

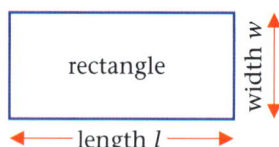

for the perimeter of a rectangle.

(c) Use your formula to find the perimeter of a rectangle with length 10 and width 2.

Remember: Perimeter is the distance around the boundary of a shape.

(a) perimeter = 2 × length + 2 × width

(b) $P = 2l + 2w$ where P is the perimeter, l is length and w is width

(c) When $l = 12$ and $w = 10$:
$P = 2 × 12 + 2 × 10 = 24 + 20 = 44$

Exercise 21F

1 The formula for the perimeter of an equilateral triangle is $P = 3l$. Work out the value of P when
(a) $l = 5$
(b) $l = 7$
(c) $l = 4$
(d) $l = 12.4$

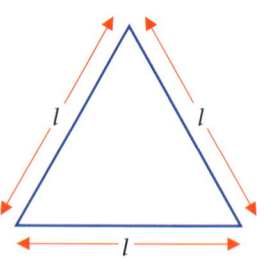

2 The formula for the area of a rectangle is $A = lw$. Find the value of A when
(a) $l = 6$ and $w = 4$
(b) $l = 5$ and $w = 3$
(c) $l = 10$ and $w = 5.6$
(d) $l = 7.5$ and $w = 3.4$

3 James uses the formula $d = st$ to work out the distance travelled, where the time taken is t and the speed is s. Find the value of d when
(a) $s = 40$ and $t = 4$
(b) $s = 50$ and $t = 2.5$
(c) $s = 70$ and $t = 3$
(d) $s = 15.8$ and $t = 5$

4 Ayesha uses the formula $v = u + at$ to work out velocity. Find the value of v when
  (a) $u = 3$, $a = 2$ and $t = 5$
  (b) $u = 5$, $a = 10$ and $t = 3$
  (c) $u = 0$, $a = 10$ and $t = 6$
  (d) $u = 2.5$, $a = 3$ and $t = 1.5$

> Remember BIDMAS. You must multiply a by t first and then add u.

5 Alex uses the formula $P = rh + b$ to work out his pay, where r is his rate of pay per hour, h is the number of hours worked, and b is his bonus.
Work out the value of P when
  (a) $r = 4$, $h = 12$ and $b = 5$
  (b) $r = 5$, $h = 40$ and $b = 10$
  (c) $r = 1.5$, $h = 4$ and $b = 1$
  (d) $r = 2.5$, $h = 6$ and $b = 2.5$

21.4 Using negative numbers

Sometimes you will need to substitute negative numbers into algebraic formulae.

The next four exercises provide practice in using negative numbers in expressions.

Exercise 21G

Work out these additions and subtractions.

1 $2 - 5$
2 $-2 + 4$
3 $-2 - 4$
4 $3 + (-7)$
5 $-3 + 5$
6 $-5 - 3$
7 $2 - (-3)$
8 $6 - (-5)$
9 $10 + (-10)$
10 $-1 - 8$
11 $1 - (-7)$
12 $-4 - (-2)$

> Remember:
> Two like signs next to each other are replaced by a +
> Two unlike signs next to each other are replaced by a −
> So
> + + = +
> + − = −
> − + = −
> − − = +

Example 8

Find (a) $a - b$ (b) $c + b$ (c) $a + c$ (d) $a - c$
when $a = 4$, $b = 6$ and $c = -3$

(a) $a - b = 4 - 6 = -2$
(b) $c + b = -3 + 6 = 3$
(c) $a + c = 4 + (-3) = 4 - 3 = 1$
(d) $a - c = 4 - (-3) = 4 + 3 = 7$

Exercise 21H

In this exercise let $a = 3$, $b = -2$, $c = -5$ and $d = 0$
Work out the value of these expressions.

1. $a + b$
2. $a + c$
3. $b + c$
4. $c + d$
5. $a - b$
6. $c - a$
7. $b - c$
8. $c - d$
9. $b - a$
10. $a - c$
11. $c - b$
12. $d - c$
13. $a + b + c$
14. $a + b - c$
15. $a + b - d$
16. $d - a$
17. $a - b + c$
18. $a - b - c$
19. $d - a + b$
20. $d - b + a - c$
21. $c - b - a$

Exercise 21I

Work out these multiplications.

1. 4×-3
2. -2×6
3. 10×-1
4. -2×-2
5. 3×-7
6. -8×4
7. -6×-5
8. -3×-9

Remember:
When you multiply two numbers:

+	×	+	=	+
+	×	−	=	−
−	×	+	=	−
−	×	−	=	+

Example 9

If $a = -5$, $b = 3$ and $c = -3$, find (a) $2a$ (b) ab (c) ac

(a) $2a = 2 \times a = 2 \times -5 = -10$
(b) $ab = a \times b = -5 \times 3 = -15$
(c) $ac = a \times c = -5 \times -3 = 15$

Exercise 21J

Let $a = -3$, $b = 2$, $c = -5$ and $d = 0$
Work out the value of these expressions.

1. $a + c$
2. $b + c$
3. $a + b + c$
4. $2a$
5. $3c$
6. $5d$
7. ac
8. ad
9. $5b + 2a$
10. $4c - 2b$
11. $5a + 2b$
12. $2a + 3b + 4c$
13. $c - a$
14. $c - 2d$
15. $ab - c$
16. $4b + 2d$
17. $3c - 2b$
18. $5a - 3c$
19. $ac - ab$
20. $abc - 2ad$
21. $3c - 2ab + 4b$

Negative numbers in algebraic formulae

Example 10

The formula $v = u + at$ is used in maths and science to work out velocities.

Work out the value of v when $u = 5$, $a = -2$ and $t = 10$.

$v = u + at$
$v = 5 + -2 \times 10$
$v = 5 + -20$
$v = -15$

Exercise 21K

1. Using the formula $v = u + at$, find the value of v when
   (a) $u = 3$, $a = -2$, $t = 5$
   (b) $u = -5$, $a = 10$, $t = 3$
   (c) $u = 0$, $a = -10$, $t = 6$
   (d) $u = -2.5$, $a = -3$, $t = 1.5$

2. Using the formula $P = a(b - c)$, find the value of P when
   (a) $a = 2$, $b = 3$, $c = 3$
   (b) $a = 2$, $b = 3$, $c = -3$
   (c) $a = 3$, $b = -2$, $c = 3$
   (d) $a = 3$, $b = -2$, $c = -3$

3. Using the formula $r = st + (t - s)$, find the value of r when
   (a) $s = 2$, $t = -3$
   (b) $s = 3$, $t = -2$
   (c) $s = -2$, $t = 3$
   (d) $s = -2$, $t = -3$
   (e) $s = 4$, $t = 2$
   (f) $s = 5$, $t = -4$

21.5 Substituting into more complicated formulae

Sometimes you have to use formulae containing powers.

Example 11

Use the formula $s = \frac{1}{2}at^2$ to find s when $t = 4$ and $a = 10$.

$s = \frac{1}{2} \times 10 \times 4^2$
$s = \frac{1}{2} \times 10 \times 16$
$s = 5 \times 16 = 80$

Remember BIDMAS.
Work out Indices before Multiplication.

Chapter 21 Formulae and inequalities

Exercise 21L

1. The formula for working out how far a ball has fallen when dropped off a cliff is:

   $s = 5t^2$

   Find the value of s when t is:
   (a) 1 (b) 2 (c) 5 (d) 10 (e) 3.5

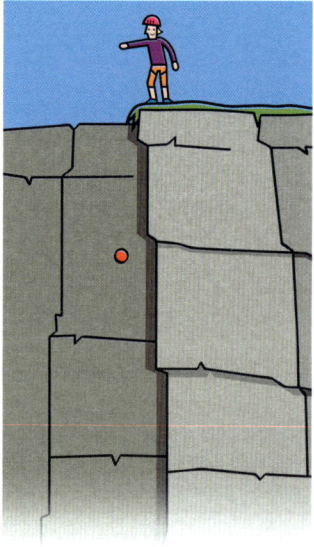

2. Copy this table of values.

x	−3	−2	−1	0	1	2	3
$y = 3x^2 + 4$							

   Complete the table by substituting the values of x into the formula to find the values of y.

3. If $a = 2$, $b = 8$ and $c = -4$ work out the value of:
   (a) $a^2 + b$
   (b) $c^2 - b$
   (c) $b^3 - a^2$
   (d) $b^2 - c^2$
   (e) $b - (a^2 + c)$
   (f) $c^2 + (a - c^2)$
   (g) $2(a + b)^2$
   (h) $c(a + b)^3$
   (i) $(a + b)^2 + (a + c)^2$
   (j) $2(b + c)^2 - 3(b - c)^2$

4. The speed of a car is given by the formula:

   $v = \sqrt{(u^2 + 2as)}$

   By substituting in values, find v when
   (a) $u = 10$, $a = 2$, $s = 5$
   (b) $u = 5$, $a = 5$, $s = 10$
   (c) $u = 5$, $a = 0$, $s = 10$
   (d) $u = -5$, $a = 2$, $s = 5$
   (e) $u = -10$, $a = -5$, $s = 10$
   (f) $u = 0$, $a = 10$, $s = 10$

More substitution

Example 12

Evaluate the expression $\dfrac{2a + b}{c}$ when $a = 3$, $b = 4$ and $c = 2$.

$2a = 2 \times 3 = 6$

so $2a + b = 6 + 4 = 10$

and $\dfrac{2a + b}{c} = \dfrac{10}{2} = 5$

> Evaluate means 'Find the value of'.

21.5 Substituting into more complicated formulae

Exercise 21M

Work out the value of these algebraic expressions using the values given.

1. (a) $4a + 1$ if $a = 3$
   (b) $3b + c$ if $b = 5$, $c = 2$
   (c) $2f - g$ if $f = 1.5$, $g = 4$
   (d) $hg - 2$ if $h = 1.5$, $g = 3$
   (e) $10 + 3x$ if $x = -2$
   (f) $2x - 3y$ if $x = 4$, $y = -2$
   (g) $2x + 3$ if $x = \frac{1}{5}$
   (h) $3ab$ if $a = \frac{1}{4}$, $b = 2$

2. (a) $2(a + 3)$ if $a = 5$
   (b) $3(s - 2)$ if $s = 7$
   (c) $4(p + q)$ if $p = 5$, $q = 3$
   (d) $r(8 - s)$ if $r = 3$, $s = 5$
   (e) $3(b + 7)$ if $b = -2$
   (f) $2(3 - c)$ if $c = -4$

   Remember BIDMAS. Brackets first.

3. (a) $5(a + b)$ if $a = 3$, $b = 4$
   (b) $4(x + y)$ if $x = 5$, $y = -3$
   (c) $\frac{a}{4} + 3$ if $a = 12$
   (d) $\frac{a}{b} + 5$ if $a = 20$, $b = 4$
   (e) $\frac{m - 4}{2}$ if $m = 12$
   (f) $\frac{7 - x}{y}$ if $x = -3$, $y = -2$

4. (a) $\frac{m + n}{r}$ if $m = 8$, $n = 7$, $r = 5$
   (b) $\frac{4q + r}{6}$ if $q = 5$, $r = 4$
   (c) $\frac{3s - r}{t}$ if $s = 8$, $r = 6$, $t = 3$
   (d) $\frac{3s}{4} - r$ if $s = 8$, $r = 3$
   (e) $x - \frac{3y}{6}$ if $x = 3$, $y = -4$

Activity – Number patterns

(a) (i) Copy and complete this table by putting values for r and t into the algebraic expression $2r + t$.
   (ii) Look for number patterns in the table.
   (iii) Try to explain the number patterns.
   (iv) Do the number patterns still hold for negative values of r and t?

$2r + t$	0	1	2	3	4
r = 0	0	1	2	3	4
1	2	3	4	5	6
2	4	5	6		
3	6	7			
4					

(columns headed by t)

(b) Repeat part (a) for other algebraic expressions involving two letters.
For example, use
r + 2t, 2r + 3t, r + t, 2(r + t), rt + 1.

(c) Find the algebraic expression used to make the table on the right.

(d) Set some problems like part (c) for your friends.

		t				
?		0	1	2	3	4
	0	0	1	2	3	4
	1	4	5	6	7	8
r	2	8	9	10	11	12
	3	12	13	14	15	16
	4					

21.6 Using algebraic equations

You can solve some problems using **algebraic equations**. Though they can look similar, an equation is different from a formula:

- **Formulae** can be used to calculate a result. For example:

    pay = rate of pay × hours worked

    You could put **any** values into these parts of the formula and get a result for the amount of pay.

- **Equations** may be true for one value or several values, but are not generally true for any value. For example:

    $3x = 6$

    This equation is **only** true when $x = 2$.
    $x = 2$ is called a **solution** of the equation.

An **algebraic equation** can be solved to find an unknown quantity.

Example 13

The perimeter of this rectangle is 30 cm.
The length is x cm and the width is 4 cm.

Work out the value of the length.

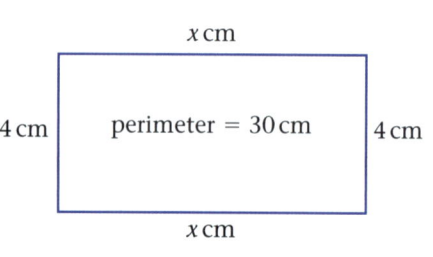

$x + x + 4 + 4 = 30$
$2x + 8 = 30$
$2x + 8 - 8 = 30 - 8$ — Subtract 8 from each side.
$2x = 22$
$x = 11$ — Divide each side by 2.

The length x is 11 cm.

Example 14

Suzanne thought of a number, multiplied it by 4 and then subtracted 3. The answer was 13.
What was the number she thought of?

$4 \times n - 3 = 13$ — n represents the number.
$4n - 3 = 13$
$4n - 3 + 3 = 13 + 3$ — Add 3 to each side.
$4n = 16$
$n = 4$ — Divide each side by 4.

Exercise 21N

1 Use the information in these diagrams to find the values of the letters.

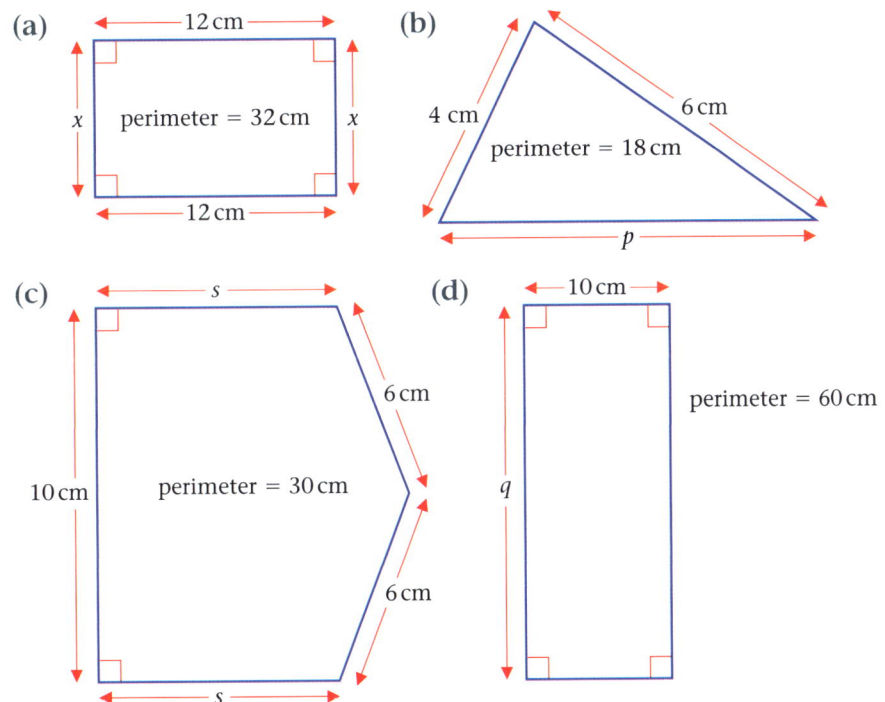

2 The perimeter of this isosceles triangle is 30 cm. Work out the lengths of the sides marked y.

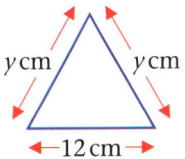

3 Gail thought of a number. She multiplied it by 5 and then added 4. The answer was 14. What number did she first think of?

4 Andrew thought of a number. He multiplied it by 6 and then subtracted 15. The answer was 27. What number did Andrew first think of?

5 Darren started a new book and read x pages of the book for each of the first four days. On the fifth day he read 12 pages and finished the book. The book had 100 pages. Work out the value of x.

6 Julia thought of a number, subtracted 5 from it and then multiplied the answer by 6 to get a final answer of 30. What number did Julia first think of?

7 There were 25 chocolates in a box. Four friends had an equal number of chocolates and this left 9 chocolates in the box.
How many chocolates did each of the friends have?

8 Trevor thought of a number, added 7 to it and then multiplied the answer by 5. This gave an answer of 55. What number did Trevor first think of?

9 Sigourney thought of a number, subtracted 12 from it and then divided her answer by 3 to get a final answer of 4. What number did Sigourney first think of?

More algebraic equations

Example 15

Use the diagram to write down an equation in terms of x. Solve your equation.

$$x + x - 10 + 3x = 180$$
$$5x - 10 = 180$$
$$5x = 190$$
$$x = 38$$
$$x = 38°$$

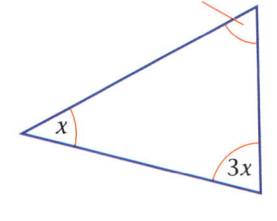

Remember:
The angles of a triangle add up to 180°.

Exercise 21O

In each question
(a) use the diagram to write down an equation in terms of x
(b) solve your equation.

1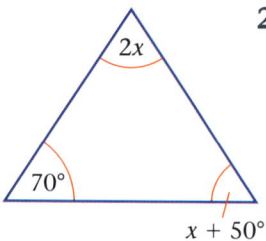

2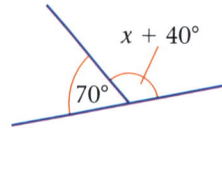

3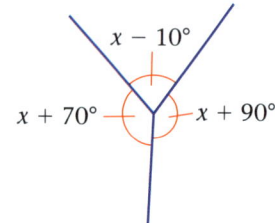

4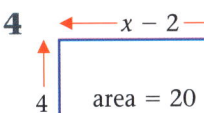

5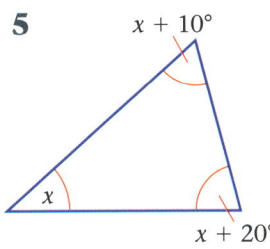

6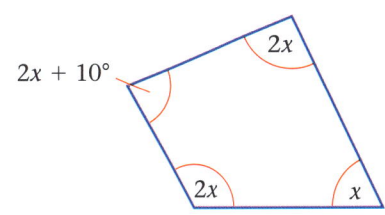

7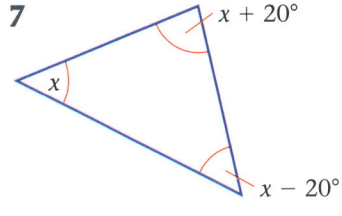

8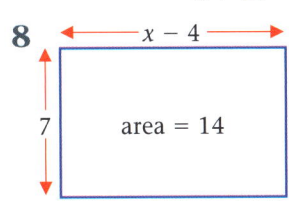

9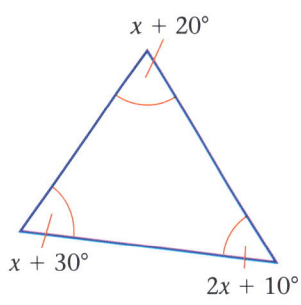

10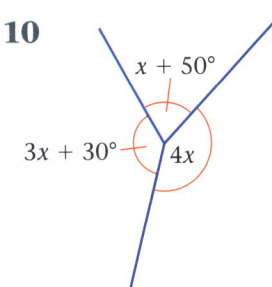

11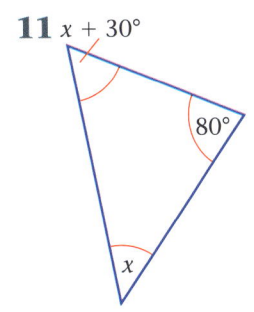

12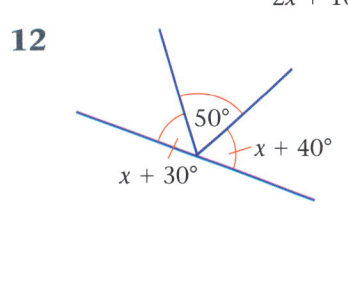

21.7 Inequalities

There are lots of apples, but there are only a few bananas. If a is the number of apples and b is the number of bananas, then a is greater than b. You can write this as $a > b$.

The smaller end of the symbol always points towards the smaller number.

The larger end points towards the larger number.

$>$ means **greater than** $<$ means **less than**
$\geq$ means **greater than or equal to** $\leq$ means **less than or equal to**

Example 16

Put the correct sign between each pair of numbers to make a true statement.
(a) 6, 7
(b) 8, 5

(a) 6 is less than 7
   $6 < 7$

(b) 8 is greater than 5
   $8 > 5$

Chapter 21 Formulae and inequalities

Example 17

Write down the values of x that are integers and satisfy these inequalities:

(a) $2 < x < 7$ (b) $-2 < x \leqslant 3$

(a) $2 < x$ means the same as $x > 2$ so the numbers must be greater than 2:
3, 4, 5, 6, 7, 8 ...
$x < 7$ so the numbers must stop before 7.
The answer is 3, 4, 5, 6.

(b) $x > -2$ so the numbers must be greater than -2:
$-1, 0, 1, 2, 3, 4, 5...$
$x \leqslant 3$ so the numbers must stop at 3.
The answer is $-1, 0, 1, 2, 3$.

> Integers are the negative and positive whole numbers including zero.

> A number **satisfies** an inequality if it makes that inequality true.
> $x = 3$ **satisfies** the inequality $x < 7$ because $3 < 7$.

Exercise 21P

1 Put the correct sign between each pair of numbers to make a true statement.

(a) 4, 6   (b) 5, 2   (c) 12, 8   (d) 6, 6
(e) 15, 8   (f) 3, 24   (g) 10, 3   (h) 0, 0.1
(i) 6, 0.7   (j) 4.5, 4.5   (k) 0.2, 0.5   (l) 4.8, 4.79

2 Write down whether each statement is true or false. If it is false, write down the pair of numbers with the correct sign.

(a) $6 > 4$ (b) $2 > 6$ (c) $6 > 6$ (d) $6 > 8$
(e) $6 < 5$ (f) $8 = 14$ (g) $7 < 6.99$ (h) $6 > 6.01$
(i) $7 < 0$ (j) $4 < 4$ (k) $6 = 4$ (l) $6 > 0.84$

3 Write down the values of x that are whole numbers and satisfy these inequalities:

(a) $4 < x < 6$ (b) $3 < x < 8$
(c) $0 \leqslant x < 4$ (d) $3 < x < 6$
(e) $1 < x \leqslant 4$ (f) $2 < x < 6$
(g) $4 \leqslant x < 7$ (h) $-2 \leqslant x < 4$
(i) $-1 < x < 5$ (j) $-2 < x \leqslant 6$
(k) $-3 \leqslant x < 3$ (l) $-4 \leqslant x \leqslant 2$
(m) $0 < x < 5$ (n) $-1 < x \leqslant 4$
(o) $-5 \leqslant x < 0$ (p) $-3 \leqslant x \leqslant 3$

Inequalities on a number line

You can show inequalities on a number line.

Example 18

Draw a number line from 0 to 10. Show the inequality

$x > 4$

x is greater than 4. You shade all the numbers to the right of 4:

Draw an empty circle at 4 since the number 4 is *not* included.

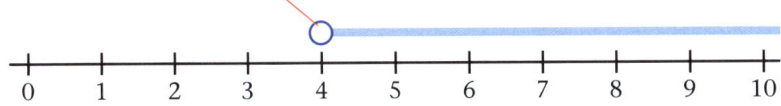

Example 19

Draw a number line from 0 to 10. Show the inequality

$3 \leqslant x < 8$

x is greater than or equal to 3 and less than 8. You shade in the numbers between 3 and 8:

Draw a solid circle at 3 since the number 3 *is* included ($x \geqslant 3$).

Draw an empty circle at 8 since the number 8 is *not* included.

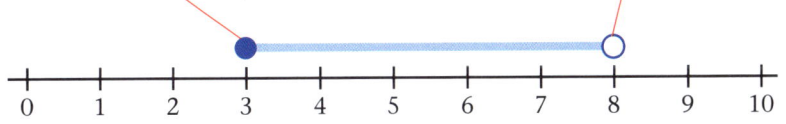

Example 20

Draw a number line from −5 to 5. Show the inequality

$-3 < x \leqslant 4$

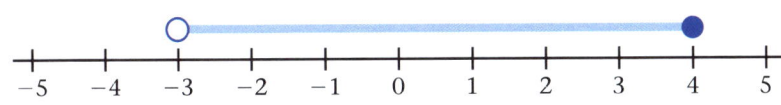

Exercise 21Q

1 Draw six number lines from 0 to 10.
   Show these inequalities:
   (a) $x > 6$
   (b) $x > 5$
   (c) $x < 4$
   (d) $x > 8$
   (e) $x < 6$
   (f) $x > 9$

Chapter 21 Formulae and inequalities

2 Draw ten number lines from 0 to 10.
Show these inequalities:
(a) $3 < x < 7$
(b) $5 < x < 8$
(c) $5 \leqslant x < 8$
(d) $7 < x \leqslant 9$
(e) $4 \leqslant x \leqslant 6$
(f) $2 < x \leqslant 8$
(g) $3 \leqslant x < 5$
(h) $4 < x < 7$
(i) $5 \leqslant x < 6$
(j) $2 < x \leqslant 5$

3 Draw ten number lines from −5 to 5.
Show these inequalities:
(a) $-3 \leqslant x < 4$
(b) $-2 < x < 5$
(c) $-1 < x \leqslant 3$
(d) $-4 \leqslant x \leqslant 0$
(e) $0 < x < 4$
(f) $-3 < x \leqslant 2$
(g) $-4 \leqslant x < 1$
(h) $0 \leqslant x \leqslant 3$
(i) $-5 \leqslant x < -2$
(j) $-2 \leqslant x < 1$

4 Write down the inequalities represented by the shading on these number lines:

(a)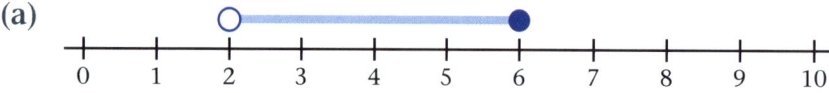

(b)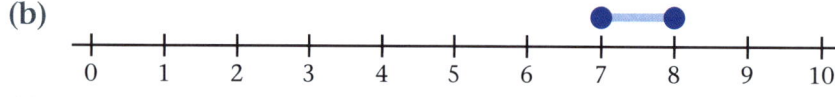

(c)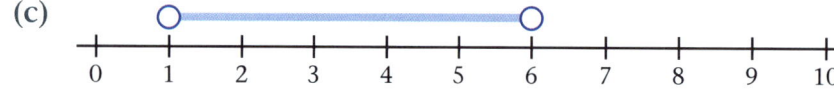

(d)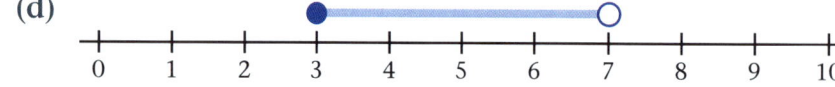

(e)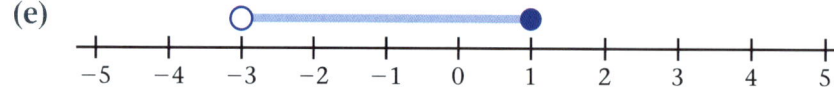

(f)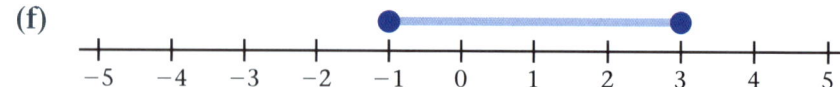

(g)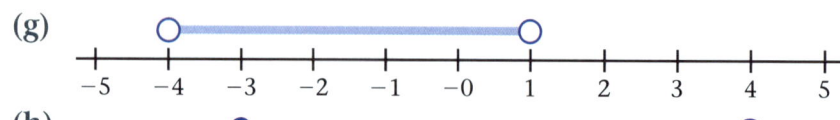

(h)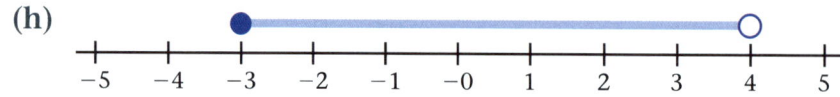

Mixed exercise 21

1 (a) Write in symbols the rule 'To find y, double x and add 1'.
(b) Use your rule from part **(a)** to calculate the value of x when $y = 9$. [E]

2 Here is the formula for working out the perimeter of a rectangle:

$P = 2(l + w)$

Use the formula to work out the value of P when $l = 6$ and $w = 4$. [E]

3 A quarterly gas bill is given by the formula

$C = S + nx$

where C is the total cost of the bill in pence
S is the standing charge in pence
n is the number of units used
x pence is the cost per unit.

Calculate the value of C when $S = 860$, $n = 152$ and $x = 7$.

4 Find the value of $x(x + y)$ when $x = -2$ and $y = 1$. [E]

5 If $a = 1$, $b = 2$ and $c = -3$, find the value of

(a) $\dfrac{c - ab}{c + ab}$ \qquad (b) $3(a + b)^2 - 2(b - c)^2$

6 To work out the cost of his mobile phone calls Derek uses this formula:

cost of calls = total time (minutes) × 10p

Work out, in pounds, the cost of a 25 minute call.

7 This word formula is used to work out the cost of placing an advertisement in a newspaper:

cost of advertisement = area (cm^2) × £15

Work out the cost of an advert which is 3 cm wide and 10 cm tall.

8 $a = 4$, $b = \frac{1}{4}$, $c = -3$

Work out

(a) $\dfrac{5a}{b} + 7$ \qquad (b) $\dfrac{6a + 2c}{3}$

(c) $3a - 6b + c$ \qquad (d) $a(a - 8b)$

9 Write down an expression in terms of n and g for the total cost, in pence, of n buns at 18 pence each and 5 bread rolls at g pence each. [E]

10 Choc bars cost 27 pence each.
Write down a formula for the cost, C pence, of n choc bars. [E]

11 The air temperature, $T\,°C$, outside an aircraft flying at a height of h feet is given by the formula $T = 26 - \dfrac{h}{500}$.

An aircraft is flying at a height of 27 000 feet.

(a) Use the formula to calculate the air temperature outside the aircraft.

The temperature outside an aircraft is $-52\,°C$.

(b) Calculate the height of the aircraft. [E]

12 Mary thought of a number and multiplied it by 5 and subtracted 4. The answer was 31. What is the number she thought of?

13 (a) Use each diagram to write down an equation in terms of x.

(i) 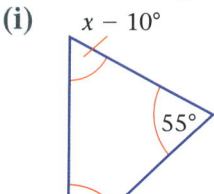 (ii)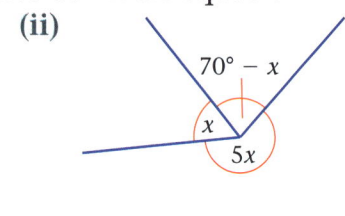

(b) Solve your equations from part (a).

14 Draw a number line from -6 to $+6$.

(a) Show in these inequalities:
   (i) $-3 < x \leq 5$ (ii) $-2 \leq x < 3$ (iii) $-5 < x < 0$

(b) List the integer values that satisfy each inequality.

15 Write down the inequalities represented by these number lines:

(a)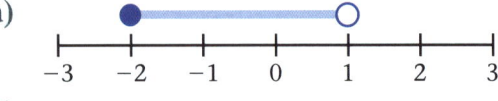

(b)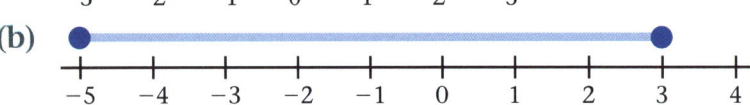

Summary of key points

1 A **word formula** uses words to represent a relationship between quantities.
   For example: pay = rate of pay × hours worked

2 An **algebraic formula** uses letters to represent a relationship between quantities.
   For example, the perimeter of a rectangle is related to its length l and width w by:
   $P = 2l + 2w$

3 An **algebraic equation** can be solved to find an unknown quantity.

4 $>$ means **greater than** $<$ means **less than**
   $\geq$ means **greater than or equal to** $\leq$ means **less than or equal to**

22 Transformations

Karen decided to rearrange the furniture in her bedroom.

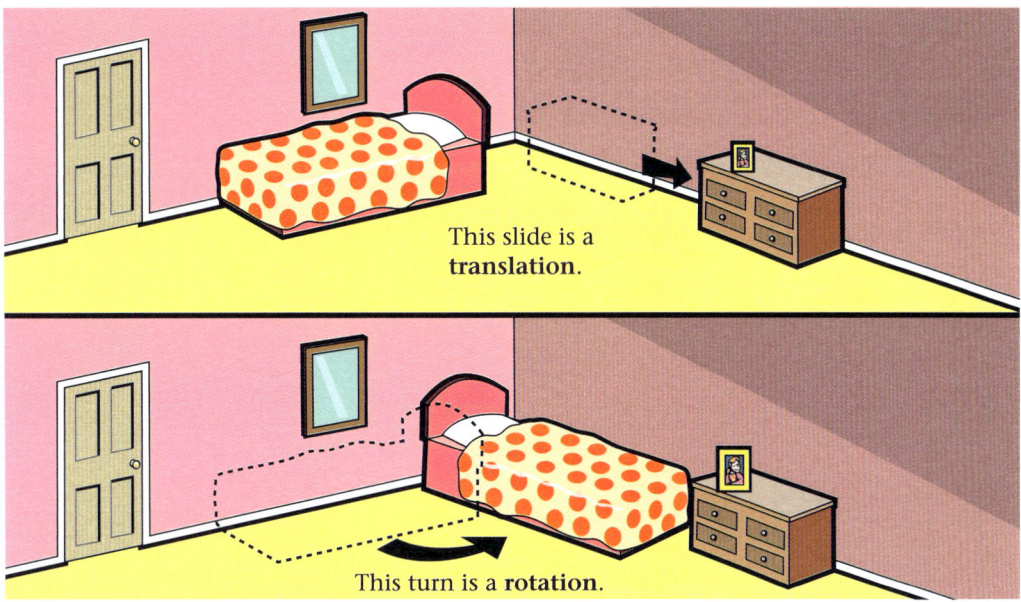

First she moved her storage unit further along the wall by sliding it.

This slide is a **translation**.

Then she turned her bed a quarter turn.

This turn is a **rotation**.

The mirror was now in a position where she could see her own **reflection** close up without the bed being in the way.

The photograph on the storage unit was rather small, so she had an **enlargement** made of it.

Reflections, rotations, translations and enlargements are all **transformations**. To help distinguish between the 'before' and 'after' positions of a shape they have special names: the starting shape is called the **object** and the finishing position of the shape is called the **image**.

22.1 Translation

The rook in these pictures has moved 4 squares forwards.

Chapter 22 Transformations

The knight has moved 2 squares forwards and 1 square to the right.

A sliding movement is called a **translation**.

Here are some examples:

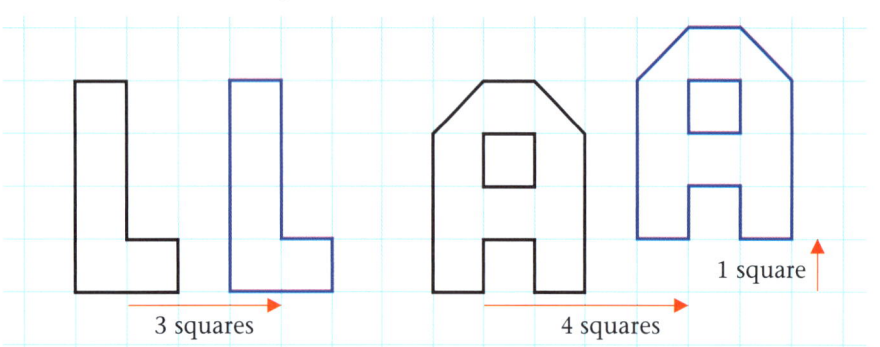

Object and image are congruent.

In a translation all the points of the shape move exactly the same amount.

Example 1

Draw the image of *ABCD* after a translation of 3 squares to the right and 1 square up.

The vertices are all going to be displaced 3 squares to the right and 1 square up.

Translate each vertex.   Join up the vertices.

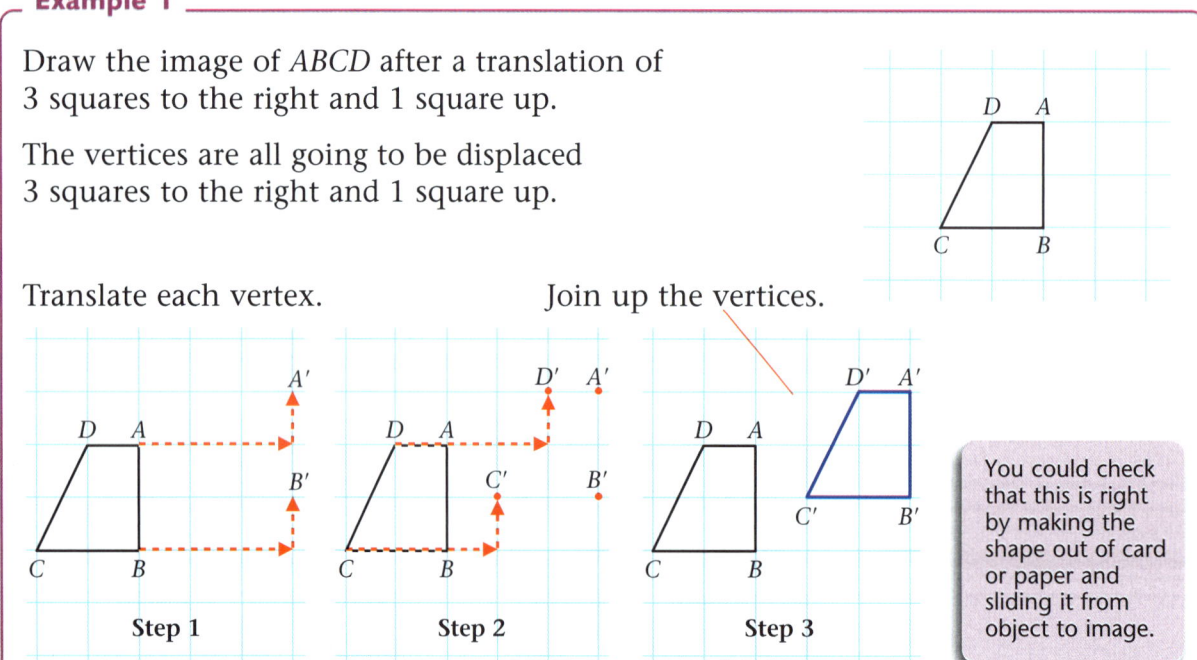

You could check that this is right by making the shape out of card or paper and sliding it from object to image.

Exercise 22A

1 Copy each shape onto squared paper and translate it by the amount shown.

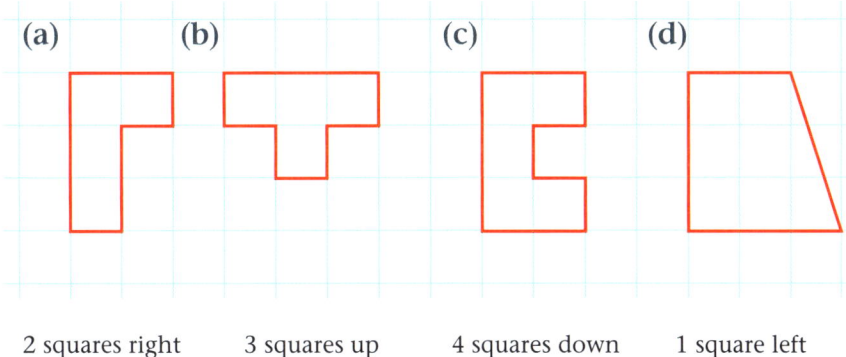

(a) 2 squares right   (b) 3 squares up   (c) 4 squares down   (d) 1 square left

2 Copy each shape onto squared paper and draw their images after translating by the amount shown.

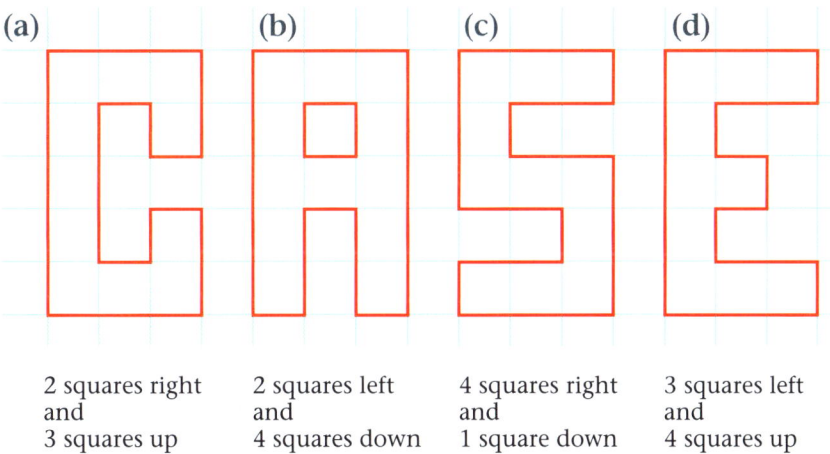

(a) 2 squares right and 3 squares up
(b) 2 squares left and 4 squares down
(c) 4 squares right and 1 square down
(d) 3 squares left and 4 squares up

3 Perform the four translations in question **2** on this shape. Draw a separate diagram for each transformation.

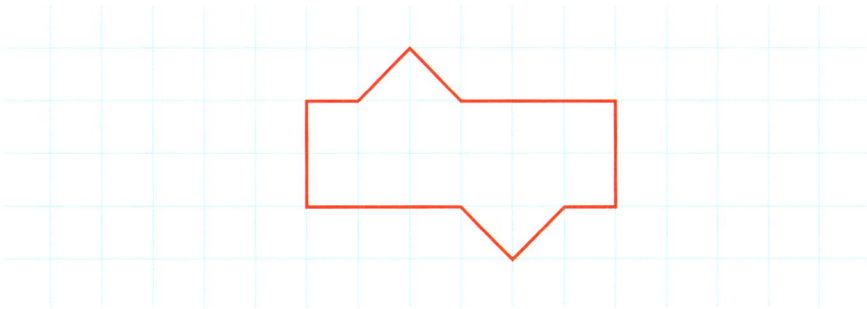

4 Describe the translation for each object–image pair.

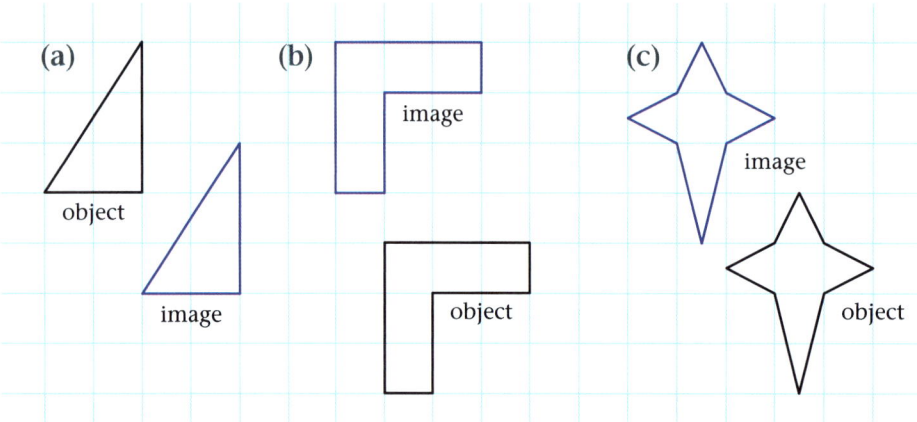

22.2 Rotation

Images of a shape which are formed by turning are called **rotations** of the shape.

The rotation can be described as a fraction of a full turn or as an angle. If no direction is given the turn is in an anticlockwise direction.

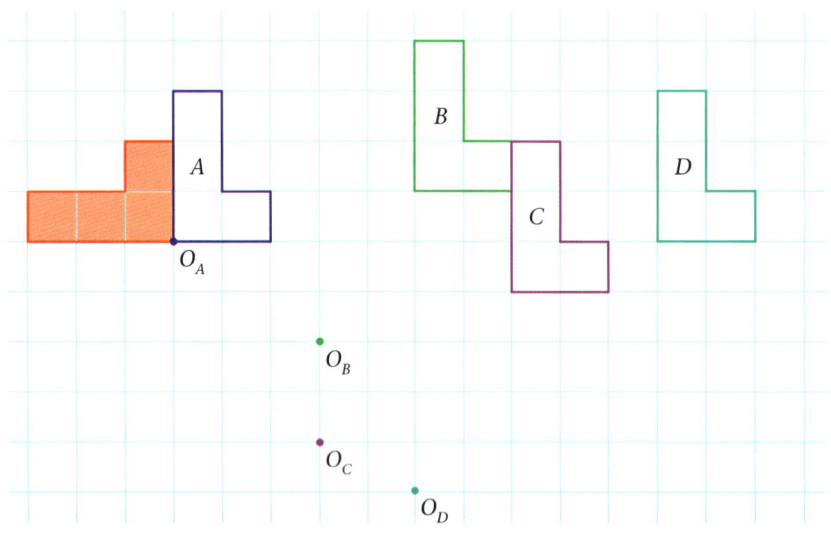

> The shaded shape rotated around point O_A becomes A.
>
> The shaded shape rotated around point O_B becomes B.

> Object and image are congruent.

> You might find it useful to use tracing paper.

The shaded shape is the object. All the others are images and they are all $\frac{3}{4}$ turns anticlockwise but they are not the same rotation.

The point about which the turning occurs is important.

The point about which the turning occurs is called the **centre of rotation**.

How to rotate a shape on paper

To rotate this shape half a turn about the point marked with a dot:

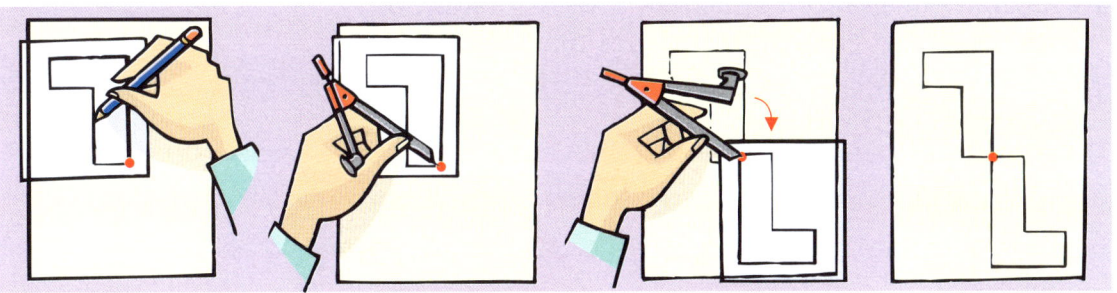

Trace the shape and the fixed point. Turn the tracing over and draw the outline on the back in pencil.

Place the tracing exactly over the original shape. Keep the point fixed using the point of a pair of compasses.

Rotate the tracing through half a turn (180°). Scribble over it to transfer the image.

Draw over the image to make it clear.

You could also do this using a card cut-out of the shape.
This pattern has been made by repeated rotations.
A is rotated to B, B is rotated to C, C is rotated to D.

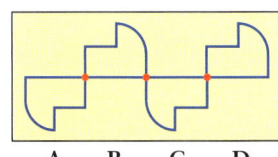

A B C D

Example 2

Draw the image of each shape after it has been rotated $\frac{1}{4}$ turn clockwise using the point O as centre.

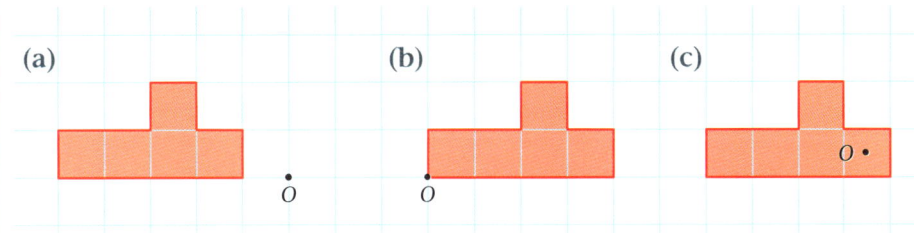

(a) (b) (c)

Using tracing paper:

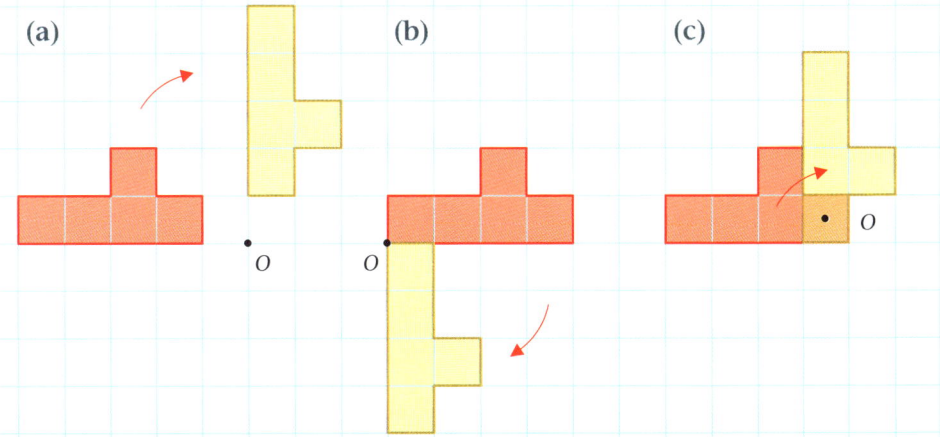

(a) (b) (c)

Notice that each line of the object has turned $\frac{1}{4}$ turn clockwise. This is obvious on this shape which is drawn on grid lines but would be true for diagonal lines as well.

Exercise 22B

1 Draw separate images for each shape after a rotation of 90° clockwise about each of the centres marked.

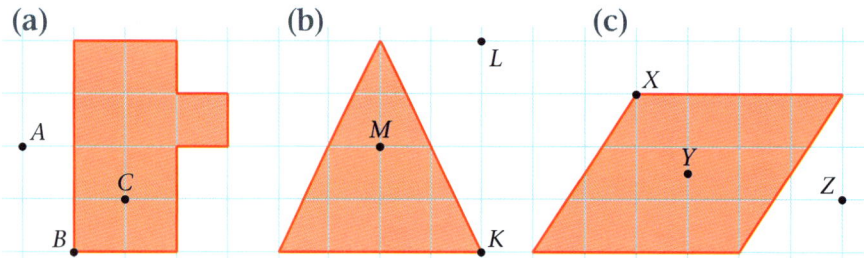

(a)   (b)   (c)

2 Copy these shapes and rotate them through a $\frac{1}{2}$ turn using the centres marked.

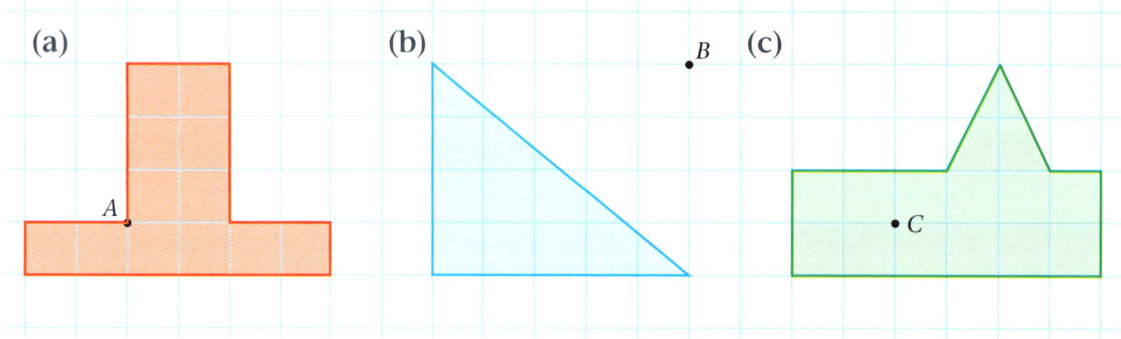

(a)   (b)   (c)

3 Each diagram shows an object and its image. Copy each diagram and write down how much the object has been rotated and the direction of the rotation. Try to identify the centre of the rotation and mark it on your diagram.

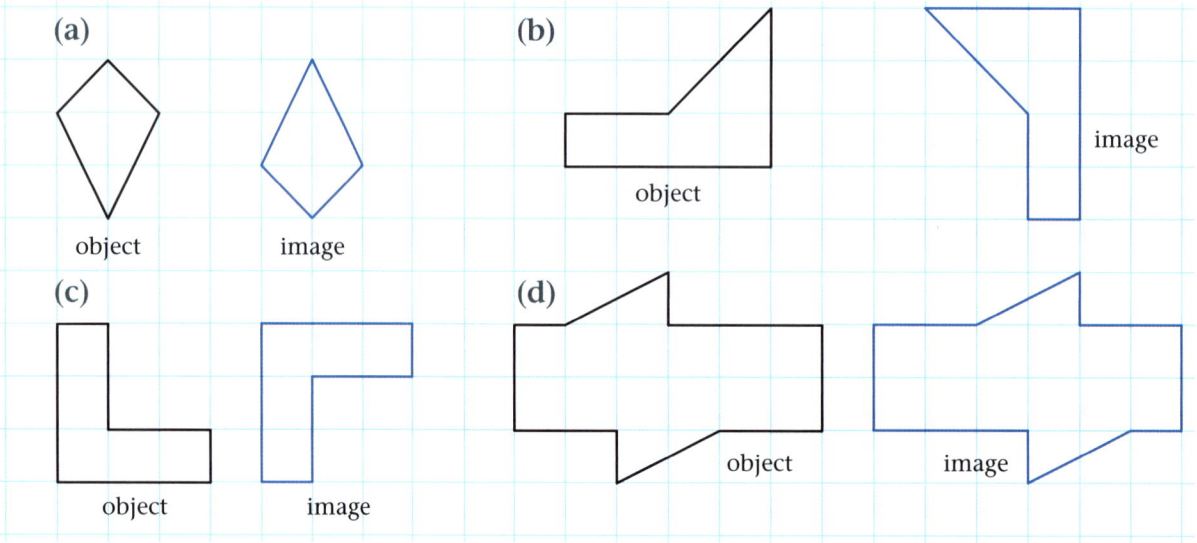

(a)   (b)   (c)   (d)

22.3 Reflection

When you next look in a mirror check to see that your image appears to be as far behind the mirror as you are in front. You can test this by moving nearer and further away from the mirror.

In a mathematical **reflection** the image is the same distance behind the mirror line as the object is in front.

Example 3

Reflect the shape in the mirror line.

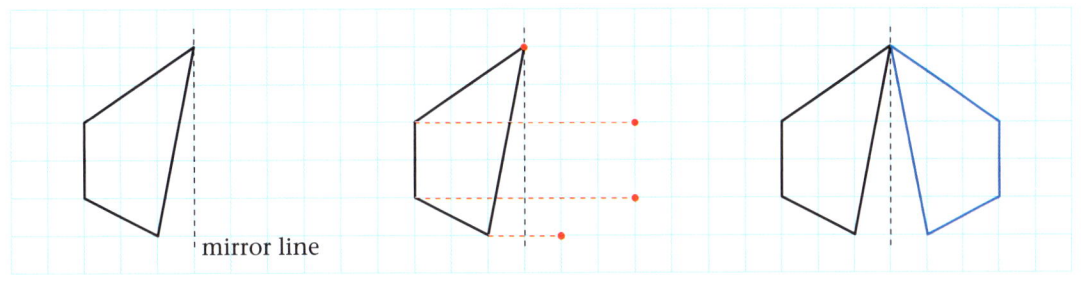

Step 1 Mark the images of the vertices. These are the same distance on the other side measured at right angles.

Step 2 Join up the vertices.

Mirror lines are **two-way**. The mirror line may go through the object, requiring reflections to go both ways.

> Object and image are congruent.

Here is a reflection which is two-way:

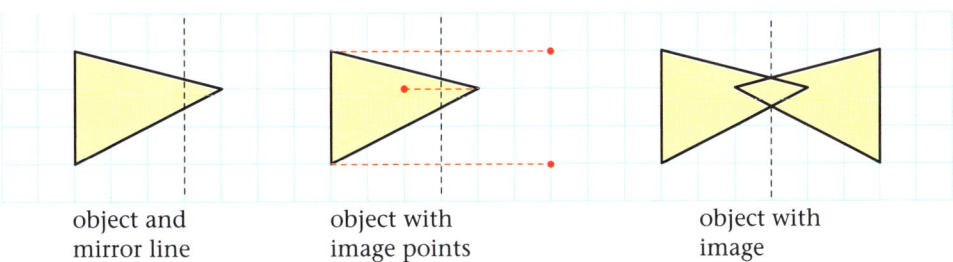

object and mirror line   object with image points   object with image

Chapter 22 Transformations

Example 4

Reflect the shape in the sloping mirror line.

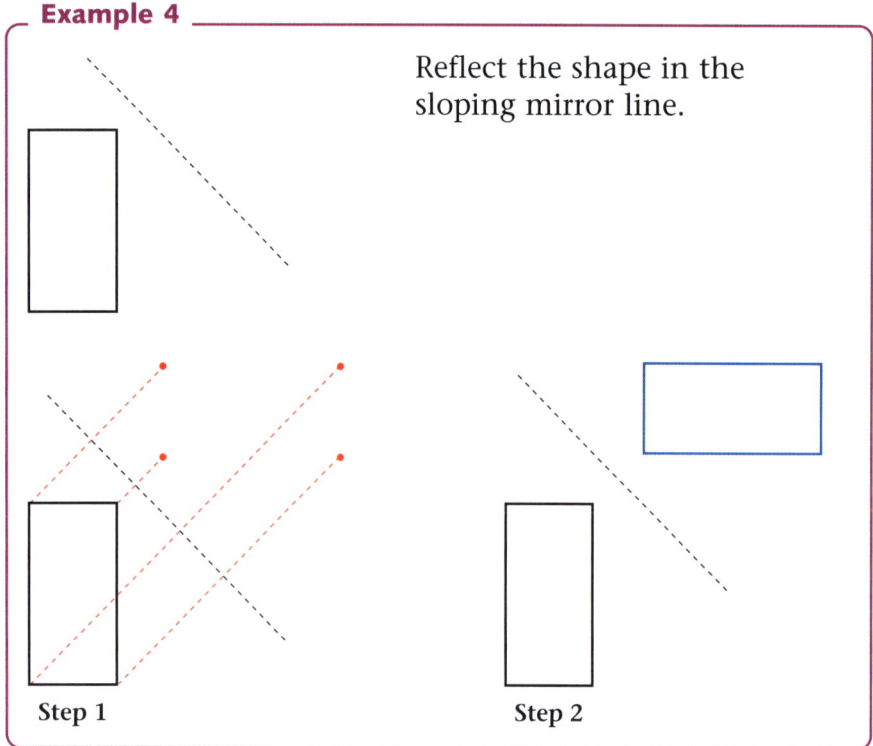

When the mirror line is sloping it is a good idea to turn the paper until the mirror line is vertical.

This way it is easier to find the images of the vertices.

Exercise 22C

1 Copy each shape onto squared paper and draw the image after reflection using the dotted line as the mirror line.

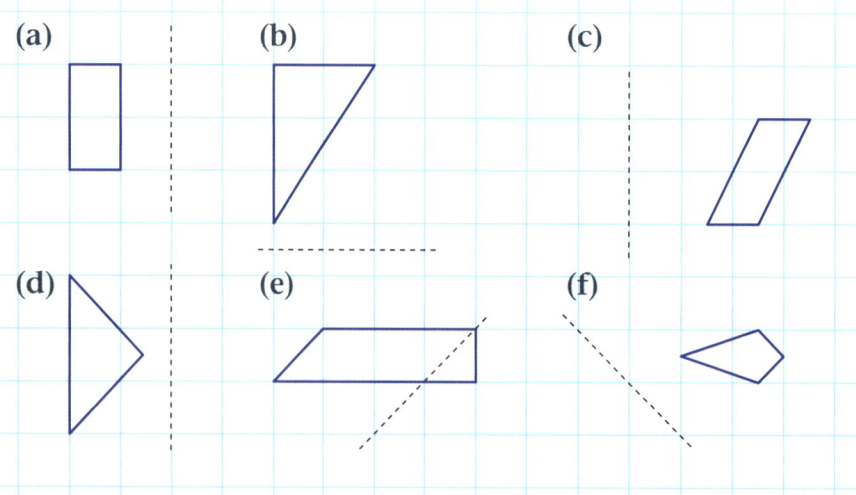

2 Each diagram shows an object with its image. Copy the diagrams onto squared paper and draw in the mirror line.

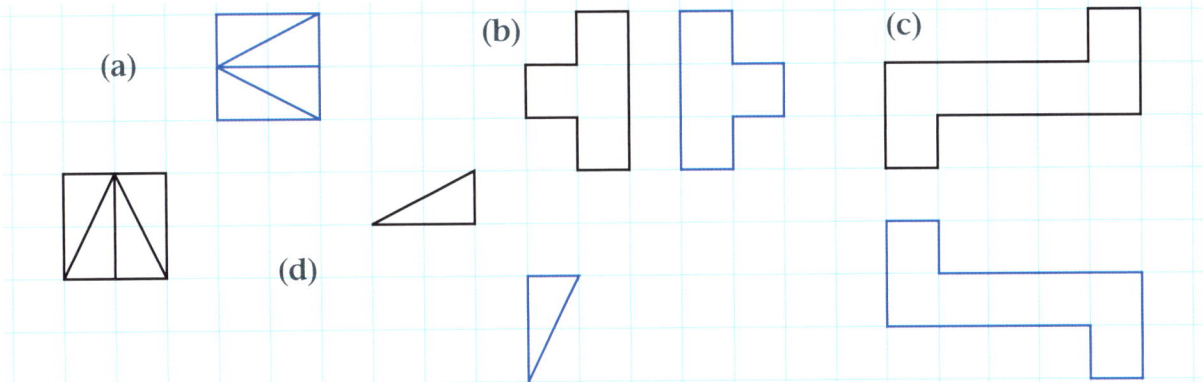

22.4 Enlargement

In an **enlargement**, all angles stay the same and all lengths are changed in the same proportion.

The **scale factor** of the enlargement is the value that the lengths of the original object are multiplied by.

This photograph has been enlarged by scale factor 2.
new length = 2 × old length
new width = 2 × old width

Example 5

Enlarge the shape *ABCD* by a scale factor of 2 using *A* as the centre of enlargement.

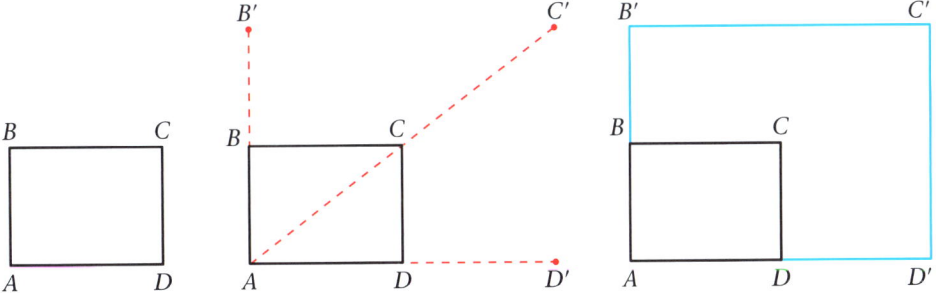

Point *A* is the centre of enlargement and is fixed. *A'* is at *A*.

All other points move 2 times as far away.

$A'D' = 2AD \quad A'C' = 2AC \quad A'B' = 2AB$

A'D' is the image of *AD*.

The **centre of enlargement** determines the final position of the enlarged image.

When one shape is an enlargement of another the shapes are called **similar shapes**.

Example 6

Enlarge shape *EFGHJ* by a scale factor of 2 using the centre of enlargement C marked inside the shape.

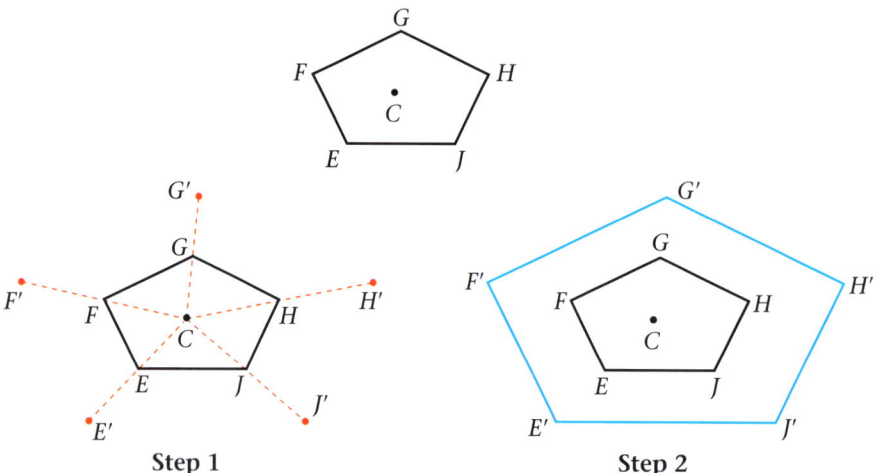

Again, all points move to image positions which are 2 times as far away from the fixed centre.

Example 7

Enlarge the shape *PQRS* by a scale factor of 2 using the centre of enlargement O marked outside the shape.

The scale factor is 2, so all the image points are twice as far away from the fixed centre as the object points.

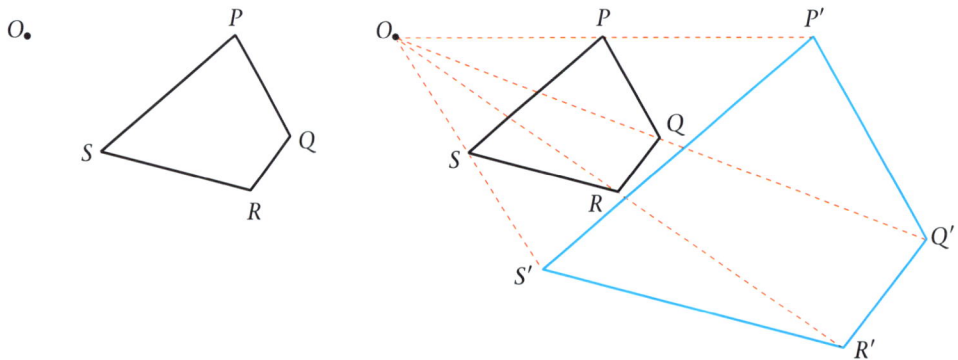

In an enlargement, image lines are **parallel** to their corresponding object lines.

You can check that sloping lines are parallel by regarding them as a combination of a sideways movement and an up/down movement.

If the shape is drawn on a grid you can see if the lines which go along the grid lines are the right length by counting.

22.4 Enlargement

Example 8

Enlarge shape *KLMN* by a scale factor of 2 and with the centre of enlargement at the origin.

K is 5 across and 2 up, so *K'* will be 10 across and 4 up. *K'L'* will be twice the length of *KL*.

LM is 2 across and 3 up.

The image *L'M'* will be 4 across and 6 up.

MN is 4 left and 1 down.

The image *M'N'* will be 8 left and 2 down.

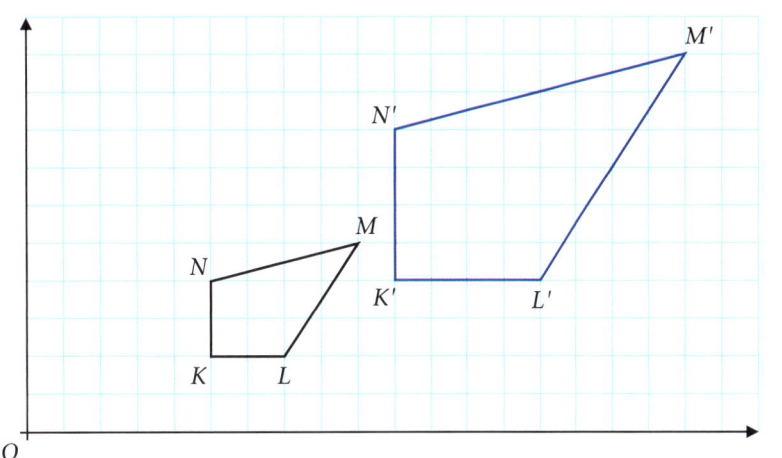

Exercise 22D

In this exercise each question has a scale factor (SF) and three possible centres of enlargement. Copy each diagram and draw the three enlargements either on the same diagram or on separate diagrams.

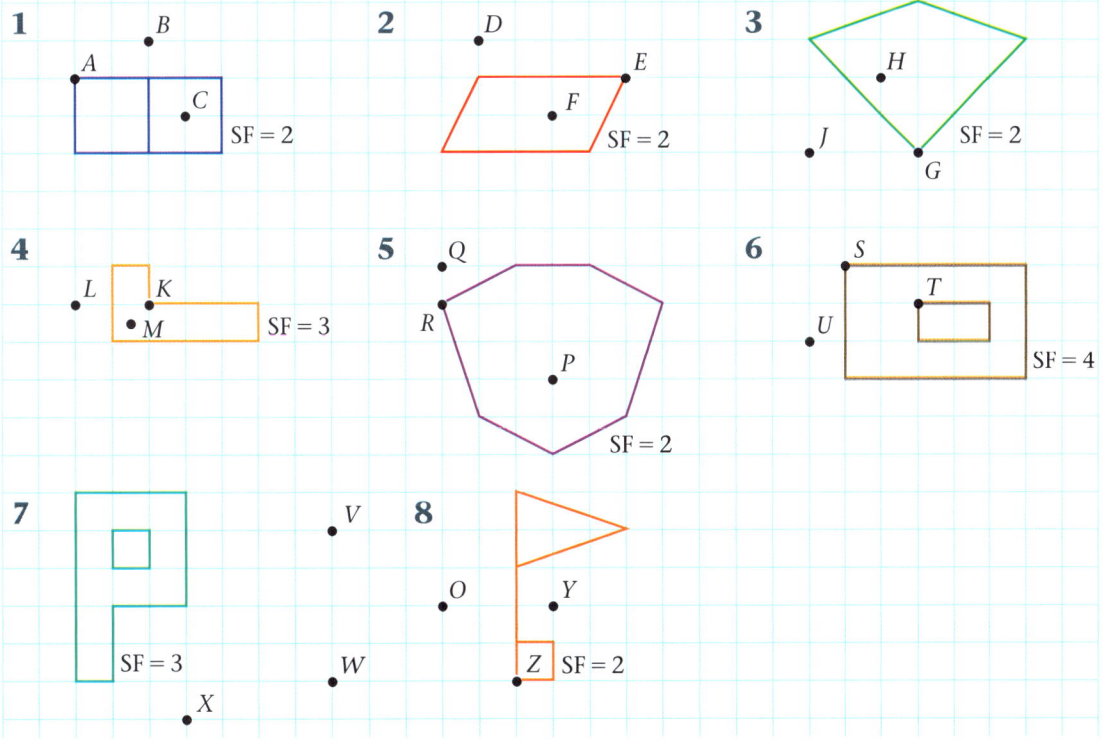

Mixed exercise 22

1. Copy this shape onto squared paper. Enlarge it by a scale factor of 3 using *P* as the centre of enlargement.

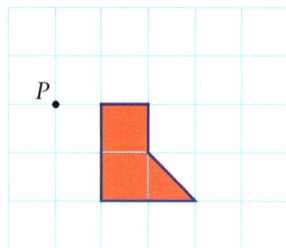

[E]

2. Copy and reflect each of the shapes in the mirror line given.

(a)
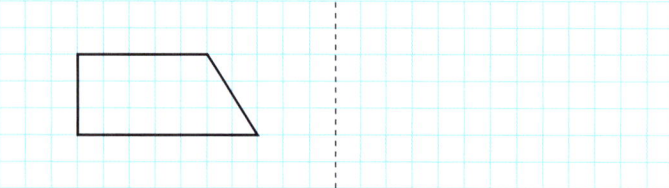

(b)
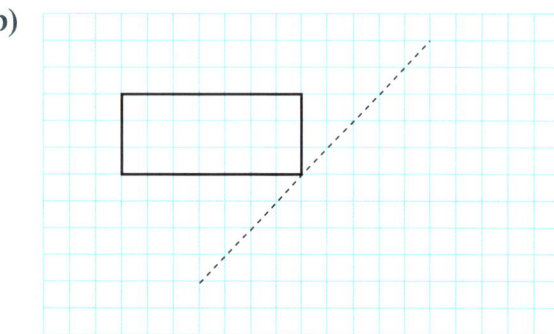

[E]

3. Copy this shape and translate it 8 squares to the right and 2 squares up.

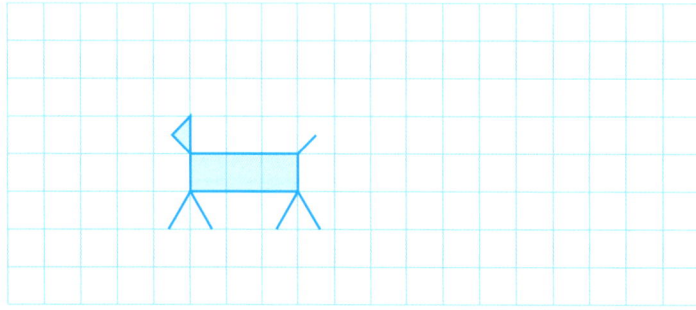

4 (a) Make a copy of the diagram. Reflect the shape A in the mirror line.

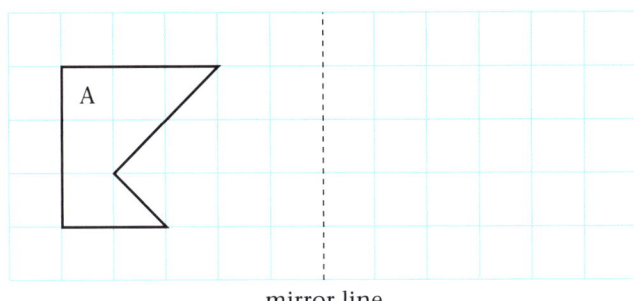

mirror line

Label the reflection B.

(b) Describe the transformation which maps the triangle C onto the triangle D.

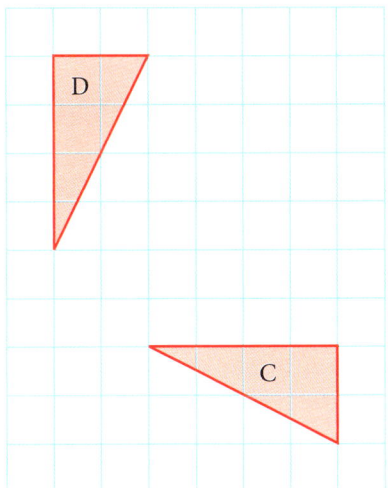

[E]

5 Copy the diagram onto squared paper, and reflect the shape in the mirror line.

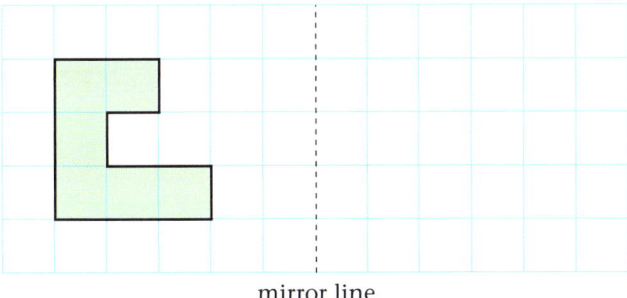

mirror line

Summary of key points

1 A sliding movement is called a **translation**.

2 Images of a shape which are formed by turning are called **rotations** of the shape.

3 The point about which the turning occurs is called the **centre of rotation**.

4 In a mathematical **reflection** the image is the same distance behind the mirror line as the object is in front.

5 Mirror lines are **two-way**. The mirror line may go through the object, requiring reflections to go both ways.

6 In an **enlargement**, all angles stay the same and all lengths are changed in the same proportion.

7 The **scale factor** of the enlargement is the value the lengths of the original object are multiplied by.

8 The **centre of enlargement** determines the final position of the enlarged image.

9 In an enlargement, image lines are **parallel** to their corresponding object lines.

23 Probability

Weather forecasts are made by studying weather data and using a branch of mathematics called probability.

Probability uses numbers to represent how likely or unlikely it is that an event such as 'a thunderstorm' will happen.

Probability is used by governments, scientists, economists, medical researchers and many other people to **predict** what is likely to happen in the future by studying what has already happened.

23.1 The probability scale

An event which is **certain to happen** has a **probability of 1**.

For example, the probability that night will follow day is 1.

An event which **cannot happen** has a **probability of 0**.

For example, the probability that you will grow to be 5 metres tall is 0.

All probabilities must have a value greater than or equal to 0 and less than or equal to 1.

This can be shown on a **probability scale**:

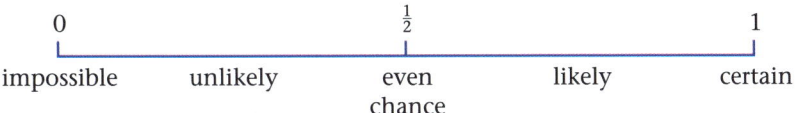

Exercise 23A

1. Draw a 0 to 1 probability scale and mark on it the probability that
   (a) it will rain tomorrow
   (b) the sea will disappear
   (c) Boxing Day will follow Christmas Day this year
   (d) you will buy a new pair of shoes soon
   (e) you will have homework tonight
   (f) the sun will not rise next week
   (g) a member of the class will be late tomorrow
   (h) if you toss a coin it will land tail up
   (i) you will see a TV star on your way home.

2. Give two examples of events that you think
   (a) are impossible   (b) are unlikely
   (c) have about an even chance
   (d) are likely   (e) are certain.

23.2 Using numbers to represent probabilities

In Exercise 23A you may have found it difficult to know where to put some of the statements on the probability scale in question **1**. It becomes easier if the probability is given a value.

When you toss a coin there are two possible outcomes: either a head or tail. One of these outcomes is tossing a head.

The probability P of tossing a head can be written:

$$\text{probability of a head} = \frac{\text{number of successful outcomes}}{\text{total number of possible outcomes}}$$

$$= \frac{1 \text{ outcome (head)}}{2 \text{ possible outcomes (head or tail)}} = \frac{1}{2}$$

In a tennis match, a coin is tossed to decide which player will serve first.

Another way of writing this is:
   P(head) = $\frac{1}{2}$

Probabilities can be written as fractions, decimals or percentages:
   P(head) = $\frac{1}{2}$
   = 0.5
   = 50%

23.2 Using numbers to represent probabilities

The probability that an event will happen is:

$$\text{probability} = \frac{\text{number of successful outcomes}}{\text{total number of possible outcomes}}$$

assuming that the outcomes are all equally likely.

Probability is a measure of *how likely* it is that something will happen on a scale from 0 to 1. If you toss a coin 10 times that does not mean you will get *exactly* 5 heads, but if you toss a coin 500 times it is *likely* that you will get about 250 heads.

If getting a head is a *success* then getting a tail is a *failure*.

Example 1

Find the probability of getting a 5 or a 6 when a fair dice is rolled.

$$P(5 \text{ or } 6) = \frac{\text{number of successful outcomes}}{\text{total number of possible outcomes}}$$

$$= \frac{2}{6} = \frac{1}{3}$$

These are two successful outcomes: 5, 6.

There are six possible outcomes: 1, 2, 3, 4, 5, 6.

The word **fair** means that each number has an equal chance of turning up: the outcomes are *equally likely*.

Exercise 23B

1 A fair six-sided dice is rolled.
What is the probability of getting:
(a) a 4
(b) a 1 or 2
(c) an odd number
(d) an even number
(e) a multiple of 3
(f) 3 or more
(g) less than 5
(h) a prime number
(i) more than 6
(j) $2\frac{1}{2}$?

2 A card is selected from a pack of 52 cards.
What is the probability it will be:
(a) an ace
(b) the ace of spades
(c) a black card
(d) a 5 or 6
(e) smaller than a 4
(f) a picture card
(g) a 3, 4 or 5
(h) a diamond
(i) a club or spade
(j) any card other than a club?

3 A token is taken from a bag containing 6 red and 5 blue tokens. What is the probability that the token will be
  (a) blue
  (b) red
  (c) yellow
  (d) red or blue?

4 A bag contains 1 white, 3 black and 5 blue beads. Omar selects a bead at random. What is the probability that the bead he chooses is
  (a) white
  (b) black
  (c) blue
  (d) not white
  (e) white or black?

5 In a game at a fete a pointer is spun. You win the amount of money written in the sector where the pointer stops. Each sector is equally likely.
Work out the probability that you win
  (a) no money
  (b) 25p
  (c) 50p
  (d) 74p
  (e) £1

6 In a raffle 5000 tickets are sold. Jasmir buys 20, Karen buys 100, Lucy buys 50 and Winston buys 25 tickets. There is one winning ticket. Work out the probability that
  (a) Jasmir wins
  (b) Karen wins
  (c) Lucy wins
  (d) Winston wins.

7 A box of sweets contains 4 toffees, 3 mints, 5 bonbons, 6 eclairs, 2 wine gums and 10 sherbet lemons. One sweet is chosen at random. Work out the probability that it will be
  (a) a toffee
  (b) a sherbet lemon
  (c) a bonbon
  (d) a wine gum
  (e) an eclair or a mint
  (f) not a sherbet lemon.

'not a sherbet lemon' means any other type of sweet.

8 A set of coloured pencils contains 1 black, 1 white, 2 red, 3 green, 3 blue, 4 brown, 2 yellow, 1 pink and 1 purple pencil. If one pencil is selected at random, find the probability that it will be
  (a) white
  (b) red
  (c) green
  (d) blue
  (e) brown
  (f) yellow
  (g) pink
  (h) purple
  (i) not yellow
  (j) not brown
  (k) red or green
  (l) mauve.

9 A letter is chosen at random from the word PROBABILITY. Work out the probability that it will be
  (a) R
  (b) Y
  (c) B
  (d) I or A
  (e) B or I

23.3 Certain and impossible events

In question 3 of Exercise 23B it is *impossible* to pick a yellow token. It is *certain* that you will pick either a red or a blue token because they are the only colours available.
If you write these probabilities as fractions you find:

P(yellow) which is *impossible* is $\frac{0}{11}$ which is 0.

P(red or blue) which is *certain* is $\frac{11}{11}$ which is 1.

The probability of an event happening is always greater than or equal to 0 (impossible) and less than or equal to 1 (certain). This can be written:

$0 \leq \text{probability} \leq 1$

Remember:
$a < 5$ a is less than 5
$a \leq 5$ a is less than or equal to 5
$5 > a$ 5 is greater than a
$5 \geq a$ 5 is greater than or equal to a

Exercise 23C

1. Write down the probability of the following:
   (a) you will grow to be 5 centimetres tall
   (b) Christmas Day will be on 25th December this year
   (c) if you toss a coin it will be a tail
   (d) you will live to be 150 years old
   (e) you will die
   (f) if you roll a dice it will be an odd number.

2. Write three statements for each of the following. The first one is started for you.
   (a) a probability of 0
       'A baby will be born with false teeth' has a probability of 0.
   (b) a probability of 1
   (c) a probability of about $\frac{1}{2}$
   (d) a probability of about $\frac{3}{4}$

3. On the right are the nets of two differently numbered dice.
   If one dice is rolled what is the probability using
   (i) Dice A   (ii) Dice B
   that you will get
   (a) a 6
   (b) a 5
   (c) a score of 4 or more
   (d) a 2
   (e) an even number
   (f) an odd number
   (g) a prime number
   (h) a square number?

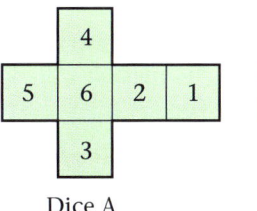
Dice A

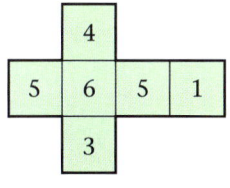
Dice B

4 A bowl of fruit contains 3 apples, 4 bananas, 2 pears and 1 orange. Norma takes one piece of fruit without looking. What is the probability that she takes

(a) an apple (b) a banana
(c) a pear   (d) an orange?

Write each answer in three ways (i) as a fraction (ii) as a decimal and (iii) as a percentage.

The first one is done for you.

(a) P(apple) is (i) $\frac{3}{10}$ (ii) 0.3 (iii) 30%

5 A hundred raffle tickets are sold. Raman buys 8 tickets, Susan 5 tickets and Gary 12 tickets. What is the probability that the first prize will be won by

(a) one of these three
(b) Raman
(c) Susan
(d) somebody other than Gary?

Write each answer in three ways: (i) as a fraction, (ii) as a decimal and (iii) as a percentage.

6 Meryl, James and Gita are playing Monopoly. The probability that Meryl will win is $\frac{1}{3}$. The probability that James will win is $\frac{1}{4}$.
What is the probability that Gita will win?

23.4 The probability that something will *not* happen

The probability of rolling a 6 on a fair dice is P(6) = $\frac{1}{6}$.

The probability of *not* getting a 6 is:

P(not a 6) = $\frac{5}{6}$

There are five ways of not getting 6: 1, 2, 3, 4, 5

The six possible outcomes are still: 1, 2, 3, 4, 5, 6

Notice that P(6) = $\frac{1}{6}$

P(not a 6) = $\frac{5}{6}$ = 1 − $\frac{1}{6}$ = 1 − P(6)

Notice also that
P(6) + P(not a 6) = $\frac{1}{6} + \frac{5}{6}$
= 1

If the probability of an event happening is *p* then the probability of it *not* happening is 1 − *p*.

Exercise 23D

1. (a) The probability that it will rain tomorrow is $\frac{1}{3}$.
   What is the probability that it will not rain?

   (b) The probability that it will snow on Christmas Day is 0.2.
   What is the probability that it will not snow on Christmas Day?

   (c) The probability that Rovers will get to the next round of a competition is 30%.
   What is the probability that they will not get to the next round?

2. This spinner is spun.
   What is the probability of getting:
   (a) a 1
   (b) not a 1
   (c) an odd number
   (d) not an odd number?

   The 3-sided spinner has landed on 2.

3. The probability of Ahmed winning his game of chess is 0.62. The probability of him drawing is 0.24
   What is the probability of him losing?

4. Susan rolls a fair six-sided dice.
   What is the probability that she will:
   (a) get a 2
   (b) *not* get a 2
   (c) get 3 or more
   (d) *not* get 3 or more
   (e) *not* get an even number?

5. Nine counters numbered 2 to 10 are put in a bag.
   One counter is selected at random.
   What is the probability of getting a counter with
   (a) a number 5
   (b) an odd number
   (c) not an odd number
   (d) a prime number
   (e) a square number
   (f) a multiple of 3?

6. A bag contains 20 coloured balls. 8 are red, 6 are blue, 3 are green, 2 are white and 1 is brown. A ball is chosen at random from the bag.
   What is the probability that the ball chosen is
   (a) blue
   (b) not blue
   (c) brown
   (d) not brown
   (e) blue or red
   (f) red or green
   (g) green or white or brown?

7 The probability of Jane scoring a 20 on this special darts board is $\frac{1}{5}$.
What is the probability of Jane not scoring 20?

8 A bag contains 20 balls. There are three different colours: green, red and blue. A ball is chosen at random from the bag. The probability of a green ball is $\frac{1}{4}$.
The probability of a red ball is $\frac{2}{5}$.
  (a) What is the probability of a blue ball?
  (b) How many balls are red?
  (c) How many balls are green?
  (d) How many balls are blue?

23.5 Finding an estimated probability by experimenting

Sometimes you will need to estimate the probability that an event will happen.

For example, you can estimate the probability of getting a head when you toss a coin by carrying out a trial.

Toss it several times and keep a record of:
- the number of successful trials (heads)
- the total number of trials (how many tosses altogether).

The **estimated probability** that an event will happen in a game or experiment is:

$$\text{estimated probability} = \frac{\text{number of successful trials}}{\text{total number of trials}}$$

The estimated probability may be different from the theoretical probability.

The **estimated probability** is given by the **relative frequency** with which the event occurs in a trial or experiment.

Relative frequency is dealt with in more detail in Section 23.8

Example 2

If you toss a coin 20 times and get 12 heads and 8 tails the **estimated probability** of getting a head is: $\frac{12}{20} = \frac{3}{5}$

The **theoretical probability** is: $\frac{10}{20} = \frac{1}{2}$

From the experiment it would seem that you are more likely to get a head than a tail. Next time you do the same experiment you may well get a different result but the theoretical probability is *always* $\frac{1}{2}$.

You can use estimated probability to predict results. If the estimated probability of Adrian winning a tennis match is $\frac{3}{4}$ then if he plays 24 matches he would expect to win 18 times. —— $\frac{3}{4} \times 24 = 18$

Exercise 23E

1 (a) Roll a dice 36 times and record your results in a frequency table like the one below. Work out the probability of rolling each number from your results.

Number	Tally	Frequency	Probability
1			$\frac{}{36}$
2			$\frac{}{36}$
3			$\frac{}{36}$
4			$\frac{}{36}$
5			$\frac{}{36}$
6			$\frac{}{36}$
		Total	$\frac{}{36}$

Use your table to answer these questions.
(b) What is the probability of rolling
    (i) a 3   (ii) a 5?
(c) What is the probability of rolling an even number?
(d) What is the total of all the probabilities?
(e) Explain your result to part (d).

2 Roll a dice another 36 times and complete a table as in question **1**.
Compare the results with those from question **1** and make comments.

3 Combine your results for questions **1** and **2** in a table and comment on the probabilities you obtain.

4 Roll two dice 36 times, add the total spots on the uppermost faces and record your results in a table like this:

Number	Tally	Frequency	Probability
2			
3			
4			
12			

Total 8

(a) What is the probability of a score being
    (i)   12   (ii) 7   (iii) 3
    (iv) 11   (v) 1   (vi) even
    (vii) greater than 8   (viii) a square number

(b) What is the total of the probabilities?

(c) What is the probability that you will not score 12?

5 Roll two dice a further 36 times and complete a table as in question **4**.
Compare the results with those from question **4**.

6 Combine your results for questions **4** and **5** in a table and make comments on your results.

7 (a) Draw a bar chart to show your results from rolling two dice. Use the data in the frequency column from question **6**.

(b) Which number occurred the most times?

(c) Which number occurred the fewest times?

(d) Write two sentences about the shape of your bar chart.

(e) Which of these numbers is most likely to occur:
    (i) 12   (ii) 6   (iii) 2?

(f) Why did the number 1 not occur?

23.6 Using a sample space diagram to find theoretical probabilities

If you roll a red dice and a blue dice what are all the outcomes? If the red dice shows 1 the blue dice could show 1, 2, 3, 4, 5 or 6. You can record these outcomes as ordered pairs, putting the red result first and then the blue result, like this:

(1, 1) (1, 2) (1, 3) (1, 4) (1, 5) (1, 6)   — red dice 1
                                                  — blue dice 6

If the red dice showed 2, the outcomes could be:

(2, 1) (2, 2) (2, 3) (2, 4) (2, 5) (2, 6)

You can represent all the outcomes on a **sample space diagram**:

```
Blue dice
6 –  (1,6) (2,6) (3,6) (4,6) (5,6) (6,6)
5 –  (1,5) (2,5) (3,5) (4,5) (5,5) (6,5)
4 –  (1,4) (2,4) (3,4) (4,4) (5,4) (6,4)
3 –  (1,3) (2,3) (3,3) (4,3) (5,3) (6,3)
2 –  (1,2) (2,2) (3,2) (4,2) (5,2) (6,2)
1 –  (1,1) (2,1) (3,1) (4,1) (5,1) (6,1)
      1     2     3     4     5     6
                  Red dice
```

The sample space diagram shows that there are 36 possible outcomes.

A **sample space diagram** represents all possible outcomes.

Example 3

Use a sample space diagram to find the probability of getting a total score of 7 when two dice are rolled.

There are 6 ways of scoring 7:

(1, 6) (2, 5) (3, 4) (4, 5) (5, 2) (6, 1)

There are 36 possible outcomes so:

P(scoring 7) = $\frac{6}{36}$ or $\frac{1}{6}$

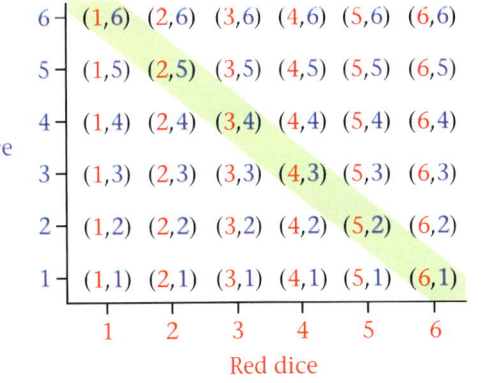

Exercise 23F

1. Use the sample space diagram in Example 3 to find the probability of
   (a) rolling a total score of (i) 5 (ii) 9 (iii) 12
   (b) rolling a score that is (i) **not** more than 4
                                (ii) **not** less than 10
   (c) rolling a 2 on either one or both of the dice
   (d) rolling a double
   (e) rolling a double 6.

2. This sample space diagram shows the outcomes when the ace, king, queen, jack, and ten from both the spades and hearts suits are placed in two separate piles and one card is taken from each pile.

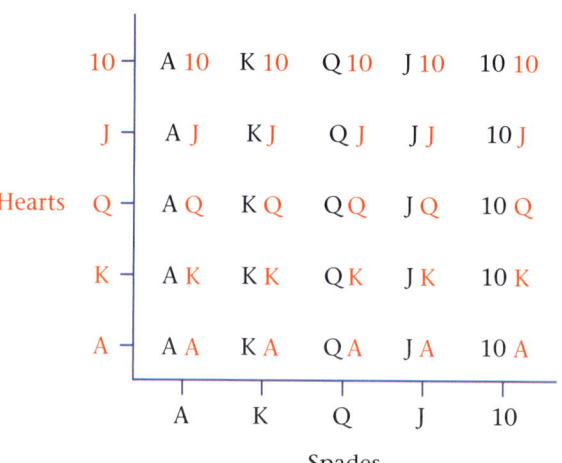

   Find the probability that
   (a) both cards will be kings
   (b) both of the cards will be either an ace or a king
   (c) both cards will be a pair
   (d) at least one card will be an ace
   (e) neither card will be a 10
   (f) neither card will be a king or a jack
   (g) one card will be a spade
   (h) both cards will be hearts.

3. Write out all the possible outcomes for each of the following pairs of events:
   (a) tossing a coin twice
   (b) obtaining an odd number followed by an odd number when a dice is rolled twice
   (c) tossing a coin and rolling a dice.

4 Work out the number of possible outcomes:
   (a) when a fair six-sided dice is thrown twice
   (b) when two discs are taken, one at a time, from a bag containing red, blue, and yellow discs (the first disc is put back in the bag before the second is taken out).

5 Four discs are placed in a bag: red, green, yellow and blue. One disc is taken at random, its colour is recorded and then it is replaced. A second disc is then taken. Draw a sample space diagram to show all the possible outcomes.

6 (a) Copy and complete this table to show the possible outcomes when a red dice and a blue dice are rolled.

Total score	Ordered pairs	Theoretical probability
2	(1,1)	$\frac{1}{36}$
3	(1,2) (2,1)	$\frac{2}{36}$
4	(1,3) (2,2) (3,1)	$\frac{3}{36}$
5		
6		
7		
11		
12		

   (b) Which was the most likely score?
   (c) What is the sum of all the probabilities? Explain your answer.

7 Nicola can turn left or right at a T-junction. List all the possible outcomes after she has passed two junctions.

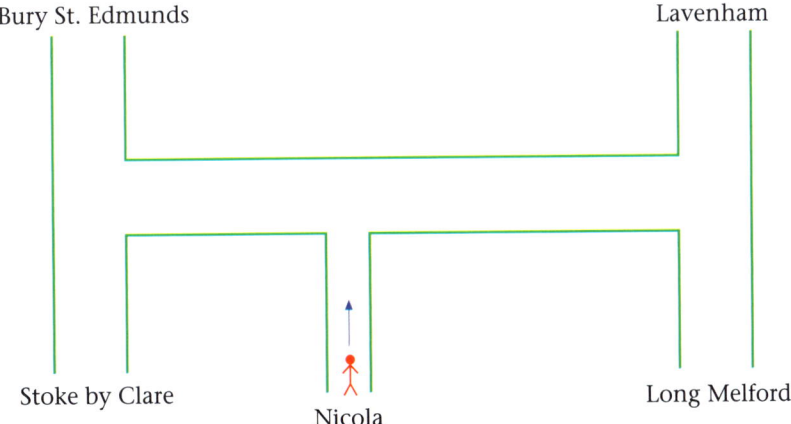

23.7 Using two-way tables to find probabilities

Another way to show possible outcomes is to use a two-way table.
You can do this even if you do not know all the outcomes.

Example 4

This table shows some information about how students in Mr Graham's maths set travel to school.
None of them come by car.

	Walk	Bus	Cycle	Total
Girls	4	p	3	12
Boys	7	q	u	t
Total	r	9	s	25

(a) Copy and complete the table.
(b) Mr Graham chooses a student at random.
   What is the probability they are:
   (i) a girl who walks to school
   (ii) a boy who cycles to school
   (iii) a student who comes by bus?

(a) Girls: $4 + p + 3 = 12$ so the number who travelled by bus p is 5.

Boys: The total who travelled by bus is 9, where $5 + q = 9$ so the number of boys who travelled by bus, q, is 4.
The total r who walked is $4 + 7 = 11$.
The total number of students is 25, where $11 + 9 + s = 25$ so the total s who cycle is 5.
The total t of boys is $25 - 12 = 13$
The number u of boys who cycle is $5 - 3 = 2$

The completed table is:

	Walk	Bus	Cycle	Total
Girls	4	5	3	12
Boys	7	4	2	13
Total	11	9	5	25

(b) (i) 4 out of 25 walked so the probability is $\frac{4}{25}$.
   (ii) 2 out of 25 cycled the probability is $\frac{2}{25}$.
   (iii) 9 out of 25 travel by bus so the probability is $\frac{9}{25}$.

Two-way tables can be used to help solve probability problems.

Exercise 23G

1. The numbers of clients interviewed by Jackie and Sam about their holidays are shown in this table:

	Monday	Tuesday	Total
Jackie	25	35	
Sam			
Total	55		100

   (a) Copy and complete the table.

   (b) How many people did Jackie interview altogether?

   (c) How many people did Sam interview on Monday?

   (d) How many people were interviewed on Tuesday?

   (e) If one of these clients is chosen at random what is the probability that they were interviewed by

   (i) Jackie on Monday

   (ii) Sam on Tuesday

   (iii) Jackie

   (iv) Sam on Monday or Jackie on Tuesday?

   > A **random** selection is one in which each person has the same chance of being chosen.

2. Jackie and Sam asked the 100 clients how they travelled to France and in which month they travelled. Some of the information is recorded in this table:

	Air	Eurotunnel	Boat	Total
July	8		10	20
August	15	5		50
September		8		
Total	30			100

   (a) Copy and complete the table.

   (b) What is the probability that a client selected at random travelled:

   (i) in July
   (ii) in August or September
   (iii) by air
   (iv) by boat
   (v) by Eurotunnel in August
   (vi) by boat in August
   (vii) not by air
   (viii) in July, but not by boat?

3 The same 100 people were asked if they had their holiday in France, went on to Italy or went elsewhere.
Some details are given in this table:

	France	Italy	Elsewhere	Total
July		10	4	20
August	18		8	
September		16		30
Total	28	50		

(a) Copy and complete the table.

(b) What is the probability that a randomly picked holidaymaker
   (i) went to Italy
   (ii) went to France
   (iii) went in July
   (iv) did not go to Italy
   (v) went elsewhere in August
   (vi) went to France in September
   (vii) went to Italy in September?

4 The same 100 people were also asked what type of accommodation they stayed in.
Part of the information is given in this table:

	Hotel	Caravan	Camping	Other	Total
July	11	4	3		
August		14		6	
September		7	4	3	30
Total	49		15	11	100

(a) Copy and complete the table.

(b) What is the probability a person selected at random
   (i) stayed in a hotel in August
   (ii) stayed in a caravan in July
   (iii) stayed in a hotel
   (iv) did not stay in a hotel
   (v) stayed in a caravan
   (vi) used other accommodation
   (vii) went camping in August?

23.8 Relative frequency

In Section 23.5 you learned that you can estimate the probability that an event will occur by carrying out an experiment or game and using the rule:

$$\text{estimated probability} = \frac{\text{number of successful trials}}{\text{total number of trials}}$$

This is also called the **relative frequency**.

$$\text{relative frequency} = \frac{\text{number of successful trials}}{\text{total number of trials}}$$

The relative frequency of an event occurring is used when the outcomes are not equally likely.

It can also be used to test whether a game of chance is fair, for example to test whether a dice is fair.

Example 5

Describe how you might undertake an experiment and set out the results to test whether a coin is fair or not.

Step 1 The number of trials (times the coin is tossed) must be large (about 500).

Step 2 Record in a table the numbers of heads (successful trials) after 50 throws, 100 throws, 150 throws and so on.

Step 3 Work out the relative frequency (estimated probability) correct to 2 d.p. and record it in the table.

Number of trials	Number of successful trials	Relative frequency
50	20	$\frac{20}{50} = 0.40$
100	45	$\frac{45}{100} = 0.45$
150	71	$\frac{71}{150} = 0.47$
200	104	$\frac{104}{200} = 0.52$
250	119	$\frac{119}{250} = 0.48$
300	146	$\frac{146}{300} = 0.49$
350	172	$\frac{172}{350} = 0.49$
400	203	$\frac{203}{400} = 0.51$
450	222	$\frac{222}{450} = 0.49$
500	245	$\frac{245}{500} = 0.49$

Step 4 Illustrate your results using a line graph.

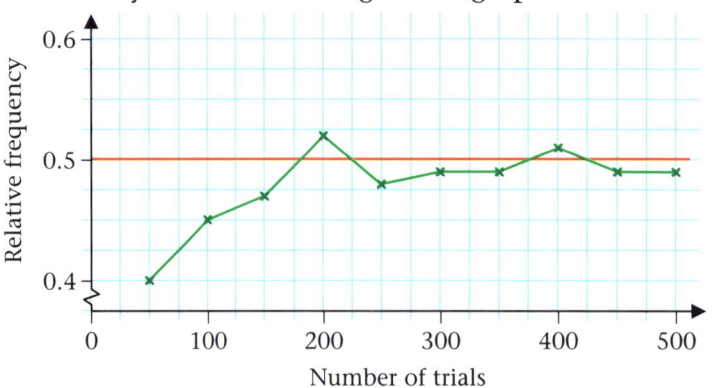

The red line shows the theoretical probability of getting a head, assuming that both outcomes are equally likely.

As the number of trials increases, the relative frequency of throwing a head (the estimated probability that you throw a head) settles down at about 0.49. This is very close to the theoretical probability of 0.5, so it is reasonable to assume that the coin is fair.

Exercise 23H

You need a dice, blue beads, red beads, a bag, card and scissors.

1. Test a dice of your own to see whether or not it is fair.

2. Ask a friend to place some of the blue beads and red beads in the bag. You must not look in the bag or ask how many there are of each colour. You need to use relative frequency to estimate the ratio of red to blue beads.

    (a) Carry out an experiment to work out the relative frequency of red beads.

    Record your results in a table and work out the relative frequency after different numbers of trials.

    (b) Record the relative frequencies on a line graph.

    (c) Read off the relative frequency where the graph 'settles down'.

    (d) Use the relative frequency to work out the ratio of red to blue beads in the bag.

3. Make a dice of your own out of card.
   Test the dice to see whether it is fair or not.

4. A dice is thrown and the score is recorded. After many trials the relative frequency of throwing a 5 is found to be 0.09. Compare this with the theoretical probability based on equally likely outcomes for a fair dice.
   Do you think the dice is fair?

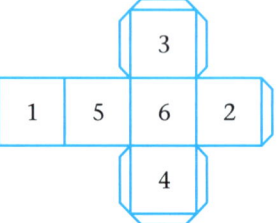

Net of dice

Mixed exercise 23

1 A box contains only blue pencils and red pencils.
   6 of the pencils are blue and 5 are red.
   A pencil is to be taken at random from the box.
   Write down the probability that
   (a) a blue pencil will be taken
   (b) a blue pencil will **not** be taken. [E]

2 Some pupils have thought of a game to use at a school fair.
   A tennis ball is rolled down a slope into one of eight holes. It can score a number from 1 to 8.
   The pupils try out their game **200 times**.
   The frequencies of the scores are shown on the diagram.

   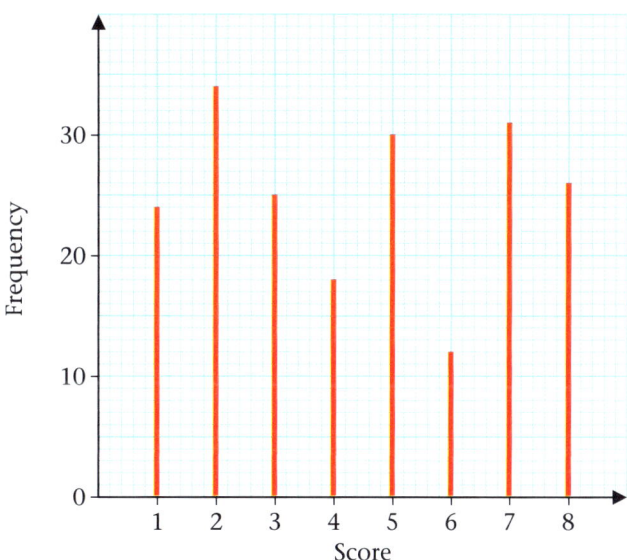

   According to the diagram, which number is
   (a) (i) the hardest to score
       (ii) the easiest to score?
   (b) Estimate the probability that the next ball rolled will score 3. [E]

3 A bag contains a red bead, a black bead, a yellow bead and a white bead.
   One single bead is to be picked out at random.
   What is the probability that the bead picked will be
   (a) red
   (b) pink
   (c) not white? [E]

4 Anil is conducting a series of tests on a biased coin.

He does 5 tests.

In each test he throws the coin 10 times and counts the number of heads.

The table shows the results of the 5 tests.

1st 10 throws	2nd 10 throws	3rd 10 throws	4th 10 throws	5th 10 throws
7 heads	6 heads	8 heads	6 heads	9 Heads

Anil then calculates the proportion of heads throughout his tests.

He sets out his calculations as shown below.

	Number of heads	Proportion of heads
1st 10 throws	7	$\frac{7}{10} = 0.7$
1st 20 throws	7 + 6 = 13	$\frac{13}{20} = 0.65$
1st 30 throws	7 + 6 + 8 = 21	
1st 40 throws		
1st 50 throws		

(a) Copy and complete the table.

(b) Explain what happens to the proportion of heads as the number of throws increases. [E]

5 80 students each visited one attraction last week.

The two-way table shows some information about these students.

	Theme Park	Aquarium	Circus	Total
Male			14	46
Female	21			
Total		29	24	80

(a) Copy and complete the two-way table.

One of the students is picked at random.

(b) Write down the probability that the student
   (i) visited the aquarium
   (ii) visited the theme park
   (iii) is female and visited the aquarium.

6 A game is played with two spinners.
You multiply the two numbers on which the spinners land to get the score.

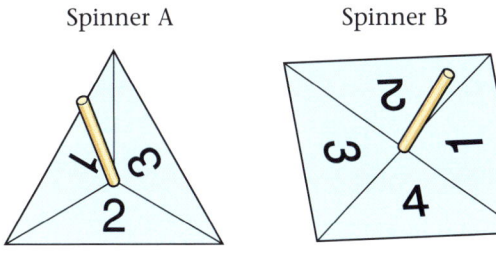

This score is 2 × 4 = 8

(a) Copy and complete the table to show all the possible scores.
One score has been done for you.

Spinner B

	×	1	2	3	4
Spinner A	1				
	2				8
	3				

(b) Work out the probability of getting a score of 6.
(c) Work out the probability of getting a score that is an odd number. [E]

7 60 British students each visited one foreign country last week.
The two-way table shows some information about these students.

	France	Germany	Spain	Total
Female			9	34
Male	15			
Total		25	18	60

(a) Copy and complete the two-way table.
One of the students is picked at random.
(b) Write down the probability that the student visited Germany last week. [E]

Summary of key points

1. An event which is **certain to happen** has a **probability of 1**.

2. An event which **cannot happen** has a **probability of 0**.

3. The probability that an event will happen is:

    $$\text{probability} = \frac{\text{number of successful outcomes}}{\text{total number of possible outcomes}}$$

    assuming that the outcomes are all equally likely.

4. The probability of an event happening is always greater than or equal to 0 (impossible) and less than or equal to 1 (certain). This can be written:

    $$0 \leqslant \text{probability} \leqslant 1$$

5. If the probability of an event happening is p then the probability of it *not* happening is $1 - p$.

6. The **estimated probability** that an event will happen in a game or experiment is:

    $$\text{estimated probability} = \frac{\text{number of successful trials}}{\text{total number of trials}}$$

    The **estimated probability** is given by the **relative frequency** with which the event occurs in a trial or experiment.

7. A **sample space diagram** represents all possible outcomes.

8. **Two-way tables** can be used to help solve probability problems.

9. The **relative frequency** of an outcome in an experiment is:

    $$\text{relative frequency} = \frac{\text{number of successful trials}}{\text{total number of trials}}$$

24 Presenting and analysing data 2

24.1 Scatter diagrams

Statements such as 'Smoking can cause lung cancer' and 'Drink driving causes accidents' are often made in the media. Sometimes they are supported by data showing, for example, whether there is a relationship between a smoking habit and the chance of getting lung cancer.

This section shows you how to compare two sets of data to see whether there is a relationship between them. For example, is there a relationship between the number of ice-creams sold at a kiosk and the average daytime temperature? James collected data to find out.

Average temperature (°C)	12	13	10	20	21	16	17	13	19	20	19	15	16	14
No. of ice-creams sold	5	9	1	51	48	20	30	15	32	42	37	23	25	14

He plotted each pair of values, (12, 5), (13, 9) and so on, on a graph. This is called a **scatter diagram** or **scatter graph**.

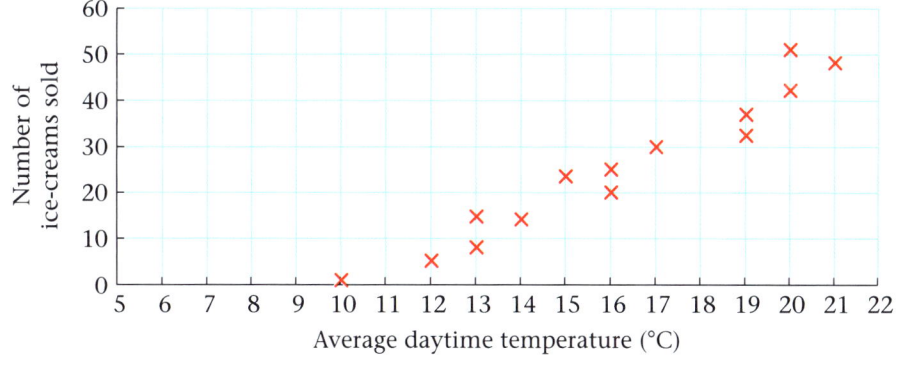

There does appear to be a relationship between the average daytime temperature and the number of ice-creams sold: the hotter it is, the more ice-creams are sold.

Here is another example. On a journey Chandra noted down how many miles there were still to go. She did this every ten minutes:

Time (mins)	10	20	30	40	50	60	70	80	90	100
Miles to go	72	60	50	42	40	32	25	18	10	0

Here is a scatter diagram showing this data:

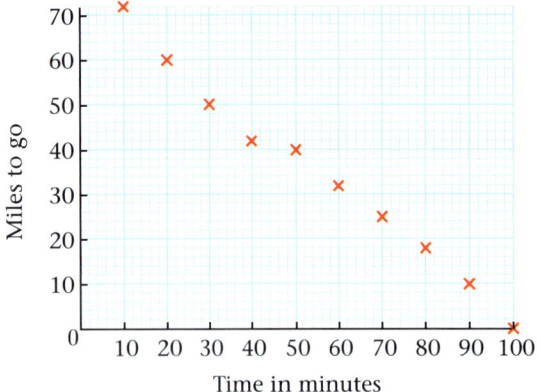

There is a relationship between the time she has been travelling and the number of miles still to go: the greater the time travelling, the fewer miles there are to go.

Sometimes there is no relationship between two sets of data Every Monday Trish recorded the temperature in °F and the rainfall in mm. Her results were:

Temperature (°F)	74	70	63	68	65	64	60	51	54	56	50
Rainfall (mm)	1	0	2	7	5	1	8	2	11	4	6

A scatter graph of this data looks like this:

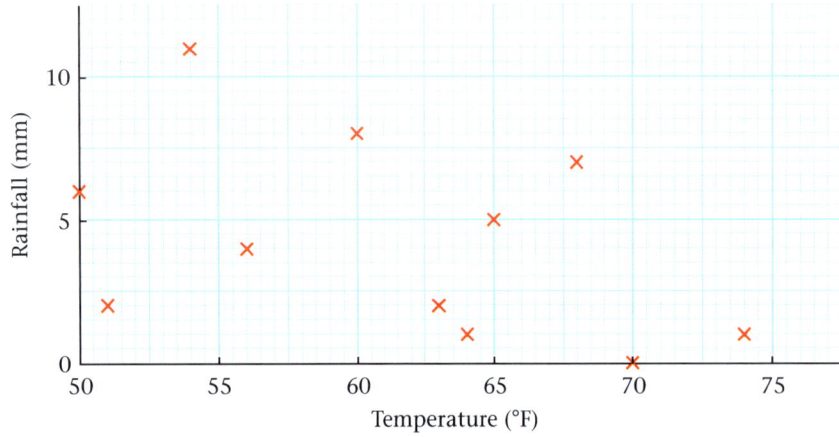

There does not appear to be any relationship.

> **Activity – Height and arm-span**
> Is there a relationship between your height and your arm-span?
> (a) Collect data for your class.
> (b) Draw a scatter graph to represent your data.
> (c) Describe the relationship.

Correlation

A relationship between two sets of data is called **a correlation**.

You need to be able to recognise different types of relationships between two sets of data. Look at these three scatter graphs:

As one value increases the other one also increases. There is a **positive correlation**.

As one value increases the other decreases. There is a **negative correlation**.

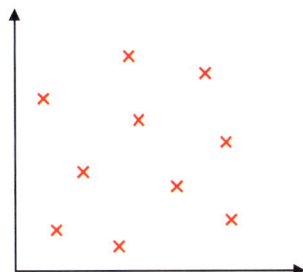

The points are randomly and widely spaced out. There is **no correlation**.

Line of best fit

When there is positive or negative correlation on a scatter diagram you can draw a line of best fit to describe the relationship between the two sets of data.

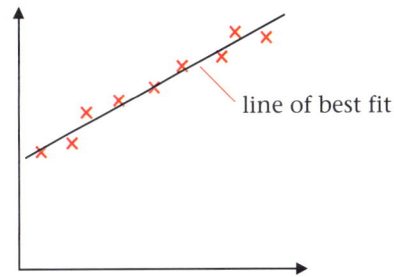

The **line of best fit** is a straight line that passes through or is as close to as many of the plotted points as possible.

For your GCSE exam you should use a ruler and draw your line of best fit by eye.

There are usually roughly equal numbers of points above and below the line.

Example 1

The table shows the acidity of seven lakes near to an industrial plant and their distance from it.

Distance (km)	4	34	17	60	6	52	42
Acidity (pH)	3.0	4.4	3.5	7.0	3.2	6.8	5.2

(a) Draw a scatter graph to illustrate this data.
(b) Draw and label the line of best fit on your scatter graph.
(c) Work out the equation of the line of best fit.
(d) Use your line of best fit to predict the acidity of a lake at a distance of 25 km.

(a), (b)

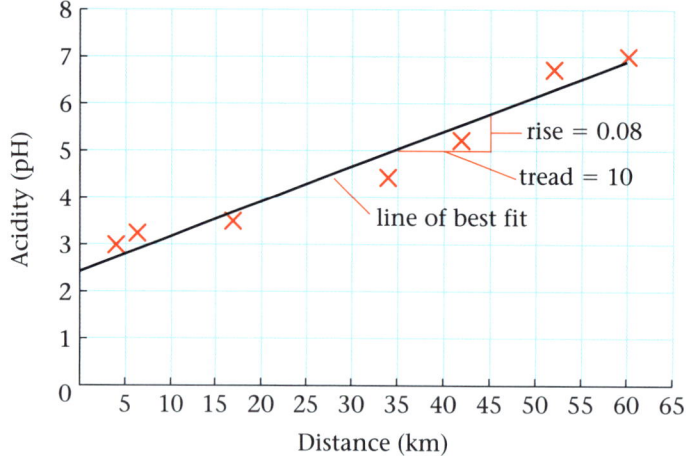

(c) The equation of the line of best fit is of the form $y = mx + c$.
m is the gradient and c is the intercept with the y-axis.
To find m, draw a right-angled triangle:

$$m = \frac{\text{rise}}{\text{tread}} = \frac{0.8}{10} = 0.08$$

From the graph: $c = 2.4$
The equation is $y = 0.08x + 2.4$

(d) Read up from 25 on the distance axis to the line of best fit, and across to the acidity axis. Using your line of best fit you can predict that the pH will be 4.3

Exercise 24A

1 The table shows the engine sizes of various cars and the distances they travel on one litre of petrol.

Engine size (litres)	0.8	1.6	2.6	1	2.1	1.3	1.8
Distances travelled (km)	13	10	5	12	7	11	9

(a) Draw a scatter diagram to represent this data.
(b) What type of correlation do you find?

2 What type of correlation would you expect if you compared the following data:
(a) heights of people and shoe sizes
(b) ages of cars and their selling prices
(c) time taken to get to school and marks in French
(d) sizes of gardens and the numbers of birds in them
(e) marks in science and marks in maths?

24.1 Scatter diagrams

3 Write down an example which you might expect would give each of the following correlations:
  (a) negative   (b) none   (c) positive.

4 A group of students went to a fitness centre. Their heights and weights were recorded and they were rated 0–40 on a number of activities.
The results are recorded in this table:

Weight	65	60	72	66	61	56	68	61	62	58	57	64
Height	175	172	182	179	174	165	176	168	172	170	162	175
Agility	24	19	32	26	23	18	34	12	35	28	16	21
Strength	29	22	32	35	26	18	25	14	30	26	20	33
Reactions	35	17	28	33	15	27	19	22	29	37	31	25
Skipping	26	34	20	18	36	28	22	36	32	28	38	16

(a) Draw scatter graphs for each of the following:
  (i) weight and height   (ii) weight and agility
  (iii) height and skipping   (iv) strength and reactions
  (v) agility and reactions   (vi) strength and skipping.
(b) For each of your scatter graphs state what type of correlation is shown, if any.
(c) If possible, draw and label a line of best fit on each of your scatter graphs.

Remember:
You can't draw a line of best fit if there is no correlation.

5 Here are sketches of six scatter diagrams:

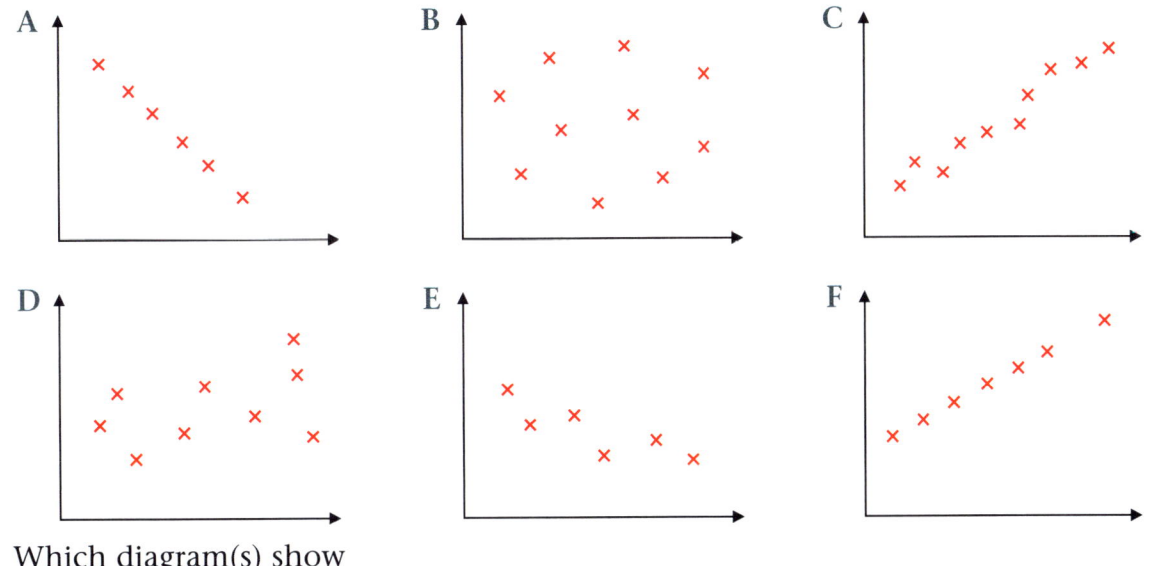

Which diagram(s) show
(a) positive correlation   (b) negative correlation   (c) no correlation?

6 This is a scatter diagram showing students' percentage scores in Paper 1 and Paper 2 of a mathematics examination:

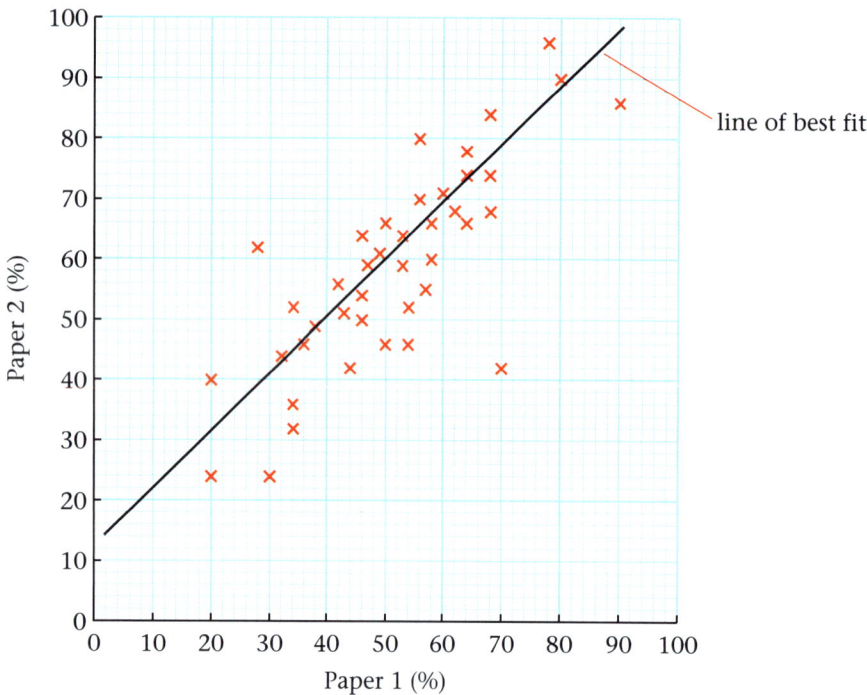

(a) What type of correlation does this diagram show?

Student A scored 43% on Paper 1, but did not take Paper 2.

(b) Use the line of best fit to estimate the percentage the student might have scored on Paper 2. [E]

24.2 Finding averages

In Chapter 20 you learned about different averages for a set of data. You should remember that:

The **mode** of a set of data is the value which occurs most often.

The **mean** of a set of data is the sum of the values divided by the number of values:

$$\text{mean} = \frac{\text{sum of values}}{\text{number of values}}$$

The **median** is the middle value when the data is arranged in order of size.

How to find the position of the median

An easy way to find the position of the median value in a set of data is to add 1 to the number of values, then divide the result by 2.

Suppose you needed to find the median value for a set of 30 data values.

$$\frac{30 + 1}{2} = 15.5$$

so the median is between the 15th and 16th values when data is arranged in order. It is the mean of the 15th and 16th values.

This method works whether there is an odd or an even number of items of data.

Exercise 24B

1. Find the mean of
   (a) 5, 11, 23, 16 and 20
   (b) 114, 107, 134, 96 and 49

2. The mean of six numbers is 12. Five of the numbers are 11, 7, 21, 14 and 9. Calculate the sixth.

3. In training Fritz ran the 100 m in 10.8, 11.1, 10.7, 10.9 and 10.8 seconds.
   (a) What was his average (mean) time?
   (b) How fast must he run in the next race to bring his average down to 10.8 seconds?

4. Use the information given to find the value of n in each of the following sets of numbers.
   (a) 5, 7, 4, 1, n, 5 : the mean is 6
   (b) 3, 1, 4, 5, 4, n : the mode is 4
   (c) 1, 7, 2, 1, n, 4, 3 : the modes are 1 and 2
   (d) 2, n, 5, 7, 1, 3 : the median is $3\frac{1}{2}$
   (e) 2.6, 3.5, n, 6.2 : the mean is 4
   (f) 4, 7, 2, n, 2, 9, 6 : the median is 5

5. A stallholder bought 5 boxes of fruit at £12.40 a box and 3 boxes at £16.20.
   What was the mean cost of the boxes?

6 The bar chart shows the number of cans of cola bought by Class 10C during a two-week period.

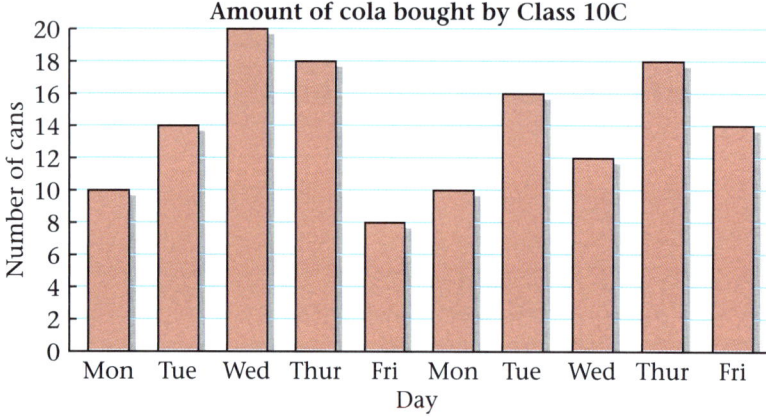

Find

(a) the mode

(b) the median

(c) the mean number of cans bought.

24.3 Averages from frequency distributions

In Chapter 12 (in Book 1) you learned that it is convenient to collect large amounts of data in a tally chart or a frequency distribution table.

This section shows you how to find the mean, mode and median when the information is given in a frequency table.

> A set of data which shows the number of times each value occurs is called a frequency distribution.

Example 2

In a survey, the number of eggs in seagulls' nests in June was counted.

The table shows the results.

Find
(a) the mode
(b) the median
(c) the mean number of eggs.

Number of eggs x	Frequency f
0	17
1	12
2	23
3	37
4	18
Total	107

(a) The mode is the value which occurs most often. In a frequency table this is the item of data which has the highest frequency. For this data the mode is 3 eggs. There are more nests with 3 eggs than any other number of eggs.

(b) The median is the middle value of the data. There are 107 nests altogether. The data in the table is in order. So the median value is the $\frac{n+1}{2}$th value.

The middle nest is nest $(107 + 1) \div 2 =$ nest 54.

   Nests 1–17 have 0 eggs
   Nests 18–29 have 1 egg
   Nests 30–52 have 2 eggs
   Nests 53–89 have 3 eggs

So nest 54 is a 3-egg nest. The median is 3 eggs.

(c) The mean is the total number of eggs divided by the total number of nests (the total frequency):

Number of eggs x	Frequency f	Frequency × number of eggs $f \times x$
0	17	0
1	12	12
2	23	46
3	37	111
4	18	72
Totals	107	241

The number of eggs in 2-egg nests is $23 \times 2 = 46$.

The total number of eggs is the sum of all the $f \times x$ values.

The mean = total number of eggs ÷ total frequency

$$= \frac{241}{107} = 2.25 \text{ eggs}$$

The mean of a frequency distribution

A short way of writing the mean uses the Greek letter sigma Σ to represent the sum of a set of values:

For a frequency distribution:

$$\text{mean} = \frac{\Sigma fx}{\Sigma f}$$

the sum of all the ($f \times x$) values in the distribution

the sum of the frequencies

Chapter 24 Presenting and analysing data 2

Exercise 24C

1 Copy and complete the table. Use your table to calculate the mean, mode and median numbers of cars per household.

> Don't forget you can use your calculator to work out the mean.

Cars per household x	Frequency f	$f \times x$
0	6	
1	20	
2	13	
3	4	
4	2	
Totals		

The frequency tables in questions **2–4** are written sideways in rows. You might find it easier to rewrite them in columns.

> Start your table off like this.

2

Dice score	1	2	3	4	5	6
Frequency	23	17	24	22	19	15

Dice score x	Frequency f	$f \times x$
1	23	23

Work out the mode, median and mean dice scores.

3 A factory takes random samples of 102 items and tests them for faults. (This is their method of maintaining standards. It is called quality control.)
Here are their results for last week:

Number of faults per sample	0	1	2	3	4	5
Number of samples	76	13	6	3	3	1

> 'Per sample' tells you that you need to divide the total number of faults by the total number of samples. So the 'number of samples' is the frequency.

Work out the mode, median and mean numbers of faults per sample.

4 Samir asked 24 people how many packets of crisps they ate last week. The results are shown in the table.

Number of packets of crisps	0	1	2	3	4	5	6	7	8
Number of people (frequency)	4	0	6	5	3	2	1	3	0

(a) Write down the modal number of packets eaten.
(b) Work out the median number of packets eaten.
(c) Calculate the mean number of packets eaten, correct to 1 d.p.

5 Some teachers were asked how many National Lottery tickets they bought last week.

The results are shown in the table.

(a) Which number of tickets is the mode?

(b) Work out the mean number of tickets.

(c) Find the median number of tickets.

Number of tickets	Number of teachers
0	2
1	7
2	5
3	2
4	0
5	3
6	1

[E]

24.4 Spread from frequency distributions

The median is the middle value, with half the data on one side and half the data on the other.

The **quartiles** are found when you divide the data up into four parts.

0   1   1   ②   3   5   5   ⑤   7   9   9   ⑩   10   11   12

Lower quartile ($\frac{1}{4}$ way along) $\frac{1}{4}(n + 1)$th value

The median or middle value $\frac{n + 1}{2}$ th value

Upper quartile ($\frac{3}{4}$ way along) $\frac{3}{4}(n + 1)$th value

◄———— Interquartile range ————►

The interquartile range is the difference between the upper quartile and the lower quartile.

Interquartile range = 10 − 2 = 8 for this data.

> Quartiles and the interquartile range will not be tested in your exam, but may be useful for your coursework.

When the data is arranged in ascending order:
- the **lower quartile** is the value one quarter of the way into the data
- the **upper quartile** is the value three quarters of the way into the data
- the **interquartile range** = upper quartile − lower quartile.

Example 3

In a school, stars are awarded for very good work. The number of stars awarded to each of 95 students is shown in this frequency table.

Number of stars	3	4	5	6	7	8	9	10	11	Total
Number of students	1	2	4	7	17	23	24	16	1	95

Work out (a) the range (b) the interquartile range.

(a) Range = highest value − lowest value = 11 − 3 = 8 stars

(b) The lower quartile is the $\frac{1}{4}(95 + 1) = 24$th value.

Adding up the number of students in order:

$1 + 2 + 4 + 7 = 14$ and $1 + 2 + 4 + 7 + 17 = 31$

As the 24th value is between the 14th and 31st values, it is one of the 17 values recorded as 7 stars. So the lower quartile is 7 stars.

Using the same method, the upper quartile is the $\frac{3(95 + 1)}{4} = 72$nd value.

Adding up the frequencies in order:

$1 + 2 + 4 + 7 + 17 + 23 = 54$ and $1 + 2 + 4 + 7 + 17 + 23 + 24 = 78$

As the 72nd value is between the 54th and 78th values, it is one of the 24 values recorded as 9 stars. So the upper quartile is 9 stars.

The interquartile range is:

upper quartile − lower quartile = 9 − 7 = 2 stars

Exercise 24D

Work out (a) the range (b) the interquartile range for the data shown in the frequency table in each question.

1 The number of letters delivered to each house in a road of 39 houses:

Number of letters	0	1	2	3	4	5	6	7
Frequency (number of houses)	8	13	9	7	1	0	0	1

2 The marks gained by 63 pupils in an examination:

Mark	10	20	30	35	40	45	50	65
Frequency	0	4	8	13	16	10	7	5

3 The number of whole months over the age of 15 years of 29 pupils in a class:

Number of months over 15 years	0	1	2	3	4	5	6	7	8	9	10	11
Frequency	1	0	1	2	3	3	3	1	2	4	5	4

4 The amounts spent by 100 people on newspapers in one week:

Amount (£)	0	1	2	3	4	5	6	7	8
Frequency	5	17	25	19	13	12	5	2	2

24.5 Averages from grouped data

In Chapter 12 (in Book 1) you also learned how to group large amounts of data in class intervals. What averages can be found from grouped data?

The manager of a hotel checks the cost of phone calls made by each guest by looking at the number of units used per call. She summarises the data from the phone calls in a frequency table, grouping it in class intervals.

Number of units	Frequency
1–5	73
6–10	161
11–15	294
16–20	186
21–25	65
over 25	11
Total	790

The median: There were 790 phone calls so the position of the median data value is the $(790 + 1) \div 2 = 395\frac{1}{2}$th value. It is in the class interval 11–15.
You cannot give an exact value for the median.

The $395\frac{1}{2}$th value is in this class interval.

> For grouped data, you can state the class interval that contains the median.

The modal class: The class interval 11–15 units per call has the highest frequency.

> For grouped data, the class interval with the highest frequency is called the **modal class**.

The modal class only makes sense as a measure of the average if the class intervals are the same.

The mean: Each class interval contains calls using different numbers of units, so you have not got the exact data you need to calculate the mean, but you can calculate an **estimate of the mean**. This is *not* a guess, but a calculation. Here is how to do it.

Assume each call in a class interval uses the middle number of units in that class interval.

Number of units used per call	Frequency f	Middle value x	$f \times x$
1–5	73	3	219
6–10	161	8	1288
11–15	294	13	3822
16–20	186	18	3348
21–25	65	23	1495
over 25	11	28	308
Totals	790		10 480

*The middle value of the class interval 1–5 is 3. The middle value of class interval 6–10 is 8 and so on.
The 161 calls did not all use 8 units each. The errors made by overestimating approximately balance those made by underestimating.
A middle value must be chosen for calls over 25 units. This is a matter of judgement. Here 28 is used.*

Now you can calculate an estimate of the mean in a similar way to that for ungrouped data:

$$\text{estimate of mean} = \frac{\text{sum of (middle values} \times \text{frequencies)}}{\text{sum of frequencies}}$$

$$= \frac{\Sigma fx}{\Sigma f} = \frac{10\,480}{790} = 13.3$$

> For more on calculating the mean see Section 24.3.

For grouped data, you can calculate an estimate of the mean using the middle value of each class interval.

In the phone calls example the data is discrete. You can use exactly the same method to find an estimate of the mean of continuous data. The method works even if the class intervals are not the same size and the middle values are not whole numbers.

> Remember:
> Discrete data can be counted. It takes a fixed number of values. Continuous data is measured. It can take any value in a range.

Exercise 24E

1 The students at Loovilla College decided to have a biscuit eating competition. A random sample of 25 students was taken. The table shows the numbers of students eating different numbers of biscuits in 4 minutes

Number of biscuits eaten in 4 minutes	Frequency f	Middle value x	$f \times x$
1–5	2		
6–10	8		
11–15	7		
16–20	5		
21–25	2		
26–30	1		
Totals	25		

(a) Calculate an estimate of the mean number of biscuits eaten in 4 minutes.
(b) Write down the modal class interval.
(c) 250 students entered the competition.
Estimate how many of them will eat more than 20 biscuits in the 4 minutes. [E]

2 In a five-leg darts match a record is kept of the scores for each throw of three darts.

Score	1–20	21–40	41–60	61–100	101–140	141–180
Frequency	3	17	25	56	8	3

(a) What is the modal class?
(b) Calculate an estimate of the mean score.

3 The heights of students in a class are measured. The table shows the results.

Height interval (h cm)	Number of students
$150 \leq h < 155$	4
$155 \leq h < 160$	4
$160 \leq h < 165$	8
$165 \leq h < 170$	7
$170 \leq h < 175$	5
$175 \leq h < 180$	2

(a) What is the modal class?
(b) Work out an estimate of the mean height.

4 Ian looked at a passage from a book. He recorded the number of words in each sentence in a frequency table using class intervals of 1–5, 6–10, 11–15, etc.

Class interval	Frequency f	Middle value x	$f \times x$
1–5	16		48
6–10	28		
11–15	26	13	
16–20	14		
21–25	10		230
26–30	3		
31–35	1		
36–40	0		
41–45	2		86
Total		Total	

(a) Copy and complete the table.
(b) Write down the modal class interval.
(c) Write down the class interval in which the median lies.
(d) Work out an estimate for the mean number of words in a sentence. [E]

5 The table shows how long couples had been married whose marriages ended in divorce in 2005.

Length of marriage in completed years	0–2	3–4	5–9	10–14	15–19	20–24	25–29	30–40
Frequency as a %	9	14	27	18	13	10	5	4

Work out an estimate for the mean length of a marriage that ended in a divorce.

Chapter 24 Presenting and analysing data 2

Mixed exercise 24

You will need graph paper.

1. The table contains information about the returns of postal surveys sent out by a market research organisation.

Issued	2000	2500	3000	2800	1400	2100	2000	1800	2400	2600
Returned	480	605	712	683	308	515	492	421	592	624

   (a) Construct a scatter graph of the postal surveys issued and returned.
   (b) Draw in a line of best fit.
   (c) Describe the correlation between the postal surveys issued and returned.

2. The ages of 12 cross-channel swimmers and their swimming times are recorded as:

   17 yrs in 15 hrs 26 min   23 yrs in 14 hrs 32 min
   36 yrs in 18 hrs 5 min   25 yrs in 11 hrs 12 min
   18 yrs in 21 hrs 21 min   28 yrs in 13 hrs 43 min
   26 yrs in 17 hrs 50 min   31 yrs in 12 hrs 7 min
   21 yrs in 15 hrs 12 min   30 yrs in 16 hrs 10 min
   42 yrs in 14 hrs 28 min   21 yrs in 11 hrs 42 min

   (a) Draw a scatter graph of the ages and swimming times of the swimmers.
   (b) Comment on the correlation between the ages of the swimmers and their swimming times.

3. This table shows the number of certificates gained by students for outstanding sporting achievement during the year.

Number of certificates	Tally	Frequency
1	||||	4
2	|||| ||||	9
3	|||| |||	8
4	|||| ||||	10
5	|||| |	6
6	|||	3

   (a) Calculate (i) the mean
               (ii) the mode
              (iii) the median.
   (b) Which one of these averages could be used to encourage students to take part?
       Explain the reasons for your choice.

4. A goal shooter has scores of 14, 18, 10, 24, 32, 26, 32 in seven games.
   How many must she score in the 8th game to bring her mean score up to 24?

5 The mean content of 11 boxes of matches is 46.
How many matches are there altogether?
The next box checked contains 49 matches.
What is the mean content when this box is included?

6 Four boys have a mean height of 160 cm.
Seven girls have a mean height of 154 cm.
What is the mean height of the eleven young people?

7 The mean of 15, 17, x, 28 and 19 is 16.
What is the value of x?

8 What mark should Leo get in his next test to get the median stated?
(a) marks so far: 1, 8, 5, 2 : median 5
(b) marks so far: 8, 2, 4, 5, 3, 8, 4, 2, 9 : median 4

9 Eleanor conducted a survey in which she recorded the shoe sizes of 40 girls. Her results are shown in the frequency table.

Shoe size	3	$3\frac{1}{2}$	4	$4\frac{1}{2}$	5	$5\frac{1}{2}$	6	$6\frac{1}{2}$	7	$7\frac{1}{2}$	8
Number of girls	1	2	2	5	5	6	7	5	4	1	2

(a) Write down the modal shoe size.
(b) Work out the median shoe size.
(c) Work out the range of the shoe sizes.
(d) Calculate the mean shoe size, giving your answer correct to 1 d.p.

10 Cole's sells furniture and will deliver up to a distance of 20 miles. The diagram shows the delivery charges made by Cole's. The table shows the information in the diagram and also the numbers of deliveries made in the first week of May 2005.

Distance (d) from Cole's in miles	Delivery charge in pounds	Number of deliveries			
$0 < d \leq 5$	15	27			
$5 < d \leq 10$	20	11			
$10 < d \leq 15$	25	8			
$15 < d \leq 20$	30	4			

(a) Copy the table and calculate the mean charge per delivery for these deliveries.
(b) Calculate an estimate for the mean distance of the customers' homes from Cole's.

11 This table gives the marks scored by pupils in a French test and in a German test.

French	15	35	34	23	35	27	36	34	23	24	30	40	25	35	20
German	20	37	35	25	33	30	39	36	27	20	33	35	27	32	28

(a) Draw a scatter graph of the marks scored in the French and German tests on a grid like this:

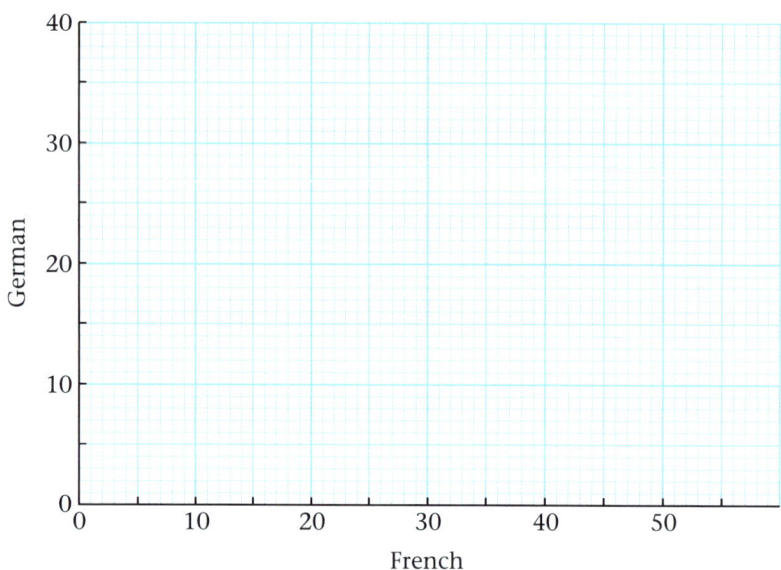

(b) Describe the correlation between the marks scored in the two tests.

(c) Draw and label the line of best fit on your scatter graph.

(d) Use your line of best fit to predict the German mark of a pupil who scored 28 in their French test. [E]

12 For each pair of variables below, state whether you think there would be:

        positive correlation
    or **negative** correlation
    or **no** correlation.

Give a brief reason for your choice.

(a) *the amount of rain falling* and *the number of people outdoors.*

(b) *the number of apples a person ate* and *the person's results in mathematics tests.* [E]

13 Jez chews bubble gum until the taste has gone. He cannot decide between two different brands. He measures his chewing times on six occasions for each brand.
This table shows his chewing times in minutes.

| Brand A | 11 | 10 | 13 | 9 | 17 | 12 |
| Brand B | 11 | 13 | 12 | 12 | 14 | 10 |

The mean and range of the chewing times for Brand A are given in the next table. Calculate the mean and range of the chewing times for Brand B.
Which brand should Jez decide to use, assuming they cost the same?
Give a clear explanation.

	Mean	Range
Brand A	12	8
Brand B		

[E]

Summary of key points

1 A relationship between two sets of data is called a **correlation**.

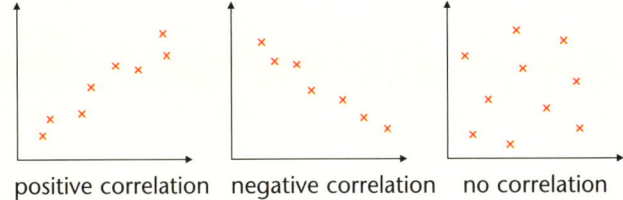

positive correlation   negative correlation   no correlation

2 The **line of best fit** is a straight line that passes through or is as close to as many of the plotted points as possible.

3 For a frequency distribution:

$$\text{mean} = \frac{\Sigma fx}{\Sigma f}$$

— the sum of all the $(f \times x)$ values in the distribution
— the sum of all the frequencies

4 When the data is arranged in ascending order:
   - the **lower quartile** is the value one quarter of the way into the data
   - the **upper quartile** is the value three quarters of the way into the data
   - the **interquartile range** = upper quartile − lower quartile.

5 For grouped data:
   - you can state the class interval that contains the median
   - the class interval with the highest frequency is called the **modal class**
   - you can calculate an estimate of the mean using the middle value of each class interval.

25 Pythagoras' theorem

This chapter shows you how to calculate the lengths of sides of right-angled triangles. This topic is regularly included in GCSE exams.

25.1 Using Pythagoras' theorem to find the hypotenuse

The longest side of a right-angled triangle is the one opposite the right angle. It is called the **hypotenuse**.

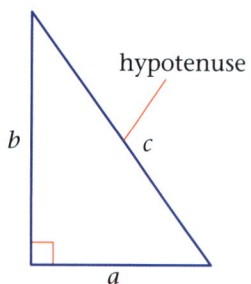

Exercise 25A

1. The right-angled triangle *ABC* has sides 3 cm, 4 cm and 5 cm. Squares have been drawn on each of its sides.

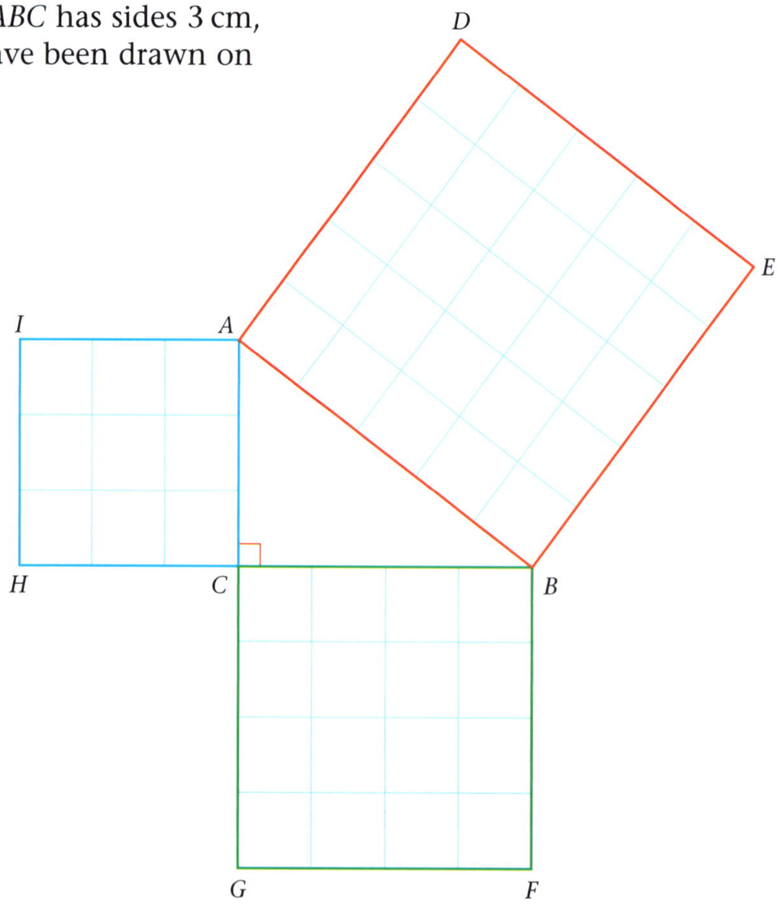

    (a) Find the number of cm squares in
       (i) the square *CBFG*
       (ii) the square *ACHI*
       (iii) the square *BADE*.
    (b) Add your answers for **(a) (i)** and **(a) (ii)**.
    (c) Write down what you notice.

25.1 Using Pythagoras' theorem to find the hypotenuse   467

2 The right-angled triangle *PQR* has sides 2.5, 6 and 6.5.
Squares have been drawn on each side of the triangle.

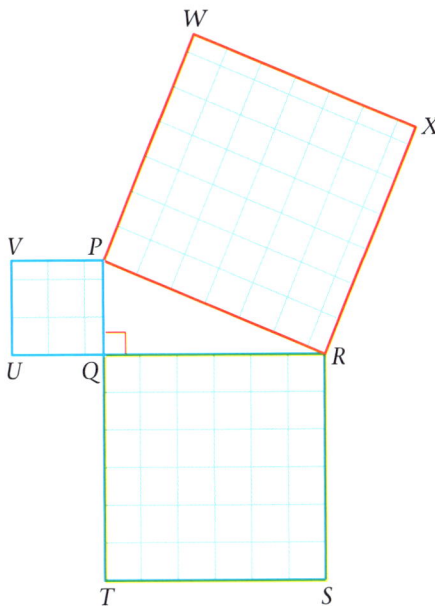

(a) Count the number of small squares in
   (i) the square *PQUV*
   (ii) the square *QRST*
   (iii) the square *RPWX*.
(b) Add your answers for (a) (i) and (a) (ii).
(c) Write down what you notice.

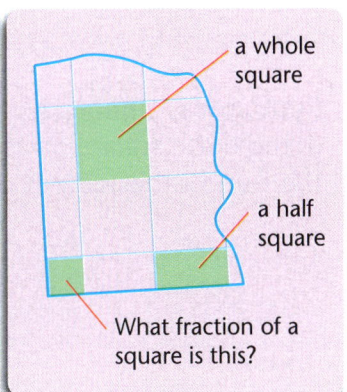

A relationship between areas

Exercise 25A shows that there is a relationship between squares drawn on the sides of a right-angled triangle.

Another way to see the relationship is to calculate the areas of the squares.

Example 1

In triangle *ABC* the square on the hypotenuse is:
$$AC^2 = 5^2 = 25$$

The sum of the squares on the other two sides is:
$$AB^2 + BC^2 = 3^2 + 4^2 = 9 + 16 = 25$$
so $\quad 5^2 = 3^2 + 4^2$
and $\quad AC^2 = AB^2 + BC^2$

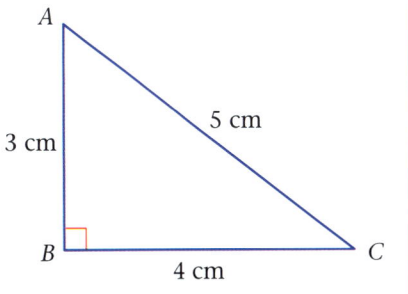

Example 2

In triangle *PQR* the square on the hypotenuse is:

$$PR^2 = 6.5^2 = 42.25$$

The sum of the squares on the other two sides is:

$$PQ^2 + QR^2 = 2.5^2 + 6^2 = 6.25 + 36 = 42.25$$

so $\quad 6.5^2 = 2.5^2 + 6^2$

and $\quad PR^2 = PQ^2 + QR^2$

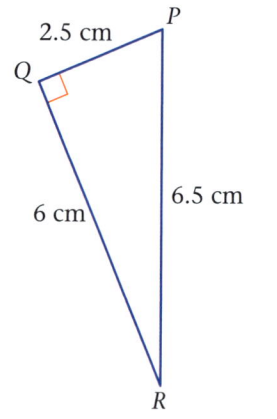

These are examples of a result, called a **theorem**, that was proved by **Pythagoras**, a Greek philosopher and mathematician who lived around 500BC.

Pythagoras' theorem states that in a right-angled triangle the square on the hypotenuse is equal to the sum of the squares on the other two sides.

$$c^2 = a^2 + b^2 \quad \text{or} \quad a^2 + b^2 = c^2$$

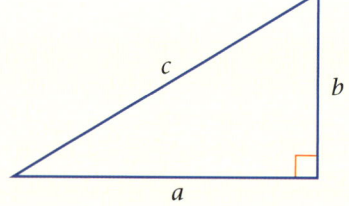

Example 3

In this right-angled triangle calculate the length of the side marked *z*.

Use $\quad c^2 = a^2 + b^2$
$\quad\quad z^2 = 12^2 + 5^2$
$\quad\quad\quad = 144 + 25$
$\quad\quad\quad = 169$
so $\quad z = \sqrt{169} = 13$ cm

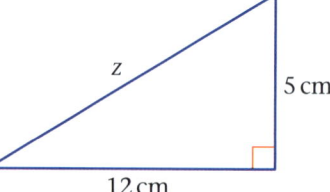

Example 4

In triangle *ABC* calculate the length of *AC* using a calculator. Give your answer correct to 3 significant figures.

$AC^2 = 5^2 + 6^2$ so $AC = \sqrt{5^2 + 6^2}$.

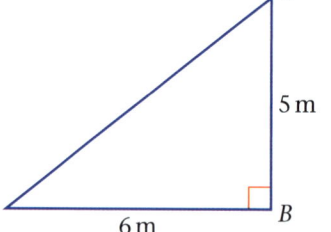

The display shows 7.8102497 so the answer is 7.81 m (to 3 significant figures).

25.1 Using Pythagoras' theorem to find the hypotenuse

Example 5

In triangle *LMN*, angle $N = 90°$,
$LN = 18.3$ cm and $MN = 7$ cm.
Calculate *LM* correct to one decimal place.

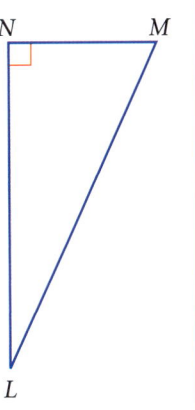

Use $c^2 = a^2 + b^2$
$LM^2 = MN^2 + LN^2$
$= 7^2 + 18.3^2$
$= 49 + 334.89$
$= 383.89$
so $LM = \sqrt{383.89} = 19.59…$ cm
$= 19.6$ cm (to 1 d.p.)

Exercise 25B

1 Calculate the lengths marked with letters in these triangles.
   For **(e)** and **(f)** give your answers correct to one decimal place.

(a) 5 cm, 12 cm, *a*

(b) 12 cm, 9 cm, *b*

(c) 3.5 cm, 12 cm, *c*

(d) 6 cm, 4.5 cm, *d*

(e) 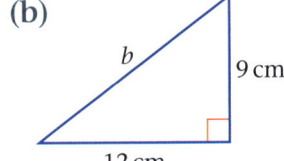 4.3 cm, 5.1 cm, *e*

(f) 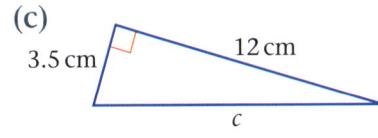 10.4 cm, 7.9 cm, *f*

2 Give your answers correct to one decimal place.

(a) Find *YZ*.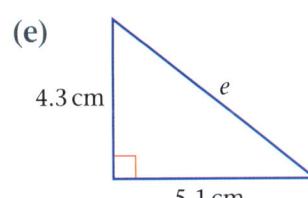
X—9 cm—Z, 7 cm, Y

(b) Find *SU*.
S, 23 cm, T—27 cm—U

(c) Find *JL*.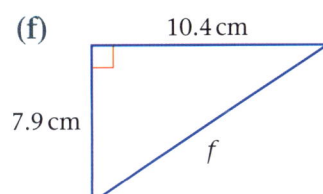
J—5.3 m—K, 4.8 m, L

(d) Find *AC*.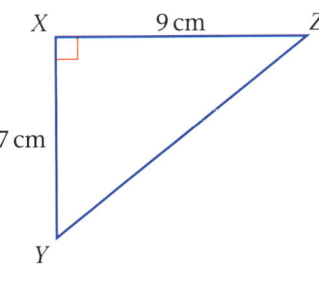
B, 13.6 m, 15.7 m, A, C

(e) Find *DF*.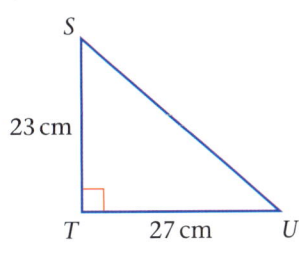
D, 4.7 cm, E—5.3 cm—F

(f) Find *PQ*.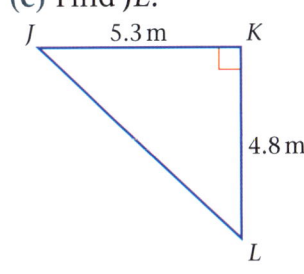
P, 3.5 cm, Q—4.8 cm—R

3 A rectangle is 13 cm long and 7 cm wide.
Work out the length of a diagonal of the rectangle.

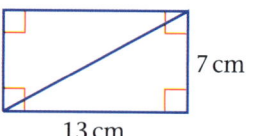

4 A boat leaves Broadstairs and sails due East for 5 km. The boat then changes course and sails due South for 3 km. Calculate the final distance of the boat from Broadstairs, giving your answer correct to one decimal place.

5 A railway at a seaside resort goes from the promenade to the top of the cliffs. The cliff top is 42 m above the promenade and the bottom of the railway is 35 m from the base of the cliff. Work out the length of the railway track.

25.2 Using Pythagoras' theorem to find one of the shorter sides of a triangle

With the formula $c^2 = a^2 + b^2$ you can calculate the longest side c of a right-angled triangle. If you need to find one of the shorter sides (a, for example) it is easier to change the formula so that a^2 is on its own on one side.

Pythagoras' theorem states:

$$c^2 = a^2 + b^2$$

To calculate either of the shorter sides a or b use Pythagoras' theorem

$a^2 = c^2 - b^2$ or $b^2 = c^2 - a^2$

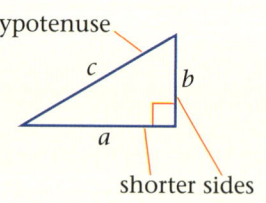

Example 6

In triangle DEF, angle F is a right angle, $DF = 5$ cm and $DE = 7$ cm. Calculate the length of EF.

Use $a^2 = c^2 - b^2$
$EF^2 = 7^2 - 5^2$
$= 49 - 25$
$= 24$
so $EF = \sqrt{24}$
$= 4.898 ... = 4.9$ cm (correct to 1 d.p.)

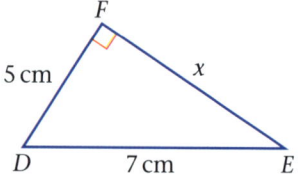

Hint: always check that the hypotenuse is still the longest side. If not, look for your mistake.

24 is not a square number, so √24 cannot be worked out exactly as an ordinary number. It is a non-terminating decimal number.

However √24 is an exact value. A number written like this (the square root of an integer) is called a **surd**. A surd is always the positive square root.

> If you were not allowed to use a calculator, you could leave your answer to Example 6 in surd notation as √24 cm.

Example 7

In triangle *STU* calculate the length of *ST* using a calculator. Give your answer correct to 3 significant figures.

$$ST^2 = 10^2 - 4^2 \text{ so } ST = \sqrt{10^2 - 4^2}$$

The display shows 9.16515139 so the answer is 9.17 m (to 3 significant figures).

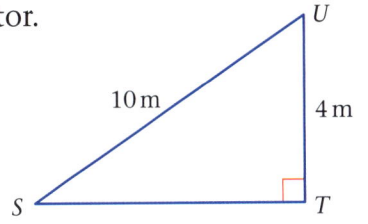

Example 8

An isosceles triangle *PQR* has *PQ* = 14.3 cm, *PR* = 14.3 cm and *QR* = 9.8 cm.

Calculate the height of the triangle correct to 1 d.p.

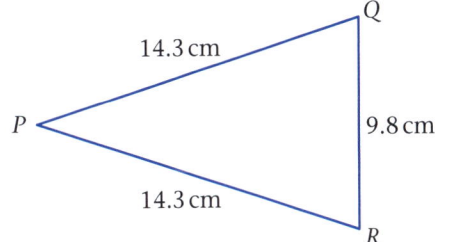

In this diagram *PN* is the height of the triangle. *PN* is a line of symmetry so *QN* = *NR*.

$$NR = \tfrac{1}{2} \times 9.8 = 4.9 \text{ cm}$$

Triangle *PNR* has a right angle at *N* so you can use Pythagoras' theorem.

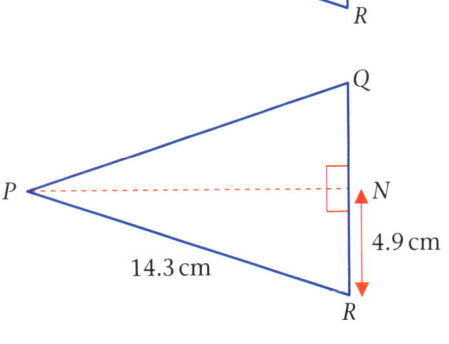

Use $a^2 = c^2 - b^2$

$$PN^2 = 14.3^2 - 4.9^2$$
$$= 204.49 - 24.01$$
$$= 180.48$$

so $PN = \sqrt{180.48}$
$$= 13.43...$$

The height of the triangle is 13.4 cm (correct to 1 d.p.)

Exercise 25C

1 Calculate the lengths marked with letters in these triangles. For parts **(c)** to **(f)** give your answers correct to one decimal place.

(a)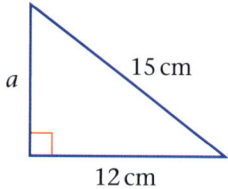

(b)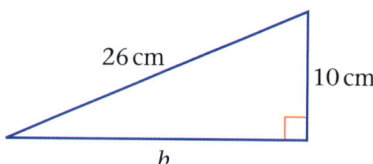

(c)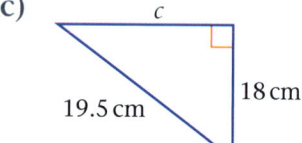

(d)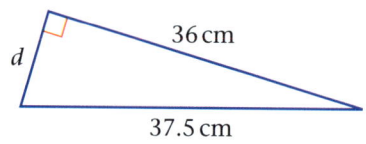

(e)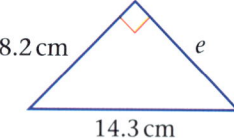

(f)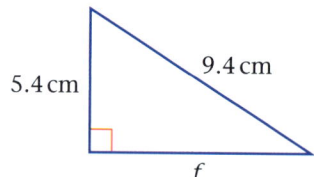

2 Give your answers correct to one decimal place.

(a) Find *ON*.
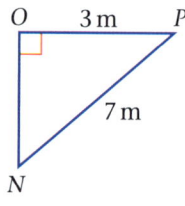

(b) Find *RS*.
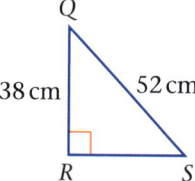

(c) Find *TV*.
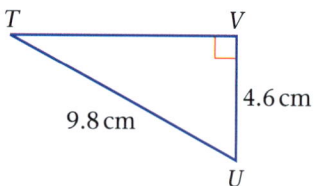

(d) Find *XY*.
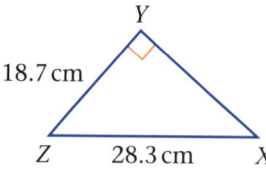

(e) Find *AB*.
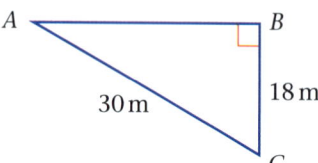

(f) Find *EF*.
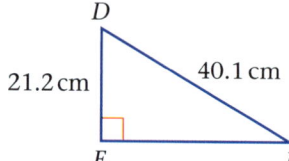

Mixed exercise 25

1 Calculate the lengths marked with letters.

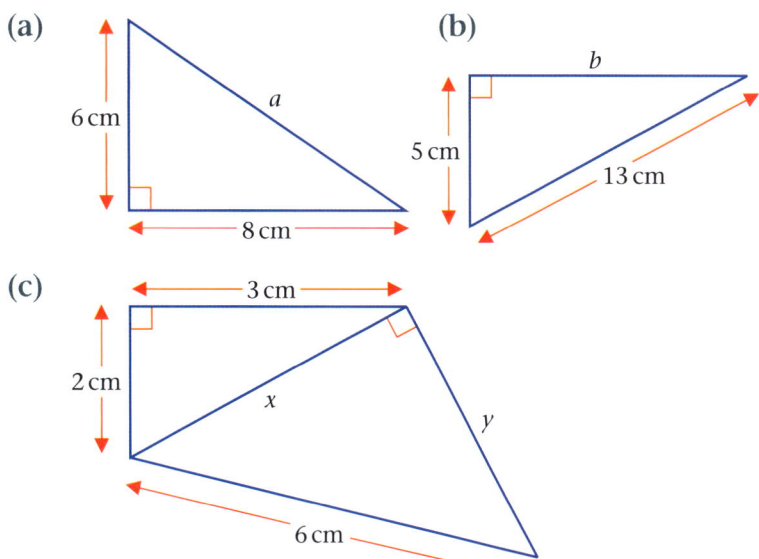

In part **(c)** leave your answers for *x* and *y* in surd notation.

2 A ladder is 5 metres long. It leans against a wall with one end on the ground 1 metre from the wall. The other end of the ladder just reaches a windowsill.
Calculate the height of the windowsill above the ground.

3 Rowena is in her helicopter above the Canary Wharf tower. She flies due West for 4.6 miles and then due North for 1 mile. She is then above Senate House. Calculate the direct distance, in miles, of the Canary Wharf tower from Senate House.

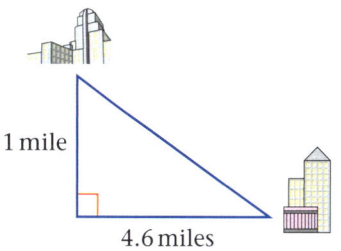

4 An isosceles triangle *ABC* has *AB* = 9.5 cm and *BC* = 9.5 cm. The height of the triangle is *BD* and *BD* = 7.2 cm.
Work out the length of *AC*.

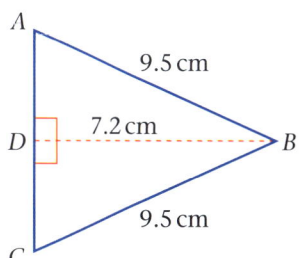

5 An isosceles triangle *XYZ* has *XY* = 26 cm, *ZX* = 26 cm and *ZY* = 18 cm.
Calculate the height of triangle *XYZ*.

6 A mother zebra leaves the rest of the herd to go in search of water. She travels due South for 0.9 km and then due East for 1.2 km. How far is she from the rest of the herd?

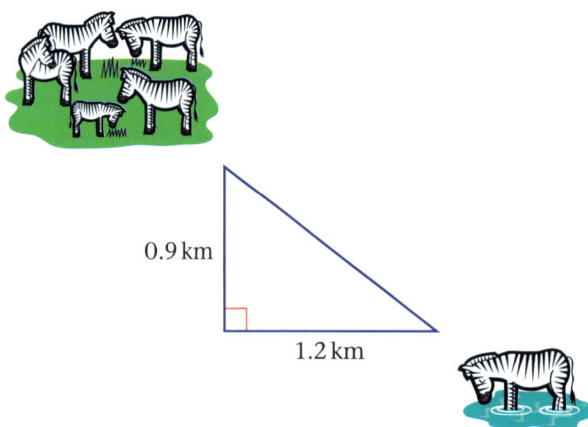

7 ABC is a right-angled triangle. AB is of length 4 m and BC is of length 13 m. Calculate the length of AC.

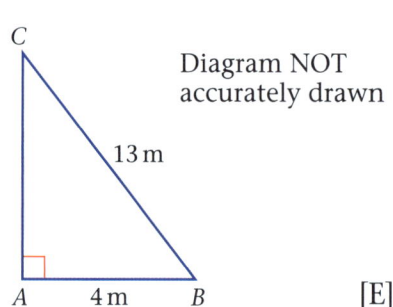

Diagram NOT accurately drawn

[E]

8 Work out the length, in metres, of side AB of the triangle.

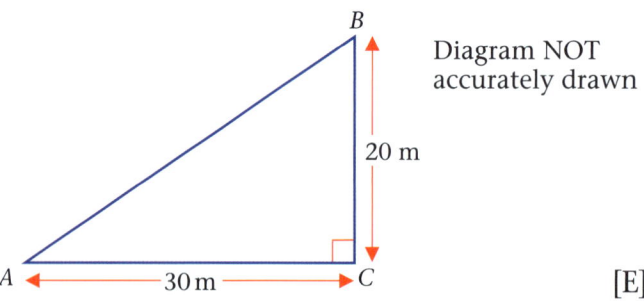

Diagram NOT accurately drawn

[E]

Summary of key points

1 Pythagoras' theorem states that in a right-angled triangle the square on the hypotenuse is equal to the sum of the squares on the other two sides.

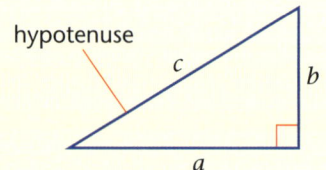

2 Use $c^2 = a^2 + b^2$ to calculate the hypotenuse.
Use $a^2 = c^2 - b^2$ or $b^2 = c^2 - a^2$ to calculate one of the shorter sides.

26 Advanced perimeter, area and volume

This chapter shows you how to find perimeters, areas and volumes for a variety of 2-D and 3-D shapes.

26.1 Perimeters and areas of 2-D shapes

You should remember these facts from Chapter 19:

The **perimeter** of a shape is the total length of its boundary:

perimeter of a rectangle = $l + l + w + w$
$= 2(l + w)$

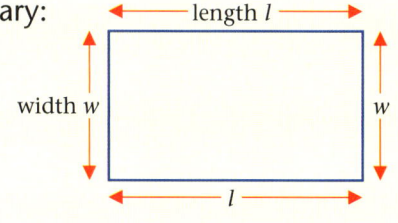

The area of a shape is a measure of the amount of space it covers:

area of a rectangle = length × width
$= l \times w$

area of a parallelogram = base × height
$= b \times h$

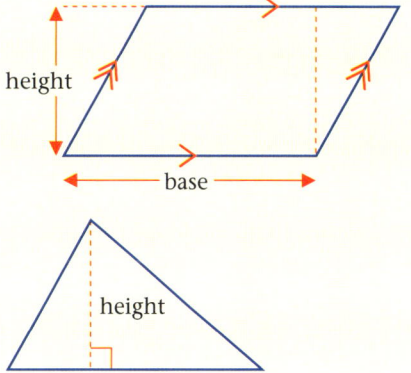

area of a triangle = $\frac{1}{2}$ × base × height
$= \frac{1}{2} \times b \times h$

Example 1

Find the shaded area.

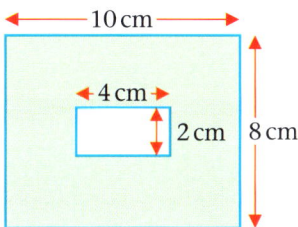

It is easiest to find the area of both the rectangles and then take away the area of the small rectangle from the area of the larger rectangle.

Area of large rectangle $10 \times 8 = 80$
Area of small rectangle $4 \times 2 = 8$
So the shaded area is $80 - 8 = 72 \text{ cm}^2$

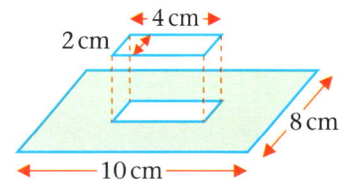

Area of a trapezium

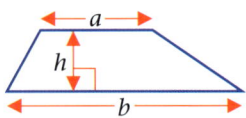

area of a trapezium = $\frac{1}{2}(a + b)h$

> $\frac{1}{2}(a + b)h$ is $\frac{1}{2}$ the sum of the parallel sides × the perpendicular distance between them.

Example 2

Use the formula to calculate the area of this trapezium.

Area of trapezium = $\frac{1}{2}(a + b)h = \frac{1}{2}(3 + 10) \times 4$
$= \frac{1}{2} \times 13 \times 4 = \frac{1}{2} \times 52$
$= 26 \text{ cm}^2$

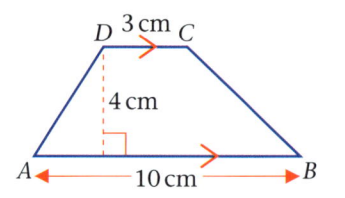

Example 3

Work out the area of this shape.

Method 1
Divide the shape into parts whose areas you can find. This can be done in several ways. One way is:

Area of rectangle **A** = $l \times w = 7 \times 4 = 28 \text{ cm}^2$
Area of trapezium **B** = $\frac{1}{2}(a + b)h = \frac{1}{2}(7 + 2) \times 4 = \frac{1}{2} \times 9 \times 4$
$= 18 \text{ cm}^2$

So the shaded area is $28 + 18 = 46 \text{ cm}^2$

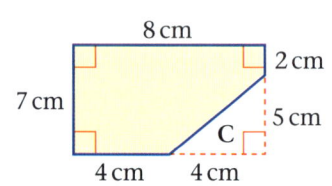

Method 2
Add on a small triangle to make a larger rectangle.

Area of large rectangle = $l \times w = 7 \times 8 = 56 \text{ cm}^2$
Area of small triangle **C** = $\frac{1}{2} \times$ base $\times$ height
$= \frac{1}{2} \times 4 \times 5 = 10 \text{ cm}^2$

So the shaded area is $56 - 10 = 46 \text{ cm}^2$

Exercise 26A

1 Calculate the areas of these shapes:

(a)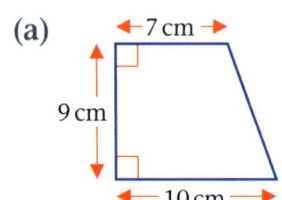

(b)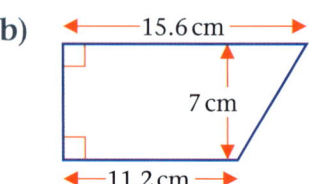

(c)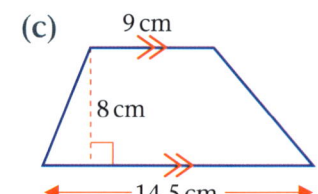

2 Work out the area of the shape *ABCDEF*.

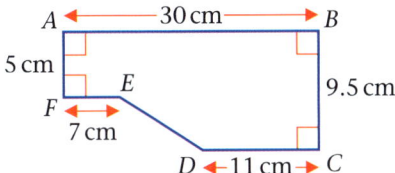

3 Find the shaded areas.

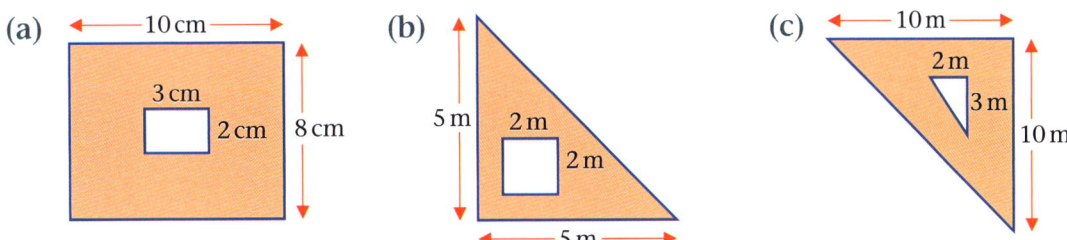

26.2 Circumference of a circle

The perimeter of a circle is called its **circumference**. The circumference of a circle is related to its diameter; Exercise 26B will help you see how.

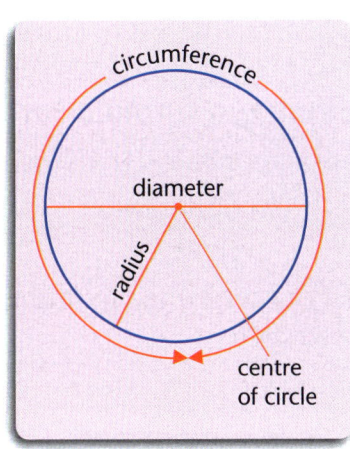

Exercise 26B

You will need a ruler, compasses and some string or thread.

1 (a) Mark a point on your paper. Use compasses to draw a circle with the marked point as its centre.

(b) Use a piece of string or thread and place it round your circle. Cut the string to fit exactly round the circumference once and measure its length. The length of the string is the same as the circumference of the circle.

(c) Measure the diameter of the circle.

(d) Work out: $\dfrac{\text{circumference of circle}}{\text{diameter of circle}}$

2 Repeat question **1** for two more circles with a different radius each time.

3 What do you notice about the ratio $\dfrac{\text{circumference of circle}}{\text{diameter of circle}}$ for each of your circles?

Introducing π (pi)

If you compare answers to Exercise 26B with your friends you should find that the circumference of a circle divided by its diameter is approximately equal to 3 each time. The actual value is a special number called π.

You cannot write down the value of π exactly. The number π is an **irrational number** (a non-recurring, non-terminating decimal) somewhere between 3.141 592 and 3.141 593.

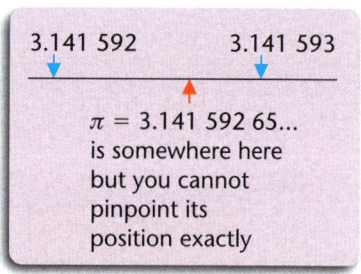

$\pi = 3.141\,592\,65\ldots$ is somewhere here but you cannot pinpoint its position exactly

If you press the π key on a calculator the value $3.141592654\ldots$ appears.

In calculations you often use the value correct to 2 d.p. (3.14) or correct to 3 d.p. (3.142).

Finding a formula for the circumference

You can rearrange the relationship

$$\frac{\text{circumference}}{\text{diameter}} = \pi \quad \text{or} \quad \frac{C}{d} = \pi$$

to give a formula to find the circumference of a circle from its diameter.

Multiply both sides by d:

$$\frac{C}{d} \times d = \pi \times d$$

so $\quad C = \pi \times d$

or $\quad C = \pi d$

You can also find a formula to find the circumference from the radius.

The diameter is twice the radius:

$\quad d = 2r$

so $\quad C = \pi \times 2r$

or $\quad C = 2\pi r$

> The perimeter of a circle is called the **circumference**:
> $C = \pi d$ where C is the circumference,
> or
> $C = 2\pi r$ d is the diameter and
> r is the radius.

Example 4

Find the circumference of a circle with diameter 5 cm.

$C = \pi d$

$C = 3.14 \times 5 = 15.7$ cm

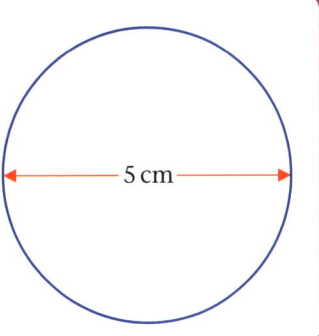

Exercise 26C

In these questions give your answers to 3 significant figures.

Use the π key or $\pi = 3.14$

1. Work out the circumferences of the circles with these diameters:
   - (a) 2 cm
   - (b) 3 cm
   - (c) 4 cm
   - (d) 10 cm
   - (e) 8 cm
   - (f) 12 cm

2. Calculate the circumferences of the circles with these diameters:
   - (a) 20 cm
   - (b) 5 m
   - (c) 50 cm
   - (d) 2.5 cm
   - (e) 3.6 cm
   - (f) 8.25 cm

Finding the circumference given the radius

Example 5

Find the circumference of a circle with radius 4 cm.

$C = 2\pi r$

$C = 2 \times 3.14 \times 4 = 25.1$ cm

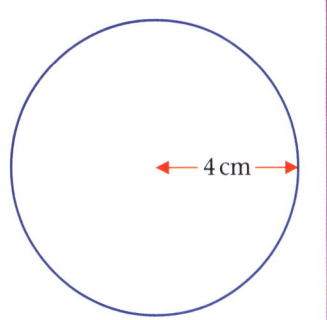

Exercise 26D

In these questions give your answers to 3 significant figures.

Find the circumferences of the circles with these radii:

Radii is the plural of radius.

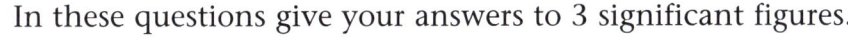

1	2 cm	2	3 cm	3	5 cm	4	10 cm
5	8 cm	6	12 cm	7	20 cm	8	5 m
9	50 cm	10	2.5 cm	11	3.6 cm	12	8.25 cm

Use the π key or $\pi = 3.14$

Chapter 26 Advanced perimeter, area and volume

Exercise 26E

In these questions give your answers to 3 significant figures.
Work out the circumference of each of the following.

 Use the π key or π = 3.14

1. a circle with a radius of 9 cm
2. a circle with a diameter of 9 cm
3. a circular table with a diameter of 90 cm
4. a circular fish pond whose radius is 60 cm
5. a circular paving slab of radius 15 cm
6. a circular flower bed of diameter 2.5 m
7. a circular candle of diameter 1.5 cm
8. a circular flower pot of diameter 6 inches
9. a pencil whose radius is 0.3 cm
10. a pen whose radius is 0.5 cm

Finding the diameter when you know the circumference

Sometimes you know the circumference of the circle and you have to calculate the radius or diameter.

Example 6

Susie's bike wheel has a circumference of 62.8 cm.
Work out the diameter and the radius of the wheel.

$C = \pi d$

so $62.8 = 3.14 \times d$

Dividing both sides by 3.14 gives:

$d = 62.8 \div 3.14$

$d = 20$ cm

To find the radius divide the diameter by 2.
The radius is 10 cm.

Exercise 26F

 In these questions give your answers to 3 significant figures. Copy this table and work out the diameter and radius of each circular shape.

Use the π key or π = 3.14

	Shape	Circumference	Diameter	Radius
1	Circle	9.42 cm		
2	Circle	12.56 cm		
3	Circular table	3.14 m		
4	Circular fish pond	10 m		
5	Circular paving slab	90 cm		
6	Circular flower bed	7.5 m		
7	Circular candle	5 cm		
8	Circular flower pot	6 inches		
9	Pencil	1 cm		
10	Pen	2.5 cm		

26.3 Area of a circle

Example 7

Here is a circle with radius 4 units drawn on a square grid. Estimate the area of the circle.

There are 44 whole or nearly whole squares.
The area of these is about 44 square units.

The shaded shapes are each about $\frac{3}{4}$ square plus $\frac{1}{4}$ square which makes about a whole square.

So the 8 shaded shapes make about 8 whole squares, with area 8 square units.

The total area of the circle is about 44 + 8 = 52 square units.

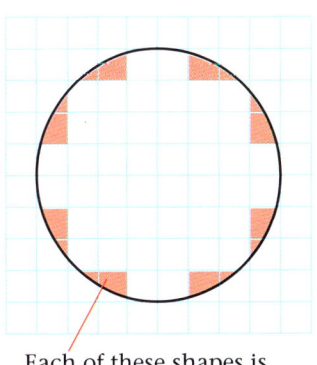

Each of these shapes is about $\frac{1}{4}$ square + $\frac{3}{4}$ square.

Chapter 26 Advanced perimeter, area and volume

Exercise 26G

You will need a ruler, compasses, a protractor, squared paper and glue.

1. (a) Draw a circle with a radius of 9 units on squared paper.
   (b) Estimate the area of the circle in square units, by counting the squares.
   (c) Divide your answer to (b) by 81 (which is 9 × 9, the square of the radius).

2. (a) Draw a circle with radius 3 cm.
   (b) Draw diameters at angles of 20° to each other to divide the circle into 18 parts.
   Carefully cut out the 18 parts.
   (c) Draw a straight line.
   Place the cut-out pieces alternately corner and curved edge against the line.
   Stick them close together.

3. Repeat question 2, but draw diameters at 10° to each other to divide the circle into 36 equal parts.

Finding a formula for the area of a circle

The shape you made with the 18 pieces in question 2 of Exercise 26G should be approximately a rectangle.

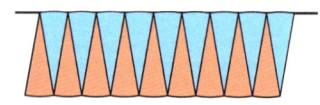

The shape from question 3 should be closer to a rectangle.

It would be very difficult to cut out the parts of the circle if you used 1° between the diameters, but the final shape would be almost an exact rectangle.

The two longer sides of the rectangle make up the whole circumference πd or $2\pi r$, so one length is πr. The width is the same as the radius of the circle, r.

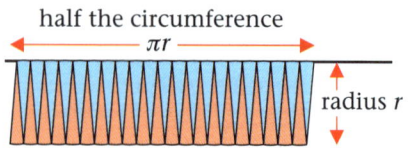

half the circumference πr

radius r

The more parts the circle is divided into, the closer to a rectangle the shape becomes.

So the area of the rectangle is length × width = $\pi r \times r = \pi r^2$.
This is the same as the area of the circle, so

area of a circle = $A = \pi r^2$

26.3 Area of a circle

Example 8

Find the area of a circle with a radius of 5 cm.

$A = \pi r^2$

$A = 3.14 \times 5 \times 5 = 78.5 \text{ cm}^2$

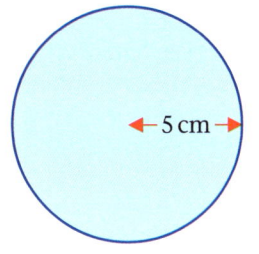

Remember:
The value of pi (π) is approximately 3.14. You may have a more accurate value on your calculator.

Example 9

Find the area of a circle with diameter 4 cm.

If the diameter is 4 cm then the radius is $4 \div 2 = 2$ cm and the area is

$A = \pi r^2$

$A = 3.14 \times 2 \times 2 = 12.56 \text{ cm}^2$

Exercise 26H

 Round your answers to 3 s.f.

Use the π key or $\pi = 3.14$

1 Find the areas of the circles with these radii:
- (a) 2 cm
- (b) 3 cm
- (c) 4 cm
- (d) 10 cm
- (e) 8 cm
- (f) 12 cm

2 Work out the areas of the circles with these radii:
- (a) 20 cm
- (b) 5 m
- (c) 50 cm
- (d) 2.5 cm
- (e) 3.6 cm
- (f) 8.25 cm

3 Find the areas of the circles with these diameters:
- (a) 2 cm
- (b) 3 cm
- (c) 5 cm
- (d) 10 cm
- (e) 8 cm
- (f) 12 cm

4 Work out the areas of the circles with these diameters:
- (a) 20 cm
- (b) 5 m
- (c) 50 cm
- (d) 2.5 cm
- (e) 3.6 cm
- (f) 8.25 cm

Exercise 26I

 Work out the area of each of the following. Give your answer to 3 s.f.

> Use the π key or π = 3.14

1. a circle of radius 9 cm
2. a circle of diameter 9 cm
3. a circular table of diameter 90 cm
4. a circular fish pond of radius 60 cm
5. a circular paving slab of radius 15 cm
6. a circular flower bed of diameter 2.5 m
7. the end of a circular candle of diameter 1.5 cm
8. the top of a circular flower pot of diameter 6 inches
9. the end of a pencil of radius 0.3 cm
10. the end of a pen of radius 0.5 cm

Finding the radius when you know the area

Sometimes you will be given the area of a circle and asked to calculate its radius or diameter.

Example 10

A circle has an area of 2826 cm². Work out its radius.

$$\pi r^2 = A$$
$$3.14 \times r^2 = 2826$$

Dividing both sides by 3.14 gives

$$r^2 = 2826 \div 3.14$$
$$r^2 = 900$$
$$\sqrt{r^2} = \sqrt{900} \text{ cm}$$
$$r = 30 \text{ cm}$$

If you need to find the diameter then you multiply the radius by 2. The diameter is 60 cm.

Exercise 26J

In these questions give your answers to 3 s.f.

Use the π key or π = 3.14

1. A circle has an area of 28.26 cm². Find the diameter.
2. A circle has an area of 12.56 cm². Find the radius.
3. A circular table has an area of 3.14 m². Work out the diameter.
4. A circular fish pond has an area of 10 m². Work out the diameter.
5. A circular paving slab has an area of 90 cm². What is the radius?
6. A circular flower bed has an area of 7.5 m². What is the diameter?
7. The end of a circular candle has an area of 5 cm². Work out the radius.
8. The top of a circular flower pot has an area of 6 square inches. What is the diameter?
9. The end of a pencil has an area of 1 cm². Work out the diameter.

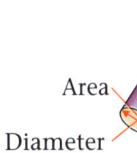

Area
Diameter

10. The end of a pen has an area of 2.5 cm². Work out the radius.

Answers in terms of π

On non-calculator papers you may be asked to leave your answers in terms of π.

Example 11

Find the area and circumference of the circle with radius 8 cm. Leave your answers in terms of π.

area = $\pi r^2 = \pi \times 8^2 = 64\pi$

circumference = $2\pi r = 2\pi \times 8 = 16\pi$

Exercise 26K

1. Work out, in terms of π, the circumference and area of a circle with radius:
   (a) 2 cm   (b) 5 m   (c) 9 mm   (d) $3\frac{1}{2}$ cm   (e) 12 cm

2. Work out, in terms of π, the circumference and area of a circle with diameter:
   (a) 6 m   (b) 8 cm   (c) 9 cm   (d) 3 m   (e) 20 cm

26.4 Parts of circles

Part of a circumference is called an **arc**.
A half circle is called a **semicircle**.

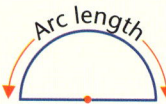

Quarter circles are called **quadrants**.

This is a **sector** of a circle.

These are **segments**.

Example 12

Find the perimeter of this semicircle.

First find the circumference of a circle with diameter 10 cm.

$C = \pi d$

$C = 3.14 \times 10 = 31.4$ cm

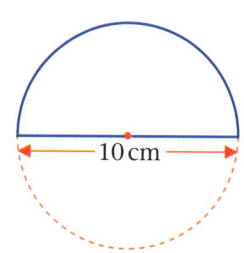

The arc length of the semicircle is *half* the circumference:

$31.4 \div 2 = 15.7$ cm

The perimeter is the curved arc length plus the straight edge of 10 cm.
So the total length of the perimeter is

15.7 cm + 10 cm = 25.7 cm

Example 13

Find the area of this quadrant.

The quadrant is one quarter of a circle.
Find the area of the circle with radius 8 cm:

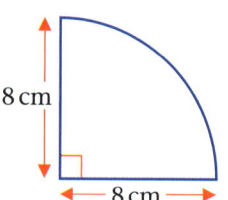

$A = \pi r^2$

$A = 3.14 \times 8 \times 8 = 200.96$ cm²

The quadrant is one quarter of the circle, so the area of the quadrant is

200.96 cm ÷ 4 = 50.2 cm² (to 3 significant figures)

26.4 Parts of circles

Exercise 26L

In questions **1–6** give all your answers to 3 significant figures.

Use the π key or π = 3.14

1 Find the perimeter of each of these shapes.

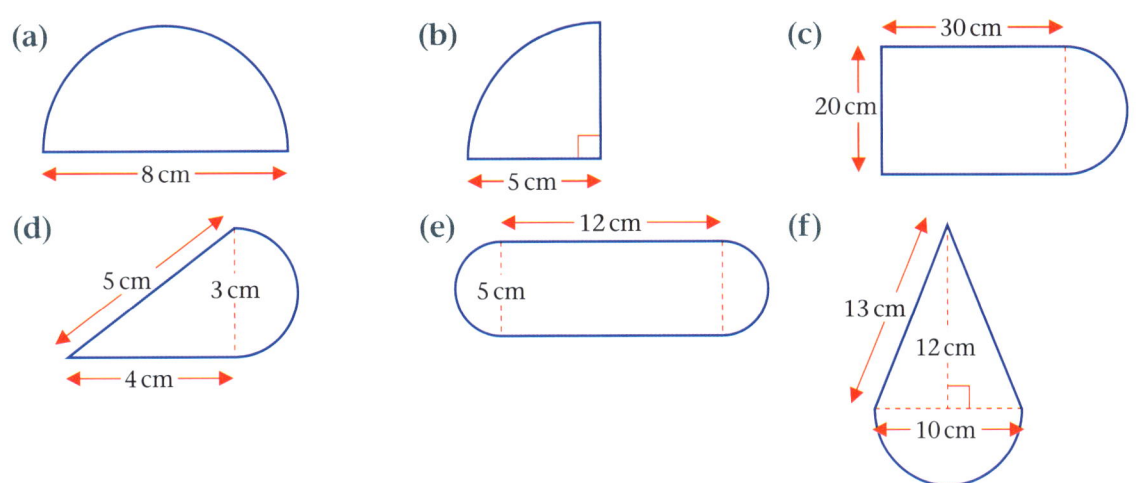

2 Find the area of each of the shapes in question **1**.

3 Find the shaded area of each in these shapes:

(a) 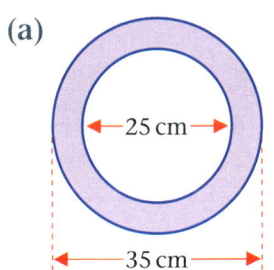 (b) 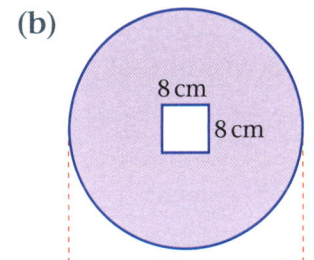 (c)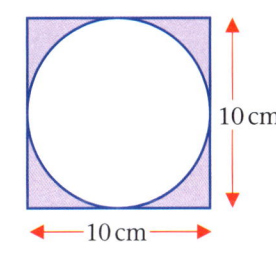

4 Calculate the area of a semicircular rug with diameter 90 cm.

5 An ice-cream wafer is in the shape of a quadrant of a circle with radius 7 cm.
Work out the area of the wafer.

6 A lawn is in the shape of a rectangle with a semicircular end.
Calculate the area of the lawn.

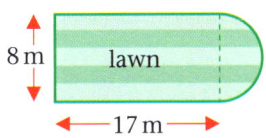

7 A circular pond has diameter 3.22 m. The pond is surrounded by a path 28 cm wide. Calculate
   (a) the area of the pond
   (b) the area of the path.
   Give your answers in m², correct to 2 decimal places.

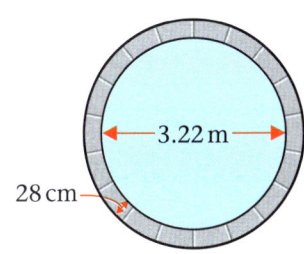

26.5 Volumes and surface areas of 3-D shapes

Volume of a cuboid

You should remember from Chapter 19 that:

The **volume** of a 3-D shape is a measure of the amount of space it occupies.

volume of a cuboid = length × width × height
$$= l \times w \times h$$

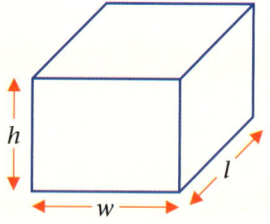

Volume of a prism

A **prism** is a 3-D shape with the same cross-section all along its length.

A cuboid can be cut in half to make a triangular prism. For example, a 4 cm by 2 cm by 3 cm cuboid can be cut in half to make this prism.

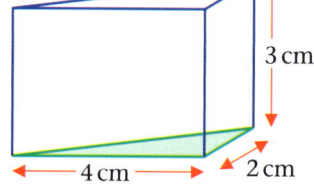

The volume of the prism is half the volume of the cuboid so it is

$$\frac{1}{2} \times (4 \times 2 \times 3) = \frac{1}{2} \times 24 = 12 \, \text{cm}^3$$

This can be thought of as

$$\tfrac{1}{2} \times 4 \times 2 \quad \times \quad 3 \quad = 12 \, \text{cm}^3$$

or **area of cross-section × height**.

Does this work for any prism? Try an octagonal prism:

To make an octagonal prism you could first make the shape of the octagonal base.

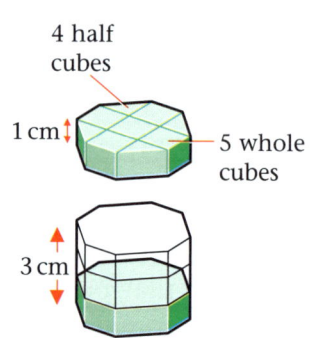

You would need 5 whole cubes and 4 half cubes.

The total number of cubes in the base would be 5 + 2 = 7.

For a prism of height 3 cm you would need 21 cubes (7 × 3).

So the volume of the prism would be 21 cm³.

This is the **area of cross-section × height**.

If the prism is lying on its side the height is called length.

26.5 Volumes and surface areas of 3-D shapes

volume of a prism = area of cross-section × length

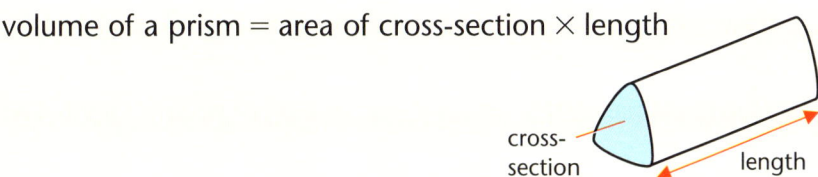

Example 14

The volume of a prism is 102 cm³.
The prism has a length of 12 cm.
Find the area of the triangular cross-section.

Volume of prism = area of cross-section × length
102 = area × 12
Divide both sides by 12
area = 102 ÷ 12 = 8.5 cm²

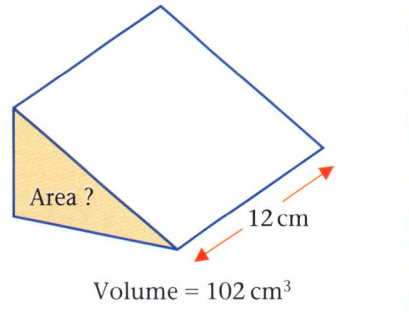

Volume of a cylinder

A **cylinder** is a special prism where the cross-section is a circle.
The area of cross-section is πr^2, so
area of cross-section × height = $\pi r^2 \times h$

volume of a cylinder = $\pi r^2 h$ Area of cross-section = πr^2

Surface area of a cylinder

You can work out the area of the curved surface of a cylindrical
can of soup by removing the label.

Cut the label parallel to the height of the cylinder. Remove the
label and open it out flat. The label should be a rectangle.

The length of the rectangle is the same as the circumference of
an end of the cylinder.

The width is the same as the perpendicular height of the cylinder.

The area is the circumference of an end multiplied by the height.

area of the curved surface of a cylinder = $2\pi rh$

Add two circular ends.

total surface area of a closed cylinder = $2\pi rh + 2\pi r^2$
total surface area of a cylinder open at one end = $2\pi rh + \pi r^2$

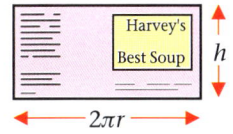
Add one circular end.

Chapter 26 Advanced perimeter, area and volume

Example 15

A cylinder has a height of 10 cm and a diameter of 6 cm.
Work out **(a)** the volume **(b)** the surface area.
Use the π key on your calculator.
Give your answers correct to 3 significant figures.

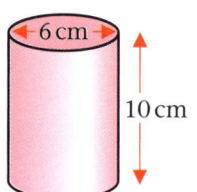

As the diameter is 6 cm, the radius is 3 cm.

(a) volume of a cylinder = $\pi r^2 h$
 = $\pi \times 3 \times 3 \times 10$
 = 90π
 = 282.743 338 8
 = 283 cm³ (to 3 s.f.)

You should write out the full answer before rounding.

(b) surface area = $2\pi rh + 2\pi r^2$
 = $(2 \times \pi \times 3 \times 10) + (2 \times \pi \times 3 \times 3)$
 = $60\pi + 18\pi$
 = 78π
 = 245.044 227
 = 245 cm³ (to 3 s.f.)

Exercise 26M

In this exercise give all your answers to 3 significant figures.

Use the π key

1 Find the volume of each of the following solids.

(a) 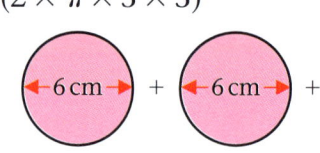   (b)    (c)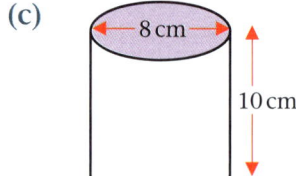

(d) 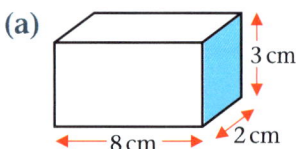   (e) 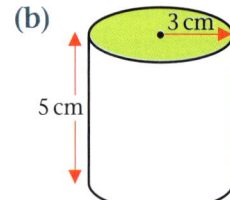   (f)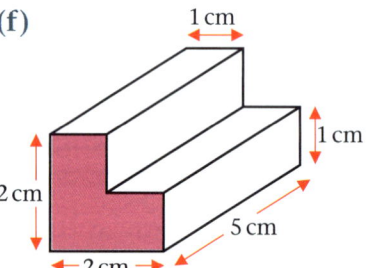

(g) 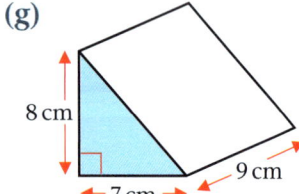   (h) 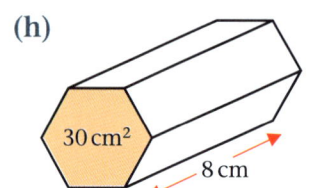   (i)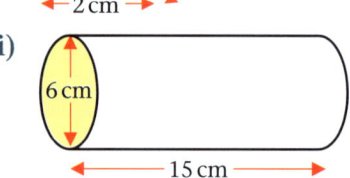

26.5 Volumes and surface areas of 3-D shapes

2 A box in the shape of a cuboid has a volume of 50 cm³. It has a length of 8 cm and a height of 2.5 cm. What is its width?

3 A cylinder has a volume of 100 cm³. Its height is 10 cm. What is the area of its circular end?

4 A cylinder has a radius of 4 mm and a volume of 230 mm³. Find the height of the cylinder.

5 A triangular prism has a length of 12 cm and a volume of 60 cm³. What is the area of the triangular end?

6 Calculate the volume of the wedge on the right, which is a triangular prism.

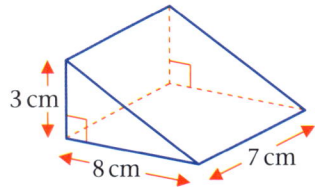

7 A closed box is a cuboid made of wood 1 cm thick. Its external measurements are 80 cm by 50 cm by 42 cm. Calculate
   (a) the internal measurements of the box
   (b) the inside volume of the box
   (c) the total surface area of the outside of the box.

Hint: sketch a diagram of the box to help you. Label the box with the dimensions.

8 The diagram shows a tank which is a prism with a trapezium cross-section.
   Calculate the volume of the tank.

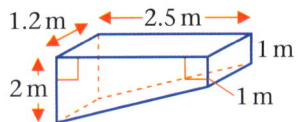

9 A gold bar is in the shape of a cylinder.
   It has a diameter of 18 cm and a length of 105 cm.
   The gold is to be recast into cuboids. Each cuboid is to be 30 cm long, 14 cm wide and 8 cm high.
   (a) Calculate the volume of the cylinder.
   (b) Calculate the volume of each cuboid.
   (c) Calculate the maximum number of cuboids that can be made from the gold bar.
   (d) What volume of gold is left over after the cuboids have been made? [E]

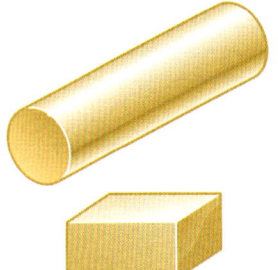

Diagram NOT accurately drawn

10 A closed cardboard box is a cuboid with a base 63 cm by 25 cm. The box is 30 cm high. Calculate
    (a) the volume of the box
    (b) the total surface area of the box.

11 The cross-section of a house is shown on the right.
    The house is 9 m long.
    Calculate the volume of the house.

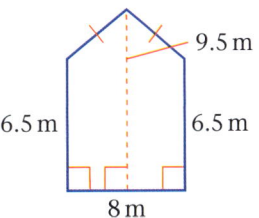

Chapter 26 Advanced perimeter, area and volume

12 A flat rectangular roof measures 15 m by 20 m.
Rainwater from the roof drains into a tank which is 1.3 m deep and has a square base of side 1.4 m.
Calculate the depth of rainfall that would just fill the tank.

13 A cuboid with a square base is 18 cm high.
The volume of the cuboid is 882 cm³.
Calculate the length of a side of the base.

14 An open waste paper bin is a cylinder.
The diameter of the base is 22 cm and the height is 28 cm.
Calculate

(a) the volume of the bin

(b) the total outside surface area of the bin.

26.6 Accuracy of measurement

Suppose you use a ruler marked in millimetres to measure a line as 237 mm correct to the nearest mm.

The true length could be anywhere between 236.5 mm and 237.5 mm.

We write this as 236.5 mm ≤ length < 237.5 mm, as all these measurements will round to 237 mm correct to the nearest mm.

So the true length could be anywhere in a range between 0.5 mm below and 0.5 mm above the recorded value:

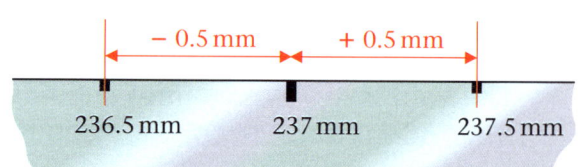

The shortest possible length is 236.5 mm.
The longest possible length is 237.5 mm.

Example 16

The time taken to walk down some stairs is measured as 10 seconds to the nearest second.

(a) What is the shortest possible time it could be?
(b) What is the longest possible time it could be?

(a) shortest possible time is 9.5 seconds
(b) longest possible time is 10.5 seconds.

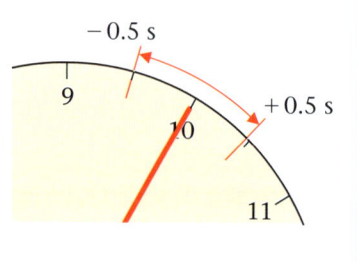

If a time is measured as 10.3 seconds to the nearest tenth of a second, it could be anything between 10.25 and 10.35 seconds.
You can write this as

$$10.25\,s \leq \text{time} < 10.35\,s$$

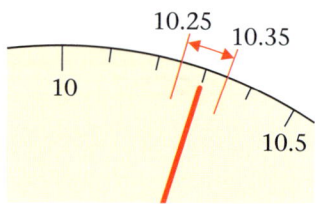

26.7 Choosing an appropriate degree of accuracy

For any measurement you make:

If you make a measurement correct to a given unit the true value lies in a range that extends half a unit below and half a unit above the measurement.

Exercise 26N

1. These lengths are all measured to the nearest millimetre. Write down the range within which each length could lie in the form shown in the examples above.
   - (a) 2.7 cm
   - (b) 3.9 cm
   - (c) 10.5 cm
   - (d) 12 mm
   - (e) 25 mm
   - (f) 36 mm

2. These lengths have all been measured to the nearest centimetre.
   For each, write down
   (i) the shortest possible length
   (ii) the longest possible length.
   - (a) 2.45 m
   - (b) 23 cm
   - (c) 4.00 m
   - (d) 14 cm
   - (e) 50 cm
   - (f) 5.34 m

3. Iain was measuring the time it took him to run 100 m. His watch was accurate to the nearest tenth of a second and he measured the time as 12.1 seconds.
   Write down
   - (a) his shortest possible time for the run
   - (b) his longest possible time for the run.

4. At a race meeting these times were measured to the nearest hundredth of a second.
   For each, write down
   (i) the shortest possible time
   (ii) the longest possible time.
   - (a) 22.35 s
   - (b) 43.67 s
   - (c) 10.02 s
   - (d) 2 min 45.34 s
   - (e) 45.00 s
   - (f) 50 s

26.7 Choosing an appropriate degree of accuracy

Sometimes when measurements are made they need to be very accurate but at other times a high degree of accuracy is not needed.

For example, the time for running the 100 metres in an international athletics competition needs to be measured to the nearest hundredth of a second. But the time needed to drive the 400 miles from London to Scotland for a holiday does not need that degree of accuracy. A measurement to the nearest half hour would be sufficient.

If you measure the width of this book the most sensible unit of measure would be millimetres. Using centimetres is too inaccurate and using tenths of a millimetre is too accurate.

Exercise 26O

In questions **1** to **4** write down the most appropriate unit you could use to measure each quantity.

1. The time taken to
   (a) run a 200 m race
   (b) walk to school
   (c) travel from London to Manchester by car
   (d) run 1000 m
   (e) walk 20 miles
   (f) watch a film.

2. (a) the shoulder height of a zebra
   (b) the thickness of this book
   (c) the length of your class room
   (d) the lengths of your fingers
   (e) the height of a large tree
   (f) the width of a pencil

3. The area of
   (a) a leaf
   (b) the school playing fields
   (c) the British Isles
   (d) the school hall.

4. The volume of liquid in
   (a) a can of cola
   (b) a car's petrol tank
   (c) a large lake.

5. Abdul and Nia are measuring the perimeter of the school field.
   (a) Write down the units they should use to measure it.
   (b) What measuring instrument should they use?
   (c) To what degree of accuracy should they give their answer?

6 Mario and Dara are carrying out an experiment with bouncing spheres. They drop spheres made from different materials from the first floor of the school building. They then measure the times the spheres take to fall and the heights to which they bounce.

   (a) Write down the units they should use to measure
      (i) the times taken
      (ii) the heights of bounce.
   (b) What measuring instruments should they use?
   (c) To what degree of accuracy should they give their answers?

26.8 Compound measures: density

Sometimes you need to work with two units at the same time. In Section 19.10 you calculated the compound measure speed. Speed is often measured in miles per hour, km per hour or metres per second.

Density is another compound measure. The density of a substance is defined as the mass per unit volume. It is worked out by the formula

$$\text{density} = \frac{\text{mass}}{\text{volume}}$$

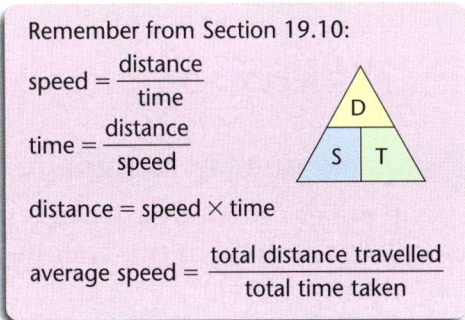

Remember from Section 19.10:

$$\text{speed} = \frac{\text{distance}}{\text{time}}$$

$$\text{time} = \frac{\text{distance}}{\text{speed}}$$

$$\text{distance} = \text{speed} \times \text{time}$$

$$\text{average speed} = \frac{\text{total distance travelled}}{\text{total time taken}}$$

The formula can be arranged to give

$$\text{volume} = \frac{\text{mass}}{\text{density}} \qquad \text{mass} = \text{volume} \times \text{density}$$

If the mass is measured in kilograms and the volume is measured in cubic metres the density is measured in kilograms per cubic metre. This can be abbreviated to kg/m³ or kg m⁻³.

Example 17

Calculate the density of a piece of metal that has a mass of 2000 kilograms and a volume of 0.5 cubic metres.

$$\text{density} = \frac{2000}{0.5} = 4000 \text{ kg m}^{-3}$$

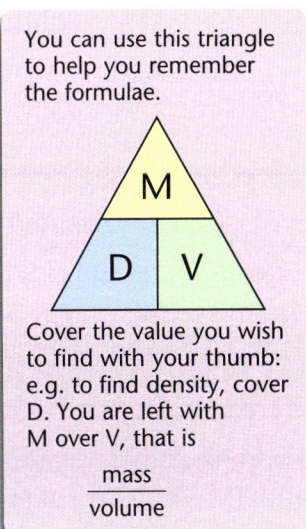

You can use this triangle to help you remember the formulae.

Cover the value you wish to find with your thumb: e.g. to find density, cover D. You are left with M over V, that is

$$\frac{\text{mass}}{\text{volume}}$$

Chapter 26 Advanced perimeter, area and volume

Exercise 26P

Calculate the densities of the following materials.

	Substance	Mass in kg	Volume in m³
1	Aluminium	5400	2
2	Copper	12 000	1.34
3	Gold	3000	0.155
4	Nickel	450	0.0506
5	Silver	2700	0.257
6	Sodium	3900	4.02
7	Tin	4000	0.547
8	Zinc	30 000	4.21
9	Lead	1	0.000 088 1
10	Uranium	10	0.000 528

Using the density formula to calculate mass or volume

If you are given the density of a material and are asked to calculate the mass or the volume then you can substitute the values into the density formula.

Example 18

Calculate the volume of a piece of oak with a density of 720 kg per m³ and a mass of 25 kg.

$$\text{density} = \frac{\text{mass}}{\text{volume}}$$

so $\quad 720 = \dfrac{25}{\text{volume}}$

Multiply both sides by volume:

$$720 \times \text{volume} = 25$$

Divide both sides by 720:

$$\text{volume} = \frac{25}{720} = 0.035 \text{ m}^3$$

Example 19

Calculate the mass of a piece of aluminium that has a volume of 1.5 m³ and a density of 2700 kg per m³.

$$\text{density} = \frac{\text{mass}}{\text{volume}}$$

so $\quad 2700 = \dfrac{\text{mass}}{1.5}$

Multiply both sides by 1.5:

$$\text{mass} = 2700 \times 1.5$$
$$= 4050 \text{ kg}$$

There is another way to work out the answers to Examples 18 and 19. You can substitute the values into the rearrangements of the density formula written on the previous page.

Exercise 26Q

 Copy this table and calculate the missing values.

	Substance	Mass in kg	Volume in m³	Density in kg m⁻³
1	Steel	2.5		7700
2	Douglas fir (wood)		1.5	600
3	Balsa wood		1	200
4	Common brick	50		1600
5	Breeze block	100		1400
6	Concrete		3.5	2300
7	Polypropylene		4	900
8	Iron	1000		7860
9	Magnesium	0.5		1740
10	Platinum	0.05		21450

26.9 Changing units

You need to be able to change units of speed between kilometres per hour, metres per second and miles per hour.

Example 20

Change 10 metres per second to kilometres per hour.

First of all you need to find how many metres are travelled in 1 hour.

So you need to multiply by 60 × 60 = 3600.

In 1 second distance travelled = 10 m
In 1 hour distance travelled = 10 × 3600 = 36 000 m

Divide by 1000 to change m to km.

In 1 hour distance travelled = $\frac{36\,000}{1000}$ = 36 km

So the speed in kilometres per hour is 36 km per hour (or 36 km h⁻¹).

There are 60 × 60 = 3600 seconds in 1 hour

Chapter 26 Advanced perimeter, area and volume

Example 21

Change 60 miles per hour to
(a) kilometres per hour (b) metres per second.
(Use 5 miles = 8 km)

(a) In 1 hour distance travelled = 60 miles
$= 60 \times \frac{8}{5}$ km = 96 km
So the speed is 96 km per hour (or 96 km h^{-1}).

(b) In 1 hour distance travelled = 96 km = 96 000 m
In 1 second distance travelled = $\frac{96\,000}{3600}$ m = 26.66 m

So the speed is 26.7 m/s (or 26.7 m s^{-1}) (to 3 s.f.).

Exercise 26R

1 Change 20 metres per second to metres per hour.

2 Change 30 km per hour to metres per second.

3 Change 60 miles per hour to miles per minute.

4 Change 15 metres per second to km per hour.

5 Change 20 metres per second to kilometres per hour.

6 Change 80 km per hour to metres per minute.

7 Sybil travels 80 kilometres in 4 hours.
   What is her average speed in metres per second?

8 An electron travels at 600 000 metres per second.
   What is this speed in km per hour?

9 A rocket must travel at 11 000 metres per second to escape the gravitational pull of the Earth. What is this speed in kilometres per hour?

10 The fastest land animal is the cheetah, which can travel at 70 miles per hour.
   Approximately what is this speed in metres per second?

26.10 Comparing measurements

To compare two measurements they need to have the same units.

> You have to compare like with like. To compare the speed of an electron with the speed of a rocket you need to change both speeds to the same units.

> 1 tonne = 1000 kg

Example 22

1 tonne of coal has a volume of 0.67 m³.

80 kg of sand has a volume of 0.05 m³.

Which material has the greater density?

$$\text{density} = \frac{\text{mass}}{\text{volume}}$$

$$\text{density of coal} = \frac{1000}{0.67} = 1492.537\ldots$$

$$= 1490 \text{ kg/m}^3 \text{ (to 3 s.f.)}$$

$$\text{density of sand} = \frac{80}{0.05} \text{ kg/m}^3$$

$$= 1600 \text{ kg/m}^3$$

So sand has a greater density than coal.

Exercise 26S

 Where needed use 5 miles = 8 km.

1. Which car is travelling faster, one at 40 miles per hour or one at 50 kilometres per hour?

2. The motorway speed limit in France is 130 km per hour and in England it is 70 miles per hour.
   Which is the faster speed?

3. An electron travels at 600 000 metres per second.
   What is this speed in miles per hour?

4. The fastest land animal (the cheetah) can travel at 112 km per hour.
   What is this speed in miles per hour?

5. A car is travelling on a motorway at 70 miles per hour.
   A peregrine falcon (bird of prey) can travel at 40 metres per second.
   (a) Change 70 miles per hour to metres per second.
   (b) Which is faster – the car or the bird?

6 In 1977 the land speed record was 283 metres per second and the water speed record was 330 miles per hour.
  (a) Change 283 metres per second to miles per hour.
  (b) How many times faster was the land speed record than the water speed record?

7 The speed of light in a vacuum is 300 000 000 metres per second. The speed of a neutron is 4500 miles per hour.
  (a) Change 300 000 000 metres per second to miles per hour.
  (b) How many times faster is the speed of light than the speed of a neutron?

Mixed exercise 26

1 Calculate the number of *complete* revolutions made by a cycle wheel of diameter 70 cm in travelling a distance of $\frac{1}{2}$ km. [E]

2 (a) Find the area of a circle of diameter 5.6 cm, giving your answer in cm² correct to two significant figures.
  (b) A fence which surrounds a rectangular field of length 300 metres and width 184 metres is taken down and is just long enough to fence in a circular paddock. Calculate the radius of the paddock. [E]

3 Light travels 300 000 kilometres in 1 second. A light year is the distance travelled by light in 1 year.
Calculate, in kilometres, how far light travels in a year of 365 days. Give your answer correct to 3 s.f.

4 Given that 1 cm³ of brass weighs 8.45 grams, calculate the weight of a solid cylinder of brass whose radius is 1.3 cm and whose height is 9.0 cm.

5 Stephanie ran 100 metres.
The distance was correct to the nearest metre.
  (a) Write down the shortest distance Stephanie could have run.

Stephanie's time for the run was 14.8 seconds.
Her time was correct to the nearest tenth of a second.
  (b) Write down
    (i) her shortest possible time for the run,
    (ii) her longest possible time for the run. [E]

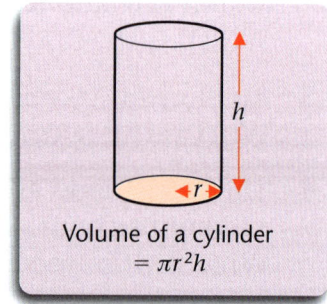

Volume of a cylinder
= $\pi r^2 h$

Mixed exercise 26

6 The diagram represents a swimming pool.
The pool has vertical sides.
The pool is 8 m wide.

(a) Calculate the area of the shaded cross-section.

The swimming pool is completely filled with water.

(b) Calculate the volume of water in the pool.

64 m³ of water leaks out of the pool.

(c) Calculate the distance by which the water level falls. [E]

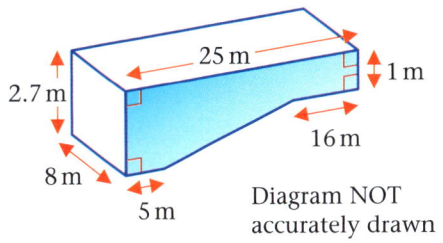

Diagram NOT accurately drawn

7 The diagram represents a chocolate box in the shape of a pyramid. The box has a square base and four triangular faces. The net of the chocolate box is shown.

(a) Work out (i) the area of the base
              (ii) the area of a triangular face
              (iii) the total surface area of the box.

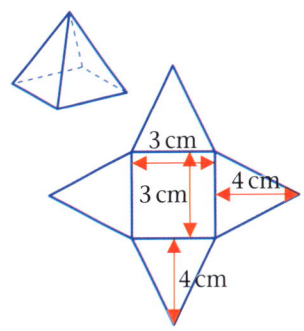

Each net is cut from a square card of area 121 cm². Any card not used for the box is thrown away.
n boxes are made.

(b) Write down a formula for the total area, *A* cm², of card which is thrown away.

(c) Construct an accurate net for the box. [E]

8 The diagram represents a tea packet in the shape of a cuboid.

(a) Calculate the volume of the packet.

There are 125 grams of tea in a full packet. Jason has to design a new packet that will contain 100 grams of tea when full.

(b) (i) Work out the volume of the new packet.
    (ii) Express the weight of the new tea packet as a percentage of the weight of the packet shown.

The new packet of tea is in the shape of a cuboid.
The base of the new packet measures 7 cm by 6 cm.

(c) (i) Work out the area of the base of the new packet.
    (ii) Calculate the height of the new packet. [E]

9 A cylindrical can has a radius of 6 centimetres.

(a) Calculate the area of the circular end of the can.
(Use the π button on your calculator or π = 3.14.)

The capacity of the can is 2000 cm³.

(b) Calculate the height of the can.
Give your answer correct to 1 decimal place. [E]

10 (a) Write down a sensible **metric** unit that should be used to measure
   (i) the height of a school hall
   (ii) the weight of a pencil.
(b) Write down a sensible **imperial** unit that should be used to measure the distance between London and Manchester. [E]

11 Change 28 miles to kilometres. [E]

12 Change 180 km per hour to metres per minute.

13 A circle has a radius of 3 cm.
(a) Work out the area of the circle. Give your answer correct to 3 significant figures.

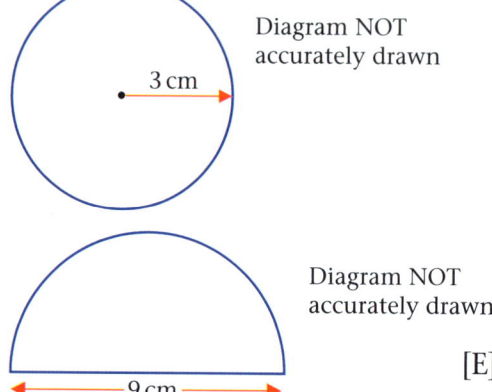

A semicircle has a diameter of 9 cm.
(b) Work out the perimeter of the semicircle. Give your answer correct to 3 significant figures. [E]

14 The density of gold is 19 320 kg m^{-3}.
Work out the mass, in grams, of 1 cm^3 of gold.

15 The density of oak is 720 kg m^{-3}.
Calculate the mass of a rectangular block of oak measuring 6 m by 0.7 m by 0.12 m.

16 The density of red cedar is 380 kg m^{-3}. Calculate the volume in m^3 of a block of red cedar with mass 212 kg.

Summary of key points

1. area of a trapezium $= \frac{1}{2}(a + b)h$

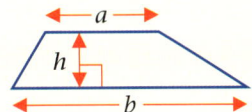

2. The perimeter of a circle is called the **circumference**:

   $C = \pi d$ where C is the circumference,
   or d is the diameter and
   $C = 2\pi r$ r is the radius.

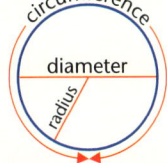

3. **area of a circle** $= A = \pi r^2$

4. Part of a circumference is called an **arc**. A half circle is called a **semicircle**.

5. Quarter circles are called **quadrants**.

   This is a **sector** of a circle.

   These are **segments**.

6. A prism is a 3-D shape with the same cross-section all along its length.

7. volume of a prism = area of cross-section × length

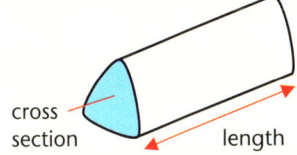

8. volume of a cylinder = $\pi r^2 h$

9. area of the curved surface of a cylinder = $2\pi rh$

   total surface area of a closed cylinder = $2\pi rh + 2\pi r^2$

   total surface area of a cylinder open at one end = $2\pi rh + \pi r^2$

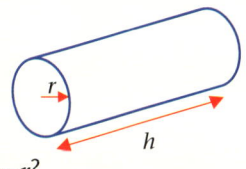

10. If you make a measurement correct to a given unit the true value lies in a range that extends half a unit below and half a unit above the measurement.

11. density = $\dfrac{\text{mass}}{\text{volume}}$ volume = $\dfrac{\text{mass}}{\text{density}}$

    mass = density × volume

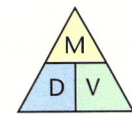

You can use this triangle to help you remember the formulae.

27 Describing transformations

Changes in the position or size of a shape are called **transformations**.

For your GCSE exam you need to know about four types of transformations: translations, reflections, rotations and enlargements.

27.1 Translations

You learned about translations in Chapter 22. You should remember that:

A **translation** is a sliding movement.

In this diagram triangle **A** is translated to **B**. All the points on **A** are moved +3 units parallel to the x-axis followed by −2 units parallel to the y-axis.

This translation is described by the **vector** $\begin{pmatrix} 3 \\ -2 \end{pmatrix}$.

To describe a translation you need to give the horizontal and vertical movements of the translation. These are written as a **vector**.

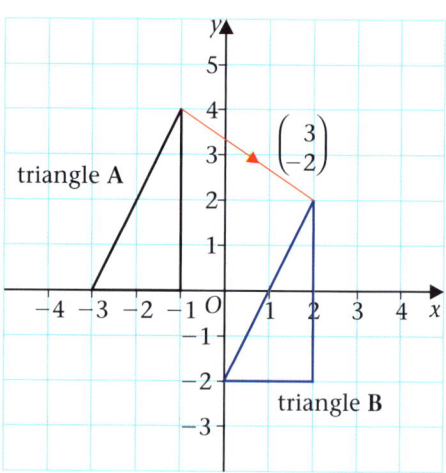

Coordinates are often used in questions involving transformations.

On the grid below, at P, $x = 3$ and $y = 1$ so the coordinates of P are (3, 1).

We say that triangle **A** 'maps on to' triangle **B**.

The object and image are congruent.

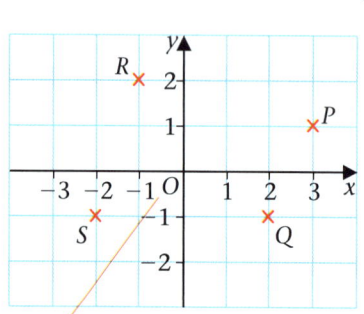

The point (0, 0) is called the **origin**.

Note:
Write the x value before the y value.

Note:
$R = (-1, 2)$
$S = (-2, -1)$
$Q = (2, -1)$

27.1 Translations

Example 1

The shape ABCD is shown on the grid.

(a) Write down the coordinates of A, B, C and D.

ABCD is translated to PQRS so that P(2, −1) is the image of A.

(b) Plot P and describe fully the translation that maps A onto P.

(c) Draw the image of ABCD.

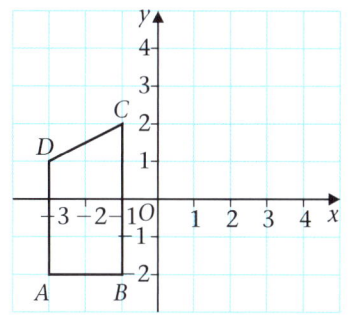

(a) A = (−3, −2), B = (−1, −2), C = (−1, 2) and D = (−3, 1).

(b) The point A(−3, −2) is translated to P(2, −1) so the x-coordinate is increased by 5 and the y-coordinate is increased by 1. This is a translation by the vector $\binom{5}{1}$.

(c) All the points on ABCD are translated by $\binom{5}{1}$.

Q is the image of B, so the coordinates of Q are (−1+5, −2+1) = (4, −1).
In the same way R = (−1+5, 2+1) = (4, 3) and S = (−3+5, 1+1) = (2, 2).

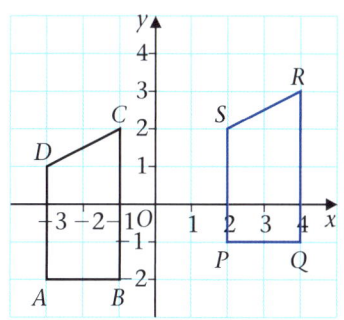

Exercise 27A

You will need isometric and squared paper and a ruler.
Tracing paper could be useful.

1 Shape **A** is shown on the grid.
   A is translated using this rule:
      Move all points +4 units parallel to the x-axis followed by +2 units parallel to the y-axis.

   This means move them by the vector $\binom{4}{2}$.

   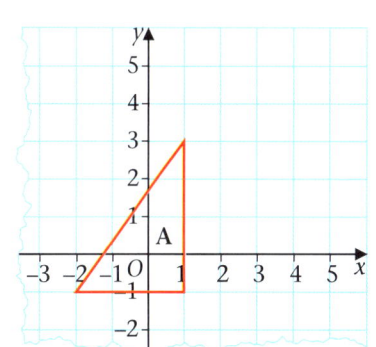

   On squared paper draw a set of coordinate axes with x and y both going from −5 to 5.

   (a) Draw the image of **A** after the translation and label it **B**.

   (b) Write down the coordinates of the vertices of shape **B**.

506 Chapter 27 Describing transformations

2 On squared paper draw a set of coordinate axes with
   x and y both going from -5 to 5.
   The corners of triangle ABC are $A(-1, 1)$, $B(-1, 4)$ and $C(1, 3)$.

   (a) Draw triangle ABC on your grid.

   Triangle ABC is translated to triangle $A'B'C'$ using this rule:
   Add 3 to the x-coordinate and subtract 4 from the
   y-coordinate.

   (b) Work out the coordinates of A', B' and C'.

   (c) Draw triangle $A'B'C'$ on your grid.

3 Describe fully the transformation which maps shape **P**
   on to shape **Q**.

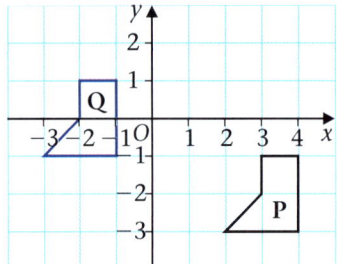

4 Make a pattern using repeated translations. You may
   use one, two or more shapes.

27.2 Reflections

You learned about reflections in Chapter 22. You should
remember that:

> A mathematical **reflection** has an image that is the same
> distance behind the mirror line as the object is in front.
>
>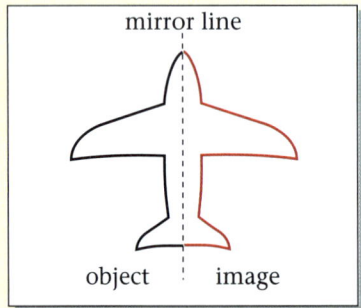
>
> Mirror lines are **two-way**. The mirror line may go through the
> object, requiring reflections to go both ways.

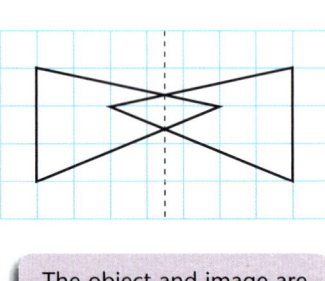

The object and image are congruent.

27.2 Reflections

To describe a reflection fully you need to give the equation of the line of symmetry.

Example 2

Describe fully the transformation that maps shape **A** on to **B**.

The image **B** is the same shape and size as the original shape **A**, but it is 'turned over'. So the transformation is a reflection.

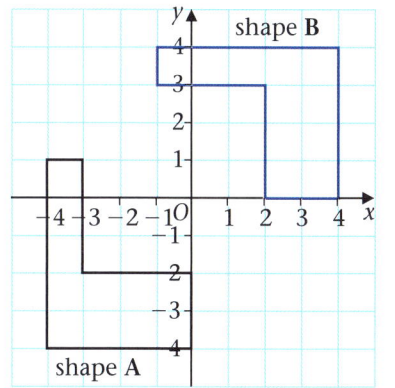

First draw the line of reflection.
Draw a line from a point on **A** to its corresponding point on **B** (shown in red on the diagram).
Find the middle point of the line. Repeat for another point on **A**. The line joining the two middle points is the mirror line (shown in black on the diagram).
The equation of the mirror line is $y = -x$. **A** maps on to **B** after a reflection in the line $y = -x$.
The transformation is a reflection in the line $y = -x$.

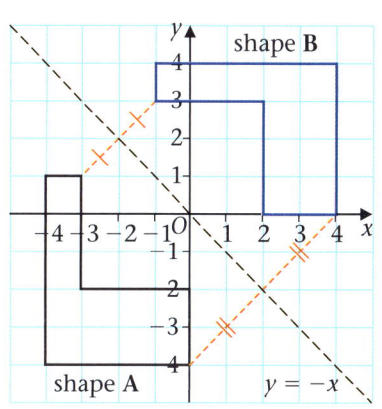

Exercise 27B

You need squared or graph paper and tracing paper.

1. Copy the grid and the shaded shape. Draw the image of the shape after a reflection in the line $y = 1$.

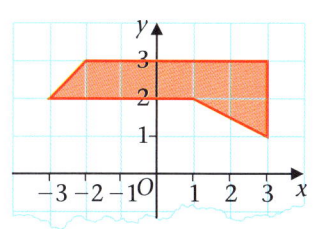

Hint: first draw the line whose equation is $y = 1$.

2. Copy triangle *ABC* and the line *TU* on squared paper. Draw the image of triangle *ABC* after it is reflected in the line *TU*. The image of the point *A* has been found for you.

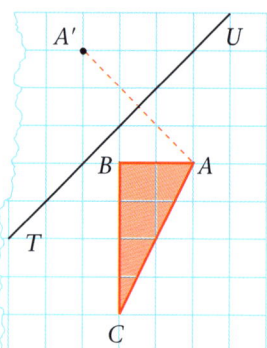

Hint: turn the page so that *TU* is vertical.

3. Draw a grid with both *x*- and *y*-coordinate axes going from −6 to 6.
   (a) Plot the points *P*(−2, 1), *Q*(0, 1), *R*(1, 0), *S*(3, 4) and *T*(−2, 4) and join them in order to form the closed shape *PQRST*.
   (b) Draw the image of *PQRST* after a reflection in the *x*-axis.

4. Describe fully the transformation that maps shape **A** on to **B**.

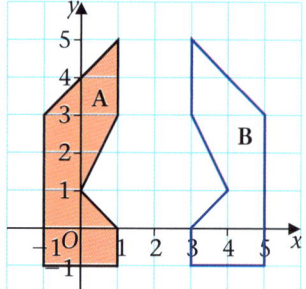

5. Use tracing paper to draw a pattern by making repeated reflections of a shape.

27.3 Rotations

You learned about rotations in Chapter 22. The minute hand of a clock **rotates** (turns) about a point near one of its ends. A blade of a pair of scissors rotates about a point part way along its length.

 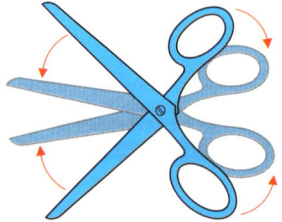

The clock hand and the scissor blade **turn through an angle** about a fixed point.

A rotation turns a shape through an angle about a fixed point.

The object and image are congruent.

Notice that the image is the same shape and size as the original shape.

27.3 Rotations

Exercise 27C

You need tracing paper, a ruler and a protractor.

1. Copy the shapes. Use tracing paper to rotate each shape half a turn about the point marked with a dot.

(a)  (b)  (c)

2. Rotate each of the shapes in question **1** a quarter of a turn anticlockwise about the point marked with a dot.

3. Copy the flag shape. Draw the image after a rotation about the point *R* of

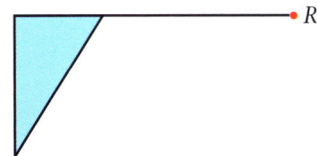

(a) a quarter of a turn anticlockwise
(b) a half turn
(c) a quarter of a turn clockwise.

4. Copy the shape. Draw the image after a rotation about the point of
   (a) 120° anticlockwise
   (b) 240° anticlockwise
   (c) 120° clockwise

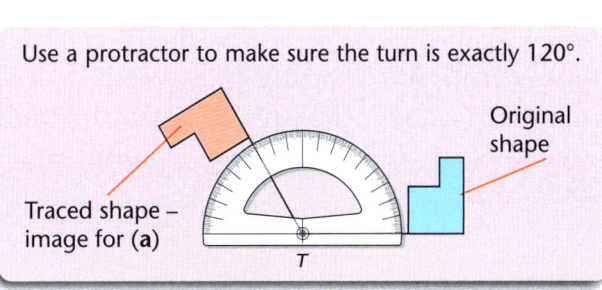

Use a protractor to make sure the turn is exactly 120°.

Traced shape – image for (a)

Original shape

When the centre of rotation is not on the object

Sometimes you need to rotate a shape about a point that is outside the shape. You can think of this as though it was the flag in question **3** of Exercise 27C without the flagpole.

Trace the shape and the dot. Then keep the dot fixed and rotate the tracing paper as before.

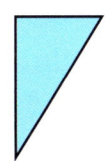

The fixed point *R* is called the **centre of rotation**.

Exercise 27D

You need tracing paper.

1. Copy the shapes and the dots. Use tracing paper to rotate each shape half a turn about the point marked with a dot.

   (a)    (b) 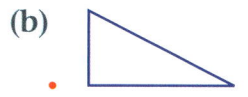   (c)

2. Rotate each shape in question **1** a quarter of a turn anticlockwise about the point marked with a dot.

3. Copy this shape and the dot.
   Make a pattern by rotating the shape about the dot through these angles:
   (a) clockwise: 60°, 120° and 180°
   (b) anticlockwise: 60° and 120°.

Rotating shapes on a grid

You can use squared paper to help you rotate shapes.

Example 3

On squared paper draw coordinate axes with x going from 0 to 7 and y going from -3 to 7. Copy the shape *ABCDEF* and draw its image after a quarter of a turn anticlockwise about the point $P(1, -1)$.

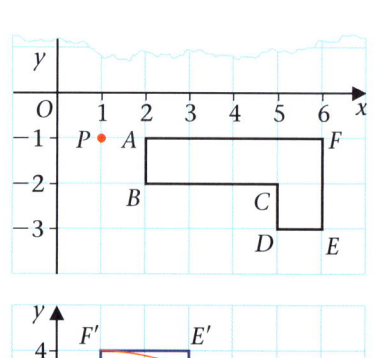

Plot image of each point on the shape and then join them to form the image.

Rotate *A* about *P* through a quarter of a turn (90°) anticlockwise and it ends up at (1, 0).

Rotate *B* about *P* through a quarter of a turn (90°) anticlockwise and it ends up at (2, 0).

F goes to (1, 4).

You could continue with the other points, but these image points are probably enough for you to complete the shape.

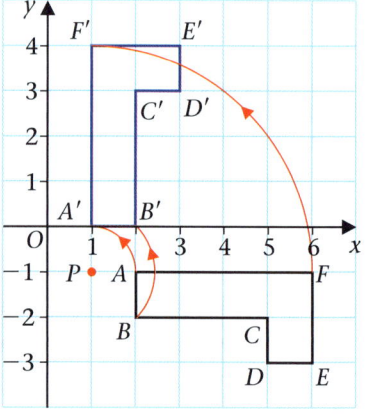

In a rotation all points in the shape rotate through the same angle. The distance of an image point from the centre of rotation is the same as the distance of the original point from the centre of rotation.

Describing rotations

To describe a rotation fully you need to give the:
- centre of rotation
- angle of turn
- direction of turn (clockwise or anticlockwise)

Example 4

Describe fully the transformation which maps shape **P** on to **Q**.

Each side of **Q** is at right angles to the corresponding side of **P** so **P** has made a quarter turn anticlockwise to get to **Q**.

To describe the rotation fully you need to say which point is the centre of rotation.

Each point on the original shape is the same distance from the centre of rotation as its image point. You might be able to see that the centre is (1, 1). So the transformation is a rotation of a quarter of a turn (90°) anticlockwise about the point (1, 1).

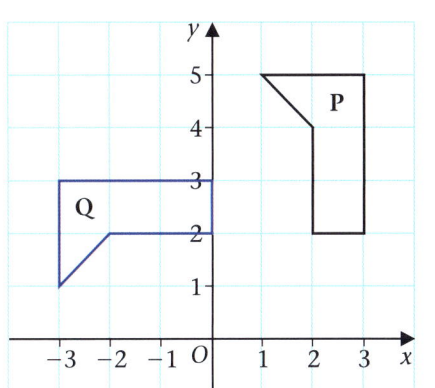

You can also find the centre of rotation geometrically. The centre is the same distance from each point and its image. So if you draw a line from any point to its image, the centre of rotation will be *somewhere* on the perpendicular bisector of the line.

To find the centre of rotation, draw lines connecting *two* points to their images. Draw the perpendicular bisectors of both lines. The bisectors are dotted lines in the diagram.

As the centre of rotation is somewhere on *both* bisectors it must be at the point (1, 1) where they cross.

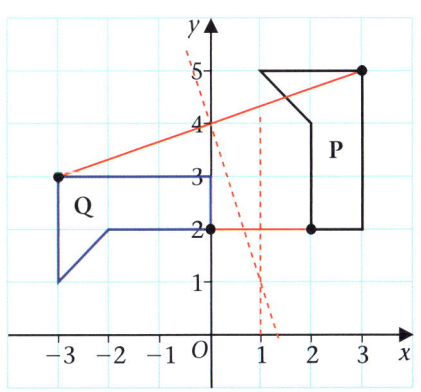

There is more about perpendicular bisectors in Section 7.7 (in Book 1).

Exercise 27E

You will need squared or graph paper.

1. Draw coordinate axes on graph paper with *x* and *y* going from −6 to 6. Copy the shaded shape.
   Draw the image of the shaded shape after
   (a) a half turn about the origin (0, 0) (label the image **A**)
   (b) a quarter turn clockwise about the origin (label it **B**)
   (c) a quarter turn anticlockwise about the origin (label it **C**).

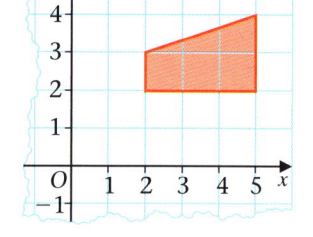

2. Draw coordinate axes on graph paper with *x* going from −6 to 6 and *y* going from −4 to 8. Copy the shaded shape.
   Draw the image of the shaded shape after
   (a) a half turn about the point *P*(0, 2) (label the image **A**)
   (b) a quarter turn clockwise about the point *P*(0, 2) (label the image **B**)
   (c) a quarter turn anticlockwise about the point *P*(0, 2) (label the image **C**).

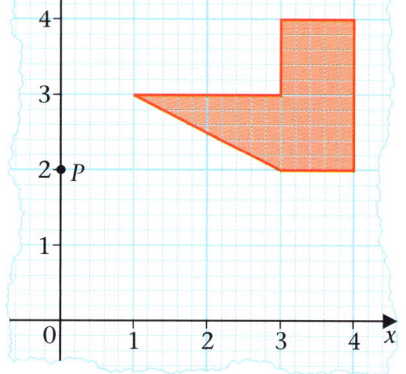

3. Describe fully the transformation which maps shape **A** on to shape **B**.

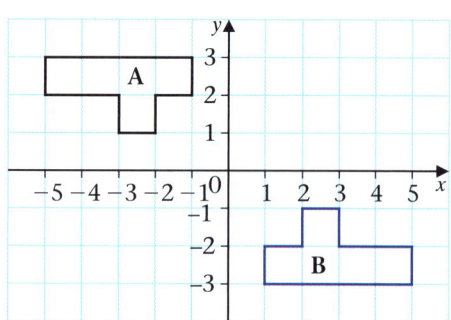

27.4 Enlargements

You learned about enlargement in Chapter 22. You should remember that:

> An enlargement changes the size but not the shape of an object. The scale factor of the enlargement is the value that the lengths of the original object are multiplied by.
>
> In an enlargement, image lines are parallel to their corresponding object lines.

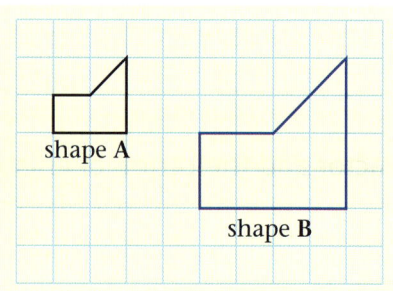

Similar shapes

In Chapter 22 you saw that

The original shape and its image after an enlargement are similar to each other.

The centre of enlargement determines the final position of the enlarged image.

$CR' = 2CR$
$CP' = 2CP$
$CQ' = 2CQ$

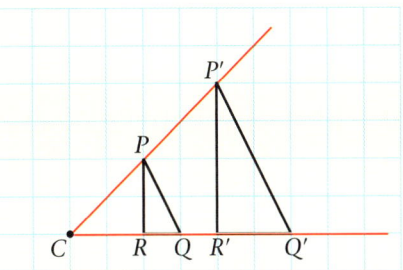

Example 5

Enlarge triangle *PQR* by scale factor 3 using *A* as the centre of enlargement.

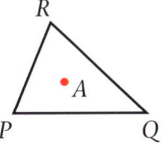

Copy triangle *PQR* and the point *A* inside the triangle.

Draw a line from *A* to *P* and continue it to *P'* so that *AP'* is 3 times *AP*. Mark the positions of *Q'* and *R'* in a similar way, then join the points *P'*, *Q'* and *R'* to form the image triangle.

The enlargement should look like this:

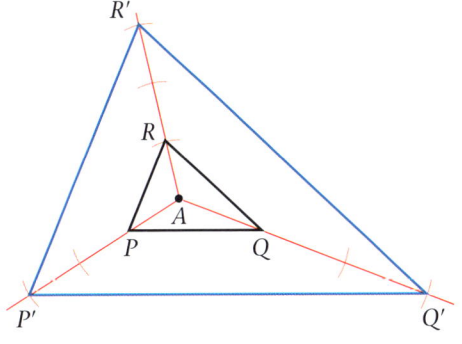

Describing enlargements

To describe an enlargement fully you need to give the scale factor and the centre of enlargement.

To work out the scale factors, compare the lengths of corresponding sides on the object and image.

> The centre of enlargement can be given by the letter of the point or by the coordinates of the point.

Example 6

Describe fully the transformation that maps *ABCD* on to *PQRS*.

PQRS is the same shape as *ABCD*. The sides of *PQRS* are all 2 times the lengths of the corresponding sides of *ABCD*. So the transformation is an enlargement by a scale factor 2.

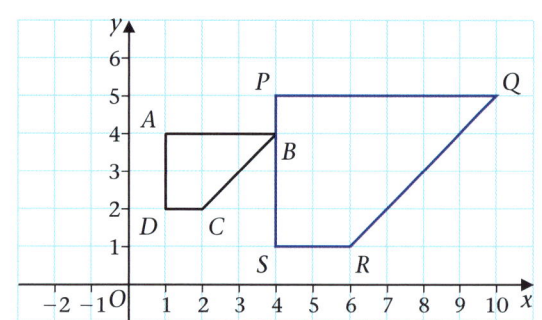

Note: you could compare the two corresponding lines as a ratio

scale factor = $\frac{PQ}{AB} = \frac{6}{3} = 2$

To describe the transformation fully you need to give the centre of enlargement.
To find the centre of enlargement, reverse the method used in Example 5.

Join *P* to *A* and continue the line.
Join *Q* to *B* and continue the line.
In the same way join *R* to *C* and *S* to *D* and continue the lines. The lines all pass through the same point (−2, 3) so this is the centre of enlargement.

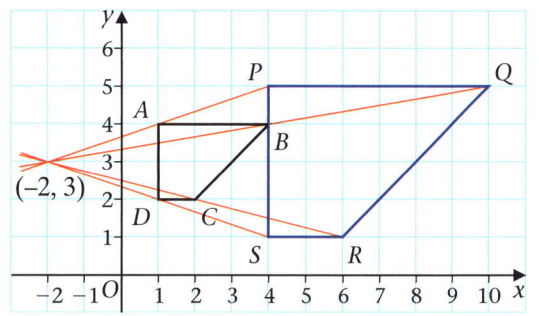

The transformation is an enlargement by scale factor 2 with centre of enlargement (−2, 3).

The scale factor of an enlargement is given by the ratio of any two corresponding line segments.

Scale factor = $\frac{A'B'}{AB}$

Enlargements with fractional scale factors

If you start with shape *PQRS* from Example 6 and transform it to *ABCD* the shape remains the same, but the size is changed, so the transformation is an enlargement.

The sides of *ABCD* are all $\frac{1}{2}$ the lengths of the corresponding sides of *PQRS* so the transformation that maps *PQRS* on to *ABCD* is an enlargement by the scale factor $\frac{1}{2}$ with centre (−2, 3).

An enlargement with a scale factor less than 1 means that the image will be smaller than the object.

27.4 Enlargements

Example 7

Draw the image of the shape *KLMN* after an enlargement by scale factor $\frac{1}{2}$ with centre *C*. Label the image *K'L'M'N'*.

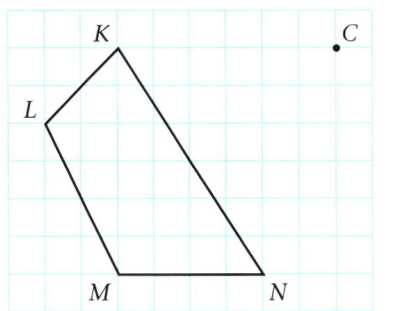

Join *CK*. *CK* = 6 units. The scale factor is $\frac{1}{2}$ so *CK'* = $\frac{1}{2}$ × 6 = 3 units.
Mark the point *K'*, 3 units from *C* along *CK*.

In the same way mark *L'* where *CL'* = $\frac{1}{2}$ *CL*, *M'* where *CM'* = $\frac{1}{2}$ *CM* and *N'* where *CN'* = $\frac{1}{2}$ *CN*.

> Hint: use the squares and their diagonals so you can do this without a ruler.

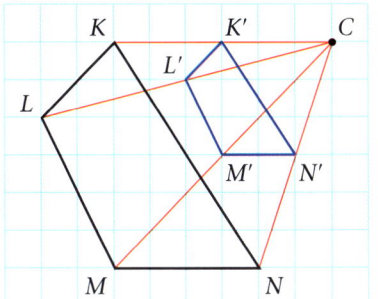

Join *K'L'M'N'* to form the image.

Example 8

Work out the scale factor of the enlargement that takes triangle *ABC* on to triangle *LMN*.

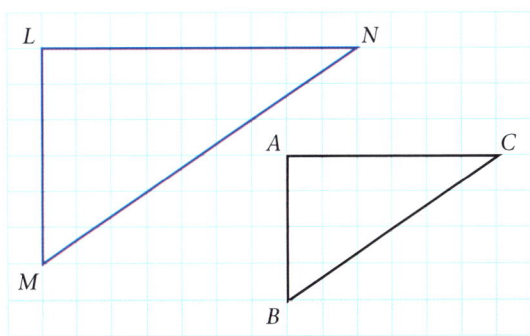

The scale factor is the ratio of any two corresponding line segments

$$\frac{LN}{AC} = \frac{9}{6} = \frac{3}{2} = 1\frac{1}{2}$$

> Or you could use $\frac{LM}{AB} = \frac{6}{4} = \frac{3}{2} = 1\frac{1}{2}$

The scale factor is $1\frac{1}{2}$.

Exercise 27F

You will need squared or graph paper and a ruler.

1. (a) Copy the diagram.
   Describe fully the transformation that maps shape **A** on to shape **B**.
   (b) Describe fully the transformation that maps shape **B** on to shape **A**.

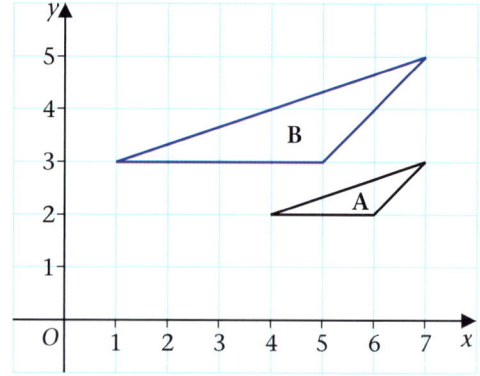

2. Copy the diagram.
   With C as centre, draw the image of the shaded shape after an enlargement by
   (a) scale factor $\frac{1}{4}$
   (b) scale factor $\frac{3}{4}$

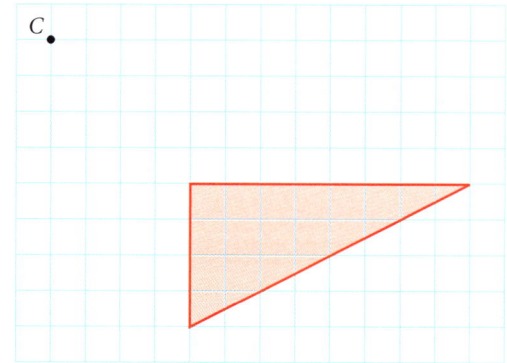

3. Copy the diagram.
   With X as centre, draw the image of the shaded shape after an enlargement by
   (a) scale factor $\frac{2}{3}$
   (b) scale factor $1\frac{2}{3}$

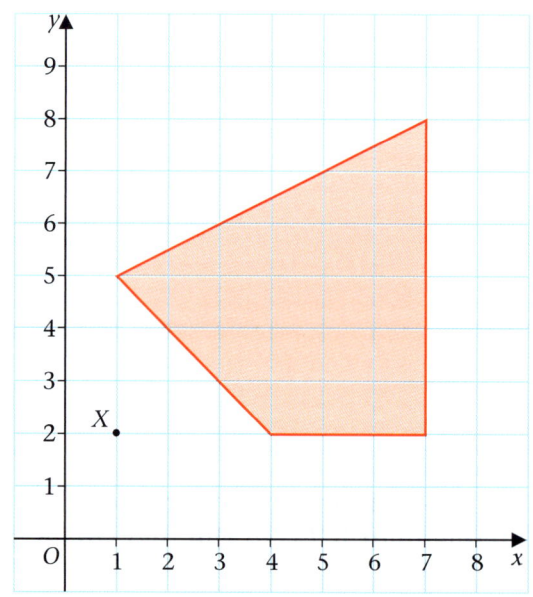

27.4 Enlargements

4 Describe fully the enlargement that
(a) maps **A** on to **B**
(b) maps **B** on to **A**.

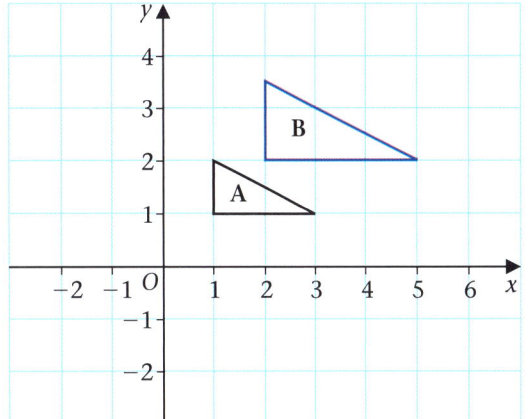

5 Describe fully the transformation that takes triangle *PQR* on to triangle *TUV*.

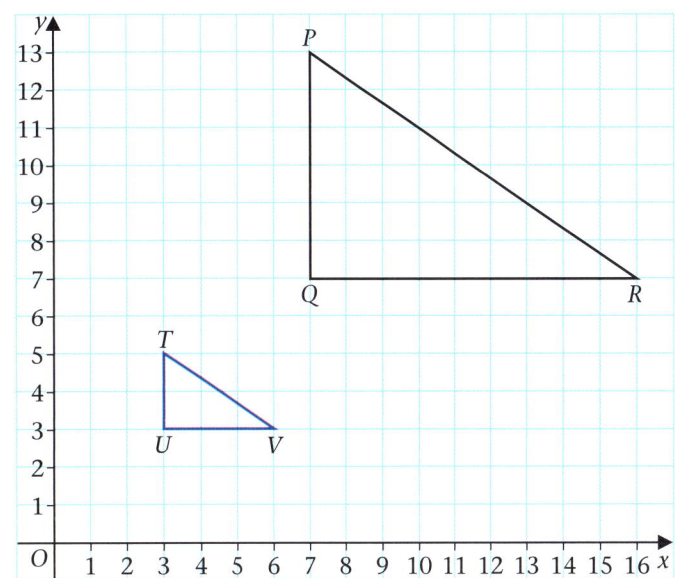

Similar circles, squares and rectangles

When two shapes are similar, one shape is an enlargement of the other.

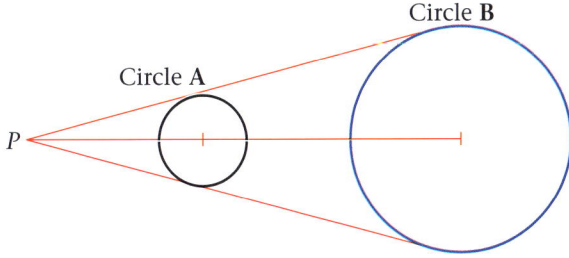

Circle **B** is an enlargement of circle **A** (the centre of enlargement is *P*), so the two circles are mathematically similar. The ratio $\dfrac{\text{radius of circle } \mathbf{B}}{\text{radius of circle } \mathbf{A}}$ is the same for all the radii of the two circles.

> This is true for **any** two circles **A** and **B**.

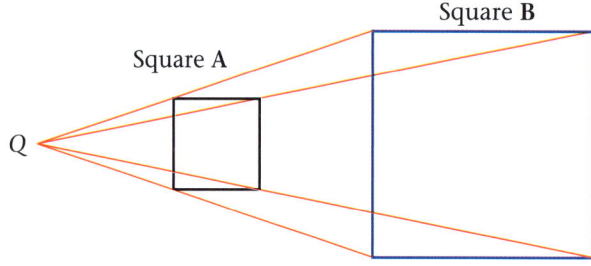

Square A is an enlargement of square B (the centre of enlargement is Q) so the two squares are mathematically similar. The ratio $\frac{\text{side of square B}}{\text{side of square A}}$ is the same for all the sides of the squares.

This is true for **any** two squares **A** and **B**.

Look at these rectangles on the right:

Length: PQ corresponds to AB. The ratio $\frac{PQ}{AB} = \frac{8}{4} = \frac{2}{1}$

Width: QR corresponds to BC. The ratio $\frac{QR}{BC} = \frac{5}{3}$

The ratios for length and width are not the same so the two rectangles are not mathematically similar.

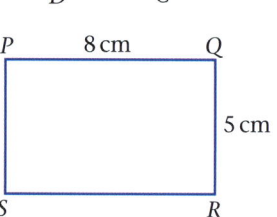

Any two circles and any two squares are mathematically similar but two rectangles may not be mathematically similar.

Mixed exercise 27

You need squared paper and a ruler.

1 (a) Copy the diagram.
   Reflect the triangle **A** in the x-axis.
   Label the reflection **B**.
   (b) Reflect the triangle **B** in the line $y = x$.
   Label the reflection **C**.

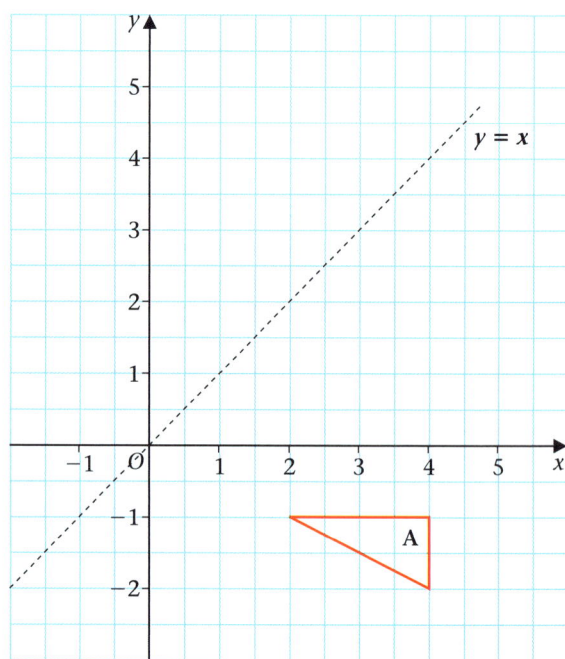

Mixed exercise 27

2 Copy and complete the coordinate grid so that
   x goes from −9 to 9 and y goes from −5 to 5.
   Copy the triangle L.
   (a) Reflect the triangle L in the y-axis.
       Label the reflection M.
   (b) Reflect the triangle M in the x-axis.
       Label the image N.

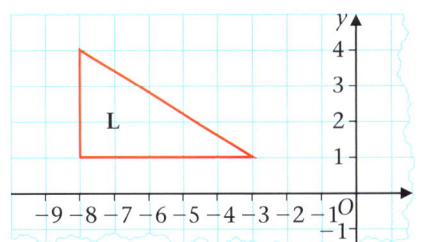

3 Write down a single transformation which is applied to
   the original tile to make each lettered part of this pattern:

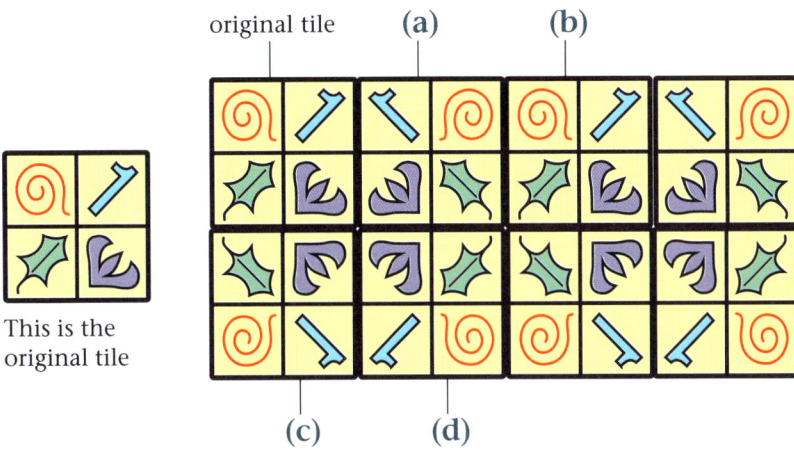

Hint: there is more than one way of doing the transformations for (b), (c) and (d).

4 On squared paper draw coordinate axes so that x and y
   both go from −6 to 6.
   (a) Plot the points (2, 2), (4, 1), (6, 2) and (4, 5).
       Join them in order and label the shape P.
   (b) Reflect P in the x-axis. Label the reflection Q.
   (c) Rotate P through 180° about the origin (0, 0).
       Label this image R.

5 Copy and complete this coordinate grid for
   x from −7 to 10 and y from −6 to 6.
   Copy shape F.
   (a) Rotate F through 180° about (0, 0).
       Label the image G.
   (b) Rotate G through 180° about (5, −3).
       Label the image H.

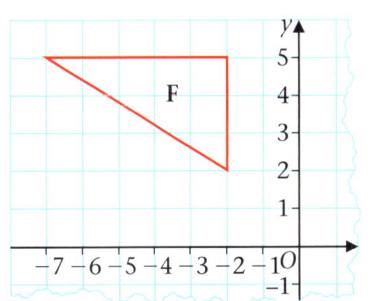

6 Copy this diagram.
  (a) Rotate triangle **A** clockwise through 90° about (0, 0). Label the image **B**.
  (b) Draw the image of **B** after a reflection in the line $y = -x$.
  Label the reflection **C**.

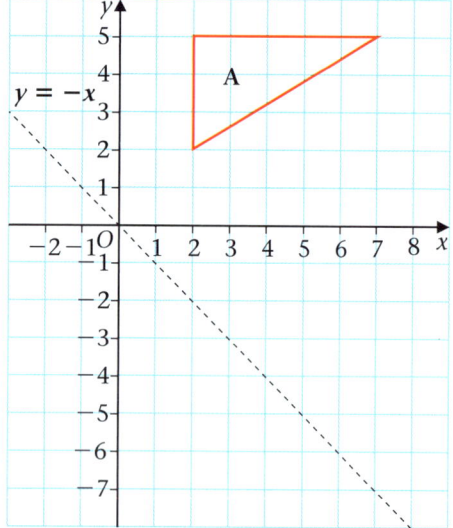

7 The triangle **Q** is an enlargement of the triangle **P**.
  (a) Write down the scale factor of the enlargement.
  (b) Work out the coordinates of the centre of enlargement.

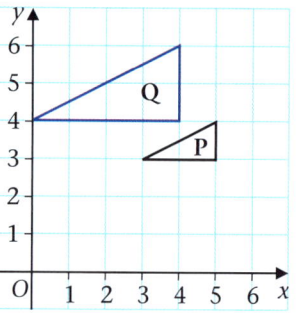

8 Draw a set of coordinate axes with x from -4 to 10 and y from 0 to 7.
  (a) Plot the points $(-2, 1)$, $(1, 3)$ and $(0, 5)$.
    Join them and label the triangle **A**.
  The triangle **A** is reflected in a line **M**. Two of the image points have coordinates $(5, 3)$ and $(6, 5)$.
  (b) Write down the coordinates of the third corner of the image.
  (c) Work out the equation of **M**, the line of reflection.

9 Rotate the triangle through 180° about centre A. On a copy of the grid draw the new position of the triangle.

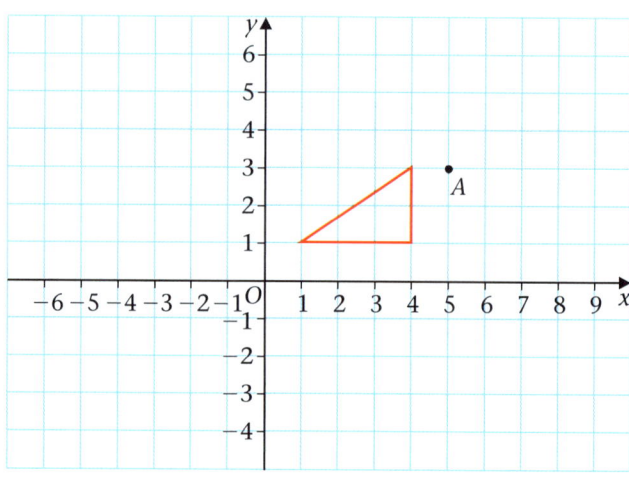

[E]

10 Draw a grid on squared paper with the x-axis from −10 to 10 and the y-axis from −14 to 4.
   (a) Plot the points A(3, 1), B(2, −4) and C(−3, 1) and join them to form triangle ABC.
   (b) Draw the enlargement of triangle ABC by the scale factor 3, using the origin (0, 0) as centre of enlargement.
   (c) Write down the coordinates of the vertices of the image triangle.

11 Copy the grid and the shaded triangle.
   (a) Draw the image of the shaded triangle after a rotation through an angle of 90° anticlockwise about the origin (0, 0). Label the image **S**.
   (b) Draw the image of the shaded triangle after a rotation through an angle of 90° anticlockwise about the point (2, 1). Label the image **T**.

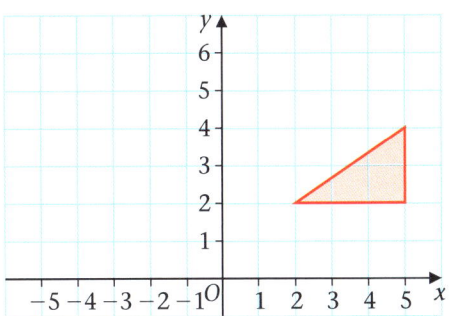

12 Draw a set of coordinate axes with x from −8 to 8 and y from −7 to 7.
   (a) Plot the points (2, 1), (6, 1) and (6, 4). Join them up and label the triangle **A**.
   (b) Reflect **A** in the y-axis. Label the reflection **B**.
   (c) Draw the line $y = x$.
   (d) Reflect **B** in the line $y = x$. Label the reflection **C**.

Summary of key points

1 Changes in the position or size of a shape are called **transformations**. Reflections, rotations, enlargements and translations are all types of transformations.

2 To describe a translation you need to give the horizontal and vertical movements of the translation. These are written as a **vector**, e.g. $\binom{5}{-2}$

3 To describe a reflection fully you need to give the equation of the line of symmetry.

4 In a rotation all points in the shape rotate through the same angle. The distance of an image point from the centre of rotation is the same as the distance of the original point from the centre of rotation.

5 To describe a rotation fully you need to give the:
  - centre of rotation
  - angle of turn
  - direction of turn (clockwise or anticlockwise)

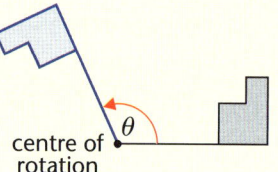

6 The original shape and its image after an enlargement are similar to each other.

7 To describe an enlargement fully you need to give the scale factor and the centre of enlargement.

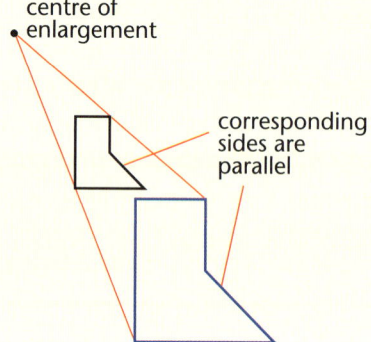

8 The scale factor of an enlargement is given by the ratio of any two corresponding line segments.

Scale factor $= \dfrac{A'B'}{AB}$

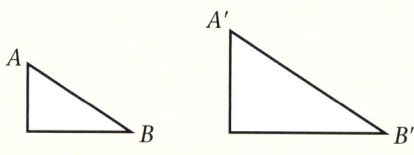

9 When two shapes are similar, one shape is an enlargement of the other.

10 Any two circles and any two squares are mathematically similar but two rectangles may not be mathematically similar.

 28 Expressions, formulae, equations and graphs

This chapter shows you how to manipulate algebraic expressions, draw and interpret graphs, rearrange formulae, and solve simple quadratic and reciprocal equations.

In Chapter 3 (in Book 1) you learned how to simplify expressions containing powers. You should remember the following key points:

To multiply powers of the same letter add the indices:

$$x^a \times x^b = x^{a+b}$$

To divide powers of the same letter subtract the indices:

$$x^a \div x^b = x^{a-b}$$

Any letter raised to the power 1 is equal to the letter itself:

$$x^1 = x$$

Any letter raised to the power 0 is equal to 1:

$$x^0 = 1 \text{ if } x \text{ is not zero.}$$

To simplify an expression containing different powers of the same letter multiplied or divided, write the expression as a single power of the letter.

> See Section 3.11 for more explanation and examples.

28.1 Simplifying algebraic expressions

In Chapter 3 (in Book 1) you learned how to simplify an algebraic expression by expanding the brackets and collecting **like terms** together. Here are some more examples:

Example 1

Simplify the expression $3(3a + 2b) + 2(a - b)$.

$3(3a + 2b) + 2(a - b)$
$= 9a + 6b + 2a - 2b$ ——— First expand the brackets.
$= 9a + 2a + 6b - 2b$ ——— Change the order for adding and subtracting to put the a terms and the b terms together.
$= 11a + 4b$

> Remember:
> This is called collecting **like terms**.

Chapter 28 Expressions, formulae, equations and graphs

Example 2

Simplify the expression $\dfrac{4n + 2}{2}$

$$\dfrac{4n + 2}{2} = \dfrac{1}{2}(4n + 2)$$
$$= \dfrac{1}{2} \times 4n + \dfrac{1}{2} \times 2 \quad \text{— Expand the brackets.}$$
$$= 2n + 1$$

Remember: the line acts like a bracket.

Example 3

Simplify the expression $x(x + 3y) + 2x(x + y)$.

$$x(x + 3y) + 2x(x + y)$$
$$= x^2 + 3xy + 2x^2 + 2xy \quad \text{— Expand the brackets.}$$
$$= x^2 + 2x^2 + 3xy + 2xy \quad \text{— Collect like terms.}$$
$$= 3x^2 + 5xy$$

Exercise 28A

Simplify the expressions in questions **1–5**.

1 (a) $2(3r + 1) + 2r$ (b) $3(4p - 2) - 10p$
    (c) $4(2x + y) + 2x - 3y$ (d) $2m - 3n + 3(m + n)$

2 (a) $4(2a + b) + 2(3a - b)$ (b) $3(p + q) + 2(p - q)$
    (c) $2(3r + s) + 4(r - s)$ (d) $3(2p - q) + 3(p + q)$

3 (a) $3(x + y) + 4(x - y)$ (b) $4(m - n) + 3(2m - n)$
    (c) $2(p - q) + 2(q - p)$ (d) $3(p - q) + 3(p + q)$

4 (a) $3(b - a) + 1(6a - 6b)$ (b) $r(r + 2) - r$
    (c) $m(n + m) + m(n - m)$ (d) $m(3 + n) + n(1 - m)$

5 (a) $3(x + 2y) + 4x$ (b) $3a + 4(5a - 6)$
    (c) $5(c - d) - 2c + 3d$ (d) $4(2p - 6q) - 3p + q$
    (e) $a(b - 2c) + 2b(a + c)$ (f) $a(b - 2) + b(a - 3)$

6 Write these expressions in a simpler form:
    (a) $\dfrac{6n + 4}{2}$ (b) $\dfrac{9n - 6}{3}$ (c) $\dfrac{10n - 20}{5}$
    (d) $\dfrac{6p + 10r}{2}$ (e) $\dfrac{4r - 8q}{4}$ (f) $\dfrac{6r - 3s}{3}$

Activity – Expressions

When an algebraic expression was simplified it became
$2a + b$

(a) Write down as many different expressions as you can which simplify to $2a + b$.
(b) What is the most complex expression you can think of that simplifies to $2a + b$?
(c) What is the simplest expression you can think of that simplifies to $2a + b$?
(d) Repeat this activity for some other simple expressions such as a, $\dfrac{a}{2}$, $2a - b$.

Dealing with negative numbers

The expression $-2(3a - 2)$ has a negative number before the brackets. To expand the brackets, multiply each term inside the brackets by -2:

$-2 \times 3a = -6a$

$-2(3a - 2) = -6a + 4$

$-2 \times -2 = +4$

Example 4

Multiply out and simplify: $4(x + 3) - 3(x + 5)$.

$4(x + 3) - 3(x + 5)$
$= 4x + 12 - 3x - 15$ —— Expand the brackets.
$= 4x - 3x + 12 - 15$ —— Collect like terms.
$= x - 3$

Example 5

Simplify the expression $4(2a + b) - 2(a - b)$.

$4(2a + b) - 3(a - b)$
$= 8a + 4b - 3a + 3b$ —— Expand the brackets.
$= 8a - 3a + 4b + 3b$ —— Collect like terms.
$= 3a + 7b$

Exercise 28B

Multiply out and simplify these expressions.

1. (a) $3(5x + 4) - 2(a + 3)$ (b) $8(2x + 1) - (x + 7)$
   (c) $7(a - 2) - 2(2a + 3)$ (d) $2(6q + 7) - 3(3p + 4q)$
   (e) $2(6x - y) - (x + y)$ (f) $2(4x + 3y) - 3(2x + y)$
   (g) $4(d - 2) - 3(d + 1)$ (h) $5(3c - 2) - 4(1 + 2c)$

2. (a) $3(d + 4) - 2(3 - 2d)$ (b) $2(2p + qw) - 3(p - q)$
   (c) $2(s - r) - 2(r - s)$ (d) $5(4b - 5) - (4 - 2b)$
   (e) $5(2y - 8) - 3(2 - 5y)$ (f) $3(2x + 5y) - 2(2x - y)$
   (g) $3(2n - 3) - 4(n - 2)$ (h) $5(4b - 2a) - 3(2a - 3b)$

Multiplying bracketed expressions

Sometimes you will need to multiply bracketed expressions by each other, for example $(e + f)(g + h)$.

This means $(e + f)$ multiplied by $(g + h)$ or $(e + f) \times (g + h)$

Look at the rectangles on the right.

The area of the whole rectangle is $(e + f)(g + h)$.

It is the same as the sum of the four separate areas so:

$(e + f)(g + h) = eg + eh + fg + fh$

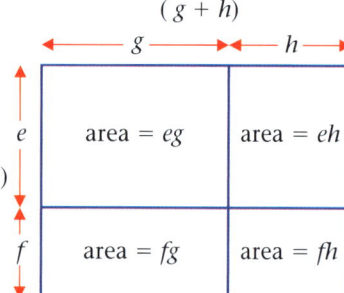

Notice that each term in the first bracket is multiplied by each term in the second bracket:

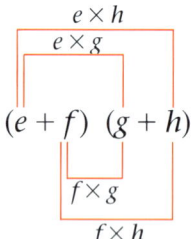

You can also think of the area of the rectangle as the sum of **two** separate parts:

$(e + f)(g + h) = e(g + h) + f(g + h)$

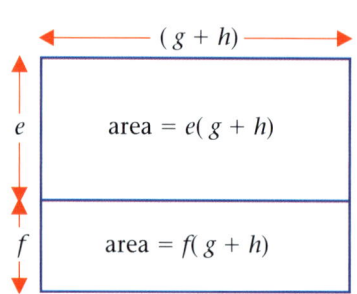

Think of multiplying each term in the first bracket by the whole of the second bracket.

These are two ways of thinking about the same process. The end result is the same.

This is called **multiplying out** the brackets.

28.1 Simplifying algebraic expressions

Example 6

Multiply out and simplify (a) $(x + 2)(x + 3)$ (b) $(x - 4)^2$

(a) $(x + 2)(x + 3) = x(x + 3) + 2(x + 3)$
$= x^2 + 3x + 2x + 6$
$= x^2 + 5x + 6$

(b) $(x - 4)^2 = (x - 4)(x - 4)$
$= x(x - 4) - 4(x - 4)$
$= x^2 - 4x - 4x + 16$
$= x^2 - 8x + 16$

> Multiply each term in the first bracket by the whole of the second bracket.

Example 7

Multiply out the brackets in the expression $(2a + 2)(3a - 4)$.

$(2a + 2)(3a - 4) = 2a(3a - 4) + 2(3a - 4)$
$= 6a^2 - 8a + 6a - 8$
$= 6a^2 - 2a - 8$

> $2a \times 3a = 2 \times a \times 3 \times a$
> $= 2 \times 3 \times a \times a$
> $= 6a^2$

Equations such as
$(e + f)(g + h) = eg + eh + fg + fh$
and $(e + f)(g + h) = e(g + h) + f(g + h)$
which are true for all values of e, f, g and h are also known as **identities**.

Exercise 28C

Multiply out and simplify these expressions.

1 (a) $(a + 4)(b + 3)$ (b) $(c + 5)(d + 4)$
   (c) $(x + 3)(y + 6)$ (d) $(a + 3)(a + 8)$
   (e) $(b + 7)(b + 4)$ (f) $(x + 6)(x + 2)$

2 (a) $(2a + 3)(a + 4)$ (b) $(3b + 2)(b + 3)$
   (c) $(4c + 3)(c + 6)$ (d) $(2a + 5)(a + 3)$
   (e) $(3b + 4)(b + 2)$ (f) $(4c + 5)(c + 2)$

3 (a) $(a - 4)(a - 3)$ (b) $(c - 5)(c - 4)$
   (c) $(x - 3)(x - 6)$ (d) $(a - 3)(a - 8)$
   (e) $(b - 7)(b + 4)$ (f) $(x - 6)(x - 2)$

4 (a) $(a - 4)(a + 3)$ (b) $(a + 5)(a - 4)$
   (c) $(x - 3)(x + 6)$ (d) $(a - 3)(a + 8)$
   (e) $(b - 7)(b + 4)$ (f) $(x + 6)(x - 2)$

5 (a) $(x+1)(x+2)$ (b) $(y+5)(y-1)$
   (c) $(d-3)(d-2)$ (d) $(g+5)(g-3)$
   (e) $(x-6)(x+2)$ (f) $(t-4)(t-2)$

6 (a) $(2a-5)(a+5)$ (b) $(3b+4)(b-6)$
   (c) $(3c-2)(c-3)$ (d) $(3a-4)(a-5)$
   (e) $(3x-4)(x+5)$ (f) $(2a+3)(a-6)$

7 (a) $(3a+1)(a-2)$ (b) $(3p+2)(4p-1)$
   (c) $(3a+2)(a+1)$ (d) $(4p+2)(3p+2)$
   (e) $(2b-3)(b-1)$ (f) $(4b-1)(2b+1)$

8 (a) $(x+3)^2$ (b) $(y-5)^2$
   (c) $(2x+1)^2$ (d) $(3y-4)^2$
   (e) $(3x+5)^2$ (f) $(6x-7)^2$

Remember:
$(x+3)^2 = (x+3)(x+3)$

9 (a) $(2x-1)(x+4)$ (b) $(y-10)(2y+3)$
   (c) $(3t-5)(2t-3)$ (d) $(m+5)(5m+1)$
   (e) $(5c+6)(5c+4)$ (f) $(3x+4)(2x-7)$

10 (a) $(6-x)(5+2x)$ (b) $(3+4x)(3x-7)$
   (c) $(2x+3)(2x-3)$ (d) $(2+5x)(3x-1)$
   (e) $(3x-4)(3x+4)$ (f) $(4-5x)(2x+3)$

28.2 Drawing graphs of simple quadratic functions

$y = 2x + 3$ is called a **function**. A function is a rule which shows how one set of numbers relates to another.

A quadratic function is a function of the type $y = ax^2 + bx + c$ in which a is not zero.
(a, b and c stand for numbers that are given.)

Here is a table of values for the quadratic function $y = x^2$:

x	-3	-2	-1	0	1	2	3
y	9	4	1	0	1	4	9

The points from the table of values are shown plotted on the graph. They do not lie on a straight line.

Exercise 28D will give you a better idea of the shape of the graph.

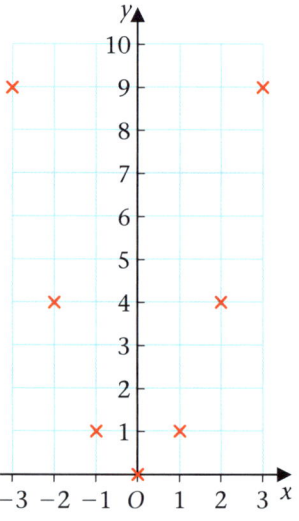

28.2 Drawing graphs of simple quadratic functions

Exercise 28D

You will need 2 mm squared graph paper and tracing paper.

1. (a) Make a full-size copy of the graph of $y = x^2$ on page 528. using 2 cm for 1 unit of x and y.
   (b) Copy and complete this extended table of values for $y = x^2$.

x	−2.5	−1.5	−0.8	−0.6	−0.4	−0.2	−0.1	0	0.1	0.2	0.4	0.6	0.8	1.5	2.5
y															

   (c) Plot these new points on your graph.
   (d) The points should appear to lie on a ∪-shaped curve. Draw a smooth curve through the points you have plotted.

   The curve should not be pointed at (0, 0).

2. On the same axes as you used for question **1**, draw the graph of $y = x^2 + 1$.

   *Use the same extra values of x in your table of values as in question **1**.*

x	−3	−2.5	−2	−1.5	−1	−0.8
y	10	7.25	5	3.25	2	

3. (a) Use tracing paper to trace the axes and the graph of $y = x^2$.
   (b) Slide the tracing paper up the y-axis to your graph of $y = x^2 + 1$.
   (c) Use the tracing paper to help you draw on the same axes the graphs of $y = x^2 + 2$, $y = x^2 + 3$, $y = x^2 − 1$.
   (d) Do any of the graphs have a line of symmetry?
   (e) Write down anything else that you notice.

   It should fit exactly.

More quadratic functions

Example 8

(a) Draw a table of values for $y = 2x^2 − 3$, using values of x from −3 to 3.
(b) Draw the graph of $y = 2x^2 − 3$.

(a)
x	−3	−2	−1	0	1	2	3
y	15	5	−1	−3	−1	5	15

(b)
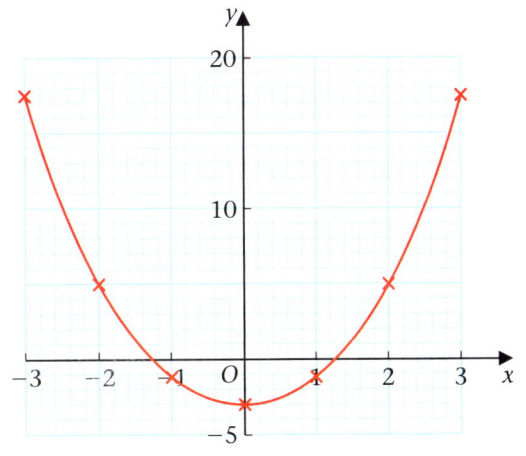

Exercise 28E

Draw a table of values and a graph for each of these quadratic functions, using values of x from -3 to 3.

1. $y = 2x^2 - 5$
2. $y = 3x^2 - 2$
3. $y = 5x^2 - 2$
4. $y = 5x^2 - 4$
5. $y = 3x^2 - 4$

28.3 Drawing graphs of more complex quadratic functions

You need to be able to draw graphs of quadratic functions accurately in order to help you solve quadratic equations.

Example 9

(a) Draw the graph of $y = 2x^2 - 4x - 3$ using values of x from -2 to 4.
(b) Draw the line of symmetry and write down its equation.
(c) What is the minimum value y can have for the function $y = 2x^2 - 4x - 3$?
(d) What value of x gives the minimum value of y?
(e) Find the values of x when $y = 5$.

(a) First make a table of values.

x	-2	-1	0	1	2	3	4
y	13	3	-3	-5	-3	3	13

When $x = -2$
$y = 2 \times (-2)^2 - 4 \times (-2) - 3$
$= 2 \times 4 + 8 - 3$
$= 8 + 8 - 3$
$y = 13$

You need to draw axes with x going from -2 to 4 and y going from -5 to 13.
Plot the points then join them with a smooth curve.

The graph should not be pointed at $(1, -5)$.

(b) The line of symmetry of the curve is the line which has the equation $x = 1$.
(c) The minimum value of y is -5.
(d) $x = 1$ gives the minimum the value of y.
(e) When $y = 5$ there are two values of x, which can be read off the graph: $x = -1.2$ and $x = 3.2$.

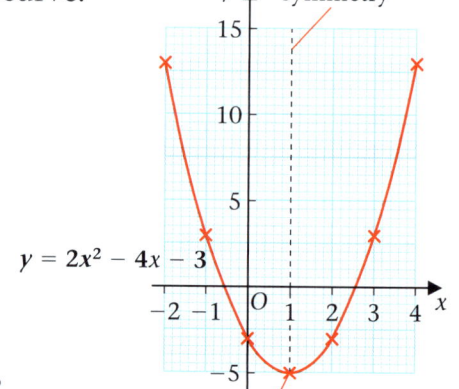

At this point y has its minimum (smallest) value.

Exercise 28F

You need 2 mm squared graph paper.

1. (a) Draw the graph of $y = 2x^2$ on graph paper. Use values of x from -4 to 4.
   (b) Draw the line of symmetry and write down its equation.

In questions **2–7** do the same as in question **1** for the functions given.

2. $y = x^2 + 5$
3. $y = x^2 - 2x$
4. $y = -3x^2 + 9$
5. $y = x^2 + 2x - 1$
6. $y = -x^2 + 3x + 5$
7. $y = 2x^2 + 3x - 5$

8. (a) Draw the graph of $y = x^2 - 7x + 10$ using values of x from 0 to 6.
   (b) Write down the minimum value of y.
   (c) Find the value of y when $x = 0.5$
   (d) Find the values of x when $y = -2$.

9. (a) Draw the graph of $y = x^2 - 3x - 4$ using values of x from -1 to 5.
   (b) Write down the minimum value of y.
   (c) Find the value of y when $x = 4.4$
   (d) Find the values of x when $y = -4$.

10. (a) Draw the graph of $y = x^2 - 2x - 8$ using values of x from -2 to 4.
    (b) Write down the minimum value of y.
    (c) Find the value of y when $x = -1.5$
    (d) Find the values of x when $y = -5$.

11. (a) Draw the graph of $y = 3x^2 - 3x - 2$ using values of x from -2 to 3.
    (b) Write down the minimum value of y.
    (c) Find the value of y when $x = 1.8$
    (d) Find the values of x when $y = 4$.

12. (a) Draw the graph of $y = 2x^2 - 5$ using values of x from -3 to 3.
    (b) Write down the minimum value of y.
    (c) Find the value of y when $x = 2.5$
    (d) Find the values of x when $y = -3$.

28.4 Solving quadratic equations

You can use a graph to solve a quadratic equation such as

$$2x^2 + 3x + 4 = 18$$

by finding the points on the graph of $y = 2x^2 + 3x + 4$ where $y = 18$, like this:

Step 1 Draw the graph of $y = 2x^2 + 3x + 4$.

Step 2 Find the value 18 on the y-axis. Draw a line through the point (0, 18) and parallel to the x-axis to meet the curve.

Step 3 Go down to the x-axis to find the two values of x which make $2x^2 + 3x + 4$ equal to 18.

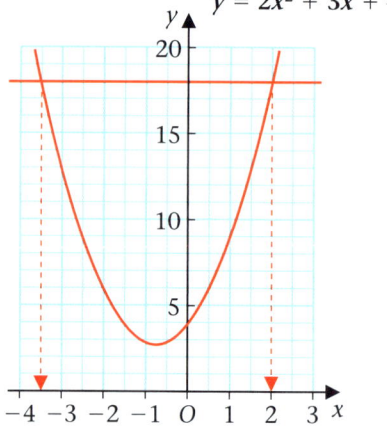

The **two possible solutions** to the quadratic equation $2x^2 + 3x + 4 = 18$ are $x = 2$ and $x = -3.5$.

You can check these answers using algebra.
When $x = 2$: $\quad 2x^2 + 3x + 4 = 8 + 6 + 4 = 18$
and when $x = -3.5$: $\quad 2x^2 + 3x + 4 = 24.5 - 10.5 + 4 = 18$
So the values $x = 2$ and $x = -3.5$ satisfy the equation.

- To try to solve the equation $2x^2 + 3x + 4 = 1$ you would draw the line $y = 1$. This line does not meet the curve so this equation has **no solutions**.
- To solve the equation $2x^2 + 3x + 4 = 2.875$ you would draw the line $y = 2.875$. This curve just touches the curve at one point (where $x = -0.75$) so there is only **one solution**, $x = -0.75$.

You can solve a quadratic equation such as $ax^2 + bx + c = d$ by drawing the graph for $y = ax^2 + bx + c$ and the line $y = d$ and seeing where they intersect.

Quadratic equations can have 0, 1 or 2 solutions.

Example 10

(a) Draw the graph of $y = 2x^2 - 3x - 2$ by first making a table using values of x from -2 to $+4$.

(b) Use your graph to solve these quadratic equations:
  (i) $2x^2 - 3x - 2 = 0$
  (ii) $2x^2 - 3x - 2 = 10$

(a) Make a table of values:

x	-2	-1	0	1	2	3	4
$2x^2$	8	2	0	2	8	18	32
$-3x$	6	3	0	-3	-6	-9	-12
-2	-2	-2	-2	-2	-2	-2	-2
y	12	3	-2	-3	0	7	18

Remember:
$-2^2 = 4$, so $2 \times (-2)^2 = 8$

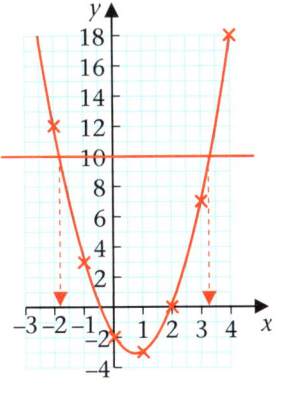

Draw axes with x from -2 to $+4$ and y from -4 to 18.
Plot the points and join them with a smooth curve.

(b) (i) To solve $2x^2 - 3x - 2 = 0$, look at the line $y = 0$.
   At $y = 0$ on the graph, $x = 2$ or $x = -\frac{1}{2}$.

$y = 0$ is the x-axis.
Read off the x values from the graph.

(ii) If $2x^2 - 3x - 2 = 10$, then $y = 10$.
    At $y = 10$, $x = 3.25$ or $x = -1.8$

Draw a line at $y = 10$. Read off the x values from the graph.

Graphs of functions of the form $y = ax^2 + bx + c$
- have a ∪-shape if a is positive
- have a ∩-shape if a is negative
- cut the y-axis at $(0, c)$.

The y-axis is only the line of symmetry when $b = 0$.

Exercise 28G

You need 2 mm squared graph paper.

1. (a) Draw the graph of $y = 2x^2 - 3x + 2$ by making a table using values of x from -3 to $+4$.
   (b) Use the graph to solve the following quadratic equations:
      (i) $2x^2 - 3x + 2 = 4$
      (ii) $2x^2 - 3x + 2 = 11$
      (iii) $2x^2 - 3x + 2 = 1$
   (c) Write down the minimum value y can take in the equation $y = 2x^2 - 3x + 2$.

(d) What value of x gives the minimum value for y?

(e) Explain why the equation $2x^2 - 3x + 2 = 0.5$ does not have a solution.

2 (a) Draw the graph of $y = -x^2 + 2x - 1$. Make a table using values of x from -3 to 5.

(b) Use the graph to solve the following quadratic equations:
   (i) $-x^2 + 2x - 1 = -4$
   (ii) $-x^2 + 2x - 1 = -1$
   (iii) $-x^2 + 2x - 1 = -9$

(c) What is the maximum value y can take in the function $y = -x^2 + 2x - 1$?

(d) What value of x gives the maximum value for y?

(e) Give a value of y for which $y = -x^2 + 2x - 1$ does not have a solution.

> When $x = -3$
> $-x^2 = -(-3 \times -3)$
> $= -(+9)$
> $= -9$
>
> When $x = 2$
> $-x^2 = -(2 \times 2)$
> $= -4$

3 (a) Draw the graph of $y = 2x^2 + 2x - 8$ using values of x from -4 to 3.

(b) Use the graph to solve the following quadratic equations:
   (i) $2x^2 + 2x - 8 = 4$
   (ii) $2x^2 + 2x - 8 = -4$
   (iii) $2x^2 + 2x - 8 = -8$

(c) What is the minimum value y can take in the function $y = 2x^2 + 2x - 8$?

(d) What value of x gives the minimum value for y?

(e) Give a value of y for which $y = 2x^2 + 2x - 8$ does not have a solution.

4 (a) Draw the graph of $y = 2x^2 + 3$ using values of x from -3 to 3.
   Use your graph to solve these equations:

(b) $2x^2 + 3 = 4$ (c) $2x^2 + 3 = 18$

5 (a) Draw the graph of $y = x^2 - 6x + 8$ using values of x from 0 to 6.
   Use your graph to solve these equations:

(b) $x^2 - 6x + 8 = 0$ (c) $x^2 - 6x + 8 = 5$

6 (a) Draw the graph of $y = x^2 - 4x + 3$ using values of x from -1 to 5.
   Use your graph to solve these equations:

(b) $x^2 - 4x + 3 = 0$ (c) $x^2 - 4x + 3 = 2$

28.5 Graphs that describe real-life situations

You do not always need an accurately drawn graph to understand the situation that the graph represents.

In this section the axes are usually labelled, but they often have no values marked. Usually the axes meet at the point (0, 0).

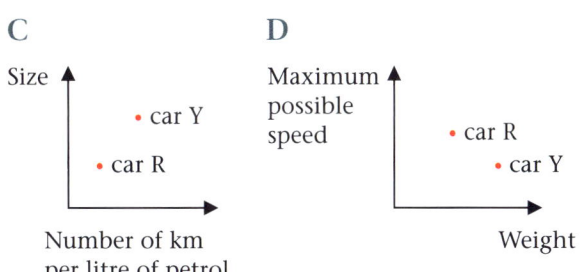

- Graph **A** shows that car Y is older than car R.
- Graph **B** shows that car R can travel faster than car Y.
- Graph **C** shows that car Y can travel further on one litre of petrol than car R.

You can use the information from graphs **A** and **B** to mark points that represent car R and car Y on this graph:

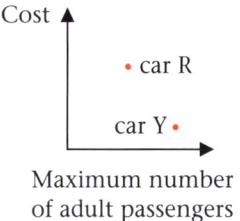

- Graph **A** shows that car R costs more than car Y so R is above Y.
- Graph **B** shows that car Y holds more adults than car R so Y is to the right of R.

You can draw **sketch graphs** to represent given information from real-life situations.

Exercise 28H

1. From graph **C** write down another statement about the cars.

2. From graph **D** write down two statements about the cars.

3. Copy each graph and mark two points to represent car R and car Y.

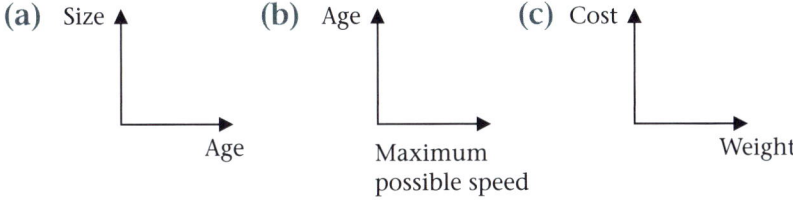

4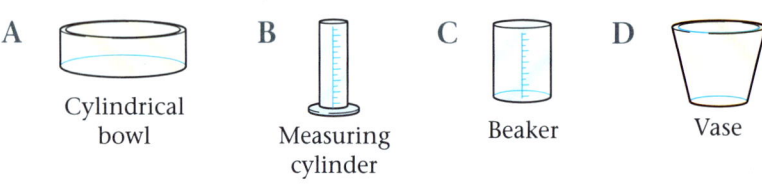

The point F on the scatter graph represents Tom.

(a) Write down the letter of each other point on the graph followed by the name of the person it represents.

(b) Use the graph to find the oldest person in the picture.

> **Activity – Filling containers**
>
> Collect several transparent containers like these:
>
> A Cylindrical bowl B Measuring cylinder C Beaker D Vase
>
> **Step 1** Turn on a tap. Let the water flow into the first container at a steady rate. Watch how quickly the water level rises.
>
> **Step 2** Repeat for the other containers.
>
> **Step 3** Write down what you notice and discuss your results.

In the activity above you should find that:
- the water level rises at a steady rate in containers like **A**, **B** and **C**
- if the container is narrow the water level rises steadily but more quickly
- in a container like **D** the water level does not rise at a steady rate. It rises quickly then more slowly. The rate decreases.

Drawing graphs to show water levels

The tanks **P**, **Q**, **R** and **S** all have circular cross-sections and they contain water.

They all start off with the same depth of water. The water is pumped out of the tanks at the same steady rate.

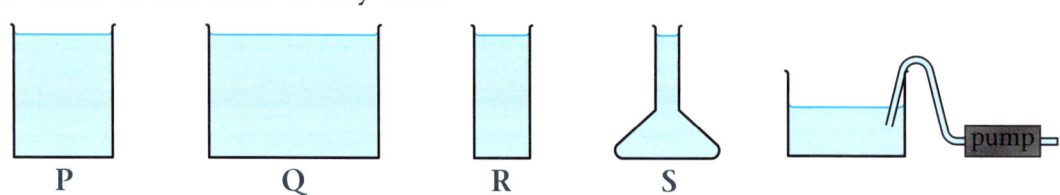

28.5 Graphs that describe real-life situations

The graph shows the relationship between the water level in each tank and the volume of water pumped out of it.

- Tank **Q** has a bigger area of cross-section than **P**. When the same volume has flowed out of each tank the water level in **Q** remains higher than in **P**. So the graph for **Q** is less steep than the graph for **P**.
- The water level in tank **R** drops more quickly than in **P**, so the graph for **R** is steeper.
- In tank **S** the level drops more quickly and steadily at first, then it gradually drops more slowly. The graph is straight to begin with (steeper than for **R**), but then it is curved as the water level drops more and more slowly.

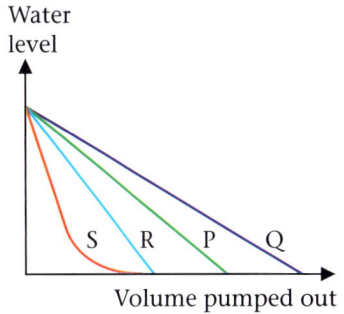

Exercise 28I

1 Here are some graphs:

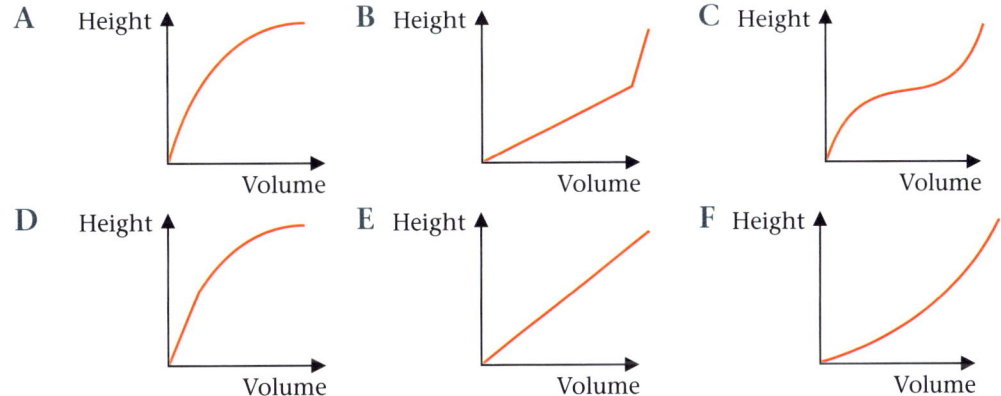

Coloured liquid is poured into each of the containers below. For each one write down the letter of the graph which best illustrates the relationship between the height of the liquid and the volume in the container.

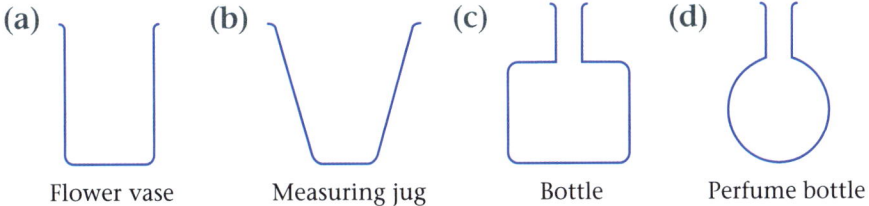

(a) Flower vase   (b) Measuring jug   (c) Bottle   (d) Perfume bottle

2 Water is poured into each of these containers. Sketch a graph to show the relationship between the water level and the volume of water in each container.

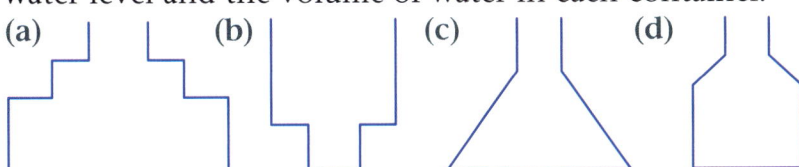

3 A DJ can control the sound level of the music he plays at a club. The sketch graph is a graph of the sound level against the time while one track was being played.

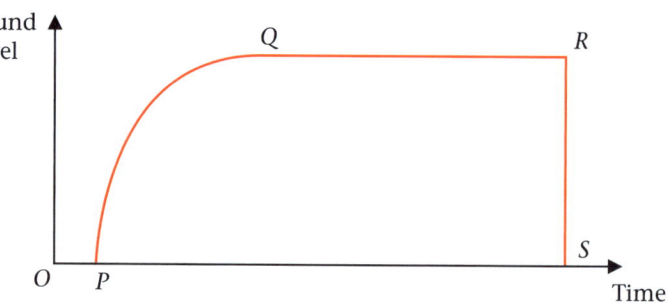

(a) Describe how the sound level changed between *P* and *Q* on the graph while the track was being played.
(b) Give one possible reason for the third part, *RS*, of the sketch graph. [E]

4 Steve kicks a rugby ball over the goal posts. He thinks about the speed of the ball as it passes over the goal posts and tries to imagine what the graph of speed against time would look like.

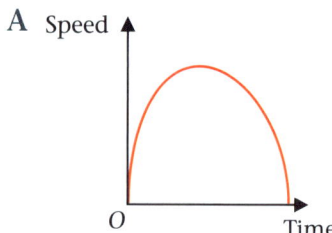
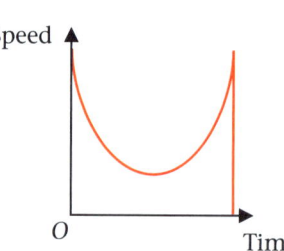
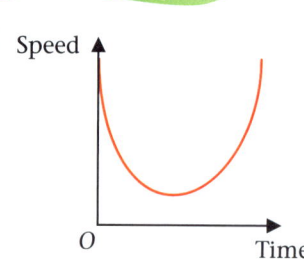

(a) Write down the letter of the graph which best illustrates the speed of the ball.
(b) Describe how the speed of the ball changes in the graph you have chosen.

5 The diagrams show the shapes of five graphs **A**, **B**, **C**, **D** and **E**. The vertical axes have not been labelled.

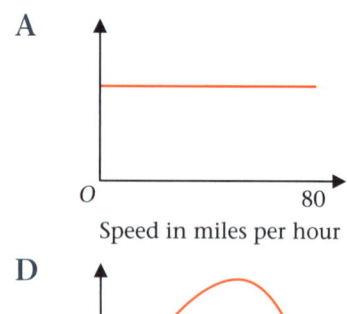
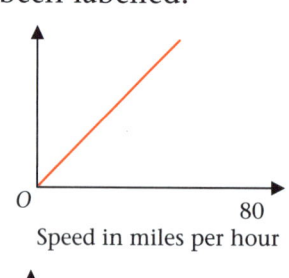
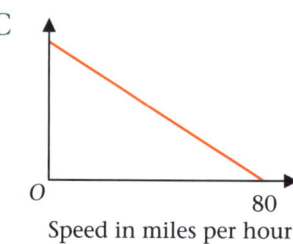
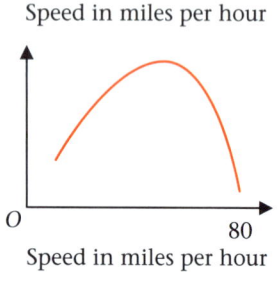
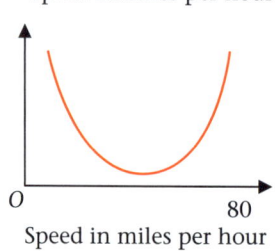

On one of the graphs, the missing label is 'Speed in km per hour'.

(a) Write down the letter of this graph.

On one of the graphs the missing label is 'Petrol consumption in miles per gallon'. It shows that the car travels furthest on 1 gallon of petrol when it is travelling at 56 miles per hour.

(b) Write down the letter of this graph. [E]

28.6 Rearranging formulae

You can build a square picture frame using small square tiles.
Call the internal length of the picture frame l tiles long.
Call the total number of tiles used t.
t and l are connected by the formula

$t = 4l + 4$

Here is how the formula can be rearranged to find l for any given value of t:

This is the flowchart for the formula $t = 4l + 4$:

This is the inverse flowchart:

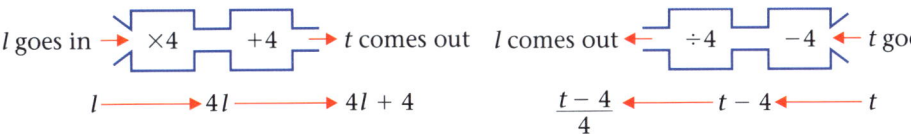

When a number machine is used to input and output letters, not numbers, it is called a **flowchart**.

So $l = \dfrac{t-4}{4}$

Changing the formula $t = 4l + 4$ so that it becomes $l = \dfrac{t-4}{4}$ is called **rearranging the formula** to make l the **subject**.

The **subject** of a formula appears on its own on one side of the formula and does not appear on the other side.

Example 11

Martin uses square tiles to make square picture frames like the one above.

Work out the internal length l, as a number of tiles, of the largest square picture frame that Martin can make using 37 tiles.

Put $t = 37$ in $l = \dfrac{t-4}{4}$

to get $l = \dfrac{37-4}{4} = 8.25$

But l can only take whole number values so $l = 8$ tiles.
The number of tiles used is $t = 4 \times 8 + 4 = 36$ and there is 1 tile left over.

Chapter 28 Expressions, formulae, equations and graphs

Example 12

Rearrange the formula $a = \dfrac{b}{4} - 5$ to make b the subject.

Method 1

$a = \dfrac{b}{4} - 5$ This is the flowchart for the formula: $b \rightarrow \div 4 \rightarrow -5 \rightarrow a$

This is the reverse flowchart: $b \leftarrow \times 4 \leftarrow +5 \leftarrow a$

so $b = 4(a + 5)$

(or $b = 4a + 20$ with the brackets expanded)

$4(a + 5) \leftarrow a + 5 \leftarrow a$

Method 2

$a = \dfrac{b}{4} - 5$

$a + 5 = \dfrac{b}{4}$ —— Add 5 to both sides.

$4(a + 5) = b$ —— Multiply both sides by 4.

so $b = 4(a + 5)$

Method 3

$a = \dfrac{b}{4} - 5$

$4a = b - 20$ —— Multiply both sides by 4.

$4a + 20 = b$ —— Add 20 to both sides.

so $b = 4a + 20$

Example 13

Rearrange the formula $r = 2(6 - s)$ to make s the subject.

$r = 12 - 2s$ —————————— First expand the brackets.

$r + 2s = 12$ —————————— Add $2s$ to both sides.

$2s = 12 - r$ —————————— Subtract r from both sides.

$s = \dfrac{12 - r}{2}$ or $6 - \dfrac{r}{2}$ —————————— Divide both sides by 2

Exercise 28J

1 Rearrange each of these formulae to make x the subject.

(a) $m = 2x - 5$ (b) $a = 4 + 3x$ (c) $p = \dfrac{k}{x}$

(d) $q = mx$ (e) $\dfrac{w}{3} = 2x$ (f) $d = 3a + x$

(g) $p = \dfrac{3x}{2}$ (h) $y = mx + c$ (i) $a = \dfrac{x - u}{t}$

(j) $d = 3(x - 4)$ (k) $f = \dfrac{9x}{5} + 32$ (l) $k = \dfrac{px}{t}$

28.7 Solving simple quadratic and reciprocal equations

2 The formula to change degrees Celsius into degrees Fahrenheit is

$$F = 1.8C + 32$$

(a) Rearrange the formula to make C the subject.

(b) What is $76\,°F$ in degrees Celsius?

3 Rearrange each of these formulae to make d the subject.
(a) $c = 3d + 2$ (b) $c = 4d + 5$ (c) $c = 5d - 6$
(d) $c = 7d + 8$ (e) $c = \frac{1}{2}d + 3$ (f) $c = \frac{1}{3}d - 4$

4 Simplify the right-hand side of each formula, then rearrange to make q the subject.
(a) $p = 2(q + 4) + 3(q - 2)$ (b) $p = 4(q + 3) - 3(q + 2)$
(c) $p = 5(q - 6) + 4(q + 7)$ (d) $p = 3(2q + 1) - 2q$
(e) $p = 6(q - 7) - 5(q - 6)$ (f) $p = 4(3 - 2q) + 2(5q - 3)$

5 Rearrange each formula to make s the subject. *See Example 13.*
(a) $r = 4(3 - s)$ (b) $r = 7(4 - s)$
(c) $r = 2(5 - 3s)$ (d) $r = 4(3 - s) + 2(s + 1)$
(e) $r = 6(s + 2) - 4(1 + 2s)$ (f) $r = 3(s + 2) - 4(s - 2)$

6 Make x the subject of each formula.
(a) $y = 3x + 5$ (b) $y = 4x - 7$ (c) $y = 2(x + 3)$
(d) $y = 3(x - 5)$ (e) $y = \frac{x - 4}{3}$ (f) $y = \frac{x + 5}{9}$
(g) $y = \frac{x}{3} + 4$ (h) $y = \frac{x}{2} - 7$ (i) $y = \frac{2x - 3}{6}$

28.7 Solving simple quadratic and reciprocal equations

A **reciprocal equation** has an x term as a denominator.

$\frac{12}{x} = 6$ is a reciprocal equation.

Some simple quadratic and reciprocal equations can be solved without having to draw graphs.

You need to rearrange the equation so the x term is alone.

Chapter 28 Expressions, formulae, equations and graphs

Example 14

Solve $3 = \dfrac{12}{x}$

$3x = 12$ ——— Multiply both sides by x

$x = 4$ ——— Divide both sides by 3

Example 15

Solve $3x^2 + 2 = 50$

$3x^2 = 48$ ——— Subtract 2 from both sides

$x^2 = 16$ ——— Divide both sides by 3

$x = \pm 4$ ——— Find the square root

There are two solutions to this equation as $4 \times 4 = 16$ and $-4 \times -4 = 16$.

Exercise 28K

Find any solutions to these equations.

1. $2x^2 - 8 = 10$
2. $9 = \dfrac{27}{x}$
3. $\dfrac{65}{x} = 13$
4. $3x^2 - 30 = 45$
5. $8 = \dfrac{64}{x}$
6. $4x^2 - 18 = 46$
7. $2x^2 - 62 = 100$
8. $\dfrac{70}{x} = 28$
9. $2x^2 - 22 = 50$
10. $3x^2 + 53 = 200$
11. $\dfrac{63}{x} = 7$
12. $8 = \dfrac{100}{x}$

28.8 Solving equations by trial and improvement

An equation such as $x^3 + 2x^2 = 2$ is called a **cubic equation**.

You can solve a cubic equation (and other complex equations) by a trial and improvement method. This gives you a good approximate answer.

Example 16

Solve the equation $x^3 + 2x^2 = 2$ giving your answer correct to 2 decimal places.

Draw a table like this one:

Put x equal to a number that you think might be the answer, for example 10.

When $x = 10$, $x^3 + 2x^2$ is bigger than 2, so try x equal to a smaller number, for example 1.

Repeat this process, trying values of x that bring $x^3 + 2x^2$ closer and closer to 2.

The solution is between 0.83 and 0.84. Try putting $x = 0.835$, half way between the two.

x	x^3	$2x^2$	$x^3 + 2x^2$	Bigger or smaller than 2?
10	1000	200	1200	bigger
1	1	2	3	bigger
0	0	0	0	smaller
0.5	0.125	0.5	0.625	smaller
0.7	0.343	0.98	1.323	smaller
0.9	0.729	1.62	2.349	bigger
0.8	0.512	1.28	1.792	smaller
0.85	0.614 125	1.445	2.059 125	bigger
0.84	0.592 704	1.4112	2.003 904	bigger
0.83	0.571 787	1.3778	1.949 587	smaller
0.835	0.582 183	1.394 45	1.976 633	smaller

The solution is between 0.835 and 0.84. Any number in this range rounds to 0.84 (to 2 d.p.). So the solution of the equation $x^3 + 2x^2 = 2$ is $x = 0.84$ (correct to 2 d.p.).

You can find approximate solutions of complex equations by **trial and improvement**.

28.9 Trial and improvement on a spreadsheet

Exercise 28L

1. Solve these equations by trial and improvement. Give your answers correct to 2 decimal places.
   (a) $x^3 + 2x = 4$
   (b) $2x^3 = 3$
   (c) $x^3 - x^2 = 3$
   (d) Find a solution bigger than 0 for $x^3 - 3x = 6$
   (e) Find a solution bigger than 1 for $x^2 + \dfrac{1}{x} = 5$
   (f) Find a solution bigger than 0 for $2x^2 - \dfrac{1}{x} = 9$

2. Solve each of these equations.
   Use a trial and improvement method, showing all your working. Give your answers to 2 decimal places.
   (a) $x^3 + 1 = 11$
   (b) $x^3 + x = 16$
   (c) $x^3 + 3x = 28$
   (d) $x^3 - x = 49$
   (e) $x^3 - 4x = 100$
   (f) $x^3 - 2x = 35$
   (g) $x^3 + x = 31$
   (h) $x^3 + 2x = 200$
   (i) $x^3 + x = 9$

3. Use a trial and improvement method to find the length of the side of a cube which has a volume of 2 litres.
   Give your answer correct to the nearest millimetre.

   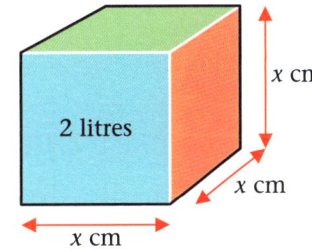

   1 litre = 1000 cm³
   10 mm = 1 cm
   1 mm = 0.1 cm

   Hint: call the length of a side of the cube x cm.

4. A cuboid has length $2x$ cm, width $3x$ cm and height x cm. The volume of the cuboid is 1100 cm³.
   Use a trial and improvement method to find the lengths of the sides, correct to the nearest millimetre.

28.9 Trial and improvement on a spreadsheet

Example 17

The width of a rectangle is 2 cm less than the length. Use a trial and improvement method to find the length when the area of the rectangle is 30 cm².
Give your answer correct to 2 d.p.

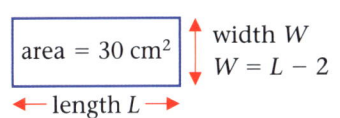

Use L for the length and W for the width of the rectangle. Put the length in column A, the width in column B and the area of the rectangle in column C.

Make sure your spreadsheet has at least 12 rows and 3 columns.

Step 1 Use your spreadsheet to try values for L from 0 to 10 in steps of 1.

Step 2 For each value of L calculate a value for W using
$$W = L - 2$$

Step 3 Multiply each value of L by the corresponding value of W to find the area of each rectangle.

Step 4 Look for the two areas which are nearest to $30\,cm^2$ and record the corresponding values of L.

Step 5 Choose new values of L between the values found in Step 4. Use values of L going up in steps of 0.1 and enter them in the cells of column A.

> Notice that the values in all the other cells change automatically. You don't need to enter the formulae again.

Step 6 Repeat Steps 4 and 5 with values of L going up in steps of 0.01 and 0.001 to get an answer correct to the accuracy you need.

values of L from 0 to 10 in steps of 1

	A	B	C
1	L	W	LW
2	0	−2	0
3	1	−1	−1
4	2	0	0
5	3	1	3
6	4	2	8
7	5	3	15
8	6	4	24	too small
9	7	5	35	too big
10	8	6	48
11	9	7	63
12	10	8	80

Values:
A2 = 0
Formulae:
A3 = A2 + 1
B2 = A2 − 2
C2 = A2 × B2

values of L from 6 to 7 in steps of 0.1

	A	B	C
1	L	W	LW
2	6	4	24
3	6.1	4.1	25.01
4	6.2	4.2	26.04
5	6.3	4.3	27.09
6	6.4	4.4	28.16
7	6.5	4.5	29.25	too small
8	6.6	4.6	30.36	too big
9	6.7	4.7	31.49
10	6.8	4.8	32.64
11	6.9	4.9	33.81
12	7	5	35

Values:
A2 = 6
Formulae:
A3 = A2 + 0.1
B2 = A2 − 2
C2 = A2 × B2

values of L from 6.5 to 6.6 in steps of 0.01

	A	B	C
1	L	W	LW
2	6.5	4.5	29.25
3	6.51	4.51	29.360
4	6.52	4.52	29.470
5	6.53	4.53	29.580
6	6.54	4.54	29.691
7	6.55	4.55	29.802
8	6.56	4.56	29.913	too small
9	6.57	4.57	30.024	too big
10	6.58	4.58	30.136
11	6.59	4.59	30.248
12	6.6	4.6	30.36

Values:
A2 = 6.5
Formulae:
A3 = A2 + 0.01
B2 = A2 − 2
C2 = A2 × B2

values of L from 6.56 to 6.57 in steps of 0.001

	A	B	C
1	L	W	LW
2	6.56	4.56	29.913
3	6.561	4.561	29.924
4	6.562	4.562	29.935
5	6.563	4.563	29.946
6	6.564	4.564	29.958
7	6.565	4.565	29.969
8	6.566	4.566	29.980
9	6.567	4.567	29.991	too small
10	6.568	4.568	30.002	too big
11	6.569	4.569	30.013
12	6.57	4.57	30.024

Values:
A2 = 6.56
Formulae:
A3 = A2 + 0.001
B2 = A2 − 2
C2 = A2 × B2

You can now see that the length L lies between 6.567 cm and 6.568 cm.

So $L = 6.57$ cm correct to 2 d.p.

> This is much easier than it looks! Remember that a computer is doing all the really hard work.

Exercise 28M

1. The length of a rectangle is 3 cm more than the width. Use a trial and improvement method on a spreadsheet to find the width when the area of the rectangle is 38 cm². Give your answer correct to 2 d.p.

2. Winford, Barry and Syreeta count how much cash they each have. Barry has 45p less than Winford, and Syreeta has £1.06 more than Winford. Altogether they have £4.54. Use a spreadsheet to find how much each person has.

   > Hint: let the amount that Winford has be W pence. Begin by entering values of W in steps of 10 in column A.

3. The height of a triangle is 2 cm less than the base. Use a trial and improvement method on a spreadsheet to find the base of a triangle with an area of 37 cm². Give your answer correct to 2 d.p.

Mixed exercise 28

1. Simplify
   (a) $x^4 \times x^5$
   (b) $y^6 \div y^3$
   (c) $12p^6 \div 4p^3$
   (d) $(3a^2)^3$
   (e) $5a^2 \times 2a^3 \times 3a^4$

2. Expand and simplify $2(3x - 1) - 2(2x - 3)$.

3. Expand and simplify
   (a) $(x + 4)(x + 5)$
   (b) $(a - 3)(a - 5)$
   (c) $(2b + 6)(3b - 2)$
   (d) $(4 - 3x)(2x + 1)$

4. Draw a table of values and a graph of these quadratic functions, using values of x from -3 to $+3$.
   (a) $y = 2x^2 + 3$
   (b) $y = -2x^2 + 7$
   (c) $y = x^2 + 3x + 2$
   (d) $y = 2x^2 + 5x - 3$

5. (a) Simplify $a^5 \div a^2$.
   (b) Expand and simplify
      (i) $4(x + 5) + 3(x - 7)$
      (ii) $(x + 3y)(x + 2y)$

6 (a) Draw the graph of $y = 2x^2 - 13x + 15$ for values of x from -2 to 7.
   (b) Use your graph to find solutions to these equations:
       (i) $2x^2 - 13x + 15 = 0$
       (ii) $2x^2 - 13x + 15 = 5$

7 Rearrange each of these formulae to make x the subject.
   (a) $y = 2x + 3$
   (b) $y = \dfrac{ax}{2t}$
   (c) $y = 3(2x - 5)$

8 Given $p = 3(3q - 4)$, find
   (a) q when $p = 24$
   (b) q when $p = -30$

9 Find any solutions to
   (a) $\dfrac{72}{x} = 9$
   (b) $3x^2 - 5 = 22$
   (c) $12 = \dfrac{100}{x}$

10 The diagram shows a water tank. The tank is a hollow cylinder joined to a hollow hemisphere at the top. The tank has a circular base.

   The empty tank is slowly filled with water.

   Copy the axes and sketch a graph to show the relation between the volume, V cm³, of water in the tank and the depth, d cm, of water in the tank.

   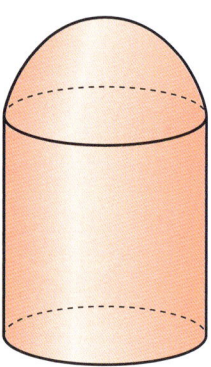

   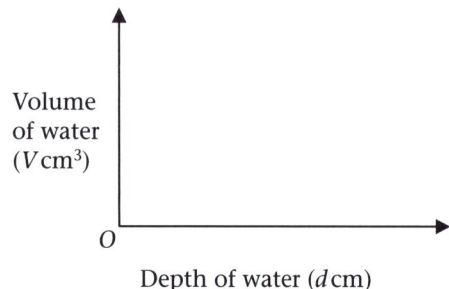

   Depth of water (d cm) [E]

11 The equation $x^3 - 2x = 67$ has a solution between 4 and 5. Use a trial and improvement method to find this solution. Give your answer correct to one decimal place. You must show all your working. [E]

12 The equation $x^3 + 3x = 47$ has a solution between 3 and 4. Use a trial and improvement method to find this solution. Give your answer correct to one decimal place. You must show all your working. [E]

Summary of key points

1. To **multiply out** bracketed expressions, multiply each term in the first bracket by each term in the second bracket:

    $(e + f)(g + h) = eg + eh + fg + fh$

    You can also think of this as multiplying each term in the first bracket by the whole of the second bracket:

    $(e + f)(g + h) = e(g + h) + f(g + h)$

2. Equations such as

    $(e + f)(g + h) = eg + eh + fg + fh$

    and $(e + f)(g + h) = e(g + h) + f(g + h)$

    which are true for all values of e, f, g and h are also known as **identities**.

3. $y = 2x + 3$ is called a **function**. A function is a rule which shows how one set of numbers relates to another.

4. You can solve a quadratic equation such as $ax^2 + bx + c = d$ by drawing the graph for $y = ax^2 + bx + c$ and the line $y = d$ and seeing where they intersect.

5. Quadratic equations can have 0, 1 or 2 solutions.

6. Graphs of functions of the form $y = ax^2 + bx + c$:
    - have a ∪-shape if a is positive
    - have a ∩-shape if a is negative
    - cut the y-axis at $(0, c)$.

    The y-axis is only the line of symmetry when $b = 0$.

7. You can draw **sketch graphs** to represent given information from real-life situations.

8. The **subject** of a formula appears on its own on one side of the formula and does not appear on the other side.
    For example:

    $t = 4l + 4$ can be rearranged to give $l = \dfrac{t - 4}{4}$

    t is the subject l is the subject

9. A **reciprocal equation** has an x term as a denominator.
    For example, $\dfrac{12}{x} = 6$

10. You can find approximate solutions of complex equations by **trial and improvement**.

Examination practice paper

Non-calculator

1 Thirty-six thousand five hundred and ninety people watched United's football match last night.
   (a) Write this number in figures.
   (b) Write this number to the nearest thousand. **(2 marks)**

2 (a) Name each of these shapes. **(4 marks)**

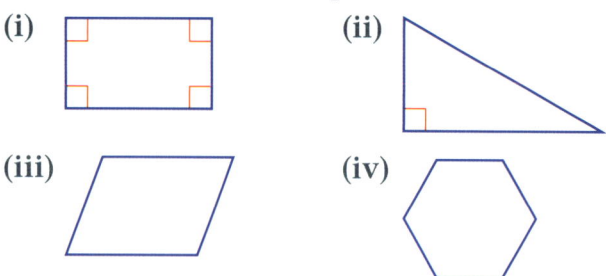

   (b) Copy the shapes that have reflection symmetry and draw in all lines of symmetry. **(4 marks)**
   (c) Write down the order of rotational symmetry for each of the shapes. **(4 marks)**

3 (a) What fraction of this shape is shaded? Write your answer in its simplest form. **(2 marks)**
   (b) What percentage of the shape is not shaded? **(2 marks)**

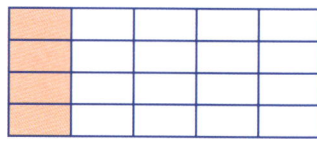

4 Choose from the numbers in the cloud and write down

   (a) two factors of 12
   (b) two multiples of 5
   (c) two square numbers
   (d) two pairs of numbers where one number is the square of the other. **(8 marks)**

5 Here is a pictogram showing the number of letters delivered at No. 23 for the last three days.

(a) How many letters were delivered on
  (i) Day 1
  (ii) Day 2
  (iii) Day 3? **(3 marks)**

(b) On Day 4, 10 letters were delivered. Draw a pictogram for Day 4 only. **(1 mark)**

6 (a) Simplify
  (i) $c + c + c + c$
  (ii) $p \times p \times p$
  (iii) $3g + 5g$
  (iv) $2r \times 5p$ **(4 marks)**

(b) Write an expression for the perimeter of the triangle.

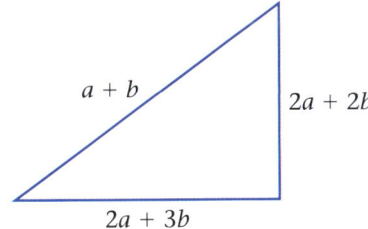

(3 marks)

7 Here is a pattern made from sticks.

Pattern 1

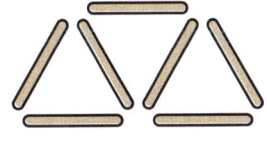
Pattern 2   Pattern 3

(a) Draw the diagram for Pattern 4. **(1 mark)**

(b) Copy and complete the table on the right for the number of sticks used in the pattern. **(4 marks)**

Pattern number	Number of sticks used
1	3
2	5
3	7
4	
10	
n	

550 Examination practice paper

8 (a) Convert $\frac{5}{8}$ into a decimal. (2 marks)

(b) Change $\frac{4}{5}$ into a percentage. (2 marks)

9 Sam bought 24 coloured pens for £44.40
(a) What was the cost of each pen? (3 marks)
Sam sold all of the 24 pens for £2.05 each.
(b) How much money did Sam collect from selling 24 pens? (3 marks)

10 Lia has a box of 20 chocolates:
   5 of them are plain chocolate
   12 of them are milk chocolate
   the rest are white chocolate.
She picks a chocolate at random from the box.
What is the probability that she chooses
(a) a milk chocolate
(b) a white chocolate
(c) a mint humbug? (5 marks)

11 Work out 70% of £3000. (2 marks)

12 Arrange these numbers in order.
Put the smallest number first.

$\frac{1}{2}$, 45%, $\frac{5}{11}$, 0.48, $\frac{2}{5}$ (2 marks)

13 (a) Write 24 : 6 as a ratio in its simplest form. (1 mark)

The recipe for making 12 plain buns is
   500 g flour
   200 g butter
      2 eggs
(b) Rewrite the recipe to make 18 plain buns. (3 marks)

14 Solve these equations:
(a) $y + 5 = 12$ (1 mark)
(b) $2x - 3 = 9$ (2 marks)
(c) $4p + 3 = 2p - 9$ (3 marks)
(d) $3(2c - 5) = 4c + 5$ (3 marks)

15 Work out the value of the angle marked
(a) r (b) t
Write down the reasons for your answers.

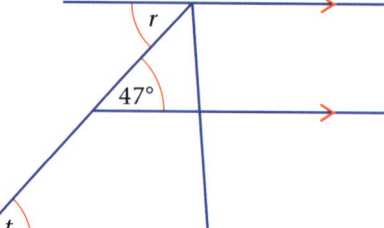

(4 marks)

16 Work out the area of this trapezium:

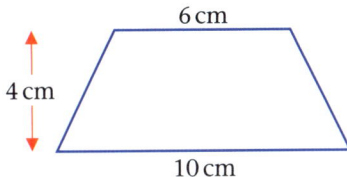

(3 marks)

17 (a) Work out the size of each exterior angle of a regular hexagon.

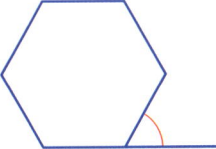

(2 marks)

(b) A different regular polygon has an exterior angle of 40°.
How many sides has this polygon? (2 marks)

18 The manager at 'Fixit' records how long in minutes it took for each repair.
Here are her results.

    18 21 15   8 12 32 25 15 18 22
    25 18 14   9 22 18 27 33 13 23
    18   7 27 18 16

(a) Draw a stem and leaf diagram to show these results. (3 marks)

(b) Use your stem and leaf diagram to work out
  (i) the median
  (ii) the range. (2 marks)

19 (a) Simplify
  (i) $g^4 \times g^3$
  (ii) $\dfrac{m^6}{m^2}$ (2 marks)

(b) Expand and simplify
  (i) $5(3p + 2) - 4(2p - 3)$
  (ii) $(x + 2)(x + 5)$ (4 marks)

20 The bearing of P from Q is 205°.
Work out the bearing of Q from P.

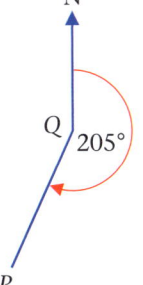

(2 marks)

21 Make t the subject of this formula:
$v = u + at$ (2 marks)

Examination practice paper

Calculator

1. (a) Write the number 72 305 in words.
   (b) What is the value of the 3 in 72 302? **(2 marks)**

2. Write down the names of these 3-D shapes:
   (a) 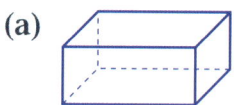   (b)   (c)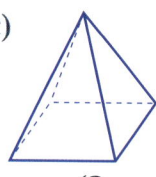
   (3 marks)

3. Joe and Bethan threw a dice 30 times.
   Here are their results.
   5, 2, 1, 4, 3, 6, 4, 5, 3, 2, 4, 5, 2, 4, 3,
   3, 2, 1, 3, 4, 2, 4, 3, 2, 1, 4, 5 6, 3, 4
   (a) Design a suitable data collection table and use it to find the frequency for each score. **(3 marks)**
   (b) Draw a bar chart to show their results. **(3 marks)**
   (c) Use your answers to work out
      (i) the mode   (ii) the median   (iii) the range.
      (5 marks)

4. (a) Find the 4th and 5th numbers in this number pattern:
      3, 8, 13, ..., ..., 28, ...   **(2 marks)**
   (b) Write down the rule that you used to work out your answer. **(1 mark)**
   (c) Work out the 20th number in the pattern. **(2 marks)**
   (d) Explain why 275 cannot be a number in the pattern. **(2 marks)**
   (e) Write down, in terms of n, the nth term of this number pattern. **(2 marks)**

5. Work out the area of these shapes:
   (a) 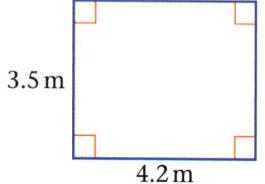   (b)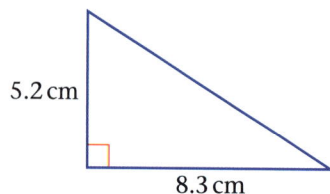
   (5 marks)

6 Copy and complete these two shapes so that they have a line of symmetry.

(a) 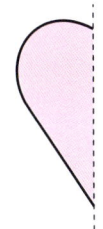   (b)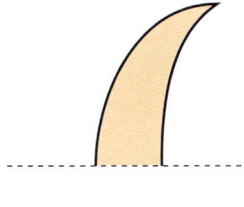

(2 marks)

7 Ella goes shopping.
She buys:
$\frac{1}{2}$ kg of apples at 72p per kg
4 bananas at 24p each
5 kg of potatoes at 25p per kg.
She pays with a £5 note.
Work out how much change she should get.   (4 marks)

8 Work out
(a) $\sqrt{12.25}$ (b) 2.4^3 (2 marks)

9 Copy the diagram. Show how the shape tessellates on the grid. You should draw at least 5 shapes.

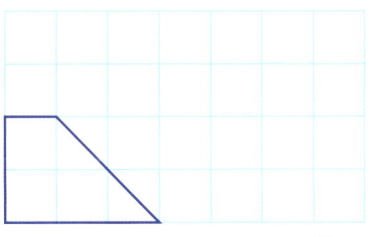

(3 marks)

10 (a) Work out the area of this shape.   (b) Work out the volume of this prism.

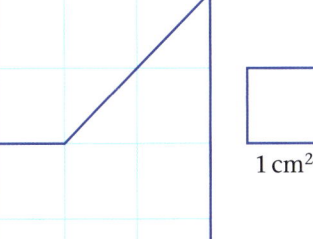   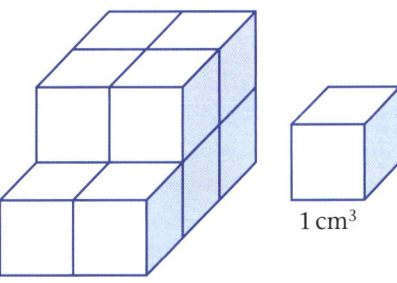

(2 marks)   (2 marks)

11 Using ruler and compasses, **construct** an equilateral triangle with side length 7 cm.
You **must** show all your construction lines.   (2 marks)

12 The two-way table shows information about the colours of cars in a school car park on a school day and on a holiday.

	White	Blue	Red	Total
School day	10			61
Holiday		7		
Total	15	26		80

(a) Write down the total number of white cars. **(1 mark)**

(b) Copy and complete the two-way table. **(3 marks)**

One of these 80 cars is to be picked at random.

(c) Work out the probability that this car will be blue. **(2 marks)**

13 Katie invests £250 for 2 years at 4% simple interest. How much interest does Katie receive after 2 years? **(3 marks)**

14 Karl invests £1000 for 2 years at 5% compound interest in a Building Society account. How much money will Karl have in his Building Society account after 2 years? **(3 marks)**

15 The table gives the highest and lowest temperatures in some cities last year.

	London	Manchester	Exeter	Newcastle
Highest	31°C	29°C	33°C	30°C
Lowest	−12°C	−16°C	−9°C	−14°C

(a) Which city had the lowest temperature?

(b) Which city had the smallest difference between the lowest and highest temperatures? **(3 marks)**

16 Gas bills are based on the amount of gas used. The cost of the gas used is worked out by this rule:

cost of gas = gas used × 21p plus £11

The amount of gas used is found from meter readings. The difference in the meter readings gives the gas used. Work out the cost of gas for these readings on the right:

First reading: 0 1 9 6 2

Final reading: 0 2 1 5 9

(5 marks)

17 A shop sells storage boxes in four different colours. The probability that a customer, choosing a box at random, will choose a box of a particular colour is given in the table.

Colour	Red	Green	Blue	White
Probability		0.1	0.2	0.3

What is the probability of choosing a red box? **(2 marks)**

18 Here are the results of a survey of the ways in which Year 11 students travelled to school.

Method of travel	Number of students
Walk	60
Car	
Bus	30
Bike	35
Moped	
Total	180

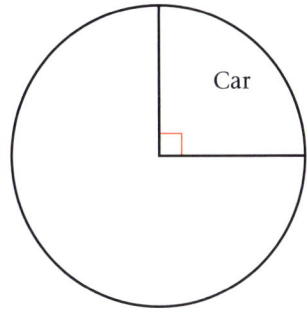

Use the information to copy and complete the table and the pie chart. **(5 marks)**

19 (a) Find the value of C when $r = 5$ in each of these formulae
   (i) $C = 3r$
   (ii) $C = 2r - 12$ **(4 marks)**
(b) Find the value of P when $x = 10$ and $y = 5$ in the formula
$$P = 2(x + y)$$ **(2 marks)**
(c) Find the value of x when $v = 10$ and $a = 5$ in the formula
$$v = 2 + ax$$ **(2 marks)**

20 Factorise
(a) $6a + 10$
(b) $x^2 - 5x$
(c) $5x^3 + 15xy$ **(6 marks)**

21 The cost of 12 pens is £2.88
Work out the cost of 20 identical pens.   **(3 marks)**

22 In this right-angled triangle,
work out the size of the side marked h.

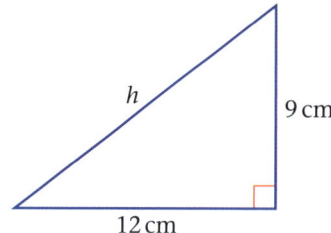

(3 marks)

23 The equation $x^3 + x^2 = 100$ has a solution
between $x = 4$ and $x = 5$.
Use a trial and improvement method to find this
solution.
Give your answer correct to 1 decimal place.
You must show all your working.   **(4 marks)**

24 Find the Highest Common Factor (HCF) of 72
and 96.   **(2 marks)**

Formulae sheet

Area of trapezium = $\frac{1}{2}(a + b)h$

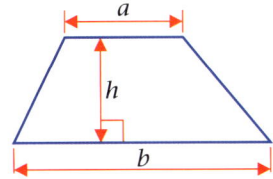

Volume of prism = area of cross section × length

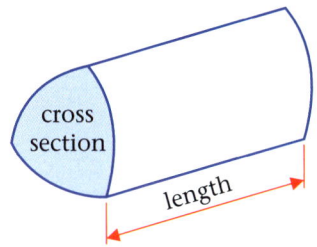

Answers

Chapter 15 Percentages

Exercise 15A

1. (a) (i) 11% (ii) 17% (iii) 18%
   (b) 54%
   (c) $\frac{27}{50}$
2. (a) (i) 11% (ii) 19% (iii) 13% (iv) 7%
   (b) 50%
   (c) $\frac{1}{2}$
3. (a) 25 grey squares (b) 40 red squares
   (c) 28 green squares (d) 7%
4. (a) 30 grey rectangles (b) 22 blue rectangles
   (c) 36 yellow rectangles (d) 12%

Exercise 15B

1. (a) (i) 1% (ii) $\frac{1}{100}$ (b) (i) 9% (ii) $\frac{9}{100}$
   (c) (i) 31% (ii) $\frac{31}{100}$ (d) (i) 59% (ii) $\frac{59}{100}$
2. (a) (i) 10% (ii) $\frac{1}{10}$ (b) (i) 20% (ii) $\frac{1}{5}$
   (c) (i) 30% (ii) $\frac{3}{10}$ (d) (i) 40% (ii) $\frac{2}{5}$
3. (a) $\frac{17}{100}$ (b) $\frac{99}{100}$ (c) $\frac{41}{100}$ (d) $\frac{3}{100}$
   (e) $\frac{3}{5}$ (f) $\frac{4}{5}$ (g) $\frac{9}{10}$ (h) $\frac{3}{10}$
   (i) $\frac{1}{10}$ (j) $\frac{7}{10}$ (k) $\frac{11}{50}$ (l) $\frac{3}{50}$
   (m) $\frac{16}{25}$ (n) $\frac{24}{25}$ (o) $\frac{3}{20}$ (p) $\frac{13}{20}$
4. (a) 0.37 (b) 0.49 (c) 0.87 (d) 0.07 (e) 0.4
   (f) 0.15 (g) 0.08 (h) 0.28 (i) 0.36 (j) 0.95
   (k) 0.45 (l) 0.03 (m) 0.035 (n) 0.065 (o) 0.125
5. $12\% = \frac{36}{300}$ $\frac{1}{12} = \frac{25}{300}$
   Jack has the better deal
6. (a) $\frac{14}{25}$ (b) 0.56 (c) $\frac{11}{25}$

Exercise 15C

1. (a) 37% (b) 59% (c) 11% (d) 10%
   (e) 36% (f) 70% (g) 3% (h) 77.1%
   (i) 9% (j) 5.5% (k) 83% (l) 56%
   (m) 7.5% (n) 12.5% (o) 67.5%
2. (a) 50% (b) 75% (c) 40% (d) 80%
   (e) 90% (f) 35% (g) 32% (h) 76%
   (i) 15% (j) 37.5% (k) 62.5% (l) 18.75%
   (m) 14% (n) 9% (o) 1.3%

3.

Percentage	Decimal	Fraction
61%	0.61	$\frac{61}{100}$
70%	0.7	$\frac{7}{10}$
35%	0.35	$\frac{7}{20}$
$8\frac{1}{2}$%	0.085	$\frac{17}{200}$
15%	0.15	$\frac{3}{20}$
12%	0.12	$\frac{3}{25}$
7%	0.07	$\frac{7}{100}$
$1\frac{1}{4}$%	0.0125	$\frac{1}{80}$
$66\frac{2}{3}$%	0.666…	$\frac{2}{3}$

4. 12.5%, 0.125, $\frac{1}{8}$

Exercise 15D

1. 99
2. 414 kg
3. £1190
4. 72
5. £25.20
6. £1.68
7. £28.70
8. £79.20
9. £1562
10. 0.75 tonnes
11. £43.20
12. 30 720 m
13. 9 km
14. 3.8 km
15. £669.12
16. 0.1728 litres

Exercise 15E

1. (a) £55 (b) 63 l (c) 480 m
   (d) £172.50 (e) 42 g (f) £504
   (g) £91.80 (h) 345 (i) 2.7 tonnes
2. (a) £35 (b) £38.50 (c) £31.50
   (d) £52.50 (e) £3.50 (f) £17.50
   (g) £28 (h) £14
3. £230
4. £2100
5. £11.25
6. £14.19, £7.92
7. £29.25
8. £89.60 + £129.60 + £45 + £50.60 = £314.80

Exercise 15F

1. (a) £108 (b) £96 (c) £114 (d) £102
2. £2700
3. £142.50
4. (a) £3.60 (b) £8.40
5. (a) (i) £12 (ii) £68 (b) (i) £111 (ii) £629
   (c) (i) £6.09 (ii) £34.51
6. (a) £295.20 (b) £137.76

Exercise 15G

1. (a) £1.75 (b) £5.25 (c) £5.60 (d) £7
   (e) £2.80 (f) £21 (g) £43.75 (h) £63
2. (a) £117.50 (b) £352.50 (c) £376 (d) £47
   (e) £188 (f) £141 (g) £2937.50 (h) £4230
3. (a) £9.17 (b) £4.90 (c) £346.50 (d) £27.79

Exercise 15H

1. (a) Sales have fallen by 4 index points.
   (b) During February to March sales fell by 8 index points.
   (c) Fall of 2%
2. (a) 2001
   (b) 2001–2002
   (c) Increase of 30%
3. (a) 2000–2001
   (b) 20
4. (a) Monday
   (b) 8% decrease
   (c) From Thursday to Friday

Exercise 15I

1. (a) 5% (b) 12% (c) 15%
   (d) $7\frac{1}{2}$% (e) $41\frac{2}{3}$% (f) $8\frac{1}{3}$%
   (g) 3% (h) 1% (i) 50%
2. (a) $7\frac{1}{2}$% (b) 20% (c) 20% (d) 4%
   (e) 4% (f) 4% (g) $6\frac{1}{4}$% (h) $\frac{1}{2}$%
   (i) 21.25% (j) $2\frac{1}{2}$%
3. 30% 4. 6% 5. 55% 6. 16%
7. $3\frac{1}{8}$% 8. 6.4% 9. 8% 10. 42.86%

Exercise 15J

1. (a) 52%, 0.53, $\frac{9}{15}$ (b) $\frac{7}{10}$, 0.71, 72%
   (c) 0.07, 8%, $\frac{1}{10}$ (d) 30%, 0.36, $\frac{3}{8}$
2. (a) maths (b) science and technology
3. pizza making 92.5%

Answers

Exercise 15K
1. (a) £20 (b) £150 (c) £20 (d) £80 (e) £10
2. (a) £21 (b) £105 (c) £20.50 (d) £81.60 (e) £5.13
3. £1166.40
4. £108.16
5. £9720
6. £5120
7. £162
8. £64 000

Mixed exercise 15
1.
    0.5   50%
  $\frac{3}{5}$ 60%
  $\frac{1}{5}$ 0.2
  $\frac{7}{20}$ 35%
    0.05 5%
2. (a) £6000 (b) £4000
3. £148.50 and £167.30
4. 25%
5. (a) £2 (b) 15%
6. Nigel (Nigel £1875, Ryan £262.50)
7. (a) £94 (b) £75.20 (c) £282 (d) £846 (e) £423
8. (a) 36%, $\frac{7}{19}$, 0.37 (b) 0.09, $\frac{1}{6}$, 19% (c) 60%, 0.62, $\frac{5}{8}$, $\frac{17}{27}$
9. (a) 4% (b) 17% (c) £58.50
10. (a) £3.36 (b) £86.79 (c) £5.23 (d) £1378.35
11. (a) 21%
   (b) Edwards 2970   Phillips 1848   Fortescue 396
12. (a) £6720 (b) £110 430
13. (a) £90 (b) £131
14. £173.40
15. £82.82

Chapter 16 Coordinates and graphs

Exercise 16A
1. (a) Cliffs (b) Lookout (c) Vantage Point
2. (a) (2,2) (b) (3,0) (c) (4,4)
3.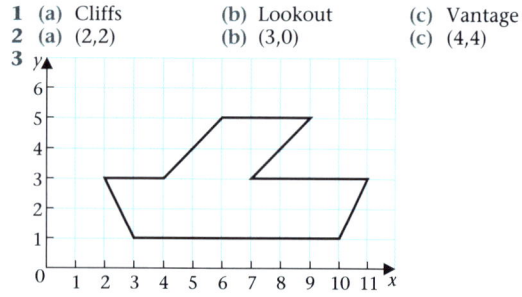
4. (1,1) (8,1) (8,4) (9,4) (7,6) (2,6) (0,4) (1,4)
5. (3,0) (8,0) (9,2) (8,2) (8,3) (7,3) (7,4) (7,5) (9,5) (7,6) (7,4) (5,4) (4,3) (3,3) (2,2) (1,2)
6.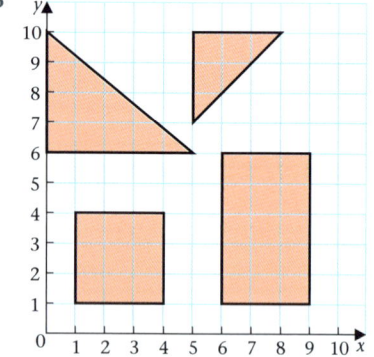

Exercise 16B
1. (a) $(2\frac{1}{2}, 2)$ (b) $(2, 6\frac{1}{2})$ (c) (8, 5) (d) $(4\frac{1}{2}, 3\frac{1}{2})$
2. (a) $(2, 2\frac{1}{2})$ (b) $(3\frac{1}{2}, 5)$ (c) $(3, 6\frac{1}{2})$ (d) (3, 4) (e) $(6, 8\frac{1}{2})$

Exercise 16C
1. (a)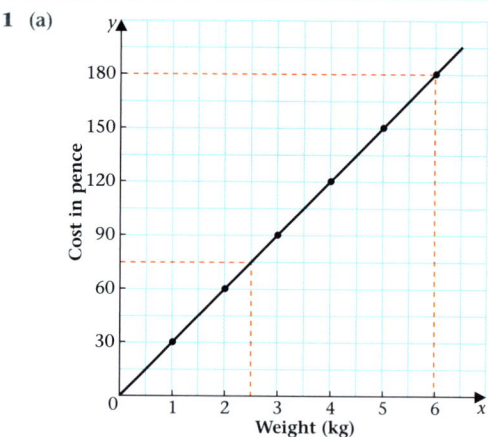
   (b) 75p (c) £1.80
2. (a)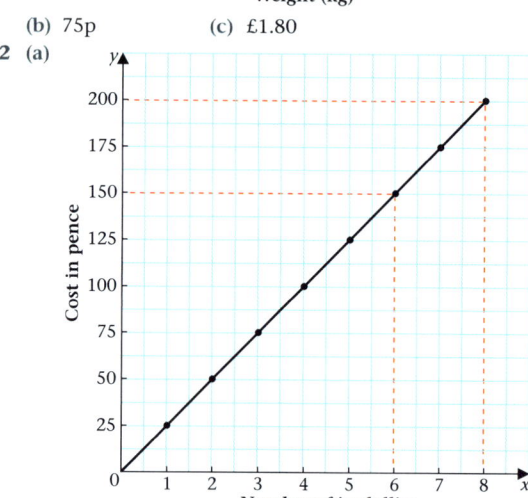
   (b) (i) £2 (ii) £1.50
3. (a)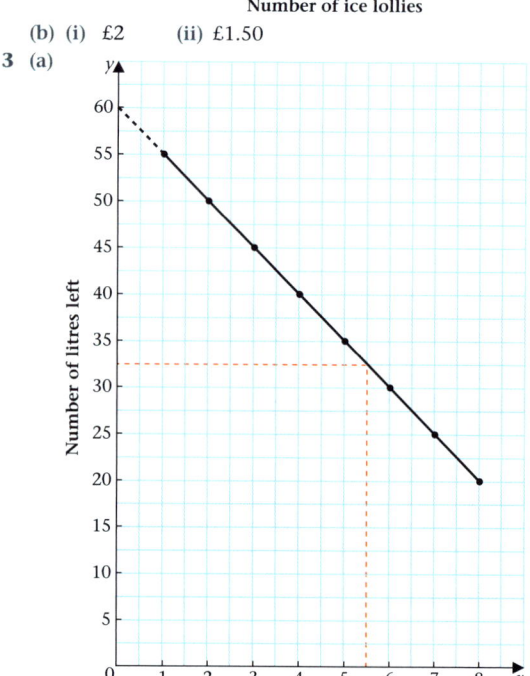

(b) 60 litres
(c) 32.5 litres

4 (a)
Distance travelled (km)	0	5	10	15	20	25
Petrol used in l	0	2	4	6	8	10

(b)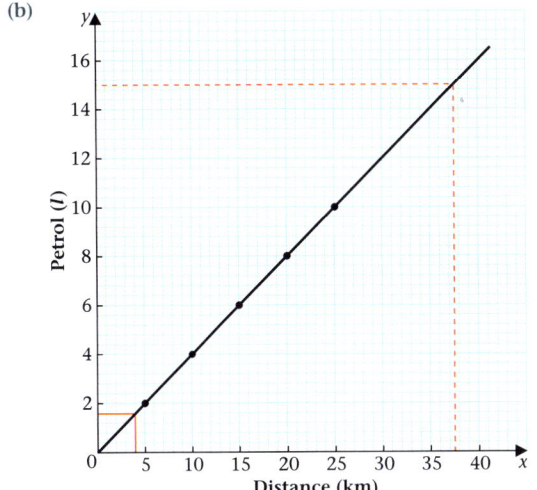

(c) 1.6 litres
(d) 37.5 kilometres

5 (a)
Weeks	0	1	2	3	4	5	6	7	8
Expected depth of water in m	144	140	136	132	128	124	120	116	112

(b)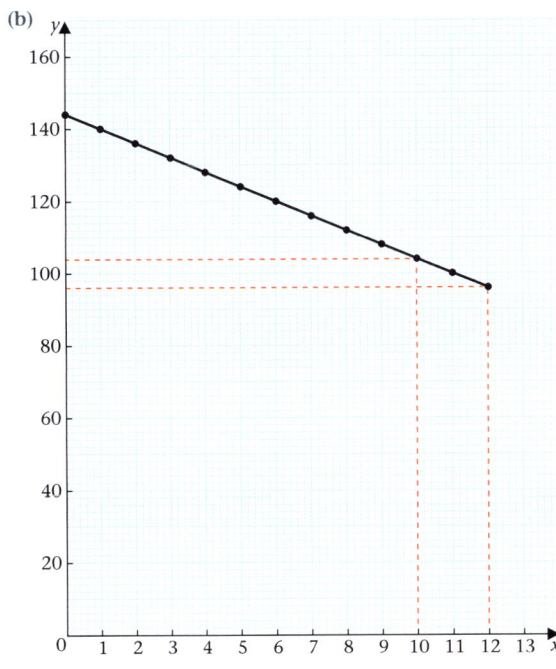

(c) 104 m (d) 12 weeks

Exercise 16D

1
°C	5	20	27	28	10	38	35	80	93	40
°F	41	68	80	82	50	100	95	176	200	104

2 (b)
Kilograms	0	4.5	9	45	30	15	22.5	6.5	35	50
Pounds	0	10	20	99	66	33	50	14	77	110

3
Inches	0	1	2	4	6	8	9	8	10	12
Centimetres	0	2.5	5	10	15	20	22.5	20	25	30

4
Miles	0	5	10	40	22.5	30	45	12.5	24	50
Kilometres	0	8	16	64	36	48	72	20	38	80

5
Hectares	0	8	12	12	15	17	9.6	18	3	20
Acres	0	20	30	30	37.5	42.5	24	45	7.5	50

Exercise 16E

1 (a) 10 minutes (b) 300 metres
  (c) 15 minutes (d) 15 minutes
  (e) 30 metres per minute or 1.8 km/h
  (f) 20 metres per minute or 1.2 km/h

2 (a) David travelled 20 km in 1 hour, he stopped for $\frac{1}{2}$ hour then travelled 40 km in 1 hour. He then stopped for one hour. He travelled the 60 km return journey in $\frac{1}{2}$ hour.
  (b) First stage 20 km/h, second stage 40 km/h, last stage 120 km/h.

3 (a) Tom set off from London at 08:00, travelled 45 km in 1 hour and then stopped for 20 minutes. He travelled the remaining 45 km in 40 minutes. He then travelled the 90 km home without stopping in 1 hour.
  (b) Sarah set off at 08:20 and travelled 30 km in 40 minutes, she stopped for 10 minutes and then travelled the remaining 60 km in 40 minutes.
  (c) Tom and Sarah passed each other at 45 km from London at 09:20.

4 Between A and B Imran turns a tap off and the water level rose 10 cm in 5 minutes.
Between B and C Imran had turned both taps off and there was no increase in water level for the 5 minutes it took him to undress and get ready for his bath.
Between C and D Imran gets into the bath and the level rises 30 cm immediately.
Between D and E Imran had his bath and the level stayed the same for 15 minutes.
Between E and F Imran let the water out of the bath and the water level dropped 60 cm in 5 minutes.

5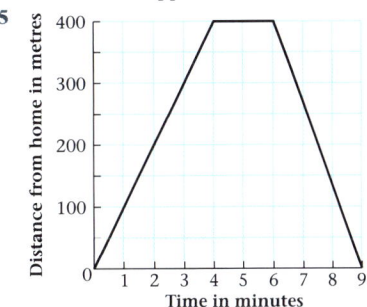

6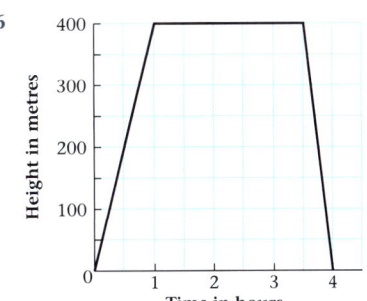

A4 Answers

7 (a)

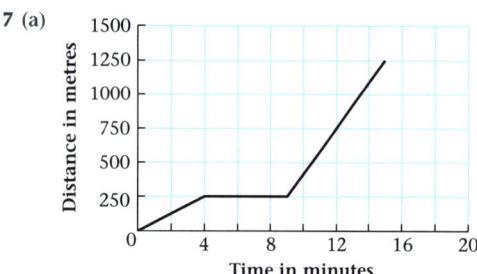

(b) 1000 metres in 6 minutes
167 metres per minute
10 km per hour

8

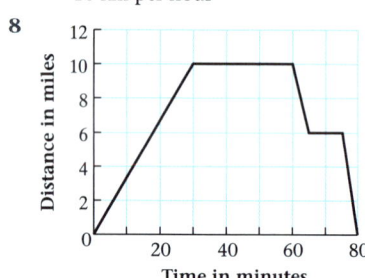

2

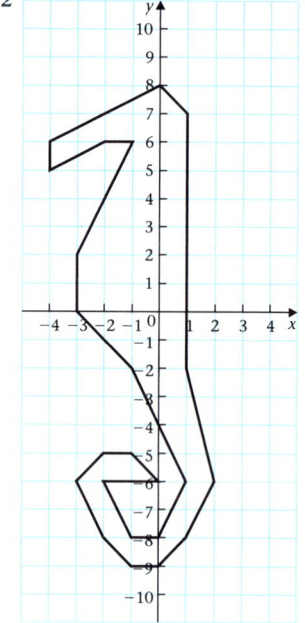

Exercise 16F

1 (a) (i) 11.5 metres   (ii) 45 metres
  (b) (i) 2.9 seconds   (ii) 2.3 seconds
2 (a) (i) 1985 m
      (ii) 1800 m
      (iii) 1530 m
  (b) (i) 11.02 and 5 seconds
      (ii) 11.02 and 39 seconds
      (iii) 11.03 and 12 seconds

3 (a)

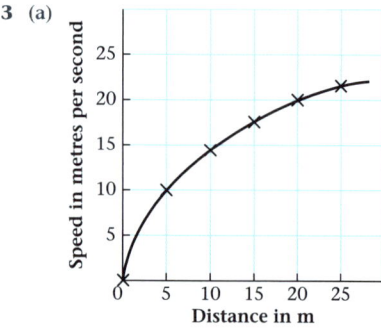

(b) 15 m/s
(c) 17 m

Exercise 16G

1 A (1, 3); B (3, 1); C (4, 0); D (3, −2); E (5, −3); F (1, −3);
G (0, −1); H (−1, −3); I (−3, −2); J (−3, 0); K (−4, 2);
L (−2, 3)

Exercise 16H

1 (a) $y = 3$ (b) $y = 1$
  (c) $y = -1$ (d) $y = -3$
2 (a) $x = -4$ (b) $x = -2$
  (c) $x = 1$ (d) $x = 4$

3

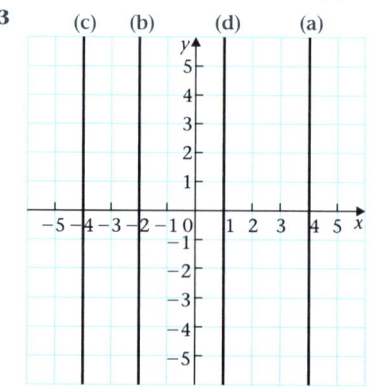

4

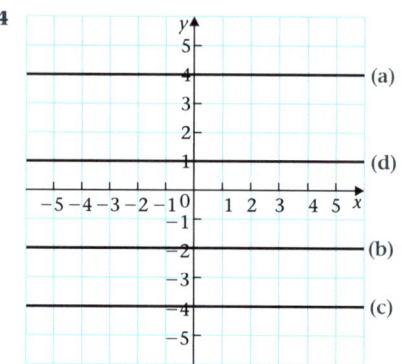

Answers

5 (b)
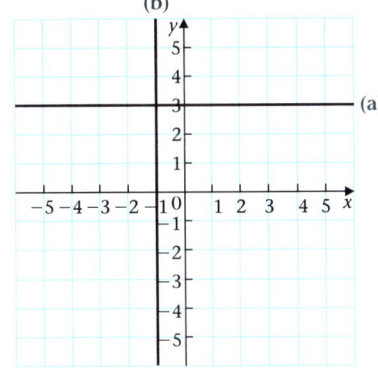
(c) (−1, 3)

Exercise 16I

1
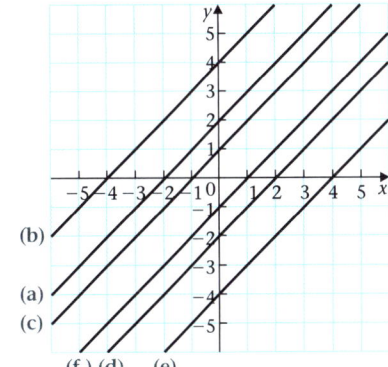

2
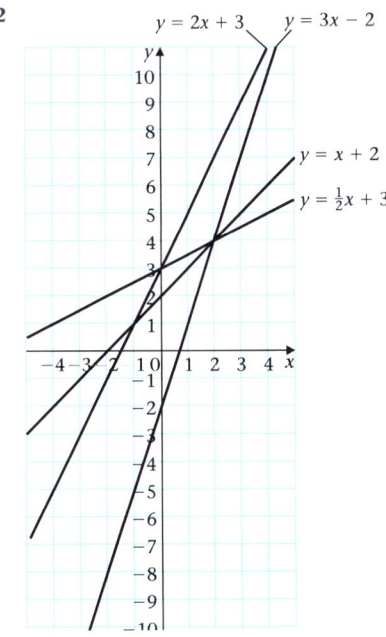
(a) $m = 1$, $c = 2$
(b) $m = 2$, $c = 3$
(c) $m = 3$, $c = -2$
(d) $m = \frac{1}{2}$, $c = 3$

3
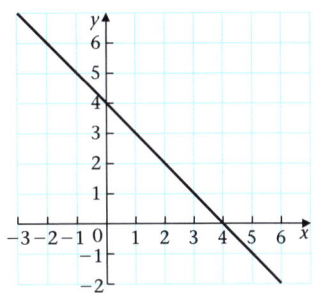

4
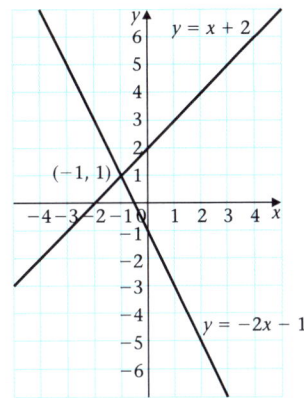

5 (a)

x	−2	−1	0	1	2	3
y	−5	−2	1	4	7	10

(b)
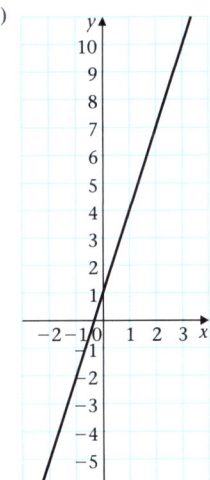

(c) $x = 1.7$

Exercise 16J

1 (a) 3-D (b) 2-D (c) 1-D (d) 3-D
2 (a) 2-D (b) 3-D (c) 2-D (d) 3-D
3 (3, 1, 1), (6, 6, 9), (4, 1, 16), (28, 1, 8)
4 (0, 0, 0), (3, 0, 0), (3, 0, 3), (0, 0, 3)
(0, 1, 3), (0, 1, 0), (3, 1, 0), (3, 1, 3)
5 (0, 0, 0), (3, 0, 0), (3, 0, −2), (0, 0, −2)
(0, −3, 0), (3, −3, 0), (3, −3, −2), (0, −3, −2)

Mixed exercise 16

1 (a) (i) P (2,3) (ii) Q (−2, −1) (c) (0 , 1)
2 (a)

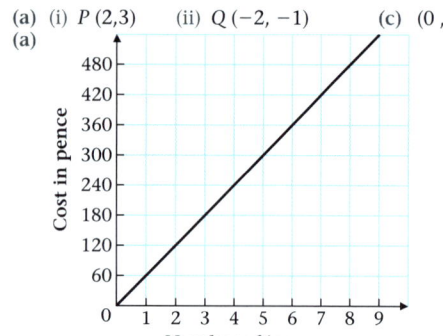

(b) (i) £5.40 (ii) £3.60 (c) 7 (d) £15
3 (b) (i) 15 cm (ii) 25 cm
  (c) (i) 10 inches (ii) 16 inches
4 (a) 48 km/h (b) join to (65,0)
5

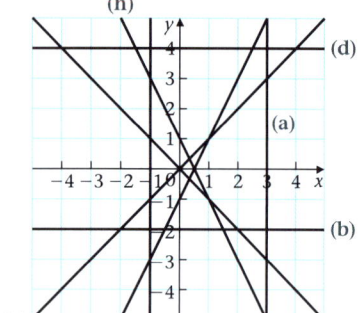

6 P ((3, 1, 0) Q (3, 1, −2) R (0, 1, −2) S (0, 1, 0)
   T (0, −2, 0) U (3, −2, 0) V (3, −2, −2) W (0, −2, −2)
7

(d) (3, 4), (4, 5)
8 (a) (i) −5, −2, 1, 4 (ii) 6, 5, 4, 3 (b) ($1\frac{3}{4}$, $3\frac{1}{4}$)
9 D (0, 0, 0) A (−3, 0, 0) B (−3, 0, −2) C (0, 0, −2)
   G (0, 2, 0) H (0, 2, −2) E (−3, 2, −2) F (−3, 2, 0)

10 (a) €450 (b) £10.50
11 £1.88 (£75 − £73.125)

Chapter 17 Ratio and proportion

Exercise 17A

1 (a) $\frac{7}{9}$, 7 : 2 (b) $\frac{1}{2}$, 16 : 16 (c) $\frac{2}{3}$, 8 : 4 (d) $\frac{4}{9}$, 12 : 15
2 (a) 80 g, 200 g (b) 120 g, 300 g (c) 200 g, 500 g
  (d) 20 g, 50 g (e) 100 g, 250 g
3 (a) 400 g, 800 g, 800 g, 8 eggs
  (b) 100 g, 200 g, 200 g, 2 eggs
  (c) 300 g, 600 g, 600 g, 6 eggs
  (d) 500 g, 1000 g, 1000 g, 10 eggs
4 (a) 21, 3, 6 (b) 28, 4, 8 (c) 7, 1, 2
5 (a) 10 kg, 5 kg, 45 kg (b) 30 kg, 15 kg, 135 kg
  (c) 2 kg, 1 kg, 9 kg
6 (a) 12 kg, 38 kg (b) 60 kg, 190 kg (c) 24 kg, 76 kg
7 680 g

Exercise 17B

1 (a) 1 : 2 (b) 1 : 3 (c) 1 : 6 (d) 1 : 4 (e) 1 : 3
  (f) 2 : 3 (g) 5 : 1 (h) 7 : 1 (i) 2 : 3 (j) 5 : 3
2 (a) 1 : 5 (b) 1 : 5 (c) 1 : 8 (d) 5 : 1
3 (a) 1 : 50 (b) 7 : 20 (c) 1 : 200 (d) 2 : 125
  (e) 15 : 2 : 6 (f) 3 : 8 (g) 17 : 60 (h) 4 : 12 : 3
  (i) 9 : 200 (j) 2 : 5 (k) 9 : 2 (l) 200 : 11
4 (a) 7 : 9 (b) 10 : 11 (c) 22 : 25
  (d) 1 : 2 (e) 9 : 7 (f) 11 : 3 : 2
5 500 : 3

Exercise 17C

1 (a) 20 (b) 28 (c) 2.5
  (d) 28 (e) 40 (f) 9
2 (a) 135 (b) 84
3 455 4 4.8 m 5 3 kg
6 20 buckets 7 96 8 15 cm

Exercise 17D

1 (a) 1 : 2.5 (b) 1 : 0.25 (c) 1 : 100 (d) 1 : 2.5
  (e) 1 : 6.25 (f) 1 : 7.5 (g) 1 : 2.2 (h) 1 : 40
2 (a) 0.75 : 1 (b) 50 000 : 1 (c) 6 : 1 (d) 7.5 : 1
  (e) 500 : 1 (f) 1000 : 1 (g) 33.$\dot{3}$: 1 (h) 0.2 : 1

Exercise 17E

1 £200, £160 2 £160, £200, £120 3 10 : 25 : 5
4 (a) 40 min (b) 1 hour 20 min
5 4 lb 3 lb 2 lb
   16 km 12 km 8 km
   28 miles 21 miles 14 miles
   36 t 27 t 18 t
   £64 £48 £32
6 (a) £4.26, £10.65 (b) £20, £25
  (c) £9.44, £42.48 (d) £14.21, £56.84, £99.47
7 (a) 360 g, 240 g (b) 12 cm, 20 cm
  (c) 3.9 l, 19.5 l (d) 6.3 m, 12.6 m, 15.75 m
8 (a) 13.68 m, 17.1 m (b) 45 cm, 30 cm
  (c) 18 kg, 30 kg (d) £51, £102, £204
9 (a) 16 (b) 12
10 60°, 50°, 70° 11 400 g 12 £132, £176, £352
13 (a) 204 g (b) 153 g 14 7000 kg

Exercise 17F

1 £120 2 £4.50 3 £10.80
4 £64 5 £3.24 6 21
7 (a) 1 hr 45 mins (b) $5\frac{1}{2}$ hours (c) 8 hours

Answers

8 (a) 64 km (b) 6 hr 15 min
9 (a) 2.4 hours (b) 2
10 (a) 12 days (b) 28.8 days (c) 48

Exercise 17G

1 £5.85   2 9 g   3 £27.50   4 £4.20
5 840   6 96p   7 £26.40   8 976 g
9 £2.25
10 2808 cm³
11 720 g flour, 1080 g fat, 3 eggs
12 (a) 18 ft (b) 8 ft (c) 5 ft
13 (a) 1400 (b) 6 hours
14 (a) 280 miles (b) 77.14 litres
15 (a) £42 (b) 12 hours

Exercise 17H

1 (a) 1.25 km (b) 1.8 km (c) 2.6 km (d) 3.1 km
2 (a) 12 cm (b) 10.4 cm (c) 16.8 cm (d) 51.2 cm
3 (a) 25 cm (b) 276 m (c) 2.19 km
4 (a) 1 : 140 (b) 30 cm
5 2 m
6 (a) 1.4 km (b) 17.4 cm

Mixed exercise 17

1 150 g sugar; 120 g butter; 3 eggs; 135 g flour; 45 ml milk
2 Ruth £110, Ben £80
3 Ice Cool 4000, old drink 3200
4 (a) £735 (b) £196
5 £8.10
6 (a) 252 m (b) 60 mm
7 9 : 11
8 25
9 £36.90
10 (a) 0.75 km (b) 13 cm
11 £14.40

Chapter 18 Symmetry

Exercise 18A

1 (a) A, D (b) B, C (c) F (d) E (e) G, H
2 (a)   (b)   (c)

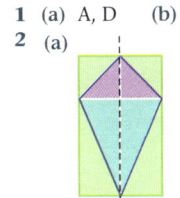    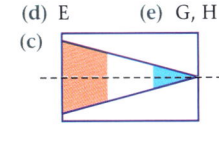

3 (a)   (b)   (c)

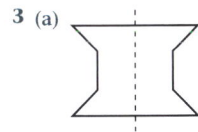 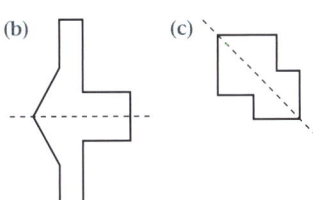

4 (a)   (b)

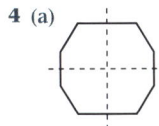 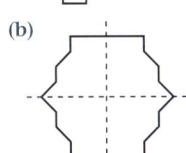

5 (a) A, B, C, D, E, K, M, T, U, V, W, Y
  (b) H, I, O, X
  (c) F, G, J, L, N, P, Q, R, S, Z

Exercise 18B

1 (a) A, C (b) D, E (c) B, F
2 (a)   (b)   (c)

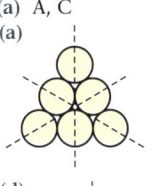 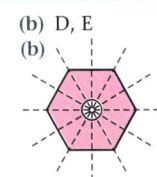 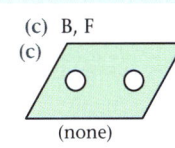

(none)

(d)   (e)   (f)

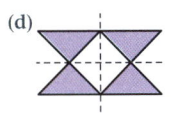 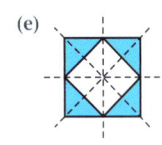 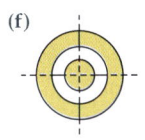

Exercise 18C

1 (a) No (b) Yes (c) Yes (d) Yes (e) No
2 (a) 3 (b) 2 (c) 4 (d) 5 (e) 5

Exercise 18D

1 (a) 3 (b) 3   2 (a) 5 (b) 5
3 (a) 6 (b) 6   4 (a) 8 (b) 8

Mixed exercise 18

1 1   2 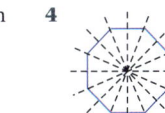   3 pentagon   4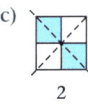

5 8
6 Equilateral triangle
7 (a) (b) (c) (d) (e)

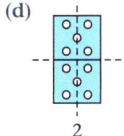 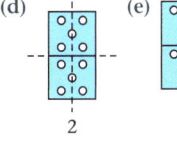

1   6   2   2   2

8 (a)   (b)

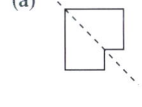 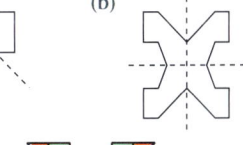

9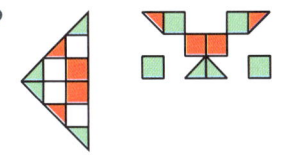

10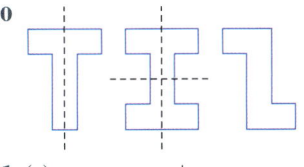

11 (a)

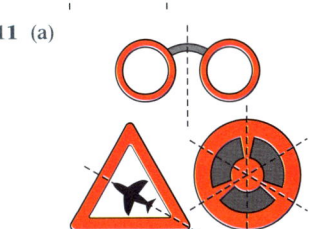

(b) Use a mirror or tracing paper
12 (a) 5 (b) 1
13 A, B, D

Chapter 19 Simple perimeter, area and volume

Exercise 19A

1. (a) 10 cm (b) 20 cm (c) 9 cm (d) 16 cm (e) 16 cm
2. (a) 20 cm (b) 12 cm (c) 18 cm (d) 16 cm

Exercise 19B

1. 20 cm
2. 22 cm
3. 21 m
4. 22 cm
5. 25 cm
6. 22 m
7. 16.9 cm
8. 13.4 cm
9. 14.5 cm
10. 14.4 cm
11. 20.7 cm

Exercise 19C

1. 8 cm²
2. 7 cm²
3. 12 cm²
4. 16 cm²
5. 7 cm²
6. 6 cm²

Exercise 19D

1. $11\frac{1}{2}$ cm²
2. $7\frac{1}{2}$ cm²
3. 10 cm²
4. $7\frac{1}{2}$ cm²
5. 15 cm²
6. 18–19 cm²

Exercise 19E

1. 16 cm³
2. 3 cm³
3. 24 cm³
4. 72 cm³
5. 44 cm³

Exercise 19F

1. (a) 8 cm² (b) 15 cm² (c) 24 cm² (d) 30 cm²
2. (a) 16 cm² (b) 64 cm² (c) 92.16 cm² (d) 146.41 cm²
3. (a) 4 cm² (b) 7.5 cm² (c) 23.4 cm² (d) 42.5 cm²
4. (a) 24 cm² (b) 40.8 cm² (c) 9.84 cm²

5.

Shape	Length	Width	Area
(a)	5 cm	6 cm	**30 cm²**
(b)	4 cm	**5 cm**	20 cm²
(c)	2 cm	**10 cm**	20 cm²
(d)	**8 cm**	5 cm	40 cm²
(e)	**5 cm**	12 cm	60 cm²

6.

Shape	Base	Vertical height	Area
(a)	10 cm	5 cm	**25 cm²**
(b)	**10 cm**	12 cm	60 cm²
(c)	**16 cm**	5 cm	40 cm²
(d)	4 cm	**16 cm**	32 cm²
(e)	16 cm	**8 cm**	64 cm²

Exercise 19G

1. (a) 20 cm² (b) 48 cm² (c) 47.7 cm² (d) 23.4 cm²
2. (a) 7.2 cm² (b) 16 cm² (c) 22.4 cm²

Exercise 19H

1. 24 cm³
2. 36 cm³
3. 108 cm³
4. 64 cm³
5. 125 cm³
6. 512 cm³
7. 160 cm³
8. 250 cm³
9. 288 cm³
10. 192 m³
11. 150 m³

Exercise 19I

1. 90 cm²
2. 102 cm²
3. 60 cm²
4. 300 cm²
5. 150 cm²
6. 408 cm²
7. 2448 cm²
8. 168 cm²
9. 472 cm²
10. 328 cm²
11. 840 cm²
12. 736 cm²

Exercise 19J

1. 4800
2. 18
3. 120
4. 100
5. 80
6. 360

Exercise 19K

1. £95.40
2. £125
3. (a) 10 tiles (b) 20 tiles (c) 800 tiles (d) £520
4. 2 tins
5. 3750 *l*
6. 2667 tiles
7. 400 strips
8. (a) 28.8 m³ (b) 8 skips

Exercise 19L

1. (a) 20 000 (b) 130 000 (c) 24 000 (d) 152 000 (e) 12 (f) 2.3 (g) 16.43 (h) 4200 (i) 300 (j) 0.3 (k) 0.01
2. (a) 7 000 000 (b) 15 000 000 (c) 3 500 000 (d) 4 780 000 (e) 4 (f) 3.78 (g) 14.789 (h) 800 000 (i) 2000 (j) 24 (k) 0.0378 (l) 0.142 (m) 0.003
3. 1.2 m²
4. (a) 1.6 m² (b) 16 000 cm²
5. 2 300 000 cm³
6. (a) 324 000 cm³ (b) 0.324 m³

Exercise 19M

1. 12 miles
2. 25 mph
3. 5 hours
4. 3.75 mph
5. 7 mph
6. 8 mph
7. $1\frac{1}{3}$ mph
8. $66\frac{2}{3}$ mph
9. 20 mph
10. 15 km/h

Exercise 19N

1.

Formula A3 = A2 + 10 (W = 100 − L) Formula B2 = 100 − A2 (A = L × W) Formula C2 = A2 × B2

	A	B	C	D
1	L	W	LW	
2	0	100	0	
3	10	90	900	
4	20	80	1600	
5	30	70	2100	
6	40	60	2400	
7	50	50	2500	
8	60	40	2400	
9	70	30	2100	
10	80	20	1600	
11	90	10	900	
12	100	0	0	

Maximum area = 2500 m²

Answers

2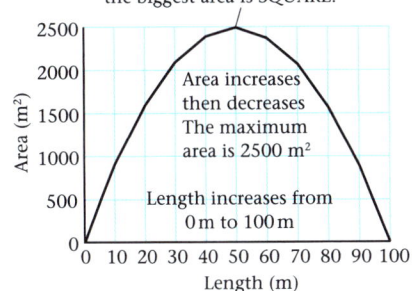
Rectangles can be long and thin or short and wide, but the rectangle with the biggest area is SQUARE!
Area increases then decreases
The maximum area is 2500 m²
Length increases from 0 m to 100 m

3

Make	Basic	Top	Price range
Audi	£21 025	£26 265	£5240
Citroen	£16 695	£20 495	**£3800**
Ford	**£14 500**	£16 680	£2180
Mazda	£15 200	**£19 200**	£4000
Nissan	**£12 650**	£15 650	£3000
Peugeot	£16 950	**£20 950**	£4000
Renault	£13 900	£18 600	**£4700**
Toyota	**£14 195**	£15 895	£1700
Volkswagen	£12 990	£18 250	**£5260**

4 (a) London 22, Paris 22, Moscow 29, New York 13, Luxor 13
(b) Moscow, London and Paris (equal), Luxor and New York (equal)
(c) e.g. To find how variable the weather is.

Mixed exercise 19

1 (a) 30 cm (b) 27 cm²
2 18.9 cm
3 26.4 cm
4 (a) (i) 5 (ii) 2 (b) 24 m (c) 22 m²
5 (a) 24 m³ (b) 68 m²
6 66 m²
7 £77.74
8 09 25
9 8 000 000 cm³
10 864

Chapter 20 Presenting and analysing data 1

Exercise 20A

1 (a) John 8, Kit 5 and 6, Mary no mode, Tina 3, 4 and 6
(b) 6 and 8
2 (a) (i) 2.3 GHz (ii) 1.4 GHz
(b) 1.6 and 1.8 GHz
3 (a) 6 (b) 5, 5 (c) 4, 4, 4
(d) 11 (e) 7, 7, 7 (f) 5, 5, 6, 6
4 (a) 0, 0, 0, 1, 1, 1, 2, 2, 2, 2, 2, 2, 3, 3, 3, 3, 4, 4, 4, 5
(b) 2 goals
(c) 20 teams

Exercise 20B

1 (a) 6 (b) 11 (c) 5 (d) $9\frac{1}{2}$
3 (a) any ≥ 5 (b) any ≤ 4 (c) any ≥ 7 (d) 5
4 (a) $7\frac{1}{2}$
(b) e.g. There are 14 marks greater than $7\frac{1}{2}$ and 14 marks less than $7\frac{1}{2}$.
5 (a) 26 (b) 32

Exercise 20C

1 (a) 13 (b) 24.25 (c) 22.5 (d) 23.75
2 (a) 162 cm (b) 161.5 cm
3 (a) 560 g (b) 1310 g
4 40.7
5 (a) 13 (b) 16 (c) 6 (d) 25

Exercise 20D

1 (a) Fiona Yass 8, Ulga Perez 5
(b) (i) Fiona Yass. She made the longest throw.
(ii) Ulga Perez. Her range was smaller.
2 (a) Tim. His range was largest.
(b) Pani.

Exercise 20E

1

	Mode	Median	Mean
(a)	6	10	10
(b)	24, 32	28	27.4
(c)	£3.60	£3.60	£4.74

2 (a) £2410
(b) (i) £200 (ii) £220 (iii) £241 (iv) £215
3 e.g. 2, 2, 2, 7, 8, 9

Exercise 20F

1 (a)

0	8, 8
1	4, 5, 7, 7
2	2, 3, 4, 4, 5, 6, 6, 6, 7, 9
3	0, 6, 6, 6, 6, 7
4	3, 3, 4, 5, 5, 9
5	2, 3, 5, 5, 7
6	7, 8, 9
7	2
8	1
9	0, 8

Key
2|7 means 27

(b) 36

2 (a)

0	4, 6, 7, 8, 9, 9
1	1, 2, 4, 5, 7, 7, 8
2	0, 2, 3, 4, 5, 6, 7, 9
3	2, 3, 4, 5, 5, 6, 7, 8, 9
4	1, 3, 4, 7, 8, 9
5	0, 2, 7, 8

Key
2|9 means 29

(b) 29 seconds

3 (a)

Marks	Tally	Frequency
0–9	I	1
10–19	IIII	4
20–29	HHT III	8
30–39	HHT HHT IIII	14
40–49	HHT HHT II	12
50–59	HHT HHT I	11

(b)

0	9
1	4, 5, 8, 9
2	0, 4, 5, 6, 7, 7, 8, 9
3	2, 4, 4, 4, 4, 5, 5, 5, 5, 6, 7, 7, 8
4	0, 2, 3, 3, 3, 4, 4, 5, 5, 6, 6, 7
5	0, 2, 2, 3, 3, 4, 5, 5, 6, 8, 9

Key
2|8 means 28

(c) (i) 30–39 (ii) 30–39
(d) 35.1 marks (e) 46%

Answers

Exercise 20G

1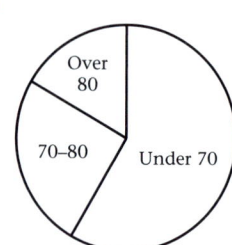

2 (a) Liberal Democrat 79°
(b)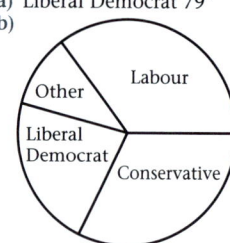

5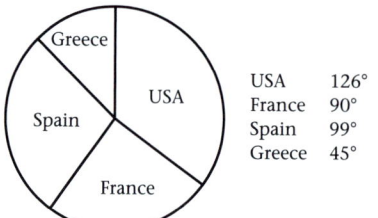

6 (a) 11, 9, 16, 19, 12
(b) Cape Town, Madrid, Melbourne, Vienna, Rome
(c) Rome

7 (a) Bus fares 48°, Going out 100°, Clothes 120°, Records 60°, Other 32°
(b)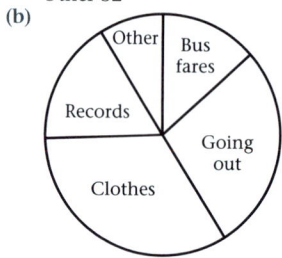

Exercise 20H

1 90
2 Gold: 75°, 5 medals;
Silver: 150°, 10 medals;
Bronze: 135°, 9 medals
3 (a) All their choices (b) chocolate
(c) orange (d) 3
(e) e.g. Number the students then pick 30 random numbers.
4 (a) Rent 90°, Travel 27°, Clothes 42°, Food 120°, Savings 60°, Spare 21°
(b) (i) Rent £60, Travel £18, Clothes £48, Food £80, Savings £40, Spare £54
(ii) Rent, Travel, Food and Savings
5 Gwyneth: 45°; Peter: 120°; Wes: 60°; Mario: 30°; Nesta: 105°
6 Standard: 190°; Student: 120°; Senior: 50°

Mixed exercise 20

1 (a) 14 (b) 29 (c) 17 (d) 14

2 (a)
0	6, 8, 9, 9
1	0, 0, 1, 1, 3, 6, 6, 6, 7
2	0, 1, 1, 5, 6
3	4, 6

Key
0|6 = 6

(b) 16 (c) 16.75

3 (a)
14	7, 7, 7, 8
15	1, 2, 3, 5, 8, 8
16	4, 5, 6, 6, 7
17	1, 2, 8
18	9, 9

Key
14|7 = 147

(b) 161

4 (a)
Month	Number of fires put out	Angle
Jan–Mar	15	60°
Apr–June	26	104°
July–Sept	35	140°
Oct–Dec	14	56°

(b)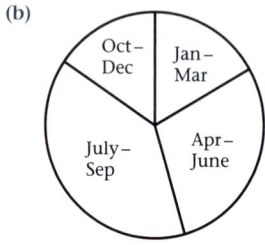

Chapter 21 Formulae and inequalities

Exercise 21A

1 (a) £210 (b) £207.50
2 (a) 180 cm (b) 150 cm
3 £4.25

Exercise 21B

1 £270   2 £150   3 £172.50   4 £14.40
5 £12   6 £3.36 7 £4.50   8 £8.40
9 £20   10 £41.40 11 12 years 12 5 coins
13 25 bars 14 12 people 15 8 sweets 16 £12.60

Exercise 21C

For example:
10 $M = NL$, M = money collected, N = number sold, L = price of a loaf
11 $P = T - M$, P = Pauline's age, T = total of ages, M = Mark's age
12 $L = S - N$, L = money lost, S = starting amount, N = money now
13 $L = H - S$, L = number of bars left, H = number the machine holds, S = number of bars sold
14 $P = C \div D$, P = number of people, C = total number of cans, D = number drunk by each person
15 $N = B \div P$, N = number of sweets each, B = number of sweets in the bag, P = number sharing the sweets
16 $P = C \div N$, P = the amount each paid, C = cost of repair, N = number of people

Exercise 21D

1 8   2 7   3 10   4 6   5 15
6 0   7 15   8 0   9 16   10 16
11 19   12 32   13 2   14 5   15 1
16 8   17 11   18 0   19 9   20 30
21 10

Answers

Exercise 21E

1 6	2 16	3 15	4 0	5 6
6 7	7 3	8 9	9 20	10 6
11 7	12 0	13 8	14 12	15 0
16 24	17 4	18 24	19 8	20 6
21 4				

Exercise 21F

1 (a) 15 (b) 21 (c) 12 (d) 37.2
2 (a) 24 (b) 15 (c) 56 (d) 25.5
3 (a) 160 (b) 125 (c) 210 (d) 79
4 (a) 13 (b) 35 (c) 60 (d) 7
5 (a) 53 (b) 210 (c) 7 (d) 17.5

Exercise 21G

1 −3	2 2	3 −6	4 −4
5 2	6 −8	7 5	8 11
9 0	10 −9	11 8	12 −2

Exercise 21H

1 1	2 −2	3 −7	4 −5	5 5
6 −8	7 3	8 −5	9 −5	10 8
11 −3	12 5	13 −4	14 6	15 1
16 −3	17 0	18 10	19 −5	20 10
21 −6				

Exercise 21I

1 −12	2 −12	3 −10	4 4
5 −21	6 −32	7 30	8 27

Exercise 21J

1 −8	2 −3	3 −6	4 −6	5 −15
6 0	7 15	8 0	9 4	10 −24
11 −11	12 −20	13 −2	14 −5	15 −1
16 8	17 −19	18 0	19 21	20 30
21 5				

Exercise 21K

1 (a) −7 (b) 25 (c) −60 (d) −7
2 (a) 0 (b) 12 (c) −15 (d) 3
3 (a) −11 (b) −11 (c) −1
  (d) 5 (e) 6 (f) −29

Exercise 21L

1 (a) 5 (b) 20 (c) 125 (d) 500 (e) 61.25

2

x	−3	−2	−1	0	1	2	3
$y = 3x^2 + 4$	31	16	7	4	7	16	31

3 (a) 12 (b) 8 (c) 508 (d) 48 (e) 8
  (f) 2 (g) 200 (h) −4000 (i) 104 (j) −400
4 (a) 11.0 (b) 11.2 (c) 5
  (d) 6.7 (e) 0 (f) 14.1

Exercise 21M

1 (a) 13 (b) 17 (c) −1 (d) 2.5
  (e) 4 (f) 14 (g) $3\frac{2}{5}$ (h) 1.5
2 (a) 16 (b) 15 (c) 32 (d) 9 (e) 15 (f) 14
3 (a) 35 (b) 8 (c) 6 (d) 10 (e) 4 (f) −5
4 (a) 3 (b) 4 (c) 6 (d) 3 (e) 5
Activity
  (c) $4r + t$

Exercise 21N

1 (a) 4 cm (b) 8 cm (c) 4 cm (d) 20 cm
2 9 cm 3 2 4 7 5 22
6 10 7 4 chocolates 8 4 9 24

Exercise 21O

1 (a) $3x + 120 = 180$ (b) $x = 20°$
2 (a) $x + 110 = 180$ (b) $x = 70°$
3 (a) $3x + 150 = 360$ (b) $x = 70°$
4 (a) $4(x − 2) = 20$ (b) $x = 7°$
5 (a) $3x + 30 = 180$ (b) $x = 50°$
6 (a) $7x + 10 = 360$ (b) $x = 50°$
7 (a) $3x = 180$ (b) $x = 60°$
8 (a) $7(x − 4) = 14$ (b) $x = 6°$
9 (a) $4x + 60 = 180$ (b) $x = 30°$
10 (a) $8x + 80 = 360$ (b) $x = 35°$
11 (a) $2x + 110 = 180$ (b) $x = 35°$
12 (a) $2x + 120 = 180$ (b) $x = 30°$

Exercise 21P

1 (a) $4 < 6$ (b) $5 > 2$ (c) $12 > 8$ (d) $6 = 6$
  (e) $15 > 8$ (f) $3 < 24$ (g) $10 > 3$ (h) $0 < 0.1$
  (i) $6 > 0.7$ (j) $4.5 = 4.5$ (k) $0.2 < 0.5$ (l) $4.8 > 4.79$
2 (a) True (b) False, $2 < 6$ (c) False, $6 = 6$
  (d) False, $6 < 8$ (e) False, $6 > 5$ (f) False, $8 < 14$
  (g) False, $7 > 6.99$ (h) False, $6 < 6.01$ (i) False, $7 > 0$
  (j) False, $4 = 4$ (k) False, $6 > 4$ (l) True
3 (a) 5 (b) 4, 5, 6, 7
  (c) 0, 1, 2, 3 (d) 4, 5
  (e) 2, 3, 4 (f) 3, 4, 5
  (g) 4, 5, 6 (h) −2, −1, 0, 1, 2, 3,
  (i) 0, 1, 2, 3, 4 (j) −1, 0, 1, 2, 3, 4, 5, 6
  (k) −3, −2, −1, 0, 1, 2 (l) −4, −3, −2, −1, 0, 1, 2
  (m) 1, 2, 3, 4 (n) 0, 1, 2, 3, 4
  (o) −5, −4, −3, −2, −1 (p) −3, −2, −1, 0, 1, 2, 3

Exercise 21Q

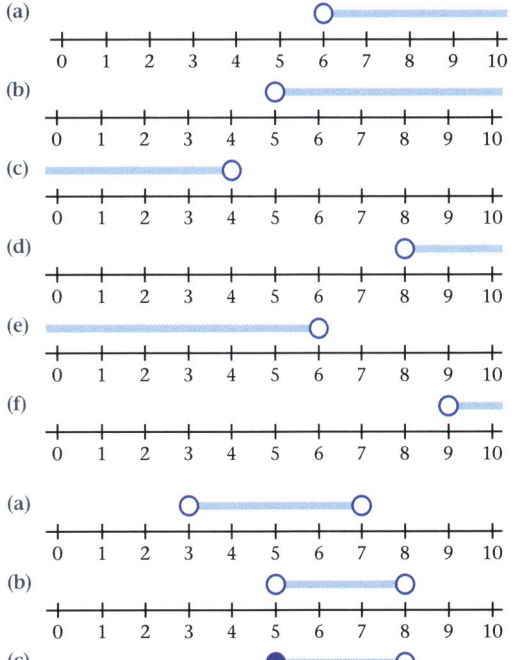

Answers

(d)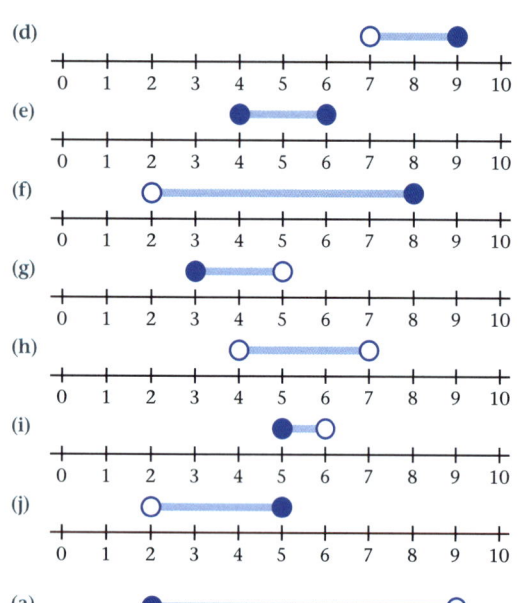
(e)
(f)
(g)
(h)
(i)
(j)

3 (a)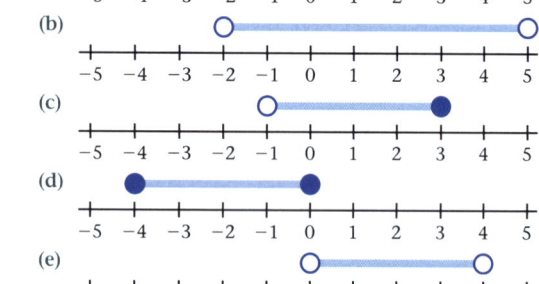
(b)
(c)
(d)
(e)
(f)
(g)
(h)
(i)
(j)

4 (a) $2 < x \leq 6$ (b) $7 \leq x \leq 8$
 (c) $1 < x < 6$ (d) $3 \leq x < 7$
 (e) $-3 < x \leq 1$ (f) $-1 \leq x \leq 3$
 (g) $-4 < x < 1$ (h) $-3 \leq x < 4$

Mixed exercise 21

1 (a) $y = 2x + 1$ (b) 4
2 20
3 1924
4 2
5 (a) 5 (b) -23
6 £2.50
7 £450
8 (a) 87 (b) 6 (c) $7\frac{1}{2}$ (d) 8
9 $c = 18n + 5g$
10 $C = 27n$
11 (a) $-28°C$ (b) 39 000 feet
12 7
13 (a) (i) $x - 10 + 2x + 55 = 180$ (ii) $x + 5x + 70 - x = 360$
 (b) (i) $x = 45°$ (ii) $x = 58°$
14 (a) (i)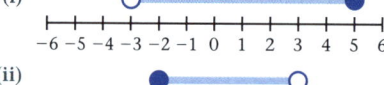
 (ii)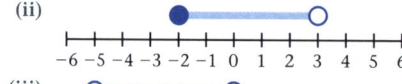
 (iii)
 (b) (i) $-2, -1, 0, 1, 2, 3, 4, 5$
 (ii) $-2, -1, 0, 1, 2$
 (iii) $-4, -3, -2, -1$
15 (a) $-2 \leq x < 1$ (b) $-5 \leq x \leq 3$

Chapter 22 Transformations

Exercise 22A

1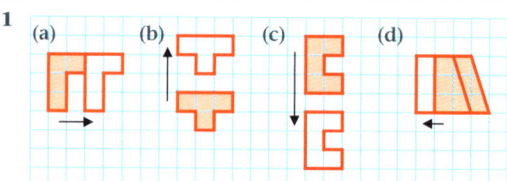

2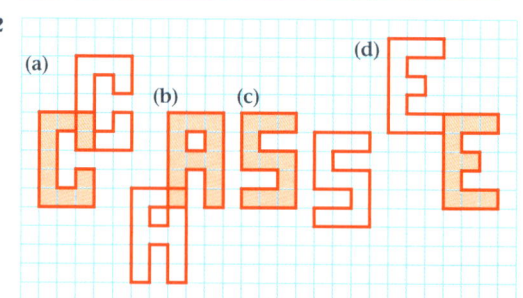

3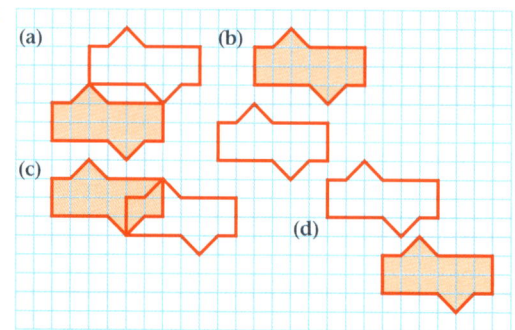

4 (a) 2 sq right, 2 sq down
 (b) 1 sq left, 4 sq up
 (c) 2 sq left, 3 sq up

Answers

Exercise 22B

1 (a)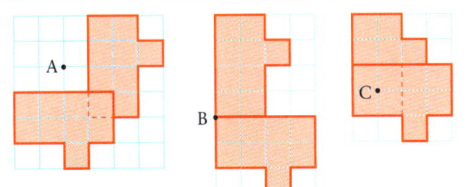

(b)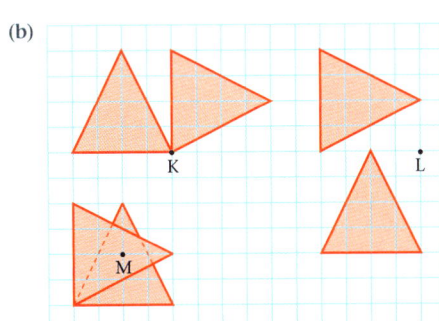

(c)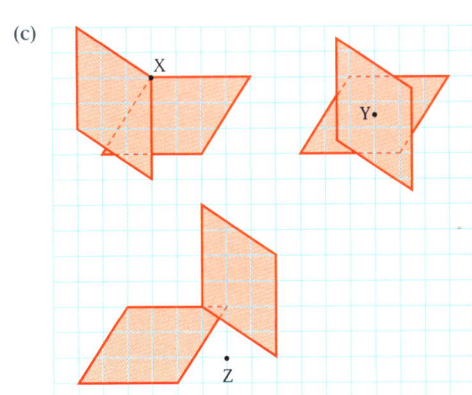

2 (a)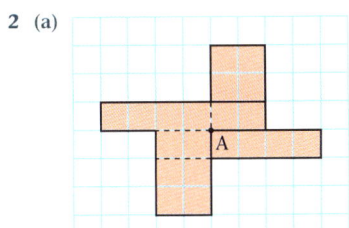

(b)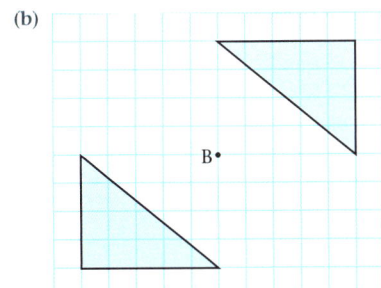

(c)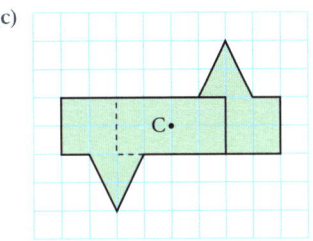

3 (a) $\frac{1}{2}$ turn clockwise or anticlockwise
(b) $\frac{1}{4}$ turn anticlockwise
(c) $\frac{1}{4}$ turn clockwise
(d) $\frac{1}{2}$ turn clockwise or anticlockwise

Exercise 22C

1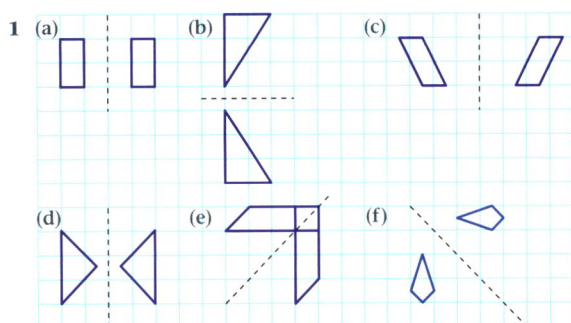

2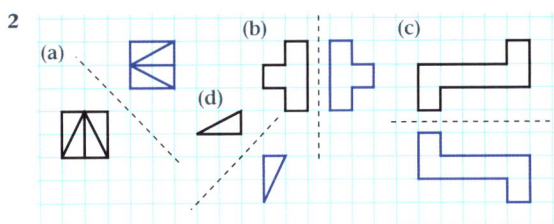

Exercise 22D

Check answers with your teacher.

Mixed exercise 22

1

2 (a)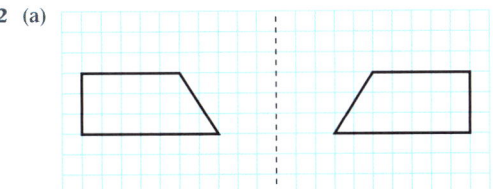

Answers

(b)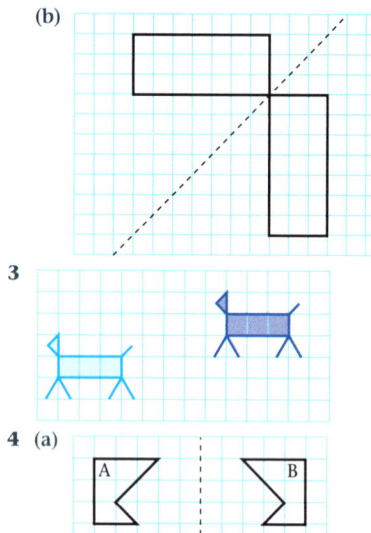

3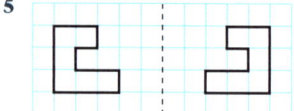

4 (a) [figure: shapes A and B with mirror line]

(b) rotation $\frac{1}{4}$ turn anticlockwise

5 [figure]

Chapter 23 Probability

Exercise 23B

1 (a) $\frac{1}{6}$ (b) $\frac{2}{6}$ or $\frac{1}{3}$ (c) $\frac{1}{2}$ (d) $\frac{1}{2}$ (e) $\frac{1}{3}$
  (f) $\frac{2}{3}$ (g) $\frac{2}{3}$ (h) $\frac{1}{2}$ (i) 0 (j) 0
2 (a) $\frac{1}{13}$ (b) $\frac{1}{52}$ (c) $\frac{1}{2}$ (d) $\frac{2}{13}$
  (e) $\frac{2}{13}$, or $\frac{3}{13}$ if Ace is low
  (f) $\frac{3}{13}$ (g) $\frac{3}{13}$ (h) $\frac{1}{4}$ (i) $\frac{1}{2}$ (j) $\frac{3}{4}$
3 (a) $\frac{5}{11}$ (b) $\frac{6}{11}$ (c) 0 (d) 1
4 (a) $\frac{1}{9}$ (b) $\frac{3}{9}$ (c) $\frac{5}{9}$ (d) $\frac{8}{9}$ (e) $\frac{4}{9}$
5 (a) $\frac{8}{16}$ (b) $\frac{4}{16}$ (c) $\frac{3}{16}$ (d) 0 (e) $\frac{1}{16}$
6 (a) $\frac{20}{5000}$ (b) $\frac{100}{5000}$ (c) $\frac{50}{5000}$ (d) $\frac{25}{5000}$
7 (a) $\frac{4}{30}$ (b) $\frac{10}{30}$ (c) $\frac{5}{30}$ (d) $\frac{2}{30}$ (e) $\frac{9}{30}$ (f) $\frac{20}{30}$
8 (a) $\frac{1}{18}$ (b) $\frac{2}{18}$ (c) $\frac{3}{18}$ (d) $\frac{3}{18}$ (e) $\frac{4}{18}$ (f) $\frac{2}{18}$
  (g) $\frac{1}{18}$ (h) $\frac{1}{18}$ (i) $\frac{16}{18}$ (j) $\frac{14}{18}$ (k) $\frac{5}{18}$ (l) 0
9 (a) $\frac{1}{11}$ (b) $\frac{1}{11}$ (c) $\frac{2}{11}$ (d) $\frac{3}{11}$ (e) $\frac{4}{11}$

Exercise 23C

1 (a) 0 (b) 1 (c) $\frac{1}{2}$ (d) 0 (e) 1 (f) $\frac{1}{2}$

3

	(i) Dice A	(ii) Dice B
(a)	$\frac{1}{6}$	$\frac{1}{6}$
(b)	$\frac{1}{6}$	$\frac{2}{6}$ or $\frac{1}{3}$
(c)	$\frac{3}{6}$ or $\frac{1}{2}$	$\frac{4}{6}$ or $\frac{2}{3}$
(d)	$\frac{1}{6}$	0
(e)	$\frac{3}{6}$ or $\frac{1}{2}$	$\frac{2}{6}$ or $\frac{1}{3}$
(f)	$\frac{3}{6}$ or $\frac{1}{2}$	$\frac{4}{6}$ or $\frac{2}{3}$
(g)	$\frac{3}{6}$ or $\frac{1}{2}$	$\frac{3}{6}$ or $\frac{1}{2}$
(h)	$\frac{2}{6}$ or $\frac{1}{3}$	$\frac{2}{6}$ or $\frac{1}{3}$

4 (a) (i) $\frac{3}{10}$ (ii) 0.3 (iii) 30%
  (b) (i) $\frac{4}{10}$ (ii) 0.4 (iii) 40%
  (c) (i) $\frac{2}{10}$ (ii) 0.2 (iii) 20%
  (d) (i) $\frac{1}{10}$ (ii) 0.1 (iii) 10%

5 (a) (i) $\frac{25}{100}$ (ii) 0.25 (iii) 25%
  (b) (i) $\frac{8}{100}$ (ii) 0.08 (iii) 8%
  (c) (i) $\frac{5}{100}$ (ii) 0.05 (iii) 5%
  (d) (i) $\frac{88}{100}$ (ii) 0.88 (iii) 88%
6 $\frac{5}{12}$

Exercise 23D

1 (a) $\frac{2}{3}$ (b) 0.8 (c) 70%
2 (a) $\frac{1}{3}$ (b) $\frac{2}{3}$ (c) $\frac{2}{3}$ (d) $\frac{1}{3}$
3 0.14
4 (a) $\frac{1}{6}$ (b) $\frac{5}{6}$ (c) $\frac{4}{6}$ (d) $\frac{2}{6}$ (e) $\frac{3}{6}$
5 (a) $\frac{1}{9}$ (b) $\frac{4}{9}$ (c) $\frac{5}{9}$ (d) $\frac{4}{9}$ (e) $\frac{2}{9}$ (f) $\frac{3}{9}$
6 (a) $\frac{6}{20}$ (b) $\frac{14}{20}$ (c) $\frac{1}{20}$ (d) $\frac{19}{20}$
  (e) $\frac{14}{20}$ (f) $\frac{11}{20}$ (g) $\frac{6}{20}$
7 $\frac{4}{5}$
8 (a) $\frac{7}{20}$ (b) 8 (c) 5 (d) 7

Exercise 23F

1 (a) (i) $\frac{4}{36}$ (ii) $\frac{4}{36}$ (iii) $\frac{1}{36}$
  (b) (i) $\frac{6}{36}$ (ii) $\frac{6}{36}$
  (c) $\frac{11}{36}$ (d) $\frac{6}{36}$ (e) $\frac{1}{36}$
2 (a) $\frac{1}{25}$ (b) $\frac{4}{25}$ (c) $\frac{5}{25}$ (d) $\frac{9}{25}$
  (e) $\frac{16}{25}$ (f) $\frac{9}{25}$ (g) 1 (h) 0
3 (a) HH HT TH TT
  (b) 1, 1 1, 3 1, 5
      3, 1 3, 3 3, 5
      5, 1 5, 3 5, 5
  (c) H1 H2 H3 H4
      H5 H6 T1 T2
      T3 T4 T5 T6
4 (a) 36 (b) 9

5

Red	RR	GR	YR	BR
Green	RG	GG	YG	BG
Yellow	RY	GY	YY	BY
Blue	RB	GB	YB	BB

Second disc (vertical axis); First disc (horizontal axis): Red Green Yellow Blue

6 (a)

Total score	Ordered pairs	Theoretical probability
2	(1,1)	$\frac{1}{36}$
3	(1,2) (2,1)	$\frac{2}{36}$
4	(1,3) (2,2) (3,1)	$\frac{3}{36}$
5	(1,4) (2,3) (3,2) (4,1)	$\frac{4}{36}$
6	(1,5) (2,4) (3,3) (4,2) (5,1)	$\frac{5}{36}$
7	(1,6) (2,5) (3,4) (4,3) (5,2) (6,1)	$\frac{6}{36}$
8	(2,6) (3,5) (4,4) (5,3) (6,2)	$\frac{5}{36}$
9	(3,6) (4,5) (5,4) (6,3)	$\frac{4}{36}$
10	(4,6) (5,5) (6,4)	$\frac{3}{36}$
11	(5,6) (6,5)	$\frac{2}{36}$
12	(6,6)	$\frac{1}{36}$

(b) 7 (c) 1, one of these outcomes must occur
7 RR – Long Melford; RL – Lavenham;
  LR – Bury St. Edmunds; LL – Stoke by Clare

Answers

Exercise 23G

1 (a)

	Mon	Tues	Total
Jackie	25	35	**60**
Sam	**30**	10	**40**
Total	55	**45**	100

(b) 60
(c) 30
(d) 45

(e) (i) $\frac{25}{100}$ (ii) $\frac{10}{100}$ (iii) $\frac{60}{100}$ (iv) $\frac{65}{100}$

2 (a)

	Air	Eurotunnel	Boat	Total
July	8	2	10	20
Aug	**15**	5	**30**	50
Sept	7	8	15	30
Total	30	**15**	55	100

(b) (i) $\frac{20}{100}$ (ii) $\frac{80}{100}$ (iii) $\frac{30}{100}$ (iv) $\frac{55}{100}$
(v) $\frac{5}{100}$ (vi) $\frac{30}{100}$ (vii) $\frac{70}{100}$ (viii) $\frac{90}{100}$

3 (a)

	France	Italy	Elsewhere	Total
July	6	10	4	20
Aug	18	**24**	8	50
Sept	**4**	16	**10**	30
Total	28	50	22	100

(b) (i) $\frac{50}{100}$ (ii) $\frac{28}{100}$ (iii) $\frac{20}{100}$ (iv) $\frac{50}{100}$
(v) $\frac{8}{100}$ (vi) $\frac{4}{100}$ (vii) $\frac{16}{100}$

4 (a)

	Hotel	Caravan	Camping	Other	Total
July	11	4	3	2	**20**
Aug	**22**	14	**8**	6	**50**
Sept	**16**	7	4	3	30
Total	49	**25**	15	11	100

(b) (i) $\frac{22}{100}$ (ii) $\frac{4}{100}$ (iii) $\frac{49}{100}$ (iv) $\frac{51}{100}$
(v) $\frac{25}{100}$ (vi) $\frac{11}{100}$ (vii) $\frac{8}{100}$

Mixed exercise 23

1 (a) $\frac{6}{11}$ (b) $\frac{5}{11}$
2 (a) (i) 6 (ii) 2 (b) $\frac{25}{200}$
3 (a) $\frac{1}{4}$ (b) 0 (c) $\frac{3}{4}$
4 (a)

1st 30 throws	21	0.7
1st 40 throws	27	0.675
1st 50 throws	36	0.72

(b) proportions get closer to a single value

5 (a)

	Theme park	Aquarium	Circus	Total
Male	6	**26**	14	46
Female	21	3	10	**34**
Total	27	29	24	80

(b) (i) $\frac{29}{80}$ (ii) $\frac{27}{80}$ (iii) $\frac{3}{80}$

6 (a)

×	1	2	3	4
1	1	2	3	4
2	2	4	6	8
3	3	6	9	12

(b) $\frac{2}{12}$
(c) $\frac{4}{12}$

7 (a)

	France	Germany	Spain	Total
Male	2	23	9	34
Female	15	2	9	**26**
Total	17	25	18	60

(b) $\frac{25}{60}$

Chapter 24 Presenting and analysing data 2

Exercise 24A

1 (a)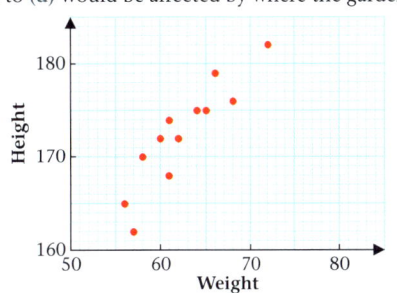

(b) Negative
2 (a) Positive (b) Negative (c) None
(d) None (positive) (e) Positive
Answer to (d) would be affected by where the gardens are.

4 (a) (i)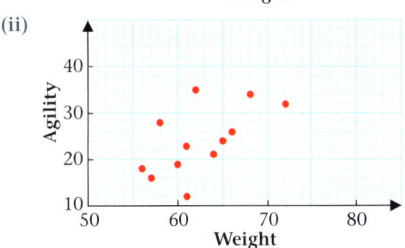

(ii)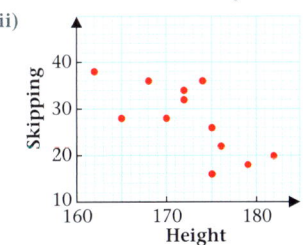

(iii)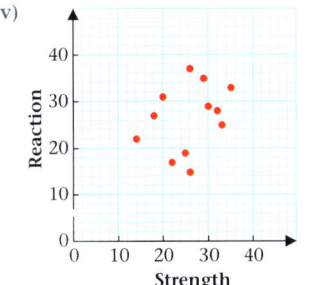

(iv)

Answers

(v)
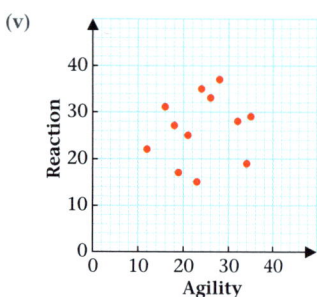

(vi)
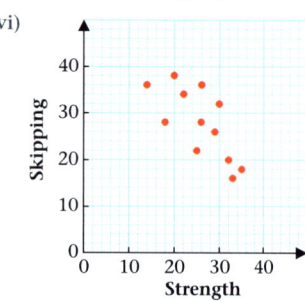

(b) (i) Positive (ii) Positive (none) (iii) None
    (iv) None   (v) None
    (vi) Negative (none)
5 (a) C, F, (D)   (b) A, E   (c) B
6 (a) Positive   (b) 53%

Exercise 24B

1 (a) 15   (b) 100
2 10
3 (a) 10.86 seconds (b) 10.5 seconds
4 (a) 14   (b) any number except 1, 3 or 5
  (c) 2   (d) 4
  (e) 3.7   (f) 5
5 £13.83
6 (a) 10, 14, 18 (b) 14   (c) 14

Exercise 24C

1 0, 20, 26, 12, 8, total f 45, total fx 66. Mean 1.47, Mode 1, Median 1
2 Mode 3, Median 3, Mean 3.35
3 Mode 0, Median 0, Mean 0.5
4 (a) 2   (b) 3   (c) 3.2
5 (a) 1   (b) 2.2   (c) 2

Exercise 24D

1 (a) 7 letters   (b) 1 letter
2 (a) 45 marks   (b) 10 marks
3 (a) 11 months   (b) 5.5 months
4 (a) £8   (b) £2

Exercise 24E

1 (a) 13 biscuits (b) 6–10 biscuits (c) 30 students
2 (a) 61–100   (b) 69.34
3 (a) $160 \leq x < 165$ (b) 164.3 cm

4 (a)

Class interval	Frequency f	Middle value x	$f \times x$
1–5	16	3	48
6–10	28	8	224
11–15	26	13	338
16–20	14	18	252
21–25	10	23	230
26–30	3	28	84
31–35	1	33	33
36–40	0	38	0
41–45	2	43	86
Total	100	Total	1295

(b) 6–10   (c) 11–15   (d) 12.95 words
5 11.79 years

Mixed exercise 24

1 (a), (b)
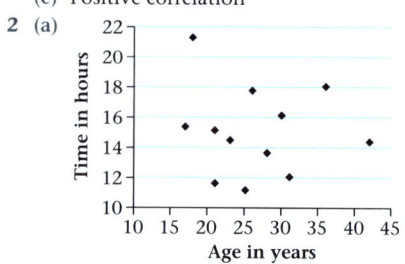
(c) Positive correlation

2 (a) [scatter graph: Time in hours vs Age in years]
(b) No correlation.
3 (a) (i) 3.35   (ii) 4   (iii) 3
  (b) Mode – gives highest number of certificates
4 36
5 506 matches, 46.25 matches
6 156.18 cm
7 1
8 (a) 5, or more   (b) 4, or less
9 (a) 6   (b) $5\frac{1}{2}$ (c) 5   (d) 5.6
10 (a) £18.90   (b) 6.4 miles
11 (a)
   (c) [scatter graph: German vs French with line of best fit]
   (b) Positive correlation
   (d) 30
12 (a) Negative correlation – when it is raining you do not go out if you do not have to.
   (b) No correlation – there is no connection between eating apples and test results.
13 Brand B: mean 12, range 4; Brand B is more consistent.

Answers

Chapter 25 Pythagoras' theorem

Exercise 25A

1. (a) (i) 16 (ii) 9 (iii) 25
   (b) 25
   (c) Area $BADE$ = Area $ACHI$ + Area $CBFG$
2. (a) (i) $6\frac{1}{4}$ (ii) 36 (iii) $42\frac{1}{4}$
   (b) $42\frac{1}{4}$
   (c) Area $RPWX$ = Area $QRST$ + Area $PQUV$

Exercise 25B

1. (a) 13 cm (b) 15 cm (c) 12.5 cm
   (d) 7.5 cm (e) 6.7 cm (f) 13.1 cm
2. (a) 11.4 cm (b) 35.5 cm (c) 7.2 m
   (d) 20.8 m (e) 7.1 cm (f) 5.9 cm
3. 14.8 cm
4. 5.8 km
5. 54.7 m

Exercise 25C

1. (a) 9 cm (b) 24 cm (c) 7.5 cm
   (d) 10.5 cm (e) 11.7 cm (f) 7.7 cm
2. (a) 6.3 m (b) 35.5 cm (c) 8.7 cm
   (d) 21.2 cm (e) 24 cm (f) 34.0 cm

Mixed exercise 25

1. (a) a = 10 cm (b) b = 12 cm
   (c) $x = \sqrt{13}$ cm, $y = \sqrt{23}$ cm
2. 4.90 m
3. 4.7 miles
4. 12.4 cm
5. 24.4 cm
6. 1.5 km
7. 12.4 m
8. 36.1 m

Chapter 26 Advanced perimeter, area and volume

Exercise 26A

1. (a) 76.5 cm^2 (b) 93.8 cm^2 (c) 94 cm^2
2. 226.5 cm^2
3. (a) 74 cm^2 (b) 8.5 cm^2 (c) 47 cm^2

Exercise 26B

1. (d), 2. (d) and 3. Approximately 3

Exercise 26C

1. (a) 6.28 cm (b) 9.42 cm (c) 12.6 cm
   (d) 31.4 cm (e) 25.1 cm (f) 37.7 cm
2. (a) 62.8 cm (b) 15.7 m (c) 157 cm
   (d) 7.85 cm (e) 11.3 cm (f) 25.9 cm

Exercise 26D

1. 12.6 cm 2. 18.8 cm 3. 31.4 cm 4. 62.8 cm
5. 50.3 cm (or 50.2 cm) 6. 75.4 cm 7. 126 cm
8. 31.4 m 9. 314 cm 10. 15.7 cm 11. 22.6 cm
12. 51.8 cm

Exercise 26E

1. 56.5 cm 2. 28.3 cm 3. 283 cm 4. 377 cm
5. 94.2 cm 6. 7.85 m 7. 4.71 cm 8. 18.8 inches
9. 1.88 cm 10. 3.14 cm

Exercise 26F

1. 3 cm, 1.5 cm 2. 4 cm, 2 cm
3. 1 m, 0.5 m 4. 3.18 m, 1.59 m
5. 28.6 cm, 14.3 cm 6. 2.39 m, 1.19 m
7. 1.59 cm, 0.796 cm 8. 1.91 in, 0.955 in
9. 0.318 cm, 0.159 cm 10. 0.796 cm, 0.398 cm

Exercise 26G

1. (b) Approximately 250 square units
   (c) Approximately 3

Exercise 26H

1. (a) 12.6 cm^2 (b) 28.3 cm^2 (c) 50.2 cm^2
   (d) 314 cm^2 (e) 201 cm^2 (f) 452 cm^2
2. (a) 1260 cm^2 (b) 78.5 m^2 (c) 7850 cm^2
   (d) 19.6 cm^2 (e) 40.79 cm^2 (f) 214 cm^2
3. (a) 3.14 cm^2 (b) 7.07 cm^2 (c) 19.6 cm^2
   (d) 78.5 cm^2 (e) 50.2 cm^2 (f) 113 cm^2
4. (a) 314 cm^2 (b) 19.6 m^2 (c) 1960 cm^2
   (d) 4.91 cm^2 (e) 10.2 cm^2 (f) 53.4 cm^2

Exercise 26I

1. 254 cm^2 2. 63.6 cm^2 3. 6360 cm^2 4. 11 300 cm^2
5. 707 cm^2 6. 4.91 m^2 7. 1.77 cm^2 8. 28.3 inches^2
9. 0.283 cm^2 10. 0.785 cm^2

Exercise 26J

1. 6 cm 2. 2 cm 3. 2 m 4. 3.57 m
5. 5.35 cm 6. 3.09 m 7. 1.26 cm 8. 2.76 inches
9. 1.13 cm 10. 0.892 cm

Exercise 26K

1. (a) Circumference 4π cm, Area 4π cm^2
   (b) Circumference 10π m, Area 25π m^2
   (c) Circumference 18π mm, Area 81π mm^2
   (d) Circumference 7π cm, Area $12\frac{1}{4}\pi$ cm^2
   (e) Circumference 24π cm, Area 144π cm^2
2. (a) Circumference 6π m, Area 9π m^2
   (b) Circumference 8π cm, Area 16π cm^2
   (c) Circumference 9π cm, Area 20.25π cm^2
   (d) Circumference 3π m, Area $2\frac{1}{4}\pi$ m^2
   (e) Circumference 20π cm, Area 100π cm^2

Exercise 26L

1. (a) 20.6 cm (b) 17.9 cm (c) 111 cm
   (d) 13.7 cm (e) 39.7 cm (f) 41.7 cm
2. (a) 25.1 cm^2 (b) 19.6 cm^2 (c) 757 cm^2
   (d) 9.53 cm^2 (e) 79.6 cm^2 (f) 99.3 cm^2
3. (a) 471 cm^2 (b) 898 cm^2 (c) 21.5 cm^2
4. 3180 cm^2
5. 38.5 cm^2
6. 161 m^2
7. (a) 8.14 m^2 (b) 3.08 m^2

Answers

Exercise 26M
1. (a) 48.0 cm³ (b) 141 cm³ (c) 503 cm³
   (d) 80.0 cm³ (e) 24.1 cm³ (f) 15.0 cm³
   (g) 252 cm³ (h) 240 cm³ (i) 424 cm³
2. 2.50 cm 3. 10.0 cm² 4. 4.58 mm
5. 5.00 cm² 6. 84.0 cm³
7. (a) 78 cm by 48 cm by 40 cm
   (b) 150 000 cm³
   (c) 18 900 cm² or 1.89 m²
8. 4.50 m³
9. (a) 26 700 cm³ to 3 s.f. (b) 3360 cm³
   (c) 7 (d) 3200 cm³ (or 3180 cm³)
10. (a) 47 300 cm³ (b) 8430 cm²
11. 576 m³ 12. 8.49 mm 13. 7.00 cm
14. (a) 10 600 cm³ (b) 2320 cm²

Exercise 26N
1. (a) 2.65 cm ⩽ length < 2.75 cm
   (b) 3.85 cm ⩽ length < 3.95 cm
   (c) 10.45 cm ⩽ length < 10.55 cm
   (d) 11.5 mm ⩽ length < 12.5 mm
   (e) 24.5 mm ⩽ length < 25.5 mm
   (f) 35.5 mm ⩽ length < 36.5 mm
2. (a) (i) 2.445 m (ii) 2.455 m
   (b) (i) 22.5 cm (ii) 23.5 cm
   (c) (i) 3.995 m (ii) 4.005 m
   (d) (i) 13.5 cm (ii) 14.5 cm
   (e) (i) 49.5 cm (ii) 50.5 cm
   (f) (i) 5.335 m (ii) 5.345 m
3. (a) 12.05 seconds (b) 12.15 seconds
4. (a) (i) 22.345 s (ii) 22.355 s
   (b) (i) 43.665 s (ii) 43.675 s
   (c) (i) 10.015 s (ii) 10.025 s
   (d) (i) 2 min 45.335 s (ii) 2 min 45.345 s
   (e) (i) 44.995 s (ii) 45.005 s
   (f) (i) 49.995 s (ii) 50.005 s

Exercise 26O
1. (a) seconds (b) minutes (c) hours (d) minutes
   (e) hours (f) minutes or hours
2. (a) cm or m (b) mm (c) m (d) cm
   (e) m (f) mm
3. (a) cm² (b) hectares or m²
   (c) km² (d) m²
4. (a) ml (b) l or gallons
   (c) litres or cubic metres
5. (a) metres
   (b) tape measure or trundle wheel
   (c) nearest 10 cm or ½ metre
6. (a) (i) seconds (ii) metres and centimetres
   (b) tape measure or metre rule and stopwatch
   (c) nearest 1 cm and nearest 0.1 s

Exercise 26P
1. 2700 kg m⁻³ 2. 8955 kg m⁻³ 3. 19 355 kg m⁻³
4. 8893 kg m⁻³ 5. 10 506 kg m⁻³ 6. 970 kg m⁻³
7. 7313 kg m⁻³ 8. 7126 kg m⁻³ 9. 11 351 kg m⁻³
10. 18 939 kg m⁻³

Exercise 26Q
1. 0.000 325 m³ 2. 900 kg 3. 200 kg
4. 0.0313 m³ 5. 0.0714 m³ 6. 8050 kg
7. 3600 kg 8. 0.127 m³ 9. 0.000 287 m³
10. 0.000 002 33 m³

Exercise 26R
1. 72 000 metres per hour 2. 8.33 metres per second
3. 1 mile per minute 4. 54 kilometres per hour
5. 72 kilometres per hour 6. 1333 metres per minute
7. 5.56 metres per second 8. 2 160 000 km per hour
9. 39 600 km per hour 10. 31 metres per second

Exercise 26S
1. 40 mph 2. 130 km/h
3. 1 350 000 mph 4. 70 mph
5. (a) 31 m/s (b) the bird
6. (a) 637 mph (b) 1.93 times
7. (a) 675 000 000 mph (b) 150 000 times

Mixed exercise 26
1. 227
2. (a) 25 cm² (b) 154 m
3. 9 460 000 000 000 km
4. 404 g
5. (a) 99.5 m (b) (i) 14.75 s (ii) 14.85 s
6. (a) 36.9 m² (b) 295.2 m³ (c) 0.32 m or 32 cm
7. (a) (i) 9 cm² (ii) 6 cm² (iii) 33 cm²
   (b) $A = 88n$
8. (a) 500 cm³ (b) (i) 400 cm³ (ii) 80%
   (c) (i) 42 cm² (ii) 9.52 cm
9. (a) 113 cm² (b) 17.7 cm
10. (a) (i) metres (ii) grams (b) miles
11. 44.8 km
12. 3000 metres per minute
13. (a) 28.3 cm² (b) 23.1 cm
14. 19.32 g 15. 363 kg 16. 0.558 m³

Chapter 27 Describing transformations

Exercise 27A
1. (a)
   (b) (2, 1), (5, 1), (5, 5)
2. (a) and (c)
   (b) $A' = (2, -3)$, $B' = (2, 0)$, $C' = (4, -1)$
3. A translation by the vector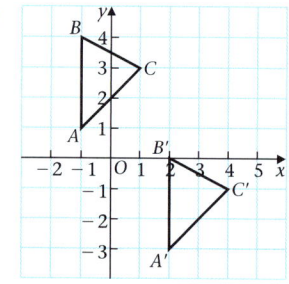

Answers **A19**

Exercise 27B

1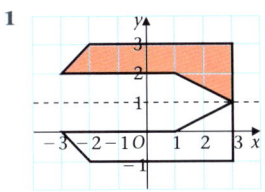
2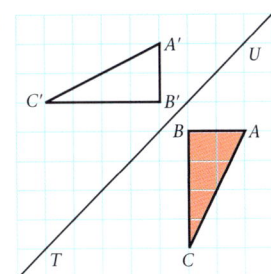

3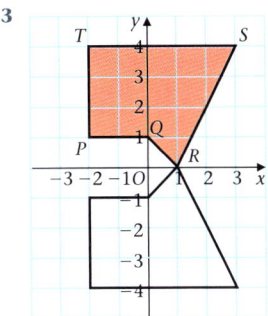

4 A reflection in the line $x = 2$

Exercise 27C

1 (a) 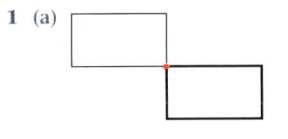   (b)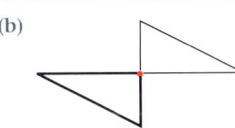

(c)

2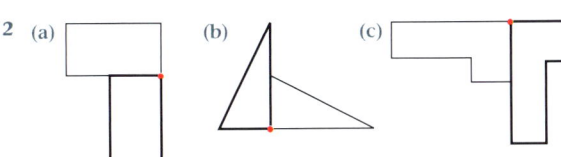

3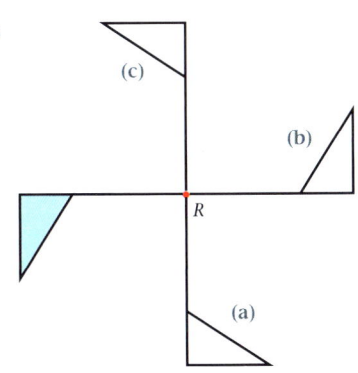

4 (a)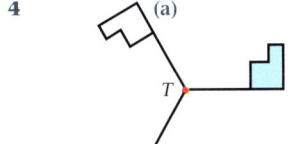

(b) and (c)

Exercise 27D

1 (a) 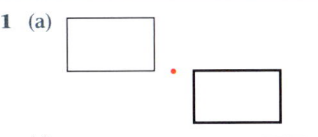   (b)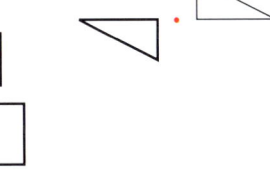

(c)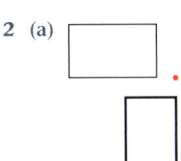

2 (a) 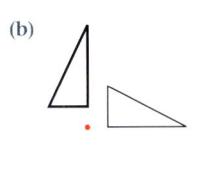   (b)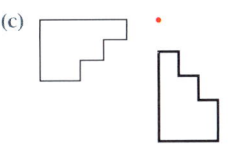

(c)

3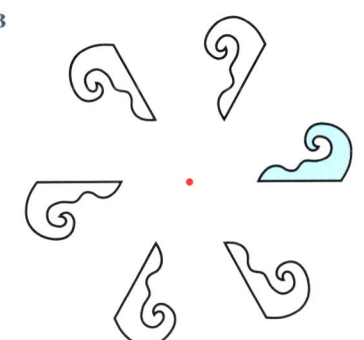

Exercise 27E

1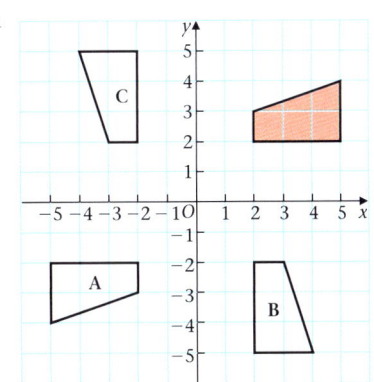

A20 Answers

2

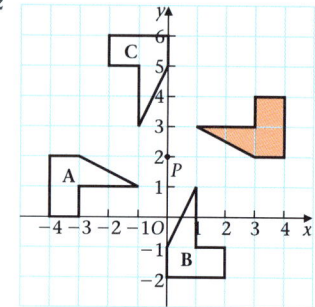

3 A rotation through 180° about the point (0, 0). (A half turn about (0, 0).)

Exercise 27F

1 (a) An enlargement by scale factor 2 and centre (7, 1).
(b) An enlargement by scale factor $\frac{1}{2}$ and centre (7, 1).

2

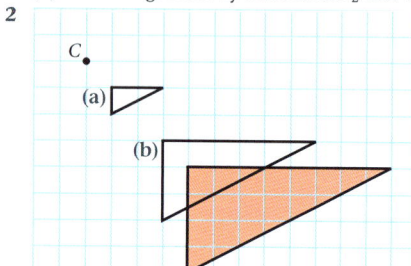

3

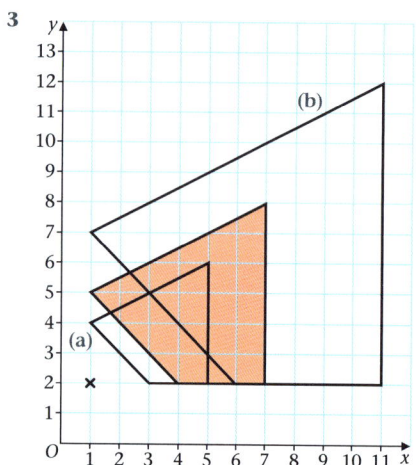

4 (a) Scale factor $1\frac{1}{2}$, centre (−1, −1)
(b) Scale factor $\frac{2}{3}$, centre (−1, −1)

5 Scale factor 3, centre (1, 1)

Mixed exercise 27

1 (a) and (b)

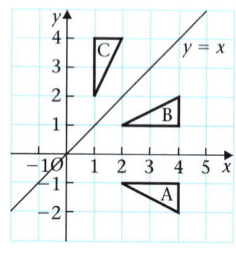

2 (a) and (b)

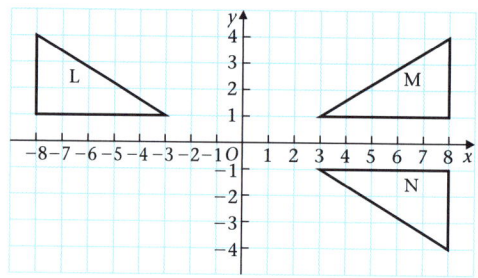

3 (a) A reflection
(b) A translation
(c) A reflection
(d) A rotation through 180°

4 (a), (b) and (c)

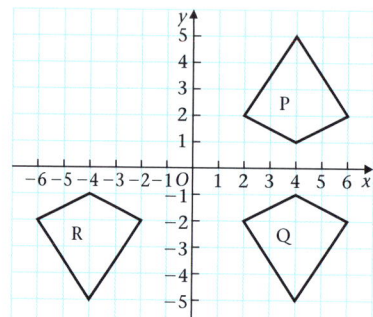

5 (a) and (b)

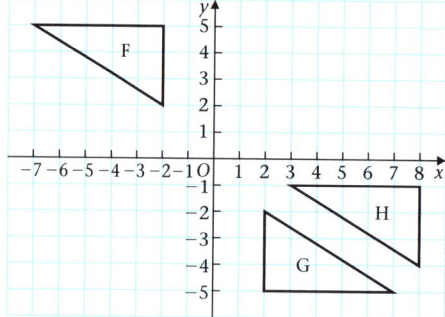

6 (a) and (b)

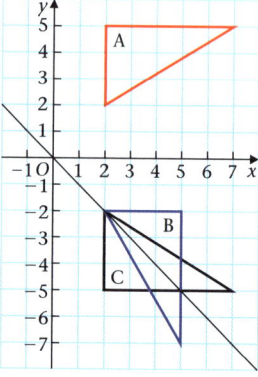

7 (a) 2 (b) (6, 2)

8 (a)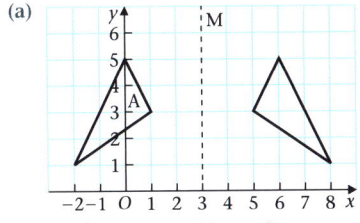
(b) (8, 1) (c) $x = 3$

9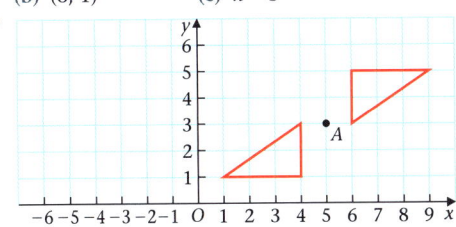

10 (a) and (b)
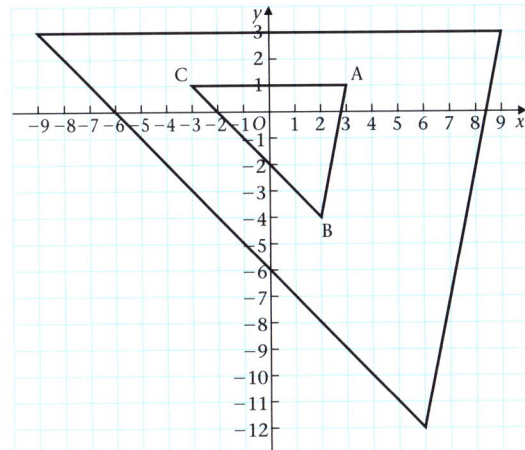
(c) (9, 3), (6, −12), (−9, 3)

11 (a) and (b)
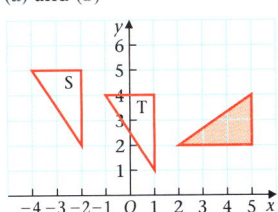

12 (a), (b), (c) and (d)
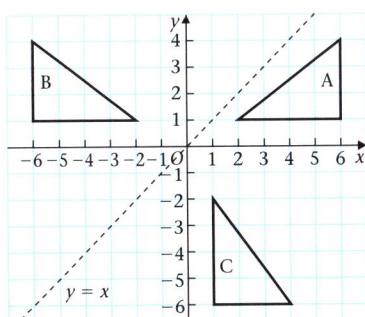

Chapter 28 Expressions, formulae, equations and graphs

Exercise 28A

1 (a) $8r + 2$ (b) $2p − 6$
  (c) $10x + y$ (d) $5m$
2 (a) $14a + 2b$ (b) $5p + q$
  (c) $10r − 2s$ (d) $9p$
3 (a) $7x − y$ (b) $10m − 7n$
  (c) 0 (d) $6p$
4 (a) $3a − 3b$ (b) $r^2 + r$
  (c) $2mn$ (d) $3m + n$
5 (a) $7x + 6y$ (b) $23a − 24$ (c) $3c − 2d$
  (d) $5p − 23q$ (e) $3ab − 2ac + 2bc$ (f) $2ab − 2a − 3b$
6 (a) $3n + 2$ (b) $3n − 2$ (c) $2n − 4$
  (d) $3p + 5r$ (e) $r − 2q$ (f) $2r − s$

Exercise 28B

1 (a) $15x − 2a + 6$ (b) $15x + 1$
  (c) $3a − 20$ (d) $14 − 9p$
  (e) $11x − 3y$ (f) $2x + 3y$
  (g) $d − 11$ (h) $7c − 14$
2 (a) $7d + 6$ (b) $p + 2qw + 3q$
  (c) $4s − 4r$ (d) $22b − 29$
  (e) $25y − 46$ (f) $2x + 17y$
  (g) $2n − 1$ (h) $29b − 16a$

Exercise 28C

1 (a) $ab + 3a + 4b + 12$ (b) $cd + 4c + 5d + 20$
  (c) $xy + 6x + 3y + 18$ (d) $a^2 + 11a + 24$
  (e) $b^2 + 11b + 28$ (f) $x^2 + 8x + 12$
2 (a) $2a^2 + 11a + 12$ (b) $3b^2 + 11b + 6$
  (c) $4c^2 + 27c + 18$ (d) $2a^2 + 11a + 15$
  (e) $3b^2 + 10b + 8$ (f) $4c^2 + 13c + 10$
3 (a) $a^2 − 7a + 12$ (b) $c^2 − 9c + 20$
  (c) $x^2 − 9x + 18$ (d) $a^2 − 11a + 24$
  (e) $b^2 − 3b − 28$ (f) $x^2 − 8x + 12$
4 (a) $a^2 − a − 12$ (b) $a^2 + a − 20$
  (c) $x^2 + 3x − 18$ (d) $a^2 + 5a − 24$
  (e) $b^2 − 3b − 28$ (f) $x^2 + 4x − 12$
5 (a) $x^2 + 3x + 2$ (b) $y^2 + 4y − 5$
  (c) $d^2 − 5d + 6$ (d) $g^2 + 2g − 15$
  (e) $x^2 − 4x − 12$ (f) $t^2 − 6t + 8$
6 (a) $2a^2 + 5a − 25$ (b) $3b^2 − 14b − 24$
  (c) $3c^2 − 11c + 6$ (d) $3a^2 − 19a + 20$
  (e) $3x^2 + 11x − 20$ (f) $2a^2 − 9a − 18$
7 (a) $3a^2 − 5a − 2$ (b) $12p^2 + 5p − 2$
  (c) $3a^2 + 5a + 2$ (d) $12p^2 + 14p + 4$
  (e) $2b^2 − 5b + 3$ (f) $8b^2 + 2b − 1$
8 (a) $x^2 + 6x + 9$ (b) $y^2 − 10y + 25$
  (c) $4x^2 + 4x + 1$ (d) $9y^2 − 24y + 16$
  (e) $9x^2 + 30x + 25$ (f) $36x^2 − 84x + 49$
9 (a) $2x^2 + 7x − 4$ (b) $2y^2 − 17y − 30$
  (c) $6t^2 − 19t + 15$ (d) $5m^2 + 26m + 5$
  (e) $25c^2 + 50c + 24$ (f) $6x^2 − 13x − 28$
10 (a) $30 + 7x − 2x^2$ (b) $12x^2 − 19x − 21$
  (c) $4x^2 − 9$ (d) $15x^2 + x − 2$
  (e) $9x^2 − 16$ (f) $12 − 7x − 10x^2$

Exercise 28D

1 (b)

x	−2.5	−1.5	−0.8	−0.6	−0.4	−0.2	−0.1	0	0.1	0.2	0.4	0.6	0.8	1.5	2.5
y	6.25	2.25	0.64	0.36	0.16	0.04	0.01	0	0.01	0.04	0.16	0.36	0.64	2.25	6.25

(c) and (d). Solid line on graph.

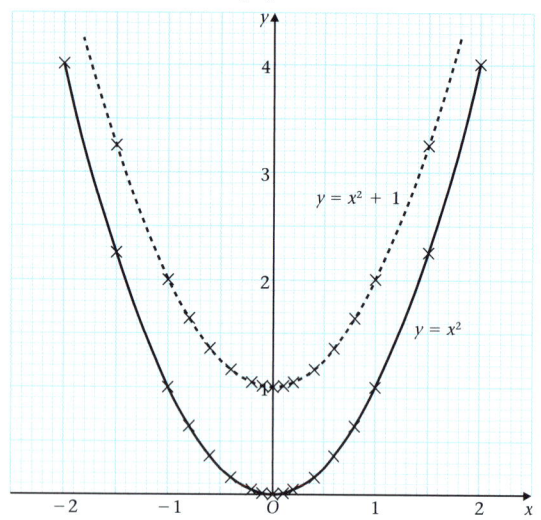

2

x	−3	−2.5	−2	−1.5	−1	−0.8	−0.6	−0.4	−0.2	−0.1	0	0.1	0.2	etc
y	10	7.25	5	3.25	2	1.64	1.36	1.16	1.04	1.01	1	1.01	1.04	

The graph of $y = x^2 + 1$ is shown by the dotted line in the answer to question **1**.

3 (c)

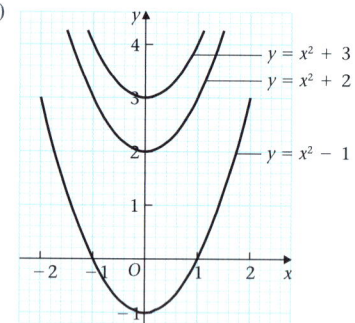

(d) The y axis is a line of symmetry for each graph of the type $y = x^2 + c$
(e) Each of these graphs cuts the y-axis at the point (0, c).

Exercise 28E

1

x	−3	−2	−1	0	1	2	3
y	13	3	−3	−5	−3	3	13

2

x	−3	−2	−1	0	1	2	3
y	25	10	1	−2	1	10	25

3

x	−3	−2	−1	0	1	2	3
y	43	18	3	−2	3	18	43

4

x	−3	−2	−1	0	1	2	3
y	41	16	1	−4	1	16	41

5

x	−3	−2	−1	0	1	2	3
y	23	8	−1	−4	−1	8	23

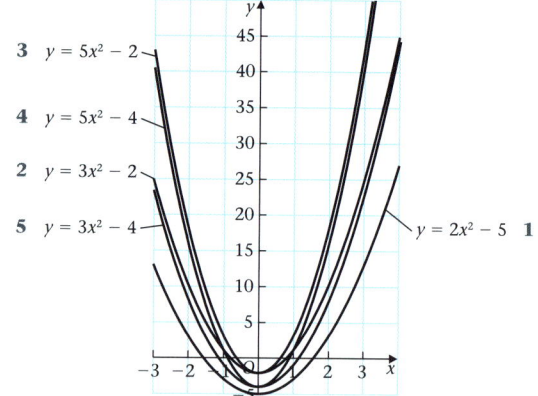

3 $y = 5x^2 − 2$
4 $y = 5x^2 − 4$
2 $y = 3x^2 − 2$
5 $y = 3x^2 − 4$
$y = 2x^2 − 5$ **1**

Exercise 28F

1 (a)

x	−4	−3	−2	−1	0	1	2	3	4
y	32	18	8	2	0	2	8	18	32

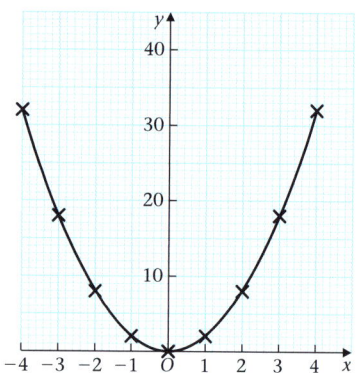

(b) $x = 0$

2 (a)

x	−4	−3	−2	−1	0	1	2	3	4
y	21	14	9	6	5	6	9	14	21

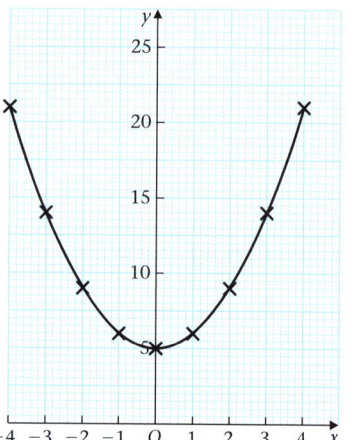

(b) $x = 0$

3 (a)

x	−4	−3	−2	−1	0	1	2	3	4
y	24	15	8	3	0	−1	0	3	8

(b) $x = 1$

5 (a)

x	−4	−3	−2	−1	0	1	2	3	4
y	7	2	−1	−2	−1	2	7	14	23

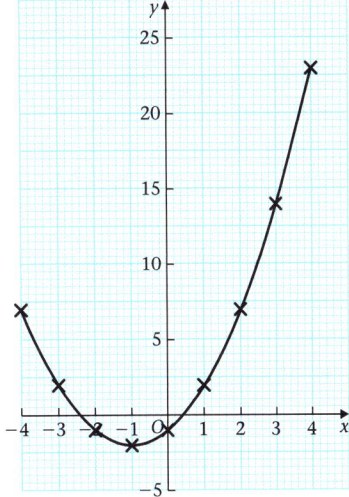

(b) $x = -1$

4 (a)

x	−4	−3	−2	−1	0	1	2	3	4
y	−39	−18	−3	6	9	6	−3	−18	−39

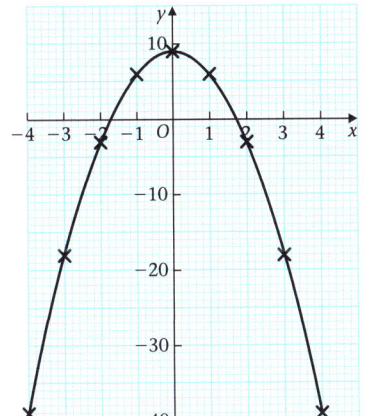

(b) $x = 0$

6 (a)

x	−4	−3	−2	−1	0	1	2	3	4
y	−23	−13	−5	1	5	7	7	5	1

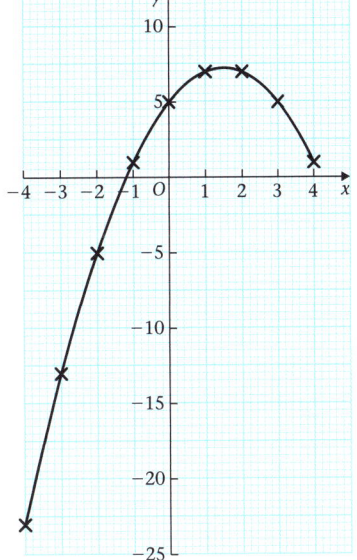

(b) $x = 1.5$

7 (a)

x	−4	−3	−2	−1	0	1	2	3	4
y	15	4	−3	−6	−5	0	9	22	39

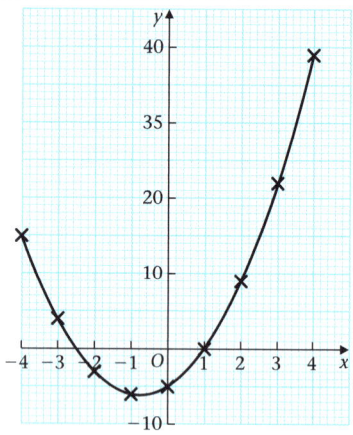

(b) $x = -\frac{3}{4}$

8 (a)

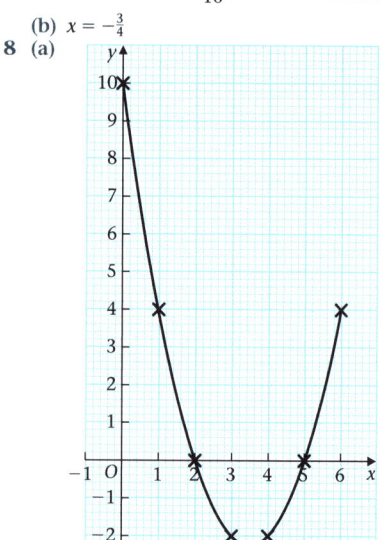

(b) −2.25   (c) 6.75   (d) 3, 4

9 (a)

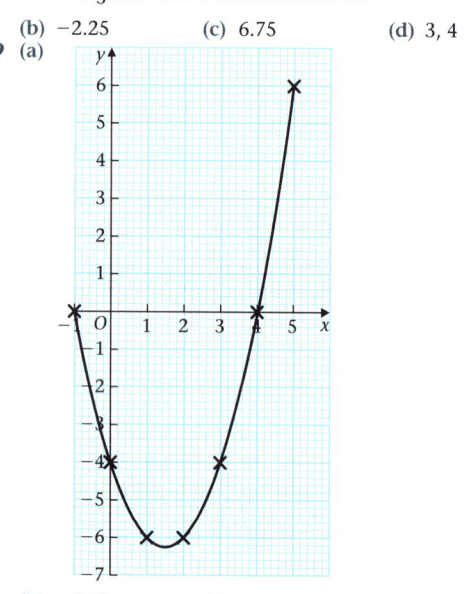

(b) −6.25   (c) 2.16   (d) 0, 3

10 (a)

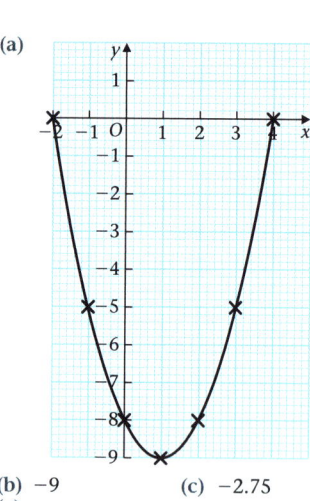

(b) −9   (c) −2.75   (d) −1, 3

11 (a)

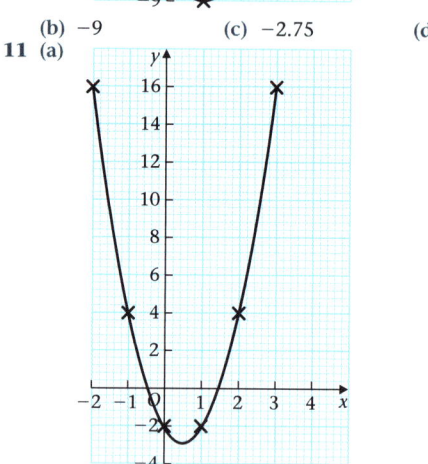

(b) −3.75   (c) 2.32   (d) −1, 2

12 (a)

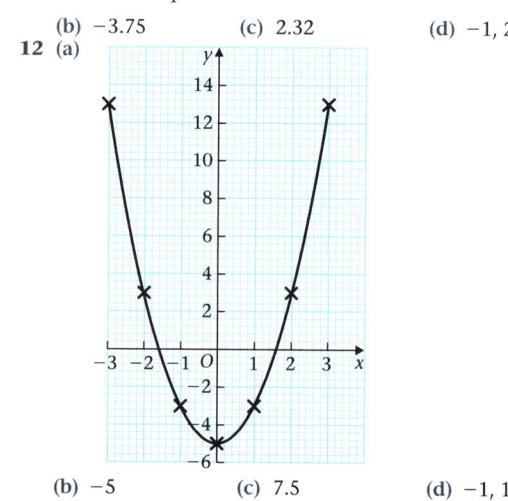

(b) −5   (c) 7.5   (d) −1, 1

Exercise 28G

1 (a)

x	−3	−2	−1	0	1	2	3	4
y	29	16	7	2	1	4	11	22

(b) (i) $x = -0.5$ or 2   (ii) $x = -1.5$ or 3
(iii) $x = 0.5$ or 1
(c) 0.875
(d) 0.75
(e) 0.5 is less than the minimum value for y.

Answers A25

2 (a)

x	−3	−2	−1	0	1	2	3	4	5
y	−16	−9	−4	−1	0	−1	−4	−9	−16

(b) (i) −1 or 3 (ii) 0 or 2 (iii) −2 or 4
(c) 0 (d) 1
(e) any value greater than 0.

3 (a)

x	−4	−3	−2	−1	0	1	2	3
y	16	4	−4	−8	−8	−4	4	16

(b) (i) $x = -3$ or 2 (ii) $x = -2$ or 1 (iii) −1 or 0
(c) −8.5 (d) −0.5
(e) any value less than −8.5

4 (a)

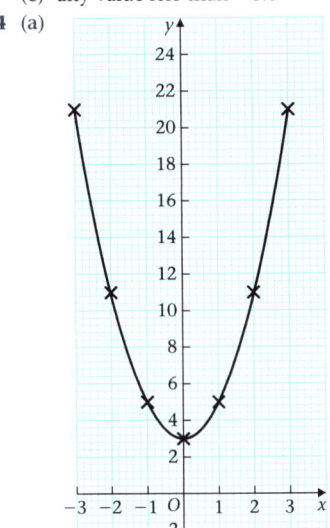

(b) $x = -0.7$ or 0.7 (c) $x = -2.7$ or 2.7

5 (a)

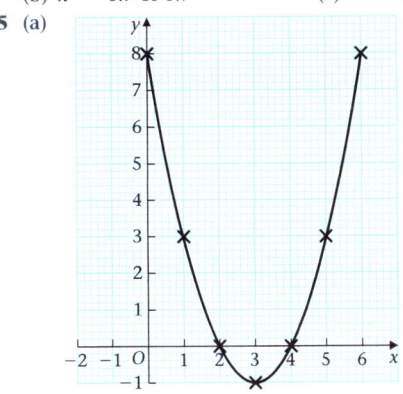

(b) $x = 2$ or 4 (c) $x = 0.5$ or 5.5

6 (a)

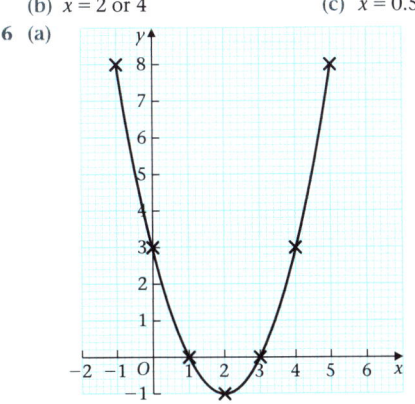

(b) $x = 1$ or 3 (c) $x = 0.25$ or 3.75

Exercise 28H

1 Car Y is bigger than car R.
2 Car Y weighs more than than car R.
Car R has a greater maximum possible speed than car Y.
3 (a) Size (b) Age (c) Cost

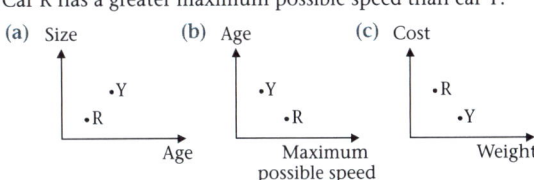

4 (a) A Kate, B Sam, C Maria, D Jamie,
E Steve F Tom
(b) Maria

Exercise 28I

1 (a) E (b) A (c) B (d) C
2 (a)   (b)

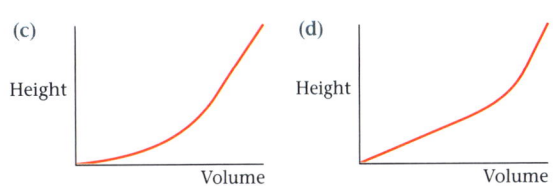

(c)   (d)

3 (a) The sound level increased rapidly then gradually levelled off.
(b) The record stopped suddenly.
Someone pulled out the plug of the record player or the record finished.
4 (a) B
(b) The speed of the ball is greatest at the start.
The speed decreases as the ball reaches its maximum height.
The speed increases as the ball falls again.
The ball stops suddenly when it hits the ground because it gets stuck in the mud!
5 (a) B (b) E

Exercise 28J

1 (a) $x = \dfrac{m+5}{2}$ (b) $x = \dfrac{a-4}{3}$
(c) $x = \dfrac{k}{p}$ (d) $x = \dfrac{q}{m}$
(e) $x = \dfrac{w}{6}$ (f) $x = d - 3a$
(g) $x = \dfrac{2p}{3}$ (h) $x = \dfrac{y-c}{m}$
(i) $x = at + u$ (j) $x = \dfrac{d}{3} + 4$
(k) $x = \dfrac{5(f-32)}{9}$ (l) $x = \dfrac{tk}{p}$
2 (a) $C = \dfrac{F-32}{1.8}$ (b) 24.4 °C

A26 Answers

3 (a) $d = \dfrac{c-2}{3}$ (b) $d = \dfrac{c-5}{4}$ (c) $d = \dfrac{c+6}{5}$
  (d) $d = \dfrac{c-8}{7}$ (e) $d = 2(c-3)$ (f) $d = 3(c+4)$

4 (a) $q = \dfrac{p-2}{5}$ (b) $q = p-6$ (c) $q = \dfrac{p+2}{9}$
  (d) $q = \dfrac{p-3}{4}$ (e) $q = p+12$ (f) $q = \dfrac{p-6}{2}$

5 (a) $s = \dfrac{12-r}{4}$ or $3 - \dfrac{r}{4}$ (b) $s = \dfrac{28-r}{7}$ or $4 - \dfrac{r}{7}$
  (c) $s = \dfrac{10-r}{6}$ or $\dfrac{5}{3} - \dfrac{r}{6}$ (d) $s = \dfrac{14-r}{2}$ or $7 - \dfrac{r}{2}$
  (e) $s = \dfrac{8-r}{2}$ or $4 - \dfrac{r}{2}$ (f) $s = 14 - r$

6 (a) $x = \dfrac{y-5}{3}$ (b) $x = \dfrac{y+7}{4}$ (c) $x = \dfrac{y}{2} - 3$
  (d) $x = \dfrac{y}{3} + 5$ (e) $x = 3y + 4$ (f) $x = 9y - 5$
  (g) $x = 3(y-4)$ (h) $x = 2(y+7)$ (i) $x = \dfrac{6y+3}{2}$

Exercise 28K

1 $x = \pm 3$ **2** $x = 3$ **3** $x = 5$
4 $x = \pm 5$ **5** $x = 8$ **6** $x = \pm 4$
7 $x = \pm 9$ **8** $x = 2.5$ **9** $x = \pm 6$
10 $x = \pm 7$ **11** $x = 9$ **12** $x = 12.5$

Exercise 28L

1 (a) $x = 1.18$ (b) $x = 1.14$ (c) 1.86
  (d) 2.36 (e) 2.13 (f) 2.17
2 (a) $x = 2.15$ (b) $x = 2.39$ (c) $x = 2.71$
  (d) $x = 3.75$ (e) $x = 4.93$ (f) $x = 3.47$
  (g) $x = 3.04$ (h) $x = 5.73$ (i) $x = 1.92$
3 $12.6\,\text{cm}$
4 $5.7\,\text{cm} \times 11.4\,\text{cm} \times 17.0\,\text{cm}$

Exercise 28M

1 width = $4.84\,\text{cm}$
2 Winford = £1.31, Barry = 86p, Syreeta = £2.37
3 base = $9.66\,\text{cm}$

Mixed exercise 28

1 (a) x^9 (b) y^3 (c) $3p^3$
  (d) $27a^6$ (e) $30a^9$
2 $2x + 4$
3 (a) $x^2 + 9x + 20$ (b) $a^2 - 8a + 15$
  (c) $6b^2 + 14b - 12$ (d) $4 + 5x - 6x^2$
4 (a)

x	−3	−2	−1	0	1	2	3
y	21	11	5	3	5	11	21

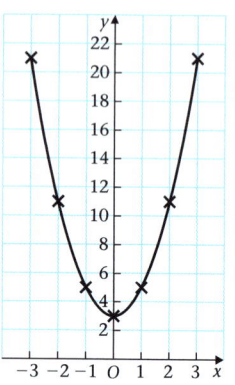

(b)

x	−3	−2	−1	0	1	2	3
y	−11	−1	5	7	5	−1	−11

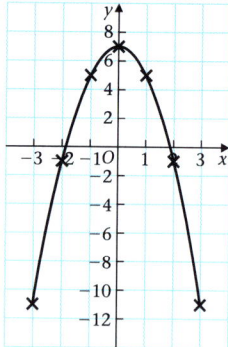

(c)

x	−3	−2	−1	0	1	2	3
y	2	0	0	2	6	12	20

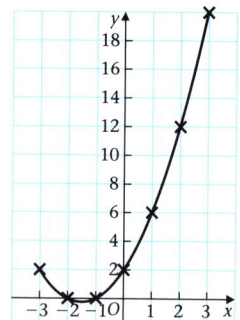

(d)

x	−3	−2	−1	0	1	2	3
y	0	−5	−6	−3	4	15	30

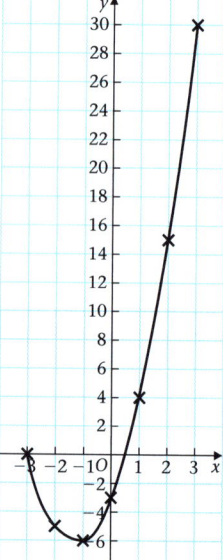

5 (a) a^3
  (b) (i) $7x - 1$ (ii) $x^2 + 5xy + 6y^2$

Answers

6 (a)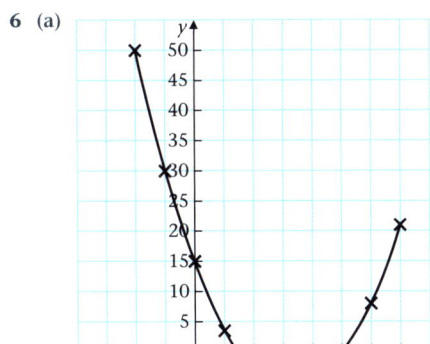

13 (a) 4 : 1   (b) 750g flour, 300g butter, 3 eggs
14 (a) $y = 7$ (b) $x = 6$ (c) $p = -6$ (d) $c = 10$
15 (i) $r = 47°$ alternate
   (ii) $t = 47°$ corresponding (or alternate to r)
16 32 cm²
17 (a) 60°   (b) 9 sides
18 (a)

0	7, 8, 9
1	2, 3, 4, 5, 5, 6, 8, 8, 8, 8, 8, 8
2	1, 2, 2, 3, 5, 5, 7, 7
3	2, 3

Key
3|2 = 32

(b) 18 minutes   (c) 26 minutes
19 (a) (i) g^7 (ii) m^4 (b) (i) $7p + 22$ (ii) $x^2 + 7x + 10$
20 025°   21 $t = \dfrac{v - u}{a}$

(b) (i) 5, 1.5   (ii) 5.6, 0.9 (approx)
7 (a) $x = \dfrac{y - 3}{2}$ (b) $x = \dfrac{2ty}{a}$ (c) $x = \dfrac{y + 15}{6}$
8 (a) 4   (b) -2
9 (a) 8   (b) ± 3 (c) $8\frac{1}{3}$
10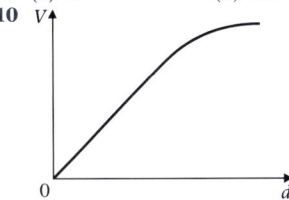
11 4.2
12 3.3

Examination practice paper: Non calculator

1 (a) 36 590   (b) 37 000
2 (a) (i) rectangle   (ii) right-angled triangle
    (iii) parallelogram   (iv) regular hexagon
 (b) (i)    (ii) none

    (iii) none   (iv)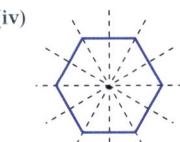

 (c) (i) 2   (ii) 1   (iii) 2   (iv) 6
3 (a) $\frac{4}{20} = \frac{1}{5}$ (b) 80%
4 (a) 2, 3 or 12   (b) 10, 15, 25 or 100
 (c) 9, 16, 25, 36 or 100   (d) 3, 9 and 10, 100
5 (a) (i) 12 letters   (ii) 6 letters   (iii) 7 letters
 (b)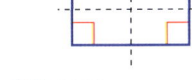

6 (a) (i) $4c$ (ii) p^3 (iii) $8g$ (iv) $10rp$
 (b) $5a + 6b$
7 (a)   (b) 4, 9; 10, 21; $n, 2n + 1$

8 (a) 0.625   (b) 80%
9 (a) £1.85   (b) £49.20
10 (a) $\frac{12}{20} = \frac{3}{5}$ (b) $\frac{3}{20}$ (c) 0
11 £2100
12 $\frac{2}{5}$, 45%, $\frac{5}{11}$, 0.48, $\frac{1}{2}$

Examination practice paper: Calculator

1 (a) Seventy-two thousand three hundred and five
 (b) 300
2 (a) cuboid   (b) cylinder
 (c) square-based pyramid
3 (a)

Score	Tally	Frequency
1					3
2							6
3								7
4									8
5						4
6				2

(b)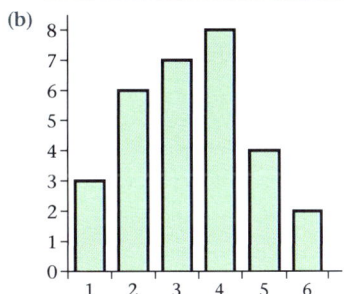

(c) (i) mode 4   (ii) median 3   (iii) range 5
4 (a) 18, 23   (b) Add 5   (c) 98
 (d) It does not end in 3 or 8   (e) $5n - 2$
5 (a) 14.7 m²   (b) 21.58 cm²
6 (a) 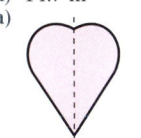   (b)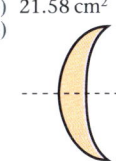

7 £5 − (0.36 + 0.96 + 1.25) = £2.43
8 (a) ±3.5   (b) 13.824
9 For example
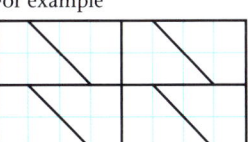

10 (a) 8 cm²   (b) 10 cm³
11

Answers

12 (a) 15 (b)

	19	32	
5		7	19
		39	

(c) $\frac{26}{80} = \frac{13}{40}$

13 £20
14 £1102.50
15 (a) Manchester (b) Exeter
16 £11 + £41.37 = £52.37
17 0.4
18 Car 45, Moped 10 Angles: Car 90°, Walk 120°, Bus 60°, Bike 70°, Moped 20°
19 (a) (i) 15 (ii) −2 (b) 30 (c) 1.6
20 (a) $2(3a + 5)$ (b) $x(x - 5)$ (c) $5x(x^2 + 3y)$
21 £4.80
22 15 cm
23

x	$x^3 + x^2$	To big or too small
4	80	small
5	150	big
4.5	111.375	big
4.4	104.544	big
4.3	97.997	small
4.35	101.235 375	big

$x = 4.3$

24 24

Index to Books 1 and 2

You can find pages 1–276 in Book 1.

A

acute angles 97–8
addition
  algebra 47
  decimals 89–90
  fractions 161–3
  negative numbers 31–2
  rule of signs 31, 32, 397
  terms in algebraic expressions 48–9
  whole numbers 8–9
algebra
  addition 47
  basics 46–7
  brackets 58–9, 60–1
  collecting like terms 49, 61
  division 52
  equations of straight lines 313–15
  expanding the brackets 60, 63
  graphs 313–15
  letter raised to a further power 58
  letter raised to the power 0 57
  letter raised to the power 1 57
  multiplication 50
  number raised to a further power 55
  number raised to the power 1 54
  summary of key points 67–8
algebraic equations
  problem solving 402–3, 404
  using 402–3, 404
algebraic expressions
  definition 48
  division 52
  factorising 64
  multiplication 51
  simplifying 523–4, 525
  summary of key points 547
  terms 48–9
algebraic formulae 394–9
  numbers 396
alternate angles 109–10, 110
analogue clocks 185–6
angle measurer 100
angles
  acute 97–8
  alternate 109–10, 110
  bearings 118–19
  bisecting 142–3
  corresponding 110
  degrees 125
  drawing 102–3
  drawing without a protractor 141–2
  'F' 110
  measurement 97–8, 100
  meeting at a point 104–5
  naming 99–100
  90° 142
  obtuse 97–8
  pie charts 383–5
  polygons 115
  protractor 100
  quadrilaterals 106
  reflex 98, 102–3
  right 97–8
  60° 141
  straight 98
  straight line 103–4
  summary of key points 122–3
  triangles 106, 113–14
  'Z' 110
approximating by rounding 20–1
arc 486
area
  circle 481–3
  composite shapes 354
  definition 349
  formulae 352–3
  irregular shapes, estimating 350
  parallelogram 475
  problem solving 360, 365
  rectangle 475
  rounding 360
  summary of key points 368, 503
  surface 357
  trapezium 476
  triangle 475
  2-D shapes 475–6
  units conversion 361–2
asymmetrical patterns 340
averages 369, 377

advantages 377
appropriate 376–7
calculating 452–3
disadvantages 377
frequency distributions 454–5
grouped data 459–60

B

bar chart 222–3
bar-line graph 233
base year 288
bearings 118–19, 139
bias 199
BIDMAS 58–9, 397, 399
bisector
　angle 142–3
　angles formed by two lines 144
　line 142–3
　perpendicular, of line 143
brackets
　basics 58–62
　expanding 60, 218
　multiplication 526–7
　negative numbers 525
　simplifying 62

C

calculator
　producing sequences 77
centre of enlargement 419
centre of rotation 414, 509
checking by rounding 22–3
chunking method 15–16
circle
　arc 486
　area 481–3
　circumference 477–9
　diameter given circumference 480
　locus 143
　quadrant 486
　radius given area 484
　sector 486
　segment 486
　semicircle 486
　similar 517–18

circular protractor 102, 119
circumference of a circle 477–9
class intervals 225
collecting like terms 49, 61, 523
cone 247, 317
congruent shapes 131, 508
continuous data 231–3, 460
conversion graphs 304–5
coordinates
　first quadrant 299
　four quadrants 312
　mid-point of line segment 300
　summary of key points 321
correlation 449–50
corresponding angles 110
cross-section 249–50, 488
cube roots 38–9, 39–40
cube [number] 36–7
cube [shape] 247–8, 253, 355–6
cuboid 247, 256, 317, 355–6, 488
curved graphs 309–10
cylinder
　properties 247
　surface area 489–90
　volume 489–90

D

data
　collection 195
　comparing 226–8
　continuous 231–3, 460
　discrete 231, 233, 460
　from database 203–4
　from internet 205
　grouped continuous 237–8
　grouping 224–5
　observation 200–1
　primary 202
　questionnaires 196, 197
　sampling 199
　secondary 202
data analysis, summary of key points 390, 465
data collection, summary of key points 210
data presentation, summary of key points 244, 390, 465
data recording, summary of key points 210
data sorting, summary of key points 244

You can find pages 1–276 in Book 1.

date calculations 271
days in month 271
decagon 118
decimal point 81
decimals
   addition 89–90
   decimal numbers 81–2
   decimal point 81
   division 92–3
   equation solutions 216
   fractions 173–4, 278–81
   multiplication 91
   ordering 82–3
   percentages 278–81
   place value diagram 81–2
   place values 81–2
   recurring 175
   rounding 84–7
   subtraction 89–90
   summary of key points 95
decreasing sequences 70
degrees 125
density 495–6
depreciation 294
digital clocks 185, 187
direct proportion 332–3
discrete data 231, 233, 460
distance–time graphs 306–7
division
   algebra 52
   algebraic expressions 52
   by 10, 100, 1000 11–12
   chunking method 15–16
   decimals 92–3
   mixed numbers 170
   negative numbers 32–4
   powers 54, 56–7
   rule of signs 33, 398
   traditional method 15–16
   whole numbers 15–16
drawing
   accurate 138–9
   angles 102–3
   angles without protractor 141–2
   line segments 134–6
   pie charts 382
   prism 250
   regular polygons inscribed in a circle 136

   scale 139
   sketch graphs 535
   triangles 135
   3-D shapes 248
   2-D shapes 130
dual bar chart 227–8

E

edges 246
elevation 254
enlargements 419–21, 512–15
equally likely 427
equations
   balance method 211–12, 213–14
   brackets 218, 220
   combining operations 214–15
   decimal solutions 216
   expanding the brackets 218
   fractional solutions 216
   letters on both sides 219
   negative solutions 216
   quadratic 532–3, 541–2
   reciprocal 541–2
   straight line 313–15
   summary of key points 221, 547
   trial and improvement 542
equilateral triangles 125
equivalent fractions 158–9
equivalent ratio 326
estimating
   area 350
   background 181
   by rounding 20–1
   capacity 182
   distance 181
   length 181
   mean 459–60
   sensibly 184
   summary of key points 194
   weight 183
even numbers 34–6
event 425, 429
examination practice papers
   calculator 552–6
   non-calculator 548–51
expanding the brackets 60, 63

F

'F' angles 110
faces 246
factor trees 41
factorising algebraic expressions 64
factors 34–6
first quadrant 299
formulae
   algebraic 394–9
   negative numbers 397–9
   powers 399
   rearranging 539–40
   subject 539–40
   summary of key points 410, 547
   word 391, 392
fractions
   addition 161–3
   decimals 173–4, 278–81
   division 170
   equation solutions 216
   equivalent 158–9
   examination 161
   improper 153–4
   mixed numbers 153–4, 163, 165
   multiplication 167–8
   numbers 151
   of a quantity 154–5
   ordering 160
   percentages 278–81
   pictures 151
   problem solving 171–2
   reciprocals 176
   scale factor of enlargement 514–15
   simplifying 156–7
   subtraction 165–6
   summary of key points 179–80
   words 152
frequency distributions 454–5, 457–8
frequency polygons 238–9
front elevation 254
function, definition 528

G

gradient 315
graphs
   algebra 313–15
   axes labels 535
   conversion 304–5
   curved 309–10
   distance–time 306–7
   linear 301–2
   quadratic functions 528–30
   real-life situations 535–7
   sketching 535
   straight line 302
   summary of key points 321, 547
grouped data 224–5, 459–60

H

heptagon 124
hexagon 115
highest common factor (HCF) 41
histograms 237–8
horizontal surfaces 245
hypotenuse 466

I

identities 527
imperial units 266, 497–8
improper fractions 153–4
increasing sequences 70–1
index numbers 288
index/indices [powers] 53
inequalities 405
   summary of key points 410
interest 283–4, 293
interquartile range 457–8
isosceles triangles 108, 125

K

kite 126, 342

L

line graph 232–3
line of best fit 449
line segments 124, 134–6
linear equations, summary of key points 221
linear graphs 301–2

You can find pages 1–276 in Book 1.

linear relationship 302, 313
lines of symmetry 338–9, 344
locus
    circle 143
    definition 143
    of a point 143–5
    points equidistant from one line 144
    points equidistant from one point 143
    points equidistant from two lines 144
    points equidistant from two points 143
long multiplication 13, 91
lower quartile 457–8
lowest common multiple (LCM) 42

M

maps 138–9, 334–5
match patterns 74
mean 373, 377, 452, 455, 459–60
measurement
    accuracy 492–4
    angles 97–8, 100
    area units conversion 361–2
    capacity 182
    comparisons 499
    density 495–6
    distance 181
    imperial units 183, 497–8
    length 181
    length accurately 191–2
    mass 495–6
    metric units 183, 497–8
    speed 363–4
    summary of key points 194, 276
    time 185–8
    unit conversion 497–8
    units choice 183
    volume 495–6
    volume units conversion 361–2
    weight 183
median 371, 377, 452–3, 455, 459–60
metric units 262, 264, 266, 497–8
mileage charts 206
mirror line 338–9, 417, 506–7
mixed numbers 153–4, 163, 165, 168, 170
mnemonics
    BIDMAS 58–9, 397, 399
    days in month 271

DST triangle 363, 495
MDV triangle 495
modal class 225, 459–60
mode 369, 377, 452, 455
money 283–4
multiples 34–6
multiplication
    addition method 91
    algebra 50
    algebraic expressions 51
    brackets 526–7
    by 10, 100, 1000 11–12
    decimals 91
    doubling method 13
    fractions 167–8
    grid method 13–14
    long 13, 91
    mixed numbers 168
    Napier's Bones 13–14, 91
    negative numbers 32–4
    powers 54, 56–7
    rule of signs 33, 398
    traditional method 13
    whole numbers 12–13

N

Napier's Bones 13–14, 91
negative correlation 449
negative numbers
    addition 31–2
    algebraic formulae 397–9
    brackets 525
    division 32–4
    equation solutions 216
    introduction 28–30
    multiplication 32–4
    subtraction 31–2
nets 250–1, 253
nonagon 116, 136
notation
    angles, naming [∠] 127
    angles, naming [⌒] 127
    angles, naming [using letters] 99–100, 127
    decimal places [d.p.] 38, 86
    greater than or equal to [⩾] 405
    greater than [>] 405
    highest common factor [HCF] 41

You can find pages 1–276 in Book 1.

less than or equal to [≤] 405
less than [<] 405
lowest common multiple [LCM] 42
parallel lines [> or ≫] 110, 124
percentages [%, pc] 277
pi [π] 478
probability of event [P(event)] 426
recurring decimals [0.ẋ] 175
right angle [⌐] 98, 124
sides of equal length [| or ||] 108, 112
significant figures [s.f.] 22, 88
square root of integer [√] 471
sum of values [Σ] 465
value added tax [VAT] 286
number facts, summary of key points 44–5
number line 7, 407
number patterns
   basics 69
   summary of key points 80
   see index entries under sequences

O

observation 200–1
obtuse angles 97–8
obtuse-angled triangles 125
octagon 124
odd numbers 34–6
1-D shape 124, 316–17
order of rotational symmetry 342–3, 344
ordering
   decimals 82–3
   fractions 160
   whole numbers 2–4

P

parallel lines 109–10
parallelogram 126, 317, 353, 475
patterns
   asymmetrical 340
   symmetrical 340
pentagon 124
percentages
   basics 277
   comparing proportions 292
   decimals 278–81
   decreasing 285
   fractions 278–81
   increasing 283–4
   quantity as percentage of another 290
   summary of key points 297–8
   value added tax 286–7
perimeter
   composite shapes 348
   definition 347
   summary of key points 368, 503
   2-D shapes 475–6
perpendicular lines 98, 124
pictograms 229–30
pie charts 381–5
place value
   decimals 81–2
   diagram 81–2
   introduction 1–2
   table 173–4
plan 254
plane 245
plane of symmetry 256
polygons
   exterior angles 115–17
   interior angles 115–17
   regular 115–16, 344
   regular, inscribed in a circle 136
   symmetry 344
positive correlation 449
powers
   calculations 52–3
   division 54, 56–7
   formulae 399
   index/indices 53
   multiplication 54, 56–7
   multiplying letters 55
   number raised to a further power 55
   number raised to the power 0 55
   number raised to the power 1 54
   simplifying 56–7
price index 288
primary data 202
prime factor form 41
prime factors 34–6, 40–2
prime numbers 34–6, 40
prism 249–51, 488–9
probability
   certain event 429

certain not to happen 425
certainty of happening 425
estimate by experiment 432–3
event 425, 429
event not happening 430
impossible event 429
numbers representing 426–7
random selection 439
relative frequency 432–3, 441–2
sample space diagram 435
scale 425
summary of key points 446
theoretical 432–3
two-way table 438
proportion
  direct 332–3
  problem solving 330–1
  summary of key points 337
  unitary method 330–1
protractor 100, 135–6, 382
protractor, circular 102, 119
pyramids 247–8
Pythagoras' theorem 466–74
  side of triangle other than
    hypotenuse 470–1
  statement of theorem 468
  summary of key points 474

Q

quadrant 486
quadratic equations 532–3, 541–2
quadratic functions, graphs 528–30
quadrilaterals
  interior angles 106
  names of special 125–6
quartile 457–8
questionnaires 196, 197

R

random sample 199
random selection 439
range 374
ratio
  definition 322–3
  direct proportion 332–3

dividing quantities 328–9
equivalent 326
form $1:n$ 327–8
form $n:1$ 327–8
lowest terms 325
problem solving 330–1
scale 138–9
simplifying 324–5
summary of key points 337
unitary form 327–8
unitary method 330–1
reading whole numbers 2–4
rearranging formulae 539–40
reciprocal equations 541–2
reciprocals 176
rectangle 126, 352, 475, 517–18
recurring decimals 175
reflections 417–18, 506–7
reflective symmetry 338–9
reflex angles 98, 102–3
regular polygons 115–16
relative frequency 432–3, 441–2
rhombus 126
right angles 97–8
right-angled triangles
  hypotenuse 466
  properties 125
  Pythagoras' theorem 466–74
rotational symmetry 342–3
rotations 414–15, 508, 509, 510–11
rounding
  area 360
  as check 22–3
  decimal places 86–7
  decimals 84–7
  overview 20–1
  significant figures 22–3, 87–8
  volume 360
rule of signs
  addition 31, 32, 397
  division 33, 398
  multiplication 33, 398
  subtraction 31, 32, 397

S

sample space diagram 435
sampling 199

You can find pages 1–276 in Book 1.

scale
  diagrams 334–5
  drawing 139
  maps 138–9, 334–5
  marks on 189–91
  ratio 138–9
  reading 188–91
scale factor of enlargement 419, 512, 514–15
scalene triangles 125
scatter diagrams 447–50
secondary data 202
sector 382, 486
segment 486
semicircle 486
sequences
  algebra used to find general rules 72–4
  basics 69
  decreasing 70
  general rules 72–4
  increasing 70–1
  nth term 73–4
  number in sequence or not 75–6
  produced by calculator 77
  rules 69–71, 71–2
  spreadsheet 77
  summary of key points 80
  terms 72–3
side elevation 254
significant figures 22–3, 87–8
similar shapes 419, 513
simple interest 293
sketch graphs 535
sphere 247
spread 457–8
spreadsheet use for
  area problems 365
  sequences 77
  trial and improvement 543–5
square roots 37–8
square [number] 36–7
square [shape] 126, 352, 517–18
square-based pyramid 247–8
stem and leaf diagrams 378–80
straight angles 98
subtraction
  brackets 61–2
  decimals 89–90
  fractions 165–6

  negative numbers 31–2
  rule of signs 31, 32, 397
  terms in algebraic expressions 48–9
  whole numbers 10
summaries of key points
  algebra 67–8
  algebraic expressions 547
  angles 122–3
  area 368, 503
  coordinates 321
  data analysis 390, 465
  data collection 210
  data presentation 244, 390, 465
  data recording 210
  data sorting 244
  decimals 95
  equations 221, 547
  estimating 194
  formulae 410, 547
  fractions 179–80
  graphs 321, 547
  inequalities 410
  linear equations 221
  measurement 194, 276
  number facts 44–5
  number patterns 80
  percentages 297–8
  perimeter 368, 503
  probability 446
  proportion 337
  Pythagoras' theorem 474
  ratio 337
  sequences 80
  symmetry 346
  3-D shapes 261
  transformations 424, 521–2
  2-D shapes 149–50
  turning 122–3
  units of measurement 276
  volume 368, 503
  whole numbers 27
surd 471
surface area
  cylinder 489–90
  definition 357
  3-D shapes 488–90
surfaces 245
symmetrical patterns 340

You can find pages 1–276 in Book 1.

symmetry
  lines of 338–9, 344
  mirror line 338–9
  patterns 340
  reflective 338–9
  regular polygons 344
  rotational 342–3
  summary of key points 346
  3-D shapes 256

T

tally chart 222–3
temperature 304–5
terms
  algebraic expressions 48–9
  sequences 72–3
tessellations 133
tetrahedron 251
theoretical probability 432–3
3-D shapes
  cross-section 249–50
  definition 124, 316–17
  edges 246
  elevation 254
  faces 246
  horizontal surfaces 245
  nets 250–1, 253
  plan 254
  properties 247
  summary of key points 261
  surface area 488–90
  surfaces 245
  symmetry 256
  vertical surfaces 245
  vertices 246
  volume 488–90
time calculations 268–70
time measurement 185–8
time series 235–6
time–distance graphs 306–7
timetables 272
transformations, summary of key points 424, 521–2
translations 411–12, 504–5
trapezium 125, 476
trial and improvement methods 39–40, 542–5
triangles
  area 352, 475
  drawing 135
  equilateral 125
  exterior angles 113–14
  interior angles 106, 113–14
  interior angles add to 180° 114
  isosceles 108, 125
  names of special 125
  obtuse-angled 125
  right-angled 125
  scalene 125
triangular prism 251
triangular-based pyramid 247
turning 96
  summary of key points 122–3
12-hour clock 185, 187–8
24-hour clock 185, 187–8
2-D shapes
  area 475–6
  congruent 131
  definition 316–17
  drawing 130
  grid paper 130
  perimeter 475–6
  properties 124
  similar 419, 513
  squared paper 130
  summary of key points 149–50
  tessellations 133

U

unitary form 327–8
units of measurement
  comparison 499
  conversion 266, 497–8
  conversion graphs 304–5
  summary of key points 276
upper quartile 457–8

V

value added tax (VAT) 286
vectors 504–5
vertex/vertices 125, 246
vertical line graph 233
vertical surfaces 245

You can find pages 1–276 in Book 1.

volume
boxes into boxes 358–9
cube 355–6
cuboid 355–6
cylinder 489–90
definition 351
prism 488–9
problem solving 360
rounding 360
summary of key points 368, 503
3-D shapes 488–90
units conversion 361–2

W

whole numbers
addition 8–9
combining 7–8
cube roots 38–9, 39–40
cubes 36–7
division 15–16
even numbers 34–6
factor trees 41
factors 34–6
highest common factor (HCF) 41
lowest common multiple (LCM) 42
multiples 34–6
multiplication 12–13
negative numbers 28–30
odd numbers 34–6
ordering 2–4
place value 1–2
prime factor 34–6
prime factor form 41
prime numbers 34–6, 40
problem solving 18
product of prime factors 40–2
reading 2–4
square roots 37–8
squares 36–7
subtraction 10
summary of key points 27
writing 2–4
writing whole numbers 2–4

Z

'Z' angles 110

You can find pages 1–276 in Book 1.